Marina Caparini, Otwin Marenin (Eds.)

Borders and Security Governance

Geneva Centre for the
Democratic Control of Armed Forces
(DCAF)

LIT

Marina Caparini, Otwin Marenin (Eds.)

Borders and Security Governance

Managing Borders in a Globalised World

Bibliographic information published by Die Deutsche Bibliothek
Die Deutsche Bibliothek lists this publication in the Deutsche
Nationalbibliografie; detailed bibliographic data are available in the
Internet at http://dnb.ddb.de.

ISBN 3-03735-005-9 (Schweiz)
ISBN 3-8258-9438-X (Deutschland)

© LIT VERLAG GmbH & Co. KG Wien,
Zweigniederlassung Zürich 2006
Dufourstr. 31
CH-8008 Zürich
Tel. +41 (0) 44-251 75 05
Fax +41 (0) 44-251 75 06
e-Mail: zuerich@lit-verlag.ch
http://www.lit-verlag.ch

LIT LEKTORAT 2006
Fresnostr. 2
48159 Münster
Tel. +49 (0)251–62 03 20
Fax +49 (0)251–23 19 72
e-Mail: lit@lit-verlag.de
http://www.lit-verlag.de

Distributed in the UK by: Global Book Marketing, 99B Wallis Rd, London, E9 5LN
Phone: +44 (0) 20 8533 5800 – Fax: +44 (0) 1600 775 663
http://www.centralbooks.co.uk/acatalog/search.html

Distributed in North America by:

Transaction Publishers
New Brunswick (U.S.A.) and London (U.K.)

Transaction Publishers
Rutgers University
35 Berrue Circle
Piscataway, NJ 08854

Phone: +1 (732) 445 - 2280
Fax: + 1 (732) 445 - 3138
for orders (U. S. only):
toll free (888) 999 - 6778
e-mail:
orders@transactionspub.com

Table of Contents

Part I: Introduction

1   Introduction to Borders and Security Governance   9
Marina Caparini and Otwin Marenin

Part II: Concepts and Approaches to Border Management

2   Democratic Oversight and Border Management: Principles, Complexity and Agency Interests.   17
Otwin Marenin

3   Towards a Rationality of Democratic Border Management   41
Alice Hills

4   Information Technology and Integrated Border Management   59
Rey Koslowski

5   Enlisting Third Parties in Border Control: a Comparative Study of its Causes and Consequences   79
Virginie Guiraudon

Part III: European Union

6   Towards a European Approach on Border Management: Aspects Related to the Movement of Persons   101
Daphné Gogou

7   Enlarging and Deepening the EU/Schengen Regime on Border Controls   125
Monika Sie Dhian Ho

8   Challenges for Non- (and Not Yet-) Schengen Countries   147
Kurt Schelter

9	Management of External EU Borders: Enlargement and the European Border Guard Issue *Peter Hobbing*	169
10	The Project of a European Border Guard: Origins, Models and Prospects in the Context of the EU's Integrated External Border Management *Jörg Monar*	193
11	Integrated Borderlands? *Eberhard Bort*	209
12	Switzerland: Between Intergovernmental Co-operation and Schengen Association *Sandra Lavenex*	233

Part IV: Comparative Perspectives

13	Border Issues: Transnational Crime and Terrorism *Louise I. Shelley*	255
14	Border Management Issues in NAFTA *Martha Cottam*	271
15	The Factor of Trust and the Importance of Inter-agency Co-operation in the Fight Against Transnational Organised Crime: the US–Mexican Example. *Edgardo Buscaglia and Samuel González-Ruiz*	291

Part V: Conclusion

16	Conclusion *Marina Caparini and Otwin Marenin*	305
	Note on Authors	313

Part I
Introduction

Introduction to Borders and Security Governance

Marina Caparini and Otwin Marenin

The chapters in this volume originated as papers delivered at the conference 'Managing International and Inter-Agency Co-operation at the Border', held in Geneva on 13-15 March 2003. The idea behind organising the conference, and its objective, was to conduct an assessment of recent developments in the governance of border security systems, both within the European region, and comparatively across other regions. Transnational movements of people, goods, and capital have become important security policy issues on national and global agendas, and the control of such movements is focused largely on efforts at borders. The powers and reach of border control systems have been enhanced by changes in law, increased political attention, an influx of resources, the utilisation of technological detection and control devices and systems, and a security discourse which stresses border management as a crucial element in ensuring the stability of states and the well-being of citizens. In short, as border guards and other state authorities have been given more authority and as their capacity to coercively control people has been magnified, the perennial question of how to control and hold accountable agencies and agents who exercise that power, often within wide margins of discretion, has risen to greater salience. At the same time, the means and mechanisms of accountability must respond to the realities of evolving forms of border management if they are to be effective and legitimate.

There are widely acknowledged reasons why borders and the accountability of evolving border control systems now matter. In an era of globally structured change and the increasing interconnections of international and local affairs, advancing integration of even remote societies into a global system of commerce, migration and production is apparent, supported by technologies of communication and transportation far more efficient and more difficult to know about and control than traditional means. All of these factors enabling legitimate traffic flows in people, capital, resources and commerce have also enabled illegitimate activities. Globalisation depends on open borders, or at least borders which can be crossed with relative ease and convenience. The increasing interdependence of global means of production and information raises practical questions of how to coordinate production and trade (such as building cars or computers with parts manufactured in many countries) and the flows of capital and profits which can only be done efficiently if traditional borders and notions of sovereignty on which they are based are devalued.

At the same time, that necessary permeability of conventional borders also allows illegitimate flows of people and capital (human trafficking, uncontrolled migration, money laundering, the trafficking of illegal goods and services) and, as well, the ingress of terrorists into target states. As economic liberalisation produces more global markets, borders need to be more carefully watched; whilst globalisation beats against the crumbling ramparts of sovereignty, security practitioners must seek more effective ways to prop up national borders. This dilemma will only worsen and complicate the very notion of the function of borders in the new era.

A second reason why borders have gained policy salience, despite the rumoured decline of the Westphalian system and the nation-state, is the emergence of regions seeking to coordinate themselves as wider systems of economic and political integration. The European Union is a prime example, as are the North American Free Trade Agreement (NAFTA) and other regional systems not as far advanced in their integration (such as MERCOSUR in South America or the ASEAN community). The creation of regional arrangements having political salience decreases the importance of internal borders and raises external borders to the status formerly occupied by international borders. The protection of the region against threats from any source begins to depend on how well external border controls can be established and sustained. The EU has advanced furthest down the road towards abolishing the security aspects of internal borders, against some quite vehement opposition at the initial stages, and has struggled with devising external border control systems which can be trusted to effectively assume the former control functions of the now internal borders.

Third, in an era of global interdependence, borders have been effectively de-territorialised and detached from their physical moorings. Borders now exist wherever they interfere with the legal flows of a global system, and border controls are often exercised quite far removed from the physical locations demarcating an imaginary line between two states.

Some of these lines, though real, create problems because they do not reflect ongoing political and economic developments. One can think of situations such as the tiny Spanish territories of Ceuta and Mellila near Africa, whose borders have become deathtraps for illegal immigrants seeking a way into the EU; or the Cabinda enclave hundreds of miles removed from its sovereign core Angola; or the leftovers of colonial empires still owing allegiance to a far distant mother country, as is the case with the islands of St. Pierre and Miquelon to France. These remnants of historical conflicts and conquests make little sense in the current global era, and they are security problems which the countries involved can ill afford to control ineffectively. The more security conditions worsen at these unreal borders, the more are their irrationalities exposed.

Lastly, there is the recognition that long-standing localised border systems are laboratories for effective and legitimate border control systems and can be incubators or catalysts for wider regional integration. Life in border regions and zones has often been substantially different in culture and ease of trans-border communication and traffic from national relations across borders.

In many border zones, e.g., Mexico–USA or France–Germany (especially in regions which have been passed back and forth into the sovereign domain of either state (such as Alsace or the Saarland), people are as familiar with the language and customs of the other nation as they are with their own. The national border has been an inconvenience to local (zonal) life rather than an issue of nationalistic pride.

Much of the discussion of border management and the need for accountability and good governance of border control systems takes place under the theoretical and policy umbrella of Security Sector Reform (SSR). SSR starts from the policy position that security for any state and its citizens is provided by many formal (military, police, gendarmerie, intelligence, border guards) and informal security providers (corporate entities, community-based groups or militias) and that the effective functioning and performance of security agencies needs to be analysed systematically and systemically. The provision of security is a system, akin to the economic or legal system, and has to be analysed holistically as a network of more or less articulated agencies all populating the security field. Each individual security agency deserves study, but so do their articulations and inter-connections to each other. And as with other governmental organs and agencies, they should be managed with procedures used in a parliamentary democracy—the checks and balances that comprise democratic control. The title of the conference—integrated management—reflected that broader understanding. Since security is a field of action, accountability mechanisms also need to be able to deal with individual actors on the field, as well as with their relations to each other.

The importance of border protection has a different salience when considered as part of a security system rather than a separate area of action (which it is). For example, the traditional reluctance of security agencies to co-operate or share information, each protecting its own turf, can be as much a problem for providing security for the state as can external threats to security. The USA found this out after investigating the relations among security agencies before the terrorist attacks of 11 September 2001. Much more information existed than was shared; if it had been effectively pooled that threat might have been detected and the attack prevented. The need for accountability, hence, requires a look at the security system or sector as well as individual agencies.

Contributors to the conference were asked to describe and assess recent border and border security developments, with a primary focus on the European Union. The editors of this volume, and the organisers of the conference, also sought out contributors who could provide insights on comparative border control developments in the North American region, and on changes in threats to the borders and the extension of border protection functions by the mandated co-optation of private and corporate companies into border controlling the flow of people, money and goods across.

The chapters in this volume are arranged thematically, and by region. Two introductory papers by Marenin and Hills discuss the broader issues faced in managing security and accountability at new and old borders, and the likely obstacles encountered in instituting accountability and good governance as part of SSR. Marenin looks closely at the challenges of democratic oversight of border control systems, drawing in part on the insights offered by policing literature, and explains why democratic oversight is more complex and difficult to achieve with border agencies than with policing systems. Greatly complicating the implementation of oversight is the fundamental change in understanding of what constitutes a border. From traditional physical demarcations between states, borders have expanded in space and time to reflect the patterns of legal and illegal flows of trade and migration. Corresponding efforts of states to influence and police those flows occur at various levels (local or subnational, national, regional and supranational) and increasingly involve private actors. Not only are the techniques and methods of border management changing in response to the pressures of globalisation, but state control of borders is ceding to multiple modes of governance. Democratic oversight lags far behind.

Hills examines the conceptual and empirical parameters of border management, defined as the rules, techniques and procedures regulating activities and traffic across defined border areas or zones, and emphasises that the specific political and historical context and multiple rationalities will play a determining role in shaping the border policing approach of any state. She applies her thesis in comparing the widely divergent border systems of three states in South East Europe, two bordering the EU, and one which recently became an EU member. The sample constitutes a microcosm of the challenges facing contemporary European border management. Hills ends with the caution that little is known about how transferable are either Schengen standards or the principle of democratic control in border policing to non-EU states.

Koslowski discusses the Janus-faced nature of information technology as a major force weakening state governance as a driver of globalisation and international migration, but also its potential for improving border management and thus reasserting the ability of the state to control its borders. However he cautions that focusing too closely on the state may cause one to overlook the involvement of non-state actors in migration control.

In the following article, Guiraudon takes up this theme and presents a precise picture of how private companies and organisations have become co-opted into the control of the movements of people, such as through carrier sanctions laws that give transport operators an important role in preventing uncontrolled migration, in particular the entry of asylum seekers. She provides evidence that law enforcement officials used the events of 11 September 2001 to reinforce immigration controls and demands on third parties. The shift in liabilities and responsibilities occurred as a result of closed-door negotiations and lack of consultation with EU watchdog bodies and those actors on whom the new demands have fallen, namely airlines.

The third section of the book focuses on developments in the EU and its neighbouring areas in terms of border management. Gogou, Dhian Ho and Schelter provide detailed accounts of the development of the Schengen regime and its relations to border control in an expanding EU. Their contributions, based on extensive participation in and deep knowledge of the decision-making process in EU bureaucracies, present and preserve a valuable historical record of a policy sphere that is undergoing rapid change. Gogou traces the development of a common approach on border management from the beginning of the European Community until the period just before the enlargement of 2004. Dhian Ho considers the implications of EU enlargement for the border control regime, including the many challenges faced by the new EU Member States in implementing the Schengen *acquis*. Schelter examines the incentives for non-EU states to cooperate with the EU border management regime, and identifies requirements for continuing integration of border management in Europe. Hobbing and Monar discuss the processes and obstacles in creating a unified European Border Police, also based on extensive involvement in the process itself. Bort argues that localised border regions can be studied as examples of transnational processes which have been able to create functioning co-operation in providing security and other services in small border regions and zones. Lavenex discusses the case of Switzerland which, claiming a tradition of neutrality, had not formally joined the Schengen agreement (this will soon change as the result of the June 2005 referendum whose in which a majority backed Swiss membership of Schengen) but also argues that in practice Switzerland has abided by many of the understandings which surround co-operation in the Schengen space.

Moving to a wider comparative perspective in the fourth section, Shelley discusses how the emergence of powerful transnational organised crime groups have changed the security landscape at the borders of all countries, and have converged with international terrorist groups through their common interest in crossing borders to realise their financial/political objectives. Cottam analyses the complexities of co-operation and conflict which exist at the northern and southern internal borders (Canada–USA, Mexico–USA) of NAFTA, and the non-security factors such as trust, historical sensitivities and sovereignty concerns which help shape the nature of such conflicts. She further examines the assumptions underlying the highly divergent approaches adopted by the US to border management along its northern border in contrast to its southern border. Buscaglia and Gonzalez-Ruiz describe the ways in which transnational and local organised crime have undermined security policies through corruption and intimidation in Mexico. They discuss the need for, and challenges to, collaboration among officials at the national, regional and international levels, as well as some of the mechanisms that have been developed to that end. In the conclusion, the editors review some of the major implications of these insightful presentations for border control and accountability, now and in the future.

The original conference resulted in informative discussion and exchanges of ideas by contributors and other participants. The experience confirmed the value of bringing a number of experts from various disciplines and backgrounds together into one room for two days, and enabling them talk about a topic in which they are truly interested. Due to the rapid pace of change in the internal security policy field in the European Union, it has proven extremely difficult in writing on border management issues not to be overtaken by events. We wish to thank the conference participants and the contributors for their papers, and for the updating that several of them did subsequently, since some time had unfortunately elapsed between the conference and the preparation of this volume.

Special thanks go to Michael Jaxa-Chamiec and Moncef Kartas, who did wonderful work helping to edit and format the papers. And, of course, we owe deep thanks to the Geneva Centre for the Democratic Control of Armed Forces (DCAF) which provided the funding for the conference, the attendance of contributors, and the preparation of this volume.

PART II

CONCEPTS AND APPROACHES TO BORDER MANAGEMENT

Chapter 2

Democratic Oversight and Border Management: Principles, Complexity and Agency Interests

Otwin Marenin

Borders are becoming fashionable, as policy and as a scholarly topic. The decline of the nation-state predicted by many seems to have been arrested as the threat of terrorism and organised transnational crime, technological advances which allow anyone to leapfrog, via cyberspace, existing borders and evade state controls on the transmission of information and ideas, and illegal trans-border trafficking in goods, people and capital have been raised to the level of a national security threat, in turn requiring safe borders to protect the state and society. Border security systems to protect the state and mitigate threats to its stability and the lives and properties of its citizens have become important items on the global security agenda. The notion of Security Sector Reform (SSR) captures ongoing dialogues among policy networks within and among states on how to conceptualise the objective needs for a security sector architecture which meets the normative and practical requirements for effective and legitimate security policies (Edmunds 2001). Border guards and security systems, as are other relevant state-based actors, are and will be central building blocks of the new domestic and global security architecture.

At the same time, processes of cultural globalisation, economic interdependence, instant and massive communications networks, and transnational mobility of trained labour have rendered borders hindrances to economic and cultural trends and dynamics which are argued to be beneficial to all in the global community, though this is not a universal feeling.

There exists an extensive scholarly and policy-driven literature, and the implications for reform of best practices and lessons learnt, for some elements of the Security Sector (e.g., police, military and intelligence services), but very little on border security systems and border guards—the professionally trained security apparatus with responsibilities, powers, functional mandates and a professional identity separate and distinct from other security providing structures; nor are the interactions of border control agents with other domestic and external security providing elements adequately described, assessed and conceptualised.

Equally unanalysed are the need for and institutional responses for effective oversight and accountability of border security systems which now exist or are in the process of being created. Yet it is likely that border security agents will be subject to the same temptations for corruption, abuse of powers, discriminatory treatment, violations of law and human rights, or co-operation with criminal elements which have been observed in other state agencies which have the power to coerce and substantial discretion concerning when, how and against whom to use their coercive capacities. The increased importance attached to border control automatically raises questions of democratic oversight, transparency and accountability of border security systems.

I will examine the nature and problems of democratic oversight of border control systems which have evolved and are being constructed, with emphasis on the external borders of the EU as these shift eastward. What oversight mechanisms are appropriate and likely to be effective in holding the emerging border control systems accountable and responsive to accepted professional standards, the rule of law, conceptions of human rights in the treatment of people, and political oversight? I will discuss the notion of borders in general; examine strategic and operational issues in border control systems; and argue the need for specific accountability mechanisms at the EU borders, drawing on insights about processes and problems of accountability from developments in comparative and international policing and border controls efforts and obstacles to successful accountability in another regional system, NAFTA (the North American Free Trade Agreement).

My argument is that democratic accountability of border systems will be more complicated and difficult to design and implement than for policing systems (even though I draw on the vast literature on how to democratise policing, largely because of the dearth of research on the occupational behaviours and cultures of border guards). The capacity by the state and civic society to impose accountability on border security systems will be complicated by these factors: the notion of what constitutes a border has changed from borders as lines to border as zones and streams; border guards are more protected against allegations of malfeasance, since their work is directly linked to national security concerns and the people they deal with are often not citizens or are suspects engaged in some illegal activity, hence are seen to lack the rights accorded citizens; there is less transparency to their work and greater secrecy surrounds what they do, partially because they deal with national security issues but also because their work locations can be out of sight and widely dispersed; private actors have been co-opted into doing security-related work; effective border guarding requires transnational co-operation and will be enmeshed in larger political issues among the countries involved; and regional border guards are a fairly new development and no regional accountability mechanisms have yet come into existence—national mechanisms still are the basic control and oversight means.

Most importantly, the notion of what constitutes a border has changed. Instead of physical demarcated lines guarded by posts and agents, borders have been extended, for purposes of security, across the world. Traditional national borders exist within border zones that frequently have created their own political and security arrangements which can be at odds with national policies

(Bort, this volume); and borders have been expanded (to use an economic metaphor) upstream and downstream, in the effort to detect, assess and control security threats before they reach the border and after they have crossed. Management and oversight issues will be much more complicated when the border is not just a line in the dirt, but exists immaterially in cyberspace or anywhere along patterns of legal and illegal trade and migration flows.

Increasingly, much of border control work is being contracted out to private companies, thereby blurring the line between state and social control and complicating questions of oversight and accountability (Bailey and Godson 1999; Huisman 2002, p.32; Lahav and Guiraudon 2000). These developments within the ambit of border control are part of a wider shift in the governance of security away from state control towards local, corporate and supra-national 'nodes of governance' (Shearing and Wood, 2000).

Since borders are guarded by two states, views on what needs to be done (what is the problem) and how to do it (domestic and trans-border organisational arrangements, policies and priorities) are likely to differ and will lead to patterns of co-operation which will fluctuate in salience and intensity as national priorities and political wills shift. For example, patterns of co-operation in NAFTA (Cottam, this volume) will reflect the functional needs and threats which exists at the internal borders of NAFTA (Canada–US; Mexico–US) but also larger ideological values, cultural stereotypes and nationalistic sentiments, leading to quite divergent patterns of trans-border trust and co-operation at the northern and southern borders of the US. Border security systems are about more issues than security at the border, and their design and implementation are influenced not only by the reality of threats and security needs but also by how such threats are perceived, categorised, interpreted and integrated into a larger securitisation discourse. In similar fashion, the structure and powers of the proposed European Border Guard (*Feasibility Study* 2002; Hobbing, Monar, this volume) will require international agreements among the 25 members of the EU, and will be shaped by multiple political, objective and subjective factors.

Borders and their Problems

The management of borders occurs in the context of fundamentally conflicting imperatives.

For one, borders must be both open and closed, be both gates and walls. The dynamics of globalisation and the rise of new threats and security ideologies will continue to demand new ways of managing border security, of dealing with economic opportunities arising within the context of a global free market while simultaneously protecting the territorial integrity, cultural identity, security of citizens, and the political stability of the state. Both legal and illegal flows of people and goods cross borders and have to be sorted out in a way that is effective and legitimate in the eyes of entrepreneurs, publics and elites. The practical 'sorting out' problem is that illegal crossings are only a tiny part of the movement of people and goods across any border.[1] Trying to detect and prevent the small portion of illegal trafficking, if done too forcefully and comprehensively, will completely disrupt the legal traffic on which trading partners depend to sustain their economies and profits.

In addition, globalisation, as Nevins notes (2002, pp.178–186), complicates gate-keeping efforts as the flow of unwanted migrants and human trafficking from poor to rich countries increases the workload of border guards. In a similar fashion, the flow of transnational crime (drugs, animals, body parts, national art) tends to go from poor countries to markets where people have a desire for and can afford to pay for these illegal commodities. (The exception to this flow pattern is hazardous waste generated in developed economies and disposed of in poor and corrupt places.) Borders which directly separate rich and poor states and citizens, such as in NAFTA and the eastern and southern borders of an expanding EU, have become lines of confrontation as well as co-operation. These pressures will only increase as globalisation's economic impacts are distributed unequally across the globe (Aronowitz 2002; Ehrenreich and Hochschild 2002; Kyle and Koslowski 2001)

A second basic dilemma is the potential conflict between power and responsibility, between autonomy and oversight. Border management requires giving controllers sufficient authorities, resources and discretion to do their job, yet without abandoning the oversight necessary to ensure that agents do not misuse their powers. Border controllers, as is true of all who have powers to enforce social control, may be tempted by situational or personal reasons to misuse their powers. They have to be watched but without undermining morale or hampering effectiveness.

This is largely a question of trust. How much trust can political elites representing civic society place in border agencies? And, conversely, how can one ensure, or have trust, that border controllers accept as a normal and legitimate part of their job that they will be watched and judged not only on the grounds of effectiveness but on the use of their powers? If the requirement for trust extends beyond one's own borders and own people, as it does at the new borders of an expanding European Union, the dilemma sharpens (CEPS 2001a).

---

[1] In practice, only a small percentage of automobiles, trucks, trains, airplanes, ships and people can be checked carefully while the rest will pass unhindered. For example, it is estimated that all of the cocaine shipped into the US could fit into fifteen standard shipping containers (heroin would fit into two or three). About eight million containers enter the US every year. Only about 3–4 percent of containers are physically checked—meaning Customs opens them, looks inside, sometimes unpacks the containers and some of its contents, and says 'looks good to us.' Unless Customs has a very good reason for suspecting something, they are not going to crawl into or unpack many containers to look inside the individual items packed into the container. Doing more than limited and cursory inspections is not feasible in terms of resources and would be unacceptable politically and economically because legal traffic must go through without much delay.

A third dilemma reflects the well-known conflict between effectiveness and due process at the local level. Control agents tend to see their job in terms of effectiveness and not so much as balancing demands for effective work (number of persons detained, amount of drugs seized, etc.) with requirements for proper obedience to law, rules and regulations. Effectiveness is what they are rewarded for by the organisation, publics and political leaders.

Fourth, there is the dilemma of how to reconcile universal with local standards of behaviour and work. Border conditions are, if not unique, situational and require different policies to work well. It is not likely that a set of policies defined by bureaucracies distant from the place in which they will be implemented will work as well, or be perceived as equally legitimate by local communities, as a set of priorities which (while still adhering to basic democratic principles of conduct) has been adapted to local conditions. As Hills notes (2002b, p.4), there is 'an increasing consensus among [observers] that locally generated benchmarks are more legitimate and realistic than outside supervision.' Local knowledge and histories matter.

Resolutions of these basic dilemmas are tied to larger security, political and ideological questions. The very notion of accountability by border security systems to democratic processes presumes the existence of effective accountability mechanisms within political systems, a willingness on the part of political leaders to insist on adherence to specified standards, and the capacity to effectively evaluate performance and sanction violations of rules and regulations by border security agencies or individual agents. The interplay between agents of control and the state and civic society they serve can take many forms, only some of which may reflect and embody the conventional benchmarks of good governance and democratic oversight—transparency, accountability, responsiveness, equity, redress, service delivery and participation (Hills 2002a, p.16).

Changing Conceptions of Border Management: NAFTA and the EU

NAFTA

In the North American context, the NAFTAisation of commercial traffic, coupled with the dominance of the US as the world's number one consumer of illegal drugs as well as being the remaining global hegemonic economic and military power, has helped create a system which cannot effectively seal the borders without a devastating impact on legal traffic. Nor can borders be so open as to allow the unfettered entrance into US national territory of drugs, people and other dangers to the well-being of the state and its citizens. The basic dilemma is how to enable an increased commerce in goods while keeping the borders closed to illegal migrants and dangerous people and goods. This has led to a border control system which pretends to be effective in order to reassure society but remains open enough to not disrupt legal traffic (Andreas

2000). There is simply too much at stake economically for the three countries involved in NAFTA to have a tight border control system.

After the September 11 terrorist attacks and the creation of a homeland security ideology and Department in the USA, condoned local trans-border interactions among communities and citizens located at the borders has been disrupted by tighter controls, especially on the US side (LeDuff 2003). The control of border zones, which used to incorporate some local autonomous patterns of policy and decision-making reflecting local situations, has been increasingly centralised, federalised and militarised (Sadler 2000).

As in other areas in the world, the USA is searching for ways in which to increase the efficiency of detecting illegal traffic while enabling legal flows, largely by enhancing technological and intelligence capacities to sort out legal from illegal traffic. The USA, Canada and Mexico have responded to this dilemma, at the insistence of the US and given NAFTA aspirations, by developing the notion of smart border control. Smart border agreements which seek to utilise technological innovations and capacities, increase transnational co-operation among border control agencies, and create forward and backward intelligence and enforcement linkages away from the borders into domestic security spheres have been signed between the USA and Canada and the USA and Mexico. Smart controls at the borders includes such means as identification cards with non-erasable biometric information (Lee 2003); giant scanning machines which can see into trucks and trains with one pass; more accurate human profiling systems; 'fast lane' crossing systems for pre-screened locals and workers; or a variety of night vision and detection devices (Schiesel 2003).

Two implications of smart border control are important. The first is that control works better if done cooperatively by agencies on both sides of border. Smart border control requires bilateral or regional border co-operation, a basic trust in the willingness and capacity of the other side to ensure the effective and fair implementation of the procedures which have been put into place.

The other implication is more interesting as an oversight and policy problem. Smart border control extends the border upstream and downstream. If control can be done before traffic reaches US borders, largely by separating legal from illegal traffic, there will be less need to do so at the border and less disruption. Pre-clearance arrangements and 'container profiling' are two examples. Presently there are agreements between US Customs and customs agencies and ports in Europe and Asia according to which items cleared there, following agreed-on procedures and standards, are considered checked and approved and will be waived through once the proper paperwork is presented at the US border.

Profiling assesses shipping agencies overseas. Containers shipped by suspect or profiled firms or coming from particular ports or flagged as suspicious by intelligence or tips will be looked at more closely. Rather than pick containers at random, or on the basis of professional hunches, or by local clues, the effectiveness of inspections can be increased by prior intelligence.

Upstream co-operation also involves private corporations. Airlines now are required to transmit passengers lists of all their flights to authorities, to allow authorities to check names against (secret) lists of suspects, in order to receive permission to land (Guiraudon, this volume).

Downstream extensions of the border exist as well. The most obvious examples from the US pertain to traffic in drugs and illegal aliens and, more recently, terror suspects. The federal government has issued an opinion that US law allows local police departments far away from the border to arrest illegal immigrants. The control of migrants should not just be the job of the now disbanded Immigration and Naturalization Service (INS) and the current Customs, Border and Protection (CBP) unit in the Department of Homeland Security. CBP has combined the Border Patrol, Customs and Agricultural Inspection agencies into 'one face' at the border (Ridge 2003). The law does not mandate that police departments do this work, and most local police departments do not want this job and most will not do it. But the legal directive is an attempt to shift the enforcement of border controls to the heart of the homeland.

The INS/CBP has always sought to track down illegal immigrants for deportation within the country at their places of employment, by roadblocks along major highways, and by sweeps through mainly non-English speaking neighbourhoods. Federal law requires that employers check the documentation of job applicants to ensure that they are legally in the country; employers have to report those who do not have the proper documentation, and will be fined if they are found to have employed non-documented workers. Since an estimated eight to nine million illegal aliens work in the USA (Lowell and Suro 2002, p.5), this system of co-opting employers into border control work clearly is not effective. Sweeps, especially, have led to a lot of friction between INS/CBP agents and local police which often, under the rhetoric of community policing, have sought to establish friendly relations with all local communities. INS/CBP agents, in co-operation with local law enforcement agencies, also man roadblocks on busy travel routes to catch illegal migrants away from the actual border line.

Drugs, of course, have always had downstream elements to them. Arrested users and dealers can be rolled up to lead to bigger fish and reveal linkages to producers and traffickers in source and transit countries. Intelligence on drug usage, such as testing of arrested suspects or local market survey of the purity and availability of drugs, can be used to estimate the effectiveness of border controls (e.g., what percentages of drugs being smuggled are seized at the borders).

Homeland security has a tremendous downstream element as well, asking citizens and professionals in certain occupations to be the informing eyes and ears of the federal government. Such attempts to link citizens to border control have happened before. But the attempt now is to integrate such practices downstream into a more coherent and federally controlled set of border control mechanisms.

The European Union

The situation of an expanding EU, and the consequent shifting of border control to the outer edges of the Schengen space, is somewhat different.[2] The basic dynamics and contours of EU enlargements are well understood and analysed by policy elites and scholars. Much of the discourse on how to protect the enlarging EU and Schengen space has focused on the themes of securitisation, evolving conceptions of borders and the importance of border zones as 'laboratories' for transnational co-operation in the provision of border security, the concept of border regimes, and the utility and limitations of technology in protecting borders.

Border control policies are evolving within a wider discourse of securitisation. As internal borders were eliminated, external borders and the increased threats from illegal activities have become essential issues in discussions of what the enlargement of the EU to include 'transitional' countries entails (Hills 2005). The security discourse reflects widespread public anxieties, identifies strangers as threats to the well being of EU member states, supports and tolerates productive law enforcement techniques against threats which would not be acceptable to members of the EU, and reinforces an emergent, us versus them, EU identity. Under the Schengen regime which new members must accept, formally open borders will now be closed to citizens left outside the Schengen space, creating a new 'Iron Curtain' (Anderson 2000, p.23) between the EU and its neighbours.

Securitisation also stresses the notion of trust. Citizens of the original EU member states can only be and feel safe if the new external borders effectively control the ingress of unwanted people, goods and threats. That requires a 'philosophy of mutual trust [as] the core idea in the establishment and development of border security systems' among policy elites, political leaders, citizen groups and border control agencies (DCAF 2001, p.19). Such trust is often in short supply.[3]

Linked to the notion of securitisation, but approaching the question from the perspective of good governance and democratisation within the

---

[2] The big difference is that people can move freely once inside the Schengen space, while in NAFTA the movement of people is still tightly controlled.

[3] That trust is not yet completely achieved. Participants at a workshop on EU border control prior to EU enlargement noted that among candidates countries 'there is a student/teacher feeling and the students (candidate countries) do not believe that the teachers (member states) are doing their homework'; that there exist double standards on the question of asylum and the application of community law to states; and that 'questions surround the intentions of member states in shifting the burden in migration management and border controls towards the new members. It appears as if the game that is being played is 'Who will get stuck with the burden of border controls?' [and] how much will the burden be shared by other member states?' (Anderson et al 2001, p.21).

concept of Security Sector Reform, are the fundamental reforms thought necessary to meet accession standards, including those which will govern the security sector. The security sector needs to be subject to democratic oversight and governance even though the specific accountability mechanisms, the transparency of organisational work, and responsiveness to societal demands will differ by the nature of the work done by particular agencies. Intelligence activities to detect, for example, planned terrorist activities upstream imply different means of oversight than does the treatment of people who have been placed under secondary scrutiny at border crossings.

Another theme has been sketched earlier and that is the extension of the borders beyond the physical line which demarcates one state from another. Borders and border security systems are now conceived as 'complex and wide entit[ies]' (DCAF 2001, p.10) requiring effective national and transnational co-operation. 'The concentration of frontier functions on the linear border is beginning to break down' (Anderson et al. 2001, p.5). At the physical border most work will continue to involve traditional forms of screening, detection, detention and protection. Most of the work away from the physical border will be intelligence and pre-screening externally and follow-up work internally. In Reimann's words (2001, p.50), 'the fundamental strategic approach' underlying border control is 'police work should not be hindered by borders.' Functional needs should override political divisions.

Reimann (2001, p.44) provides an extensive and detailed description of the tactics and strategies pursued by the German border police to achieve the four basic goals of 'securing the borders; measures in the countries of origin; international co-operation; [and] national co-operation'. What is interesting is the large variety of skills and personnel required to carry out these varied duties. At the very least, providing border security within the context of a securitisation discourse and a widened border involves: customs personnel to check the transit of goods; immigration officers to check the flow of long-term migrants, tourists and daily workers crossing the borders; border guards to patrol and protect the borders between crossing stations, at the blue borders and in the air (some of these forces are heavily militarised, or work with military forces, depending on the nature of border threats, civil turmoil in adjacent countries, or massive organised crime involved in smuggling activities).[4]

---

[4] In the US, which faces no real military threat at any of its borders, militarisation of border controls has a long history. Blue borders have been patrolled by the Coast Guard, which is considered a military organisation (for example, it has its own academy as do the other branches of the armed forces) even though it was located in the Department of Transportation and now has been moved to Homeland Security. Internal security at airports has been the duty of local and federal police forces with civilian assistance to screen passengers; screening is now federalised and part of Homeland Security; and land borders have been patrolled in between checkpoints by the Border Patrol, often in close cooperation with military units and local law enforcement. Assisting border control efforts has been a massive in-

The increase in perceived threats from foreign terrorists and a rhetoric of war suggest a further expansion of control efforts: the militarisation of border control will likely increase; intelligence collection and risk analysis personnel will be deployed in and outside the country; liaison personnel of various sorts (police advisers, trainers and observers, customs and drug enforcement officers, documents experts, delegates to regional and international planning groups and international/regional organisations) will be stationed outside the country; undercover operatives to detect organised illegal and criminal activities and plans will work globally; and a massive managerial capacity and staff to coordinate strategies, policies and activities will have to be developed. If the border security zone is extended to include legal authorities to prosecute violators; guards at detention centres for illegal immigrants, asylum seekers and other suspects; or professionals involved in international extraditions and mutual assistance, the complexity of the security system is even more apparent. What this list, which could be extended by specific examples, makes obvious is that border security is not of one piece nor can it be done by one organisation.[5] Accountability and oversight, hence, will require different mechanisms with different rules for transparency, disclosure and external oversight.

There appears in some of the writings on the future of border guarding and control in the EU (e.g., DCAF 2001; Reimann 2001) a yearning for and advocacy of a unified, professionally trained, hierarchically organised, autonomous and somewhat militarised single agency, with all agents receiving similar training, which does all of border control at the borders and is subject to one national department. Underlying this sentiment is a search by border guards for identity, status and professional respectability akin to the police or military. That appears to be an unlikely development, nor would it be effective or legitimate. The sentiment is normally attached to a the notion of 'border guards' but is at odds with the new, broader definition of what constitutes the border and border security. The search and advocacy of a professional and distinct identity for border police or guards, a kind of in-between identity and occupation located in the space between a military force oriented by norms and culture to defeating an enemy by force and a police service meeting whatever

---

telligence gathering and analysis system involving military, law enforcement and civilian personnel.

[5] Anderson (2000, p.25), summarises these developments: 'There has been a certain deterritorialisation of border controls in the sense that controls are now exercised in the consulates located in most countries of the world, by transportation companies through the use of carrier liability legislation, by third countries by the pressure on east central European countries to accept Schengen norms, by internal controls on identity by police and other public services, and by the Schengen external frontier and associated arrangements. In other words, the controls that were formally concentrated at national border posts are now exercised by a variety of means.'

order and safety demands are placed on them by the public, is not likely to evolve. It is clear from the discussion of broader security systems having national and transnational aspects that border guards will be only a small part of the overall border system. A far more likely development is the creation of specialised units and agencies loosely grouped under the label of border management and control, and subject to different forms of democratic oversight.

A third common theme is the notion of border regimes. As defined by Anderson (2000, pp.15–16) border controls are embedded in 'frontier regimes.' Frontier regimes consist of: agreements about borders with neighbouring states, whether bilateral or multilateral; the practices that have grown up around them; the administration and management of borders controls; related systems of police and customs co-operation; and institutions and arrangements for transfrontier co-operation. Implicit in these regimes are the various conceptions of functions that are fulfilled or that, it is thought, should be fulfilled by borders. Also central to the regimes are territorial ideologies—perceptions of the meaning and significance of frontiers held by policy-making elites, the population of frontier regions and, more generally, by the inhabitants of a country.

Border regimes point to the interplay of formal and informal, universal and local, and agency and public interests and point to the complexity and multi-functionality of border management.

Border control cannot be understood, or the subject of oversight, only as a system of formal institutions, roles and powers. Its dynamics are much more complicated. As Reimann argues (2001, p.53), 'in Europe at the beginning of the 21st century "border security arrangements" in the traditional, particularly military sense, are neither feasible no politically desirable.' Border security must be as flexible and adaptive as the new contexts and threats which will arise.

Lastly, responding to new threats and increasing economic integration, border control has become more technologised and intelligence oriented. To preserve a semblance of effectiveness in controlling illegal border crossings and sorting out legal from illegal traffic, border management has resorted to technological means, in turn requiring different specialised training, detection routines and decision-making skills. The 'fifth sense' of experienced customs agents which they fall back on to detect and further investigate suspicious people and cargo has been replaced by bureaucratic decision-making rules, technical expertise and a reliance on 'intelligence.'

Oversight and Accountability: Issues and Means

The need for accountability

Given these emerging realities and problems of border control, what should the border systems be accountable for, and to whom? In this new control environment, as borders have widened into international and domestic spheres, have incorporated new forms of surveillance and intelligence gathering, have become increasingly technologised and multi-functional, and retain their regime characteristics, what forms of oversight are available and will work? As the borders of countries and regions become subject to different mechanisms of control, exercised by an often quite complex set of national and transnational institutional arrangements and overlapping powers, what happens to the capacity of democratically elected elites and societal groups to effectively oversee border management agencies and hold them accountable to emergent global standards of human rights, due process, the rule of law and the non-discriminatory, dignified and respectful treatment of all the people border control agents encounter in their work. What mechanisms can be put into place when, in the case of the EU, border controls have become effectively de-territorialised and subject to EU guidelines while effective political oversight and control remains at the level of member states?[6] Since few accountability mechanisms exist at the level of the EU (beyond statements of principles, bureaucratic directives, and some legal institutions) accountability and oversight will revert to the new border states, which often and almost by definition (being 'transitional' countries), have little history and experience in establishing and running effective accountability processes which seek to control the state's coercive forces.

Establishing effective oversight, hence, will require 'some innovative thinking about the precise complex of subnational, national and supranational mechanisms best suited to the task of rendering European [border control] more democratically responsive' (Loader 2002, p.139).[7] Given the complexity of border security agencies, tasks and activities, Hills' conclusion (2002a) that the 'key to accountability is to be found in multiple structures, at multiple levels of control' is right on point. DCAF (2001) suggests three levels: internal, external and, in the background, legislative oversight. And that conclusion also accords with studies of accountability of the police. The OSCE (2002, p.7) suggests 'five levels of supervision: internal affairs, external oversight, Parliamentary oversight, police/media policies and procedures, and local police/community relations.' But it is not made clear which mechanisms should apply to which element of border systems.

As many observers have noted, the regulations concerning practices and principles of border control for the EU have been developed within secretive bureaucracies, their specific contents are often unknown to the public, and regulatory mechanisms to deal with violations of them are conducted and

---

[6] Under the Schengen *acquis*, which will govern border security systems at the external EU borders, 'co-operation models cannot be comprised of shared responsibilities or combined border patrols as the full responsibility of the external borders remains in the hands of the EU candidates' and is based on a 'national strategy' (Niemenkari, 2002, p. 5).

[7] Loader is talking about policing, but the argument applies to border management and oversight as well.

imposed, if they are, out of sight. As Anderson suggests (2000, p.28, notes 14 and 16), the exact contents, beyond general principles, of the approximately 3000 pages of the Schengen *acquis* are unknown and efforts to determine what the *acquis* actually requires are stymied.[8] The basic principles and guidelines of Schengen are summarised in Niemenkari (2002). Interestingly, there is nothing in his depiction of the Schengen principles which relates to oversight and accountability (except for a brief mention of data protection in the SIS system).

It is widely accepted, as well, to use Loader's (2002, p.139, 133) words, that the 'opaque, self-corroborating modes of rule one encounters in the EU, a system that exhibits profound shortcomings as regards its democratic credentials', at best, has led to a 'thinly accountable policy network increasingly organized around an ideology of European security' (see chapters by Sie Dhian Ho and Schelter, this volume, for more detailed descriptions of the complexities of decision-making within the EU context).

As Hills notes (2002b, p.3), 'there is no coherent or comprehensive set of formal internationally recognized policies or programmes dedicated to achieving the objective' of 'providing a framework with which to meet the political imperatives of democracy, security and public confidence' in the management of border security systems. Sheptycki (2002, p.9), talking about policing, argues that 'specifying the political structures for fostering police accountability is an indispensable step on the road to clarifying the practical strategies for enhancing public safety and human rights. Fostering a better interplay of the structures of police accountability at the local, national and transnational level is one of the abiding tasks of our time'. The 'baleful effects of inter-governmentalism on the transparency and accountability of decisions making' within the security field need to be minimised (Loader 2002, p.148). The argument applies to border control as well.

Border agents, as are police, are accountable for two types of actions: things they should not do but do anyway—corruption, abuse of power, criminal acts, or violations of law and professional standards; and acts for which they have an affirmative obligation—acts they should and must do but fail to do. Much of the discussion of accountability is framed in terms of prohibited acts by state agents; less attention is paid to acts which they fail to do. The accountability problem for negative acts is to prevent their occurrence and to sanction agents who do wrong. The problem and the prescription are straightforward. Accountability which focuses on acts which should have been done are harder to define and more difficult to enforce. Accountability for affirmative obligations requires that agents be made to do work which, often for reasons which seems quite legitimate to them, they do not wish to do.

---

[8] Snyder (2000, p.222) notes that the 'common external border is the first major EU policy whose outlines have been shrouded in secrecy. It has been difficult, even for national governments, to establish just what the Schengen system is.' What is clear is the exclusion felt by non-members. 'The expression "Schengenized", meaning excluded from Europe, is heard more and more often' (p.223).

Corrupt agents know that corruption is wrong. But agents are less convinced that not performing affirmative obligations is equally wrong.

A typical example comes from human trafficking at the Mexico–US border. People being smuggled by traffickers, or *coyotes*, are frequently victimised by their traffickers and guides. They are robbed, raped, beaten and sometimes left to die. This has occurred with some frequency recently as increased border control near urban areas at the border has forced illegal migrants to try to cross at less populous areas, which typically are desert. Migrants are abandoned by *coyotes* without food and water, and do not know where to go, become disoriented, and die of thirst. Illegal migrants are helpless.[9] They are, after all, illegally in the US and who are they going to complain to? If they go to the police they will be deported and lose the money they paid to the traffickers.

It is an affirmative obligation of border agents to protect all persons against criminal attacks, and that includes illegal immigrants, and to seek to catch and turn over traffickers who commit criminal acts against the people they smuggle to the authorities. This requirement strikes many border agents as legally correct but also goes against their dominant occupational values. As they see it, their job is to catch, arrest and deport illegal migrants, not to protect them. The victimisation of illegal migrant is not their problem. If migrants do not want to be victimised, they should not come across illegally.[10] The stories of human trafficking at other international borders are quite similar. Migrants and trafficked humans are exploited in many ways.

Other instances of affirmative obligation which are not easily done by agents, and are justified on the basis that this is not really their job, include: informing on fellow officers who are corrupt or abusive or engaged in criminal acts; treating ordinary citizens and criminals equally as regards threshold norms of civil rights; or even the minimal obligation to do a day's work for a day's pay for street-level workers and financial accountability for an agency's budget by managers and planning staffs. In a larger view, the notions of responsiveness, efficiency and effectiveness are affirmative obligations as well.

---

[9] There are now citizen groups who go into the desert area known to be used by smugglers to find abandoned illegal immigrants and rescue them. Initially, local police and the border patrol were vehemently opposed to such groups, even arrested them for helping commit the crime of illegal border crossing. But public outcry and common sense has prevailed. Rescued immigrants are saved but still turned over to the border patrol.

[10] Sometimes, the police will form special groups whose job it is to seek out and protect illegal migrants against victimisation by traffickers and fellow law enforcement agents. The San Diego police, in the late 1970s, formed a special task force whose members posed as immigrants in the borderlands and offered themselves as bait for victimisation (Wambaugh 1984); the Mexican police in the Tijuana area created *Grupo Beta* in the 1990s to protect illegal immigrants against corrupt police and *coyotes* (Rotella 1998, pp.90–116). But such concerted efforts are rare.

Impediments to accountability

Analogies to oversight processes and problems which have appeared in the policing field can provide some insights on how to proceed, as can examples drawn from other border management experiences. Some principles can be suggested. These are taken from the literatures and policies on oversight and accountability in policing, a field that has seen a vast expansion of policing activities and a massive eruption of scholarly attention and analyses. The meaning, principles and means for accountability have been widely discussed and have led to a basic understanding of what works, why, and how what works can be implemented. The obstacles and impediments to effective democratic oversight, transparency and accountability in policing are quite likely to be found in border control systems as well. The general functional and occupational requirements of social and border control are similar in that both forces assert legal and coercive powers and authority over the freedom of people encountered.

The major impediment to accountability is that border security systems combine formal and informal dynamics and respond to and reflect contextual pressures and ideologies. As noted earlier, frontier regimes exist and will continue to develop and they will have an 'autonomous' (Anderson 2000, p.16) impact on the course of events.

What Anderson does not emphasise in the quotation given earlier, which the police literature would, is hidden in the phrase 'the practices which have grown up around them.' The people who do the work are directly and effectively responsible for creating many of such practices. The police and border agents will contribute to the creation of practices based on their organisational and occupational cultures acquired through experience and passed on to new recruits by examples and anecdotes. The formal frameworks (legal powers and obligations, trans-border and inter-agency organisational arrangements, administrative regulations, managerial priorities, the enumeration of roles and tasks) function as constraints on informal re-interpretations by agents, but formal frameworks do not prohibit or seriously inhibit informal elaborations and discourses by workers in the field.[11]

Another element missing in Anderson's listing of characteristics of frontier regimes are oversight practices and means. These may be contained

---

[11] An extreme example of shaping the work to perceived organisational demands and one's own career aspirations occurred in the INS office in California. Two employees shredded 'as many as 90,000 documents to reduce a growing backlog of unprocessed paperwork' (Broder 2003), documents related to visa, passport, work permit and asylum applications. The employees worked for a government contractor. Their shredding was discovered by a government supervisor and led to their indictment on criminal charges after an audit by the Inspector General of the Justice Department. Why they shredded the documents is obvious. It got rid of work, made them look more efficient, and the victims were unimportant.

within formal regulations, civil services requirements, or conditions of employment but, as is true for the interplay of formal and informal organisational dynamics anywhere, the force of regulatory mechanisms on the conduct of agents will be mediated by informal cultures. In policing, as noted by two scholars with vast experience observing the police in many countries, the police do not generally take well to being overseen by outsiders. Nor do they have a strong belief in the inviolability of legal demands on them. As stated by Bayley (2002, p.133), 'among police there is a nearly universal mindset that abiding by the rule-of-law and adhering to recognized standards of human rights is sometimes too restrictive, preventing victims from obtaining justice, allowing criminals to go unpunished, and placing society at unacceptable risk.' This occupational understanding by the police raises problems concerning the place of the police in a democratic society that wants to be governed by law. Chevigny (2002, p.15) calls these sentiments 'The Belief [which] is widely held by the police and often by large parts of the public as well.' The Belief leads the police to reject allegations of (minor) wrongdoings as unfounded, unrealistic, and not based on a correct understanding of the nature of the work and tasks faced by the police.

All I wish to suggest here is that border control agents will also have a strong occupational culture as they attain a separate identity, and that The Belief is likely to have a central position in that culture's set of values and practices. This is not a prediction but an assessment of probabilities. The Belief is not an arbitrary or whimsical set of values and orientations; it is anchored in the strong desire by the police to have a degree of autonomy and discretion in work; they take great pride in their skills, knowledge and familiarity with their job and do not believe that outsiders know as much about the job as they do. I would suspect that other skilled workers, including border agents, have or will develop similar occupational outlooks.[12]

It is not impossible to control the tendency of agents to shape their work to their liking, to engage in illegal and corrupt activities, or to neglect affirmative obligations, but that requires consistent managerial enforcement and external attention, as well as the creative use of political authority. Lessons from the policing field suggest that this will not be easy. Efforts to ensure the democratic accountability of police in transitional and developing countries have been going on for quite some time now, and the meaning of democratic policing is well understood and laid out in numerous international and regional conventions. Yet as Das and Palmiotto observe (2002, p.220), 'it is unfortunate that both authors have found in their informal surveys of police departments in the United States, Canada, India, and various other countries that police officers, including the top ranking personnel, do not even have basic knowledge of the international human rights instruments.' If managers do not

---

[12] Police cultures have been extensively studied, as have the processes by which they are acquired by new recruits and how occupational culture affect work performance. It would be interesting to conduct similar studies of border agents.

know or understand the implications and contents of accepted international conventions they are not likely to insist that their officers follow them. In the management of borders specific conventions analogous to conventions governing the police use of force or codes of conduct do not even exist, and are at best implied by general conventions on human rights and the use of force.

Another impediment is the existence of local transborder relationships which have developed independently of national priorities, formal prohibitions against interactions, and notions of sovereignty held by national elites. Local interactions in effect create a cooperative system of governance for which the international border is simply an impediment, not a prohibition. Rodriguez and Hagan (2001, p.115; also Witt 2001), in their studies of two twin city pairs at the Mexico–US border found a 'variety of formal and informal local practices that create what are effectively transborder communities. These communities reproduce themselves on a daily basis despite national regulations, such as US enforcement campaigns to regulate migration, that attempt to divide them.' This seems to be a typical pattern at all borders where local communities are situated closely together and are integrated economically and by family relations.

The centralisation of border control, as it has occurred in NAFTA and may occur in the EU, will strip border communities of their local capacity to work together and will seek to impose a border control regime suited to national and regional rather than local priorities. As Sadler (2000, p.172) notes in his discussion of the transformation of local regimes at the Mexico–US border, when the border became a 'sexy' political issue because of the war on drugs and the threats of organised crime and national bureaucrats and agencies saw organisational and personal benefits in working at the borders, local knowledge (including mutual abilities to speak the language) and priorities were devalued and existing transborder regimes which had worked effectively to provide mutual assistance in problems were disrupted.

> Now that the border was hot, Washington cowboys and Mexico City *chilangos* were deciding who did what and where. Senior officials (district directors) who did not know Spanish (and had no inclination to learn even a few courtesy terms) and hated Mexico, Mexicans in general, and Mexican officials in particular, suddenly populated most of the major US customs districts. (Sadler 2000, p.172).[13]

Though somewhat stringent in his views of US officials, the main point holds true. National officials will have quite different views on what needs to be done and how; local control, autonomy and responsiveness will lose out when

---

[13] Sadler's personal observations and characterisation of the sentiments of US officials are based on long involvement in border research and border governance.

border control become a national priority. Garcia (2002) describes the development of security regimes at the border in similar fashion. They incorporate local and national priorities as these shift over time, sometimes allowing local autonomy and enterprise and sometimes shutting down long standing transborder interactions and community connections. Centralisation, as it occurs, will be a loss for accountability.

Local autonomy and informal interactions provided a rough and pragmatic accountability of border control tactics, both in the quid pro quo arrangements which developed among border control agencies on both sides ('you do something which helps me and I will owe you one') and by the necessary responsiveness of border tactics to local community concerns expressed through economic umbrella organisations and political leadership, often in quite informal settings. These mechanisms were disrupted by the takeover of control by national agencies and no effective accountability mechanisms took their place.[14] Lack of familiarity with local conditions combined with adherence to national and supranational norms lessened accountability to the publics most directly affected by new control policies.[15]

Another impediment, which is typical of cooperative systems, is that agencies involved in the same field of control will not always see eye-to-eye and work together, despite their common mandate to protect the state and region. Rather, they will compete for resources, lead status and public recognition. The notion of an integrated, smart border management and oversight system is more easily depicted on paper than achieved in reality. The interests and values of agencies and agents do not accommodate themselves frictionless to the demands of outsiders to perform their work by priorities and values specified by other agencies.

An obvious point of friction is the sharing of information. In theory, information should be shared easily and freely for greater effectiveness for the greater good, but that is not how most agencies will see the matter. Information is what guarantees their survival and expansion, their professional autonomy and claims for specialised expertise. Even strong political pressures will have trouble overcoming resistance to giving up part of what makes an agency different and powerful. This has always been a problem in border control in NAFTA. Sharing information among Mexican and US agencies has been hampered by mutual suspicions that have been difficult to overcome. And sharing information among US agencies themselves has not been much

---

[14] Sadler (2000) also argues that the displacement of local control by national bureaucracies increased corruption in border control agencies.
[15] The CEPS (2001b, p.1) Declaration on Friendly Schengen Borders lists six border areas in which close cooperation between neighbors at borders will be disrupted as the Schengen curtain descends.

smoother.[16]

It is also clear from studies of police accountability that, ultimately, oversight will only lead to accountable and responsive behaviour if the values which support oversight become part of the organisational and occupational cultures of control agencies, and are enforced in the day-to-day practices of the organisation. Merely providing training without practical follow-up does not ensure obedience to norms and rules. This same argument can be made for border agencies; and the more professionalised they become, the more the argument holds true since one aspect of professionalisation is the devolution of powers, authority and discretion to individual agents.

The reason is simple. The formal requirements of law and professional codes of conduct are only some of the pressures which shape the behaviour of control agents. To be effective, values supportive of democratic policing, and border control, have to be accepted within the cultures typical of agencies and agents. 'Democratic rights are protected most robustly when there is a cultural commitment to human, civil and democratic rights that is universally accepted, including among the ranks of the security forces' (Waddington 2001, p.5). The Belief has to be superseded by an acceptance by the police, and border agents, that they are accountable for their actions to outsiders.

Concluding Comments[17]

The most basic lesson to be gained from studies of accountability in the policing field and comparative border security studies is that accountability can and must be demanded from the top down, but, in order to be effective, it has to be built from the bottom up as well. From the top, by developing effective plans for accountability which can be enforced by managers, and from the bottom by influencing the nature, content and powers of occupational cultures. Efforts to implement accountability, oversight, and transparency will not work unless they take into account the specific nature of the work done by agents who will be held accountable, and the occupational cultures, values and practices which have evolved and which give meaning to their work. To argue this is not to abdicate demands for accountability or to accept practices and

---

16   One can expect that national border control agencies in the EU will be as reluctant to share information unless and until a stronger EU identity has gained greater salience in the thinking of border control managers and agents.

17   The discussion is of the physical border. Much illegal border trafficking is not confined to physically moving across a demarcated line on the ground. Money laundering, transfers of capital, information and plans to carry out organised crime or terrorist acts, VAT fraud, the theft of trademarks and copyrights, depositing bribes in numbered overseas accounts, or visa frauds can be done without even noticing a border (other than being aware of the territoriality of legal and enforcement processes). Such transborder violations and crimes are not deterred by the physical controls at existing borders.

values which deviate from established standards and norms. All that is implied by this argument is that demands and practices which do not make sense to people who do the work will most likely be avoided, distorted, compromised and fitted to what experience has shown enables agents to do an effective, safe and rewarding job. In that sense, border control agents are no different from any other occupation. As new systems for accountability are drawn up, equal attention must be paid on how and why such systems would be implemented by border control agents.

The second lesson from the policing field is that accountability can be imposed but it requires time, persistent efforts, technical and organisational capacities to detect violations,[18] and an organisational and managerial ethos and set of practices, linked to the career aspirations of officers, which insists that accountability is a normal and important part of the job.

Third, as with policing, accountability cannot be demanded and achieved by the same means for different agents and their diverse occupational tasks. Accountability mechanisms, demands for transparency, standards of conduct and professional work, or sanctions imposed have to be tailored to some degree to the specifics of the job. Principles and values are the same, but the means to achieve adherence to rules and norms have to be different. Guards at a detention facility for illegal immigrants or asylum seekers have a different job than armed guards patrolling a green and distant border. The temptations for corruption are different; their capacity to use force unobserved are different; the consequences of abuses of power are different. All this means is that accountability requires knowing what agents actually do, what are likely or probable violations of standards, and what is likely to prevent such violations.

Fourth, specific guidelines and job descriptions for appropriate behaviour have to be developed and applied. A statement of principles is not enough. Personnel doing the job, and observers judging performance, will need to know what is the appropriate behaviour within the limits of authorised discretion. Proper behaviour will, of course, vary according to the nature of the job.

Fifth, reform in the security sector is best thought of as process rather than a specific outcome. The capacity to be adaptive, flexible and responsive to new contexts has to be built into the institutional dynamics of the border control system. Flexibility, or discretion in their work, has to be incorporated

---

[18] Corruption at the borders requires little effort; it can be almost completely passive. A high ranking Mexican official explained to me once one way in which drug smugglers get across the border with the US. Having agreed with a corrupt US customs official on the deal, smugglers will call up and say 'tomorrow, between 1 and 2 pm, we will come across in a blue Toyota (or some other make) pickup.' All the officer has to do is go about her/his normal job, inspect trucks, talk to drivers, but in the 1 to 2 pm period not examine blue Toyota pickups too closely. An observer would not be able to detect anything unusual in the behavior or work of the officer.

into formal and informal teaching and be part of the socialisation agents experience as they enter the organisation and as they move through their careers. Discretion implies judgment, and judgment implies having a basic understanding of the norms which should guide judgment. One of the orthodox findings from studies of police training is that judgment and standards for exercising judgement which are in accord with societal norms are not often or extensively taught to new recruits, nor reinforced through in-service training. Border agent training must avoid this weakness.

Sixth, mechanisms to minimise competition among border control agencies should be instituted. Competitions will occur and require the establishment of a external oversight capacity to keep agencies in line and on target.

Last, more mechanisms for accountability are better than a few or a single one. Combinations of external (legal, political, community, media) and internal means to seek out, prevent or deter, and sanction violations are more likely to be effective than either external or internal means alone. Ultimately, internal mechanisms are needed to translate external demands into effective organisational policy. But external oversight is a spur to internal oversight which could lapse when external oversight has weakened or collapsed and agents and supervisors know that has happened.

As effective security systems at the external borders of the EU become more institutionalised and varied, enhanced efforts to create the variety of accountability mechanisms to sustain the legitimacy of new arrangements and practices are equally important. Ultimately, developing fair and effective accountability systems requires as much transnational co-operation as is needed to develop effective and trusted border control systems. The two should go hand-in-hand. So far that has not happened in either NAFTA or the EU. So far, accountability has been trumped by securitisation, transparency by a 'need' for secrecy, and oversight by the reluctance of member states to create regional oversight bodies.

References

ANDERSON, MALCOLM. 2000. 'The Transformation of Border Controls: A European Precedent?' In *The Wall Around the West. State Borders and Immigration Controls in North America and Europe*, eds. Peter Andreas and Timothy Snyder, 15–29. London: Rowman and Littlefield Publishers.

ANDERSON, MALCOLM, JOANNA APAP AND CHRISTOPHER MULKINS. 2001. 'Policy Alternatives to Schengen Border Controls on the Future EU External Frontier'. Proceedings of an Expert Seminar, Warsaw 213, 24 February 2001. Brussels: CEPS.

ANDREAS, PETER. 2000. *Border Games: Policing the US–Mexico Divide*. Ithaca: Cornell University Press.

ARONOWITZ, ALEXIS A. 2002. 'The United Nations Programme Against Trafficking in Human Beings: Research and Lessons Learned'. *International Journal of Comparative and Applied Criminal Justice*, 26 (2): 257–275.

BAILEY, JOHN AND ROY GODSON, eds. 1999. *Organized Crime and Democratic Governability. Mexico and the US–Mexican Borderlands*. Pittsburgh: University of Pittsburgh Press.

BAYLEY, DAVID H. 2002. 'Law Enforcement and the Rule of Law: Is There a Tradeoff?' *Criminology and Public Policy*, 2 (1): 133–153.

BRODER, JOHN M. 2003. 'I.N.S. Workers Accused of Shredding Files'. *New York Times*, 31 January 2003, A18.

CENTER FOR EUROPEAN POLICY STUDIES. CEPS, 2001a. SITRA FOUNDATION AND STEFAN BATORY FOUNDATION. 2001a. 'New European Borders and Security Cooperation: Promoting Trust in an Enlarged European Union'. Conference Report, CEPS: Brussels, 6–7 July.

CENTER FOR EUROPEAN POLICY STUDIES. CEPS, 2001b. 'A Political Declaration on Friendly Schengen Border Policy'. CEPS: Brussels.

CHEVIGNY, PAUL. 2002. 'Conflict of Rights and Keeping Order'. *Criminology and Public Policy*, 2 (1): 155–160.

DAS, DILIP AND MICHAEL J. PALMIOTTO. 2002. 'International Human Rights Standards: Guidelines for the World's Police Officers'. *Police Quarterly*, 5 (2): 206–221.

DCAF. 2001. 'Border Security Models Put to the Test. First Report of the 'Lessons Learned from the Establishment of Border Security Systems' Workshop'. Geneva (December).

EDMUNDS, TIMOTHY. 2001. 'Defining Security Sector Reform'. In *Proceedings of the Geneva Centre for the Democratic Control of Armed Forces (DCAF)–IISS Workshops, Geneva, 23–25 April 2001*, 15–19. London: The International Institute for Strategic Studies.

EHRENREICH, BARBARA AND ARLIE RUSSELL HOCHSCHILD, eds. 2002. *Global Woman. Nannies, Maids, and Sex Workers in the New Economy*. New York: Henry Holt and Company.

'Feasibility Study for the Setting up of a 'European Border Police''. Final Report. Rome, 30 May 2002. Available at: <http://jurrit.jur.kun.nl/cmr/docs/61.pdf>

GARCIA, JOSÉ Z. 2002. 'Security Regimes on the US–Mexico Border'. In *Transnational Crime and Public Security. Challenges to Mexico and the United States*, eds., John Bailey and Jorge Chabat, 299–334. La Jolla: University of California, San Diego, Center for US–Mexican Studies.

HILLS, ALICE. 2002a. 'Border Control Services and Security Sector Reform'. DCAF Working Paper (February). Geneva.

_____ 2002b. 'Consolidating Democracy: Professionalism, Democratic Principles and Border Services'. DCAF Working Paper (July). Geneva.

_____ 2005. *Border Security in the Balkans: Europe's Gatekeepers.* Adelphi Paper No. 371. London: Institute for International and Strategic Studies.

HUISMAN, SANDER. 2002. 'Transparency and Accountability of Police Forces, Security Services and Intelligence Agencies (TAPAS). A Draft Comparative Assessment of the Effectiveness of Existing Arrangements in Seven Countries: Bulgaria, France, Italy, Poland, Sweden, the United Kingdom and the United States of America'. Groningen, The Netherlands: Centre for European Security Studies.

KYLE, DAVID AND REY KOSLOWSKI, eds. 2001. *Global Human Smuggling. Comparative Perspectives.* Baltimore: The Johns Hopkins University Press.

LAHAV, GALLYA AND VIRGINIE GUIRAUDON. 2000. 'Comparative Perspectives on Border Control: Away form the Border and Outside the State'. In *The Wall Around the West. State Borders and Immigration Controls in North America and Europe,* eds., Peter Andreas and Timothy Snyder, 55–77. London: Rowman and Littlefield Publishers.

LEDUFF, CHARLIE. 2003. 'Border Towns Are Close Enough to Touch But Worlds Apart'. *New York Times,* 24 February 2003, A11.

LEE, JENNIFER. 2003. 'Progress Seen in Border Tests of ID System'. *New York Times,* 7 February 2003, A14.

LOADER, IAN. 2002. 'Policing, Securitisation and Democratisation in Europe'. *Criminal Justice,* 2 (2): 125–153

LOWELL, B. LINDSAY AND ROBERTO SURO. 2002. 'How Many Undocumented: The Numbers Behind the US–Mexico Migration Talks'. Washington, DC: The Pew Hispanic Center; Available at URL <http:\\www.pewhispanic.org>

NEVINS, JOSEPH. 2002. *Operation Gatekeeper. The Rise of the 'Illegal Alien' and the Making of the US–Mexico Boundary.* New York and London: Routledge.

NIEMENKARI, ARTO. 2002. 'EU/Schengen Requirements for National Border Security Systems'. DCAF Working Paper. Geneva.

OSCE, LAW ENFORCEMENT DIVISION. 2002. 'Co-operation Programme to Strengthen the Rule of Law. Council of Europe and OSCE Joint Final Report on Police Accountability in Serbia'. OSCE and Council of Europe, first draft.

REIMANN, JURGEN. 2001. 'Session 3: German Case Study'. DCAF, Workshop on the 'Criteria for Success and Failure in the Establishment of Border Security'. Geneva.

RIDGE, TOM. 2003. 'Remarks of Secretary Tom Ridge to the American Enterprise Institute: Securing An [sic] Post 9/11 World', at <www.DHS.gov>, Press Room, 3 September 2003.

RODRIGUEZ, NESTOR AND JACQUELINE HAGAN. 2002. 'Transborder Community Relations at the US–Mexico Border: Laredo/Nuevo Laredo and El Paso/Ciudad Juarez'. In *Transnational Crime and Public Security. Challenges to Mexico and the United States*, eds., John Bailey and Jorge Chabat, 88–116. La Jolla: University of California, San Diego, Center for US–Mexican Studies.

ROTELLA, SEBASTIAN. 1998. *Twilight on the Line. Underworlds and Politics at the US–Mexico Border*. New York: W.W. Norton and Company.

SADLER, LOUIS R. 2000. 'The Historical Dynamics of Smuggling in the US–Mexican Border Region, 1550–1998: Reflections on Markets, Cultures and Bureaucracies'. In *Organized Crime and Democratic Governability. Mexico and the US–Mexican Borderlands*, eds., John Bailey and Roy Godson, 161–176. Pittsburgh: University of Pittsburgh Press.

SCHIESEL, SETH. 2003. 'Inspectors at Customs Checkpoints Put Advanced Technology to Work as Their Focus Shifts from Drug Shipments to Potential Terrorist Weapons'. *New York Times*, 20 March 2003, E1ff.

SHEARING, CLIFFORD AND JENNIFER WOOD. 2000. 'Reflections on the Governance of Security: A Normative Inquiry'. *Police Practice and Research*, 1 (4): 457–476.

SHEPTYCKI, JAMES. 2000. 'Policing and Human Rights: An Introduction'. *Policing and Society*, 10 (1): 1–10.

SNYDER, TIMOTHY. 2000. 'Conclusion: The Wall Around the West'. In *The Wall Around the West. State Borders and Immigration Controls in North America and Europe*, eds., Peter Andreas and Timothy Snyder, 219–227. London: Rowman and Littlefield Publishers.

WADDINGTON, P.A.J. 2001. 'Negotiating and Defining 'Public Order''. *Police Practice and Research*, 2: 1–14.

WAMBAUGH, JOSEPH. 1984. *Lines and Shadows*. New York: Bantam Books.

WITT, ANDREA. 2001. 'National Borders: Images, Functions, and Their Effects on Cross-Border Cooperation in North America and Europe'. In *Caught in the Middle. Border Communities in an Era of Globalisation*, eds. Demetrios G. Papademetriou and Deborah Waller Myers, 166–199. Washington, D.C: Carnegie Endowment for International Peace.

Chapter 3

Towards a Rationality of Democratic Border Management

Alice Hills

Developing a regionally appropriate model of border security has been a priority for the European Union (EU) in recent years and pressure has been brought to bear on adjacent countries to adopt not only the EU's functional standards, but also its understanding of democratic management. Many countries in Europe's fragile regions confront challenges similar to those of EU applicant and candidate countries, and the EU's standards, as embodied within the Schengen *acquis* (which lays out the written rules and commonly accepted standards for border management within the Schengen sphere), are seen as providing a benchmark for measuring the convergence of regional border services to appropriate standards (Niemankari 2002). Despite this there is little systematic or comparative analysis of the theory and practice of democratic border management.

In this chapter I argue that the transferability of the EU's model of border management to countries outside the Schengen area cannot be assessed, nor the transformation it seeks to achieve be explained, unless the empirical and conceptual parameters of comparative border management are first identified.[1] This is more problematic than it might appear because border management is not based on a coherent theoretical framework but on a number of competing assumptions, political imperatives, functional necessities, and social realities. Democratic oversight—which is taken here to epitomise the EU's legitimising ideal—is merely one such theme, and there are too many variables involved to allow for an easy linkage between it, EU functional standards, and effective security practice.

This premise is considered by means of two questions: (1) what are the empirical and conceptual parameters of functional border management; and (2) what rationalities of security and governance are implicit in contemporary practice? It would be useful to consider these questions primarily in terms of EU pronouncements and policies. The answers offered are instead based on developments in three countries on the EU's south-east frontiers, one of which

---

[1] Special thanks are due to the members of DCAF's International Border Security Advisory Board: Aare Evisalu, Arto Niemenkari, Andrus Öövel, Jürgen Reimann and Zoltan Szabo. The opinions expressed here are nonetheless mine alone.

is now a member state. The recent creation of a state border service in Bosnia and Herzegovina (BiH) is considered first on the basis that Bosnia is in effect a European colony, which makes the assumptions underpinning its system explicit. To explore the possibilities for generalising from Bosnia's experience, a comparison is made with the more extreme situation in Slovenia, where harmonisation with Schengen standards has been achieved, and Albania, where there is no functioning border system. The choice of these countries acknowledges the importance of regional dynamics but avoids the possibility of producing too narrow and specific an explanation. Together they are indicative of the rationalities underpinning contemporary European border management.

Parameters of Border Management

Border management concerns the administration of borders. Its precise meaning varies according to national context, but it usually concerns the rules, techniques and procedures regulating activities and traffic across defined border areas or zones. Most European definitions have a strongly legislative or bureaucratic flavour. Hence in the EU's sphere of influence border management concerns the rules, techniques and procedures regulating activities and traffic across defined border areas or zones. It is defined in terms of border checks and border surveillance; border checks on people, their possessions and vehicles are carried out at authorised crossing points, while surveillance is carried out between authorised crossing points (EU Schengen Catalogue 2002).

Border guards who have received specialised training usually provide border management.[2] Guards trained in the border departments of professional academies are familiar with their national security policies, criminal law and procedures, and with specialities such as international obligations, criminal reconnaissance, risk assessment, alien policing, traffic control, communications, or logistics; some will be knowledgeable about management studies; and some will speak a foreign language. Some receive instruction in the theoretical and philosophical aspects of border control (Zrínyi Miklós 1999). But such levels of knowledge are unmatched outside professional circles. Border management is usually analysed in terms of identity politics or European integration, rather than functional security, and guarding is benignly neglected. Distaste for the old defence roles of border guards has been replaced by the perception that guarding is a technically-focused subset of policing that does not deserve specific attention. That assumption is questionable.

---

2 The terms *border guard* and *border police* are often used interchangeably but *border guard* is the preferred term here, not least because its use emphasises that within the EU's sphere of influence border forces should be independent and specialised organisations, subordinate to ministries of the interior but not forming part of a national police force.

Empirical Parameters

The influence of the EU ensures that the legal and empirical parameters of guarding across Europe are increasingly identifiable. Within its sphere of influence, the EU's written and unwritten rules governing border security exert significant influence even in countries that as yet can only aspire to closer association with the Union. Even so, the extent to which it is appropriate to generalise from the EU's rules is debatable.

There is undoubtedly a political and 'professional' consensus regarding many aspects of guarding across the geographical region. The function of border guards is generally agreed to be that of protecting the territorial integrity of states from incursion or infiltration by illegal immigrants or traffickers. This is judged to be an essentially policing, rather than military, task and reflects today's broad concept of security. The EU's written and unwritten rules governing border security lay out the bureaucratic boundaries of the task in great detail.

Empirical and legislative guidelines were laid down in the Schengen *acquis* that was integrated into the EU framework in 1999 when the Treaty of Amsterdam came into force. The *acquis* provides standards regarding the organisation, tactics and procedures for border authorities, as well as rules and regulations, many of which are clarified by the *EU Schengen Catalogue* of recommendations for Schengen's correct application and best practice (Niemankari 2002). But whether such context-specific bureaucratic processes and procedures are indicative of the unique parameters of the field is less clear; to explain or describe border guarding solely in terms of Schengen's recommendations is like analysing policing only in terms of UK-style policing. For this reason Schengen's understanding may best be categorised as a regional and time-specific parameter, and its fundamental explanatory value is best judged in relation to its transferability to non-member states on the EU's periphery.

The key to understanding the parameters of the wider European border guard field is to be found in the balance between political imperatives, social realities and functional legacies. A brief survey of border developments in the region illustrates the way in which the balance shifts according to circumstances. During the Cold War border management in central and south-east Europe was designed to protect the state. There were naturally differences between state approaches. Albania had a rigorous control system of its own, Hungary was bound by Warsaw Pact rules on entry and exit, while the former Yugoslavia (Serbia and Montenegro) had a relatively tolerant system for movement by its citizens and visiting tourists. But all were primarily military in structure and philosophy.

With the ending of the Cold War, exit controls were abolished and most military frontier guard structures were transformed into civilian border police. Some states (notably Hungary and Slovenia) began to adapt their systems to EU specifications, but elsewhere in the region instability and conflict ensured the continuation of a more military-oriented culture. Bosnia, for example, had no external borders or border force in the early 1990s, but its police transitioned from law enforcement to war fighting easily during the war that began in 1991 because their paramilitary role in the Yugoslav All People's National Defence system had equipped them with heavy weapons such as anti-tank and anti-aircraft guns (Dziedzic and Bair 1998). In addition, paramilitarism was linked to organised crime throughout the region; Bosnia's nationalist politicians, for example, expected the police to control their respective regions and contribute to smuggling, gun running and ethnic cleansing.

Since then the parameters have shifted to accommodate new political objectives, including democratisation as a vehicle for creating regional stability. Thus a number of programmes, financed and promoted by the EU, the UNHCR, and the Stability Pact of the Organisation for Security and Co-operation in Europe (OSCE) have been designed to develop democratic management. Such programmes not only emphasise the importance of democratic oversight and professionalism, but they also widen the parameters of the guarding field to include an international dimension that is usually presented in terms of co-operation. Yet the environments in which such plans must develop are shaped by wars that led to several million refugees and the revival of traditional Balkan smuggling routes, leaving a legacy of serious organised crime, uncontrolled migration, and the widespread trafficking of illegal migrants, stolen cars, drugs and weapons. Furthermore, much of the region lacks the administrative and judicial capacity needed to develop or support effective border management. Poverty, corruption, and low educational levels further complicate its development. As a result political calls for democratic forms of border security are offset by institutional incapacity, pervasive corruption amongst officers, and chronic insecurity. Macedonia's border guards, for example, must deal with insurgent gangs armed with missile launchers and sub-machine guns. In other words, social realities and functional imperatives retain relevance; it is their relative balance that has changed.

In summary, the formal parameters of border guarding within the EU's sphere of influence are now clear: The major legal and technical features of border guarding within Europe are indicated by the Schengen *acquis*, which acts as a regional standard despite the social realities of the states in which it is to be influential. Yet many questions concerning the nature of border guarding remain unanswered. Indeed, the dominant—and politicised—nature of the EU's requirements suggests that the factors shaping the wider border guard field remain under-explored. This is particularly evident when the conceptual parameters of border guarding are discussed.

Conceptual Parameters

The empirical and theoretical parameters of border guarding are linked in that political developments directly affect the way we understand the subject, with the conceptual parameters of border guarding shifting to accommodate political demands and contemporary norms. Thus border guards performed a military or paramilitary role protecting state frontiers during the Cold War whereas consequent shifts in our understanding of the nature of security and protection in Europe means that guarding is now understood as a policing matter (Bruinsma and van der Vijver 1999).

Cold War forms of border protection are no longer required. The border management department of Hungary's Zrínyi Miklós University of National Defence, for example, has not conducted officer training in the framework of a 'land forces/all-weapons command course' or presented obligatory military subjects since the mid-1990s (Konya 1999). Border surveillance and policing troops are no longer required, and Hungary, in common with many European countries, has phased out the use of conscripts. These trends are reflected in today's emphasis on border services rather than forces, and by the increasingly common title of border police.

This blend of new and old suggests that Schengen's context-specific provisions cannot provide definitive conceptual parameters to the border management field. To some extent the EU accepts this. As the *Schengen Catalogue* notes, its provisions refer 'to ideas or concepts connected with the administration of borders, the terms of which are not uniformly defined or codified in the Schengen States' (*EU Schengen Catalogue* 2002). In practice these concepts refer to favoured organisational or ordering models such as the Integrated Border Security (IBS) model, rather than border guarding per se.

The IBS model, which is based on a set of complementary measures that are implemented on four complementary tiers or filtering levels, reflects the EU's political vision and is both expensive and sophisticated. The four tiers, for example, are activities in third countries (as in the collection of information by liaison officers), international border co-operation, measures at external borders, and further activities inside the territory of Schengen states or between them. The successful application of the model depends on its implementation across the EU's sphere of influence, and the key elements in its successful ('correct') application are co-ordination, accurate and reliable situational assessment, the use of specialised trained professionals, and the development of trust between the various actors involved. The methodologies used are those of policing; IBS's vocabulary is based on risk analysis, intelligence, data-flow management, situational awareness, reaction capability and information exchange (*EU Schengen Catalogue* 2002). The successful use of such techniques requires motivated and trained guards, i.e., a professional force. In so far as the conceptual parameters of IBS are considered by policy makers, they are taken to be those of policing, albeit specialist policing. The problem with relying on this is that it avoids the question of what is special or unique to border guards.

Contemporary literature on border management focuses on the general task of policing borders, on the need for co-operation, and on measures to stop trafficking (Salt et al. 2000), rather than on the functional necessities or the agents—guards—responsible for border policing. It rarely addresses the unique nature of border guarding. The neglect stems from the assumption that border guarding is merely a subset of policing, a technical or administrative task performed by a specialist police. This is reflected in, for example, the categorisation used by the OSCE, whose 2001 Police Reform Co-ordination Conference included border policing within six priority areas for police reform in Serbia (Monk 2001). At the same time, however, there is an EU consensus that border guards should be similar to, but distinct from, public police; that they should be a separate and multi-purpose police, answerable to civilian interior ministries. Border management is also treated as an activity dependent on administrative and technical networks in which border guards work alongside public police, immigration and customs officers, and private transport and security companies (Bigo 1999).

The EU's political programme, with its conflation of security and crime, external and internal security, and promotion of a European border police, drives this understanding forward. The trend is strengthened by the paramilitary nature of many European policing traditions, and by the regional realities of violence and criminality: organised crime, illegal trafficking, and terrorism (which are essentially enforcement matters) are generally recognised as the gravest threats to European order. Indeed, the programme's validity is emphasised by the EU's urgent need to manage uncontrolled migration and human smuggling on its borders, a challenge that straddles its need to guard its frontiers and police trafficking while acting in accordance with humanitarian legislation. That border management is seen as a policing role, designed to filter out problems at borders, is further reinforced by the belief that crime and insecurity are synonymous. Border guarding has, moreover, become specialist policing because, as Bigo points out, 'The routine identity check carried out according to the Schengen Convention is motivated by a kind of rationality different from that of earlier frontier checks concerning foreigners. All those who pass the frontier now are suspected of being potential criminals' (Bigo 2000). Nowadays border security has more to do with filtering, monitoring, protection and law enforcement than traditional defence or guarding.

The assumption that border guarding is a policing matter is in many respects legitimate. Most border guards are capable of acting as conventional police, most perform a wide range of duties, and many are integral parts of their state's police organisation. Policing accordingly plays a defining role in conventional understanding of border management. But there is still a need to identify the relevant policing paradigms and to assess the extent to which they are applicable to border guarding.

Part of the problem in so doing is that the basic parameters of the policing field are themselves indeterminate. Bittner's classic notion of legitimate force as the essence of the police as an institution, for example, aids understanding of what guards sometimes do, but it is not sufficient to explain what they do outside times of crisis or emergency (Bittner 1980). Contrast a more recent multi-variable definition that refers to policing as 'those organised forms of maintenance, peacekeeping, rule or law enforcement, crime investigation and prevention and other forms of investigation and associated information-brokering—which may involve a conscious exercise of coercive power—undertaken by individuals or organisations, where such activities are viewed by them and/or others as a central or key defining part of their purpose' (Jones and Newburn 1998). This is comprehensive, but does not really explain what public police do, or what is unique to their role.

So what defines the border policing field? Why do we distinguish between public police and border guards/police? The answer appears to be that the conceptual parameters of border guarding are primarily as in policing, but there are significant differences between the two. Discipline, for example, is relevant, as are the notions of high/low policing, and the policing of territory and populations. The notion of policing as being about 'securing territory' (including surveillance) and thereby controlling 'suspect populations' seems especially relevant (Ericson quoted in Sheptycki 2000, p.10), particularly in the frontier zones where guards have formal authority; when territory cannot be secured then the surveillance and control of its permanent or transient occupants is impossible. For such reasons, EU border management forms part of a system of surveillance and control that depends on police co-operation across the EU. It must be seen in the broad context of the police area of the EU's sphere of justice and home affairs.

Rising crime rates, terrorism, uncontrolled migration, violence and instability appear to call for a policing response to border-related problems. Accountability and discretion seem to apply to border guarding as much as they do to policing too, though regional realities mean that notions of personal accountability or discretion are alien to some police cultures. Coercion is also relevant (escort duties are coercive), though guards are distanced from involvement in other aspects of criminal justice. The removal measures involved in managing illegal migration, for example, are not punishment; that departure may be involuntary does not make enforced removal punishment. This understanding is reflected in the increasingly common use of the term 'uncontrolled' (rather than illegal) migration.

These observations suggest that there are significant differences between border guards and public police, and the most significant difference is that border security is about protection and monitoring—about guarding—rather than coercion per se, though guards clearly have specific coercive powers. Effective border management naturally requires co-operation between border guards and police,[3] but, even so, it is clear that while border guards can perform many police duties, not all police can perform border duties. This is primarily the result of the technical and operational demands associated with EU standards, and is especially strong where the application of Schengen standards requires specialised knowledge and training.

This general interpretation supports the European approach to democratic forms of border management, though its application elsewhere in the world may be difficult to justify. It also raises the question of the extent to

---

[3] It also requires co-operation with customs, transportation authorities and the judiciary, though it does not mean they are similar.

which it is reasonable to generalise from Schengen standards. It may be that we should simply accept that the picture is more nuanced than we would wish: the linkage between border guards and the police (or military) varies according to political context and historical legacy.

Implicit Rationalities

Border management is based on a number of competing assumptions, so it is additionally necessary to identify the assumptions and rationalities of security and governance implicit in contemporary border management. How, for example, does border management reflect our assumptions about the nature of European security? What are the implications of today's emphasis on tighter border regimes and greater co-operation between law enforcement and intelligence agencies? What does contemporary practice tell us about the principles of knowledge underpinning border management?

Contemporary European guarding practice is underpinned by multiple rationalities, of which the following five—policing, security, politics, institutional, and functional—are representative.

First, policing's rationalities offer a key to border security within the EU's sphere of influence. Not only are enforcement issues such as uncontrolled migration, terrorism and transnational crime regarded as more serious threats than conflict, but also the EU has been organisationally well placed to shift international attention from the concerns characteristic of the Cold War to those associated with today's more diffuse threats (Grabbe 2000). Indeed, Schengen expresses the EU's model of internal security, which developed in response to EU perceptions of its increasing vulnerability to trans-border threats; today's security agenda is primarily concerned with managing such threats and developing the conditions for stability and peace (rather than preventing conflict and instability as such) and so allows border policies to lie at the heart of security debates.

The EU has been able to shift attention to such concerns, and effectively legitimise its response, because it has long enjoyed a sense of legitimacy in this area. But policing is not the whole story because more conventional security challenges are also present, especially in the EU's border regions where NATO retains a role. For this reason, policing (or enforcement) rationalities tend to merge into those associated with more conventional definitions of security.

Second, the EU's security fears also cluster around uncontrolled migration, the trafficking of illegal drugs, and terrorism. These issues are often difficult to disentangle, and their prioritisation varies according to circumstances, but border security is generally thought to represent an important line of defence against all three; uncontrolled migration offers profitable business opportunities to the organised crime that supports terrorism, so guards check for forged documents and illegal or suspicious loads, and they patrol the green or blue borders that illegal migrants cross. In this way

EU border policies reflect the Union's understanding of the nature of European security.

Third, politics must be factored in. Security is a matter of perception, but it is also constructed by the agents involved, and manipulated for political or institutional purposes. It has been argued, for example, that the prominence given to uncontrolled migration and transnational organised crime within the EU reflects the instrumental demands of law enforcement agencies for greater resources. Politicisation and securitisation also refer to the overtly political desires of some member governments and organisations to promote forms of border organisation consistent with tighter political integration (Benyon 1996). This is not to suggest a crude attempt to shape border management so much as to emphasise the role of political imperatives; the desire for European integration and the promotion of expanded notions of security shape contemporary border management just as strongly as politico–military requirements moulded guarding during the Cold War. Additionally, the European integration project involves managing national borders in more consensual ways so as to enhance stability, and Schengen is the ordering device associated with this. The rationalities implicit in border management may therefore be taken to include power relationships (and population control) within and without the EU, as well as politics and national security strategies (Bigo 1998).

The fourth factor, institutional and bureaucratic interests, cannot be discounted either, for the reorganisation required by Schengen is not always in the interests of the security forces concerned. Indeed, all the rationalities referred to here are ultimately accommodated, adapted or subverted by the functional agents involved. A 'canteen culture' comparable to the sub-culture observed in many police forces is probably present, but little analysis of occupational cultures has been conducted. Guards may, for instance, act in the belief that they alone hold back chaos and keep out undesirable groups even though this may conflict with managerial objectives emphasising human rights. And national understandings of what constitutes good guarding probably exist too (Das 1997).

Lastly, the functional imperatives of managing borders, which are the fifth rationality, cannot be discounted. Guarding mountainous or forested areas requires paramilitary capabilities and rapid reaction forces, while green and blue borders may also demand special skills.

In other words, multiple rationalities are present, so the extent to which Schengen's functional and political standards can fundamentally shape European border security is questionable. This has policy and practical implications for the transferability of democratic forms of border management.

Relating Theory to Practice

The development of democratic forms of border management in Europe's borderlands is, not surprisingly, a key issue for organisations such as the EU and OSCE. In the case of the EU, the effective management of its area of freedom, security and justice rests on candidate and aspirant countries sharing its values and practices, hence the utility of Schengen's standards. Similarly the Stability Pact judges the reform of border management in South Eastern Europe, and the harmonisation of regional border control to EU standards, as a priority: 'Without such reforms and co-operation, organized crime will make use of porous borders, and ill-equipped and low-paid border staff. Proper and modern border control is also a prerequisite for the increase of tourism, for the facilitation of the exchange of persons, services and goods to foster economic growth, and for a well functioning customs control, bringing stable incomes to state budgets' (Stability Pact 2001).

Schengen standards clearly represent a critical tool for achieving this, but focusing on them alone ignores fundamental questions regarding democratic border management. Are democratic forms of accountability a normative priority, for example, a legitimising principle, or an organising device? Is democratic border management a matter of bureaucratic accountability and transparency, or a matter of professional standards and values? How does change in the rationale and meaning of borders translate into institutional structures? Partial answers to such questions can be found in border forces outside the core Schengen area. The case of the State Border Service (SBS) of Bosnia and Herzegovina (BiH), for example, shows that border guarding is based on a number of competing assumptions and functional necessities, of which democratic control is merely one. To explore the possibilities for generalisation BiH is compared to the more extreme examples of Slovenia, which became a member in 2005, and Albania. Together they illustrate the range of possibilities and dilemmas facing European border management.[4]

---

[4] BiH has approximately 1,666 km of border, an area of 51,129 sq km, and a population of 3.8 million. Albania's borders are 1,082 km in length, its area is 27,398 sq km, and its population 3.5 million, while Slovenia's borders are 1,382 km, its area 20,723 sq km, and its population two million.
BiH's SBS deployed 1,750 officers in early 2002 (the projected figure for late 2002 was 2,700); Albania's border police were estimated as 500 in 2002; and Slovenia's police numbered 4,500 (907 new officers were employed in 2001–02). The BiH figures are taken from ICG 2002, p.16; those of Albania from IISS 2003, p.64; Slovenia's were provided by the Slovenia Police.

State Border Service of Bosnia and Herzegovina

The BiH State Border Service (SBS) is important here for three reasons: it is new; it is explicitly shaped by political imperatives; and its formal objectives and organisation are based on internationally acceptable norms, structures, and objectives. It thus provides an indication of where the balance between effective control and democratic oversight may lie.

Pre-war BiH did not have an international border or border force. The SBS was created in 2000 and ratified by the State Parliament in the summer of 2001. The United Nations Mission's High Representative imposed the law creating it, and the UN Mission in Bosnia and Herzegovina (UNMIBH)'s Border Service Department effectively controls its development and management. Its integrated border control management model is based on EU standards, and its equipment and training reflects international standards and approaches; SBS had inherited little in the way of resources so almost all the equipment and training programmes were needed. Many countries, including Austria, Germany, Hungary, Italy, the Netherlands, Sweden, Switzerland, Italy, the UK and the USA, gave bilateral financial assistance, donations, and training programmes. Inter-governmental organisations provide additional assistance. Thus standard UNMIBH courses for all police include advice on 'human dignity', the UNHCR provides training in the handling of asylum seekers, while the EU's IMMPACT team trained approximately more than 1,500 officers in forgery detection, interviewing and profiling in the SBS's first two years (*Borderline 2002*).

SBS's formal organisation and objectives reflect the philosophy of such donors, for whom democratic forms of border management in BiH are a normative priority, a legitimising principle, and an organising device. SBS is a specialist police that is described as a law enforcement agency, and its creation is seen as an important contribution towards police reform in BiH. This was reflected in announcements that the EU police-training mission in Bosnia would train the police in border control, and that customs regulations harmonisation with the EU was to be achieved by 2005. SBS's duties include discovering and preventing indictable offences and searching for those committing them, and investigating border-related criminal offences within its jurisdiction, as well as supervision of the state border, ensuring security at BiH's airports, and controlling official crossing points. SBS is expensive but it is amongst the most advanced border services in the region and its creation is a major achievement. It has enhanced the authority of the state, increased its revenues, and made a genuine contribution to fighting cross-border crime (ICG 2002). But SBS has yet to escape from its social and political environment.

Local capabilities rarely match international standards.[5] The notion that SBS exists to enforce the law rather than the wishes of the government of the day means little because notions such as personal accountability are largely absent from the existing police culture; there is little notion that officers are servants of the law. Corruption, low quality recruits and incompetence are real problems. So too is SBS's powerlessness in the face of well organised smuggling operations enjoying political protection. Similarly, SBS cannot touch the most profitable forms of organised crime in Bosnia (human trafficking, terrorism and smuggling) because they are a regional rather than local problem, and regional co-operation leaves much to be desired. Working relationships between the relatively well-paid state-level SBS and the police and entities' customs officers are often poor.

Domestic realities must be balanced by international realities. Much international aid is prompted by the EU's desire to use the SBS as a filter mechanism for its own security (Bosnia is still seen as a security problem), but much is prompted by national concerns. As a result, there is little co-ordination between the various national training programmes. In 2001, for instance, courses teaching specialist-interviewing skills were provided by the UK and Denmark, and the UNHCR, working in isolation, while the US Immigration and Naturalization Service (INS) ignored the UNMIBH's Border Service Department and worked directly with the SBS (ICG 2002, p.8). This pattern continues. In other words, BiH's SBS is underpinned by multiple rationalities.

As far as democratic control is concerned, SBS is a good answer to a real problem but it is not the whole answer. International political pressure for democratic oversight as a norm, principle and organising device is, as ever, offset by social realities.

Slovenia

The Slovenia border system is also new, having been created on independence in 1991. Its formal objectives and structures also mirror internationally acceptable norms, and its equipment and training reflect internationally acceptable approaches. But there are significant differences that go beyond these factors, and are suggestive of different rationalities.

In contrast to BiH's dedicated border service, Slovenia does not have a special independent border police. There are specialised border police units operating at the local level but the police units carrying out border tasks are an integral part of the regular police, which conducts all border guard duties. Thus the combined police units operating at the local level provide both border checks and surveillance, and all other police tasks within their regional jurisdiction. A specialised police unit for border surveillance was created in

---

[5] Though some international capabilities are tainted by, for example, association with prostitution. See ICG 2002, p.33.

2002 but the State Border and Foreigners Section of the Uniformed Police Directorate, which is part of the General Police Directorate, provide border security. State border control, surveillance, and the supervision of foreigners are the main tasks of police border units, but other units, including those used for general police tasks, traffic and more specialised roles (such as airports, railways, and dogs) also perform these tasks. Good co-ordination between the various units is critical.

More importantly, the development of Slovenia's border management has been shaped by its political objective of becoming a full-fledged member of the EU. A number of significant points are identifiable. The State Border Control Act of 1991, for example, made a number of important statements indicative of future developments. Not only was the 'border zone' and restrictive movement regime abolished, but the importance of police discretion was established; the objectives of border control formally include 'strengthening the subjective responsibility of police officers'—ie., encouraging the acceptance of personal responsibility (personal communication from Dušan Burian, 5 November 2002.).

A strategic policy document stating that Slovenia would implement the Schengen regime (and, by extension, procedures that are conducive to democratic control) was issued in 1996. National visa policy was harmonised with EU policy in 1998, and bilateral agreements with Austria and Italy signed. The following year saw the initiation of a number of twinning projects addressing topics such as surveillance (Germany and Austria), migration (Austria), organised crime (with Italy and Spain), and police co-operation (Spain). Technical support from the EU and a programme of financial realisation for the establishment of control on the EU's external borders facilitated harmonisation, and by 2002 the adoption of a new border surveillance act, the preparation of cadre and equipment plans, training procedures and compensatory measures, plus further legal and technical changes resulted in complete harmonisation with the *acquis*. These developments suggest that the role of Slovenia's political elite has been critical in ensuring that the ideals of democratic border security have transferred to the police.

Other factors include the small size of the country, its geographic position, and recent history—all of which mean that police–community relations are relatively good, with citizens reporting suspected illegal migrants to the authorities, and approximately ten percent of calls received relating to border issues (personal communication from Dušan Burian, 5 November 2002). When Slovenia faced an influx of illegal migrants in 2000, good community relations ensured that the police were able to identify, apprehend and return some 40 percent of those thought to have entered the country; 70 percent of 2001's entrants were estimated to have been returned in 2002. Democratic control and personal accountability do not appear to be controversial issues, and morale amongst border police seems reasonable.

Democratic control is a legitimising priority and an organisational device for Slovenia's border police. Slovenia's case is special, but its experience provides a useful source of information on the relative importance of political rationalities, functional needs and social realities in shaping border management, each of which must be addressed if effective border security and civilian oversight is to be achieved.

Albania

In contrast to the situation in BiH or Slovenia, the capacity and desire of the Albanian state to develop effective border security, let alone transfer democratic forms of management to its border police, is low. Notions such as democratic control make little headway in a society with a weak tradition of respecting the law, and an administrative culture developed for a repressive state.

Theoretically the empirical and conceptual parameters of its border security are conventional. The Law on the State Police charges the Central Directorate of Border Police with the obligation to control the state border, and various multinational border regimes and readmission agreements are acknowledged. Admittedly the past decade has been marked by political and economic instability, violence, and the rise of organised crime, but Albania's small western-trained elite is increasingly concerned about its image abroad, and the government began talks with the EU on a Stabilisation and Association Agreement (similar to those signed with Croatia and Macedonia) in 2003. Nevertheless, member states are concerned about the government's commitment to improving law enforcement and reducing the pervasive corruption (Hope 2002). In practice Albania is one of Europe's poorest countries and Albanian border management is marked by inefficiency, corruption, lethargy, and a non-functioning structure.

There is no separate, fixed, or formal border police. Indeed, the system hardly functions. There are separate border policing units inside the state police structures—the Central Directorate of Border Police is part of the General Directorate of the State Police—but the border police do not have their own resources or, indeed, career paths. The border police have a fixed number of staff (about 1,680), but officers are rotated between the various state police units and none are specialists. Most trained officers were trained under the old regime, but more than half the police have not been trained at all; professionalism means little amongst impoverished and untrained generalists, while the few who have received training from international projects do not use their training because they are moved between units. Add harsh weather and poverty to deep-rooted corruption and an almost total lack of resources, and the rationalities of Albanian border management become only too clear, as the small, dark and broken-down premises of many of Albania's border crossings show.[6]

---

[6] A simple comparison between the resources available to Albanian border guards and those of BiH make the importance of social and political context obvious. In

Conclusions

Contemporary border management, like contemporary security itself, reflects a number of competing assumptions and functional necessities, of which democratic control is merely one. It follows that the transferability of the EU's style of border management cannot be understood, nor the democratic transformation it seeks to achieve be explained, unless the parameters and rationalities of comparative border management are first identified.

Based on trends within European border management, three linked rationalities deserve emphasis: (1) border security is a specialist policing function, and many of the paradigms of public policing are useful in identifying the field's parameters; (2) border guards operate at the intersection of a number of competing priorities, norms, and functional necessities; and (3) social realities matter as much as political objectives and functional necessities. To this list might be added structural factors, but we still do not know how or why border security is structured as it is within certain types of state.

The Schengen *acquis* is undoubtedly a significant factor shaping our understanding of the procedures and purposes of border management within Europe. But it is primarily a project about political order, and its ability to affect the fundamental rationalities of border guarding may be transitory or superficial outside the EU core. Member states rely on the EU to provide a regional consensus on functional border management—Schengen standards act as an ordering device within the European region—but we do not know much about transferring either EU models or, indeed, democratic control into effective practice outside a small number of sample countries.

References

BENYON, JOHN 1996. 'The politics of police co-operation in the European Union'. *International Journal of the Sociology of Law*, 24 (4): 353–379.

BIGO, DIDIER 1998. 'Frontiers and Security in the European Union: The Illusion of Migration Control'. In *The Frontiers of Europe*, eds., Malcolm Anderson and Eberhard Bort, 148–164. London: Pinter.

———— 1999. 'Landscape of Police Co-operation'. In *The Boundaries of Understanding: Essays in Honour of Malcolm Anderson*, eds., Eberhard Bort,

---

the summer of 2004 the SBS received 18 surveillance vehicles as part of a package from the German Border Police that included 21 mini buses, computer equipment, passport inspection devices, photocopiers, and training. In contrast, most Albanian controllers have little more than a pen, a notebook and an old telephone; they rarely have working radios or vehicles. In late 2002 the entire border police had approximately 90 hand held radios and 10 vehicles. (Personal communication, Geneva, March 2003.)

and Russell Keat, 59–75. Edinburgh: University of Edinburgh, International Social Sciences Institute.

_____ 2000. 'Liaison officers in Europe: New officers in the European security field'. In *Issues in Transnational Policing*, ed. J.W.E. Sheptycki, 67–100. London: Routledge.

BITTNER, EGON. 1980. *The Functions of the Police in Modern Society*. Cambridge, MA: Oelgeschlager, Gunnand Hain.

BORDERLINE. 2002. 3 (14).

BRUINSMA, G. J. N. and C. D. VAN DER VIJVER, (eds). 1999. *Public Safety in Europe*. Enschede, Netherlands: International Police Institute. 1999

COUNCIL OF THE EUROPEAN UNION. *EU Schengen Catalogue*, 16.

_____ *EU Schengen Catalogue*, 9.

COUNCIL OF THE EUROPEAN UNION, GENERAL SECRETARIAT. 2002. *EU Schengen Catalogue: External Borders Control, Removal and Readmission*.

DAS, DILIP. 1997. 'Challenges of policing democracies: a world perspective'. *Policing*, 20 (4): 609–630.

DZIEDZIC, MICHAEL and ANDREW BAIR. 1998. 'Bosnia and the IPTF'. In *Policing the New World Disorder: Peace Operations and Public Security*, eds., Robert Oakley, Michael Dziedzic and Eliot Goldberg, 253–314. Washington, DC: National Defense University.

ERICSON, R. V., quoted in *Issues in Transnational Policing*, ed. J.W.E. Sheptycki, p.10. London: Routledge.

GRABBE, HEATHER. 2000. 'The Sharp Edges of Europe: Extending Schengen Eastwards', *International Affairs*, 76 (3): 519–36.

HOPE, KERIN. 2002. 'Albania: Crackdown Follows EU Pressures', *Financial Times*, 18 December 2002.

INTERNATIONAL CRISIS GROUP. 2002. *Policing the Police in Bosnia: A Further Reform Agenda*. Sarajevo/Brussels.

IISS. 2003. *The Military Balance 2002–2003*. Oxford: Oxford University Press.

JONES, TREVOR AND NEWBURN, TIM. 1998. *Private Security and Public Policing*. Oxford: Oxford University Press.

MONK, RICHARD. 2001. 'Study on Policing in the Federal Republic of Yugoslavia'. OSCE, Vienna.

NIEMANKARI, ARTO. 2002. 'EU/Schengen Requirements for National Border Security Systems'. DCAF Working Paper Series No. 8. Geneva

Personal communication from Dušan Burian, 5 November 2002.

Personal communication from Dušan Burian, 5 November 2002.

Personal communication from Josef Konya, June 1999.

SALT, JOHN, JENNIFER HOGARTH, JUDIT JUHÁSZ, MAREK OKÓLSKI, TATIANA KLINCHENKO, OLGA MALYNOVSKA, IGOR MINGAZUTDINOV, and OLEG SHAMSHUR. 2000. *Migrant Trafficking and Human Smuggling in Europe: A Review of the Evidence with Case Studies from Hungary, Poland and Ukraine*. Geneva: International Organization for Migration.

SPECIAL CO-ORDINATOR OF THE STABILITY PACT FOR SOUTH EASTERN EUROPE. 2001. *National and Regional Management and Development of Border Control*. Regional Conference, Bucharest 2001.

ZRÍNYI MIKLÓS, UNIVERSITY OF NATIONAL DEFENCE. 1999. *Border-Policing and Defence Management Course: Course Description*. Budapest: Faculty of Military Science 4.

Chapter 4

Information Technology and Integrated Border Management

Rey Koslowski

Integration of immigration and asylum policy has fallen short of initial expectations at the time of the signing of Amsterdam Treaty and the follow-on Tampere European Council. However, the Amsterdam Treaty's incorporation of the Schengen Convention into the EU Treaties and several key new initiatives have taken European co-operation on border controls to the point of integration in increasingly sensitive areas of state sovereignty, such as border control enforcement, government surveillance, data collection and exchange. In anticipation of enlargement, the EU and its member states have increased budgets, staffing and information technology for border controls.

The prospect of lifting internal EU borders and shifting the common external EU border to new member states prompted increasing discussions of integrated border management, which has a wide variety of means and definitions inside and outside of Europe (Hobbing 2005). Integrated border management refers to the modernisation and cross-agency co-ordination of border control activities within individual states as well as increasing co-operation (and, to a certain extent, integration) of border control functions across the member states of the European Union. Integrated border management at the European level is perhaps best embodied in the establishment of the European Agency for the Management of Operational Co-operation at the External Borders of the Member States of the European Union, better know as FRONTEX (from the French *frontières extérieures*), which is located in Warsaw and became operational in June 2005. Increasing use of information technology for border control has become a hallmark of border security agency modernisation efforts, inter-agency co-operation within EU member states as well as an essential component of integrated border management at the European level.

Border control technology deployments, however, have not been solely driven by intra-EU integration, EU enlargement and political agendas aimed at increasing control over migration to the EU. In response to the 11 September 2001 attacks, EU member states not only passed anti-terrorism legislation and committed to joining the US in Afghanistan but they tightened borders and accelerated border control information technology programs. There has also been increasing practical co-operation between the European Commission and the US that attempts to produce a more secure common transatlantic space for international travel based on the use of new technologies such as biometric e-passports and advanced electronic submission of manifests and passenger name records. The European Commission also is endeavouring to bring the new EU member states into this transatlantic space as they develop sufficiently robust border control capabilities of their own and connect to the Schengen Information System II, which is a prerequisite for the eventual lifting of internal border controls between current Schengen member states and the new members of the EU.

This chapter will consider the role of information technology in integrated border management both within modernisation efforts of EU member states as well as across the EU. First, I provide an overview of European co-operation on migration and border control. Second, I consider EU responses to al Qaeda attacks on the US, Spain and the UK. Third, I examine the increasing use of border control information technologies within several EU member states. Fourth, I examine the development of Europe-wide information technology initiatives and evaluate their place in integrated border management.

European Regimes and Global Mobility

Advances in transportation and communications technology increase the potential for international migration around the world. As international migration becomes less inhibited by physical or economic constraints and becomes more of a function of legal constraints imposed by states, it becomes an increasingly important issue in politics among states. As such, international migration is an issue area for possible international co-operation within international organisations or through the formation of less formal international regimes.

The number of international regimes has increased greatly over the past few decades in an expanding breadth of areas, but international co-operation among states to regulate international migration has been very limited. Putting the international refugee regime aside, there is little in the way of international co-operation on international migration at the global level—no international migration regime exists.

At the regional level, migration regimes have developed within and to the EU. A regime governing intra-EU migration was first articulated in the Treaty of Rome, reaffirmed in the Single European Act (SEA) and formally codified in the European Citizenship provisions of the Treaty on European Union (TEU) signed at Maastricht. A regime governing migration into the EU from non-member states began to emerge with the 1990 Dublin Convention on jurisdiction for asylum applications, the 1990 Schengen Convention on border controls and Title VI of the 1992 Maastricht Treaty dedicated to Co-operation in Justice and Home Affairs (JHA), and then became more fully articulated with the 1997 Amsterdam Treaty.

During the 1980s, intra-European trade and intra-European travel increased while at the same time shipments increasingly went by truck and more Europeans drove cars. This became a recipe for huge backups at borders as trucks and tourists were stopped for passport inspections. To address this problem, Germany, France, Belgium, the Netherlands and Luxembourg signed the Schengen agreement in 1985 to gradually abolish internal border checks. The associated Schengen Convention signed in 1990 called for a common visa policy, harmonisation of polices to deter illegal migration and an integrated automated Schengen Information System (SIS) so as to coordinate actions regarding individuals who have been denied entry. All customs controls at internal borders within the newly established European Union were lifted in 1993 and the Schengen Convention went into effect in 1995, lifting internal border controls while establishing a common external border.

Title VI of the 1992 Maastricht Treaty formalised longstanding co-operation among the member states regarding border controls, migration and asylum. Co-operation in the fields of Justice and Home Affairs (JHA) formed one of three 'pillars' of the EU along with the First Pillar of the original European Community and the Second Pillar of Common Foreign and Security Policy (CFSP). The pillar structure effectively kept this co-operation on an 'intergovernmental basis' outside of the original Treaty on European Community (TEC).

The 1997 Amsterdam Treaty incorporated the Schengen Convention into the EU treaties and set out a plan to put policies on visas, asylum, immigration and external border controls under Community procedures and into the Community legal framework by May 2004. Shortly after the Amsterdam Treaty went into force in 1999, European policy makers were beginning to accept the long-term demographic implications of low fertility rates and the realities of their aging populations as well as the economic impacts these changing demographics had on pay-as-you-go pension schemes. This led them to enact policies that foster greater political incorporation of their present resident alien populations and consider policies to prepare for those to come. The European Commission then issued a broad outline of its proposal for a Community Immigration Policy, which refers to replacement migration as a partial solution to the aging of the European populations and advocates opening 'channels for immigration for economic purposes to meet urgent needs for both skilled and unskilled workers' (European Commission 2000, 13). Some aspects of this policy integration, particularly on asylum, family reunification, long term residents, and residence permits for victims of trafficking had been realised by the deadline, but the Council could not agree on a directive for the admission of third country nationals for employment purposes (European Commission 2004), proving a broader EU immigration policy to be much more elusive.

As policy makers recognise that economic development in many source countries depends upon migrant remittances and that destination countries increasingly depend upon immigration to support aging populations, there have been more discussions beyond just within the EU of establishing a regime facilitating the international movement of labour similar to the international trade regime based on the General Agreement on Tariffs and Trade (see e.g., Ghosh 2000; Straubhaar 2000). The fundamental obstacle to international co-operation on labour migration, as Ari Zolberg (1991;1992) and James Hollifield (1992) have pointed out, is that migrant destination countries have little incentive to join such a regime because foreign labour, especially low-skilled labour, is in abundant supply. If labour shortages develop during periods of economic growth, states can get as much labour from abroad as they like with bilateral agreements or simply by opening labour markets to migrants while at the same time avoiding any commitment to keep labour markets open during economic downturns. A global migration regime may make sense in terms of increasing economic efficiency world-wide (Staubhaar 2000) and ensuring poorer migrant source countries' access to richer migrant destination country markets for the sake of international development and reducing global inequalities (United Nations Development Program 1992). However, the additional economic gains to individual destination countries of joining such an international regime, as opposed to maintaining the unilateral status quo, are negligible in comparison to the non-economic costs of large-scale immigration on a destination country's security, society and culture. Such non-economic costs, whether real or just perceived, have domestic political consequences and make a policy of multilateral engagement on migration even more difficult for destination state policy makers to sell to sceptical publics than international free trade agreements.

Although international co-operation on migration for the sake of economic considerations has languished, security concerns in the wake of the attacks on 11 September 2001 have motivated international co-operation on international mobility that encompasses migration and travel. In addition to the 175 million international migrants, which the UN defines as the number of people who have lived outside of their country of nationality for at least one year, there are the millions of tourists, students and business people who travel internationally for shorter stays including most of the 19 hijackers who attacked the World Trade Center and the Pentagon, thereby precipitating changes in US visa policies and border control processes in ways that have reverberated around the world.

An international regime for orderly migration has greater security value in the post-11 September world. Previously, the security threats posed by illegal migration and human smuggling were those of 'disruptive movements of people' (Ghosh 2000, p.221) that could provoke immediate border security problems because of the scale of such movements or adverse domestic political reactions to perceived governmental 'loss of control' of borders. Now the threat may come from small groups or even individuals within larger illegal flows. By increasing the share of migration that is orderly, properly documented, pre-screened and comes through ports of entry rather than around them, an international migration regime can help border authorities focus their limited resources on travellers and visitors who potentially pose the greatest security risks.

The member states of the EU have taken international co-operation on migration further than any other states in the world. EU member state co-operation on migration greatly exceeds that of international co-operation on a global level and it also goes way beyond that of other regional organizations of comparable advanced industrialised states. The decades of economic and political integration that has laid the groundwork for the lifting of border controls among EU member states may prove extremely difficult, if not impossible, to replicate in other regions (see Koslowski 2005). Moreover, given existing border control capabilities, proactive border control policies and the prospects of increasing integration of border control functions, the EU may itself become a leader in the development of a global mobility regime.

While the EU may provide the best example of an international migration regime, it is perhaps inappropriate to use it as a point of comparison for other regions, let alone a global migration regime. In fact, European co-operation on migration, asylum policy and border control may even be at cross-purposes with global co-operation in these areas. Much like the dilemma posed to global free trade by the formation of regional economic blocs with discriminatory policies that favour members over non-members, if co-operation aimed at free movement within the EU prompts policies that are less open to the rest of the world, EU migration regimes may limit rather than further global co-operation on migration as a whole. For example, after the Maastricht Treaty established the Justice and Home Affairs (JHA) Council as an institutionalised framework for articulating the common principles, rules, norms, and decision-making procedures that made up the emerging EU migration regime, the JHA Council agreed to a common definition of refugee as its first legally binding joint position in November 1995. Based on a strict interpretation of the 1951 Geneva convention, which defines a refugee as someone with a well-founded fear of being persecuted for reasons of race, religion, nationality, membership in a particular social group or political opinion, the new common EU definition effectively excluded those who flee civil wars, generalised armed conflict and persecution by 'non-state agents' such as armed militias and insurgent groups. Before the common definition was issued, Germany, France, Italy and Sweden were the only member states that did not define those persecuted by non-state agents as refugees. The UNHCR criticised the common position as contrary to the spirit of the 1951 Convention and as a step backwards that could imperil refugee protection throughout the world (European Insight 1995).

To hear it from Secretary General Kofi Annan, European co-operation on asylum policies may very well be responsible for the demise of what little global co-operation on migration that does exist—the refugee regime. Speaking to the European Parliament Annan said that 'when refugees cannot seek asylum because of offshore barriers, or are detained for excessive periods in unsatisfactory conditions, or are refused entry because of restrictive interpretations of the (1951 Refugee) Convention, the asylum system is broken and the promise of the Convention is broken, too' (Annan 2004). Simply put, increasing European co-operation on migration need not lead to liberal outcomes that benefit asylum seekers and would-be migrants seeking to enter the EU. International co-operation is by and for states, and if states collectively opt for more restrictive policies, international co-operation may reduce migration rather than lift barriers to it.

Migration and Border Controls in the EU After 11 September

In the immediate aftermath of the attacks on the World Trade Center and the Pentagon, the extraordinary European Council of 21 September invited member states to strengthen controls at external borders and strengthen surveillance measures provided for in the Schengen Convention. The Council advocated vigilance when issuing identity documents and residence permits, recommended more systematic checking of identity papers for document fraud, asked for more input to the Schengen Information System from member states and asked for consular co-operation and stepped-up information exchanges between member states regarding visas (European Council 2001).

Within ten days of the extraordinary European Council, the EU coordinated 'Operation High Impact' which involved more than 10,000 police officers from 15 member states and 10 candidate countries and lasted from 29 September to 8 October. Police apprehended 1,350 illegal migrants and 34 migrant smugglers. Shortly thereafter, the Justice and Home Affairs Council began discussions towards a common border police force. Police exchange programs and liaison work have become increasingly common under the aegis of the Schengen Convention as, for example, when Germany sent border police to assist in Italy. Prompted by 11 September, the Council and Commission have endeavoured to initiate a more coherent strategy. This involves the development of a harmonised curriculum for training border control officials and the development of a European Border Guard School. Nevertheless, despite the momentum behind the concept, and the support of states such as Germany and Greece, proposals for a common border guard were blocked in December at the Laeken European Summit because, as Swedish Prime Minister Goran Persson explained, EU leaders did not want an additional layer of bureaucracy (Migration News Sheet 2002). While this explanation may put a good public face on the lack of consensus, the integration of member state border police into a common border guard represents a major transformation of state sovereignty that some member states might have been less willing to accept than others, even in the face of the threats of terrorism and asymmetric warfare that they might be better able to combat with a unified force.

In the end it was decided to establish a new 'European Agency for the Management of Operational Co-operation at the External Borders of the European Union', or FRONTEX, which will co-ordinate the implementation of common policies by member state border police but lacks policy-making or implementing powers of its own (European Commission 2003). The agency was set up by a regulation in October 2004 (European Council 2004) and after extensive negotiations Warsaw was chosen as its administrative location in

April 2005. The agency's mission is to: 'coordinate operational co-operation between Member States in the field of management of external borders; assist Member States in the training of national border guards, including the establishment of common training standards; carry out risk analyses; follow up the development of research relevant for the control and surveillance of external borders; assist Member States in circumstances requiring increased technical and operational assistance at external borders; provide Member States with the necessary support in organising joint return operations' (FRONTEX 2005). FRONTEX will also implement the updated border code on movement of persons across borders and so facilitate the free movement of persons within the Schengen area. Although the new agency fell short of earlier proposals for a European border guard, FRONTEX is viewed by border control professionals as an important step in this direction.

The heightened security on the external EU border also had a major impact on states applying for EU membership. In October 2001, Gunter Verheugen, EU Commissioner for Enlargement made clear to candidate countries that they would have to meet current member states' internal security and border control capacities before accession. Before 11 September, the EU had conceded that it would permit a grace period after accession within which candidate states could bring up their border control capacity to EU levels (Migration News Sheet 2001).

In terms of the development of a common immigration policy, the attacks of 11 September have stalled Council action on Commission proposals and delayed the initiation of proposals by the Commission itself. For example, the Belgian Presidency placed a high priority on harmonising policy on family reunion. The 11 September attacks pushed this issue off of the EU's agenda as a compromise solution was rejected on 27 September and another attempted compromise failed in November 2001 (Migration News Sheet 2001a). The fate of more dramatic common policies that would enable increased labour immigration, both high and low skilled, quickly became much more in doubt. The impact of 11 September was also reflected in the lack of progress in adopting measures to meet the goals of the 'scorecard' (European Commission 2001a). Focusing on delays in the JHA process, the Laeken European Council called for more frequent and more focused JHA meetings, i.e., a one-day meeting with a limited agenda every month (European Council 2001a).

With respect to the impact on asylum policy, some EU member states, such as Austria, stopped processing asylum claims lodged by nationals of Afghanistan (Migration News Sheet 2001b). Moreover, member states, such as Greece, expressed concerns that they would be overwhelmed by a wave of Afghan asylum seekers (Migration News Sheet 2001c). Afghani nationals comprised one of the largest groups of smuggled asylum seekers entering the EU before 11 September and it was feared that their numbers would increase dramatically, much as had been the case when the military intervention began in Kosovo.

Although the implementation of asylum policies was clearly affected by 11 September, the Commission expressed the opinion that current legislation could handle the needs of greater internal security while at the same time adhering to international commitments (European Commission 2001a). The Commission went on to advocate that member states take full advantage of escape clauses that enable states to take actions limiting asylum and rights of asylum seekers for the sake of national security, although fallout from the attacks also prompted member states to propose reception centres outside of the EU itself to which Kofi Annan alluded to above.

The 11 March 2004 Madrid bombings then prompted the European Council to establish the position of an EU counter-terrorism coordinator and take even more measures to strengthen border security. The terrorist attacks raised many concerns about increasing illegal migration—especially the prospect of terrorists being smuggled into the EU or entering by visa fraud. A group linked to the Madrid bombings, Ansar al-Islam, had been running a human smuggling and document fraud operation to fund terrorist actions as well as to smuggle its own members into countries like Spain and Iraq.

The establishment of an EU counter-terrorism co-ordinator drew comparison to the establishment of the Office, then the Department of Homeland Security in the US. There is however, no exact EU or EU member state counterpart to the US Department of Homeland Security. Interestingly, the new Department of Homeland Security is much closer in organisation to European interior ministries that implement most border control functions than the previous dispersal of border control functions across the US federal government. The border control divisions of EU member state interior ministries, however, are collectively much larger than their US equivalent.

US Bureau of Customs and Border Protection (CBP) staffing is quite modest compared to border control agencies of other advanced industrialised countries with large-scale immigration flows, such as Germany, especially in relation to the length of their respective land borders. CBP has 40,828 employees (DHS 2005, p.23) of whom 10,739 are Border Patrol agents (DHS 2005, p.27) and 18,000 are CBP officers at ports of entry. This is roughly equivalent to the size of Germany's *Bundesgrenzschutz* (Federal Border Police), renamed *Bundespolizei* (Federal Police) in July 2005, with 40,000 employees (30,000 of whom are officers with 21,000 stationed at border crossing points). Although roughly comparable, the *Bundesgrenzschutz* does not have the same array of functions as the CBP in that it also includes the Federal Railway Police (the US counterpart would be Amtrak Police) but it does not include customs inspectors (which CBP) does. Poland has 16,000 border guards and plans to hire 5,300 more by 2006 (Kole 2004). In 2001, Hungary had 11,000 border guards and planned to increase the total to 14,000 (European Commission 2001b). It is also worth noting that only 688 miles of Germany's borders (with Poland and the Czech Republic) are external Schengen borders that are patrolled and have border crossing check points. Once the Schengen Convention becomes effective with Poland and the Czech Republic and internal borders are lifted, German border guards at these border points will no longer be necessary and they can be reassigned to other posts and missions.

Border Control Information Technology in EU Member States

As the EU endeavours to erect a common external border, member state border authorities increasingly use an array of remote sensors and surveillance technologies to stop clandestine crossings of illegal migrants who are increasingly assisted by smugglers.

Germany

Beginning in the mid-1990s the German Federal Border Police, *Bundesgrenzschutz* (BGS), now Federal Police, increasingly modernised operations by installing computers in offices and in the field.

In terms of information technology deployments, the number of workstations increased from 2,900 at the end of 1997, to 4,000 in 1998 to 6,200 in 1999 to 11,200 by 2001 (BGS 1996/97; 1998; 1999; 2000/01). During the mid-1990s, the BGS rapidly increased the number of mobile identity document readers at the border, doubling the number from 300 in 1997 to 600 in 1998 to (BGS 1996/97; 1998) and border guards also received night vision equipment and carbon dioxide sensors to combat illegal migration (BGS 1996/1997). Working together with Germany's Länder, the BGS put into practice the concept of an integrated European digital network for security agencies that would carry audio, data and pictures in the Berlin-Potsdam area in 1998, and initiated a pilot project in the Aachen area in 1999 (BGS 1998; 1999). In 1999, the BGS developed connections between its information systems and a common information system used by the federal and Länder police (BGS 1999), and in 2000 was connected to the extranet of the federal and Länder police (BGS 2000/01). By June of 2001 the digital network pilot project in Aachen also included digital mobile communications (2000/01).

In response to the 11 September attacks, the German government passed a first package of anti-terrorism legislation on 19 September 2001 which provided DM 3 billion to upgrade national security and included provisions to be able to better screen airport personnel by easing data protection laws giving relevant authorities access to intelligence and other government databases (Bundesregierung 2002). More comprehensive measures were also proposed in a second package which ultimately contained measures to increase resources for information exchange between German security authorities, tighten border controls, and identify extremists, as well as to improve the security features in personal identification documents and passports (Bundesregierung 2002a).

As the Cabinet of the German government approved the first package of anti-terrorist measures on 19 September 2001, the Interior Minister Otto Schily said that the central registry for foreigners and visa data should be made more accessible, while Cem Ozdemir, the Green Party's spokesperson for domestic affairs at the time, argued that the efficacy of any changes in data privacy rules must be first examined (FAZ 2001). One week later, German Länder officials admitted that they were using data-mining for computer-aided profiling to attempt to identify terrorist 'sleeper cells' while those Länder that did not have laws permitting such computerised profiling quickly passed laws to be able to do so (FAZ 2001a).

Another point of controversy within the SPD/Alliance90/Green coalition government concerned Minister Schily's proposal on biometric data in the second anti-terrorism package of legislation. The Interior Ministry originally demanded inclusion of fingerprint data in identification documents and passports while the Greens proposed using hand and facial geometric data. A compromise emerged to leave open the type of biometric data used while agreeing that the ban on fingerprints in the passport law would be lifted (FAZ 2001b). The Greens won further concessions in that biometric data on ID cards and passports would not be recorded in a central data bank, meaning that this data could only be used for verification of identity and not for data-mining in criminal investigations (FAZ 2001c). The second package was passed on 20 December 2001 and went into effect on 1 January 2002. Additional provisions have been made to establish a central database of passport photos to thwart identification substitution, reduce restrictions on exchanging data, particularly between carriers and authorities on passenger bookings, and selective fingerprinting of visitors upon arrival (International Organization for Migration 2002).

One less controversial use of biometrics is the 'Automated and Biometrics-Supported Border Controls' (ABG), a voluntary registered traveller pilot program at Frankfurt Airport aimed at expediting frequent travellers through border controls. Enrolment is open to citizens from EU/EEC countries and Switzerland entitled to unrestricted freedom of movement who are 18 years or older and hold a machine-readable passport. Federal Police query the German INPOL police database and the Schengen Information System (SIS). If cleared, the applicant looks into an iris recognition camera, which produces a biometric template of the iris scan. This is added to the participant's personal data, encrypted and filed under his or her passport number in a local ABG database. To enter an auto-control lane, travellers place their passport on a document reader and data from the machine-readable zone to check whether the passport holder is enrolled. If so, the automatic doors open and the traveller enters the inner control area, where an IRIS scan is submitted then compared to the template generated at enrolment. If verification is successful and the traveller is not listed on a watch list, he or she may cross the border.

United Kingdom

The United Kingdom has also turned extensively towards technology solutions for border control. By virtue of the fact that it is an island nation and not a Schengen Convention signatory state, border control primarily involves inspections of some 81,000 ships and aircraft and 90 million passengers at ports of entry (Home Office n.d.). The British authorities have been very keen to deploy sensor technologies, especially since June 2000 when 58 Chinese immigrants suffocated in a truck crossing the English Channel by ferry. In April 2001 the Home Secretary announced that the Immigration Service of the Home Office would purchase Gamma X-ray scanners to detect humans being smuggled in vehicles and that some scanners belonging to Customs would be used as well (Home Office 2001). Gamma X-ray scanners have been complemented by the deployment of carbon dioxide detectors, heart beat detectors and passive milimetric wave imaging at the Dover crossing (European Council 2002). With French co-operation, high technology was also deployed before vehicles embarked at Calais so that by the end of 2002 all vehicles going to England through Calais were searched for illegal migrants. The UK is also providing detection equipment for use at other French ports— initially at Cherbourg and Dunkirk—as well as to Belgian ferry ports (Home Office 2002).

In order to detect visa abuse and document fraud at ports of entry as well as to intercept potential terrorists, new immigration and asylum legislation announced in April 2002 includes provisions that enable data-sharing between government departments and government and the private sector to facilitate data-mining for profiling and detecting high-risk passengers (International Organization for Migration 2002). The legislation also set up 'right to carry' schemes whereby carriers must confirm that passengers do not present a security risk nor are at risk of breaking immigration law before those passengers are permitted to board UK-bound airplanes. Such carrier sanctions complement efforts to automate immigration controls through a combination of data-sharing and the use of biometric identification systems to speed legitimate passengers through and allow border control officers to concentrate their efforts on more high risk travellers (Home Office 2002a). The UK also developed a new 'Borderguard' system, which uses electronic recording and facial recognition technology to detect forged documents and uncover abusive asylum claims (Home Office 2002b) and deployed it in 'Operation Hornet' at Dover (Home Office 2002a).

Led by the Home Office's Immigration and Nationality Directorate (IND) and engaging partnerships with the UK Immigration Service (UKIS), HM Revenue & Customs (HMRC), UKvisas and the Police Service, the e-Borders Programme aims to use electronic processing of information relating to travellers to and from the UK in order to establish an intelligence-led border control and security framework. At this stage, the programme has two pilot projects, Semapore and IRIS. Semaphore is an operational prototype to trial e-Borders concepts and technology. The pilot involved collection of data on 10 air routes but will be expanded. The Iris Recognition Immigration System (IRIS) is a biometric automated barrier entry system. The voluntary program is aimed at frequent travellers from non-EU member states. Travellers may submit a no-cost application to immigration officers staffing enrolment centres in airport departure lounges who immediately run background checks. If deemed eligible for the program, travellers then submit photographs of their eyes and face. Patterns of their iris are stored in a database and linked to passport data, immigration status and photograph. When enrolled travellers present themselves at UK border controls that have the IRIS system they may opt to use the automated IRIS lane. After travellers enter an enclosed automated barrier unit, they must only look into the biometric reader. If identity is confirmed and watch list checks are clear, a gate opens and the traveller continues past passport controls without any interactions with immigration officers and then enters the UK. IRIS went live in June 2005 at Heathrow's Terminals Two and Four. Eleven units will eventually be deployed at ten sites (Home Office 2005).

The overhaul of British immigration and asylum legislation also includes measures to issue smart cards to asylum applicants for identification and tracking as well as to use biometrics to help identify potential terrorists among asylum seekers (International Organization for Migration 2002). In February of 2003, the UK joined the launch of EURODAC, an EU-wide database that records the fingerprints of asylum applicants, as will be discussed below (Home Office 2003).

Although Germans and other continentals have long carried national ID cards, 11 September prompted UK Home Secretary Blunkett to break with British tradition and propose a national ID card which would include personal data, a digital photo and a biometric, such as a fingerprint. The draft bill and pilot scheme was introduced to a mixed response.

Other EU member states

Netherlands is intensifying visa controls enhanced by fingerprinting and examining the role of other biometrics in passports (International Organization for Migration 2002). According to Giuseppe Mistretta, the first counsellor of the Italian embassy in the UK, Italian citizens approved of the plan to introduce a new high tech national ID cards (Jones 2003). Drexler Technology, an international supplier of digital governance products, reported that the first phase of the Italian national ID card program utilised 200,000 of Drexler's LaserCard(R) Smart/Optical(TM) cards and associated read/write devices. Drexler also reported that a Permanent Resident Card permitting non-citizens to reside and work in Italy is under consideration (Business Wire 2003). Finland's Frontier Guard has deployed sophisticated radar, sensors, and camera surveillance systems. Border control authorities have about 2,000 workstations and these stations have on-line connections to databases (Niemenkari 2002). Portugal is considering improving technology after a strike by border guards (de Queiroz 2003).

Information Technology and European Integrated Border Management

As noted earlier, in the immediate aftermath of the attacks on the World Trade Center and the Pentagon, the extraordinary European Council of 21 September 2001 invited member states to strengthen controls at external borders and strengthen surveillance measures provided for in the Schengen Convention.

The Schengen Information System (SIS) is a critical component of the Schengen Convention designed to enforce the common external border and build confidence in this common border so as to enable member states to remove all internal border controls among signatory states. Integration into the SIS is necessary before provisions of the Schengen Convention become effective for any signatory state. All EU member states (except the UK) plus Norway and Iceland are connected to the system. The SIS contains data on illegal migrants, lost and false travel documents, wanted or missing persons, stolen goods and counterfeit notes. As of June 2002, approximately 10 million people were listed in the SIS. Most entries were for forged or stolen passports and IDs but 1.3 million were entered into the alert system as convicted and suspected criminals (European Report 2002). The SIS is made up of two parts: national SIS systems (NSIS) in each of the Schengen signatory states and a central technical support system known as the Central SIS (CSIS), located in Strasbourg, France. SIS costs about 5 million Euros (2000 Budget) per year to maintain (European Report 2001). 'NSIS enables designated national authorities to carry out searches in SIS. CSIS ensures that data files of the national sections are updated and kept identical at all times by online transmission of information' (Kabera Karanja 2002).

Not only is the SIS critical to implantation of the Schengen Convention, SIS is central to the development of integrated border management at the European level. As Peter Hobbing (2005, p.17) argues, 'without the SIS linking relevant authorities—regardless of their geographical location in central offices in the capitals, as border staff right on the front line or consular representations abroad—a coordinated operation of border matters would be unthinkable.' Member state border police may share information through their NSIS or directly; however, the SIS can only electronically transmit text and figures, not photos and fingerprints (European Report 2002a) and it is not large enough to accommodate all member states. Therefore it may have been essential to integrated border management, but its role is greatly limited by these technical constraints.

Since the SIS is only capable of working with no more than 18 members states and cannot handle the increased data processing demands of EU enlargement, the European Commission proposed the Schengen Information System II (SIS II). SIS II will also store digital images and biometric data and answer police requests within five seconds (European Report 2003). Internal border controls with new member states will not be lifted until they are included in the Schengen Information System and this has a target date of 2007. The European Commission set out a proposed legal basis for SIS II (European Commission 2005) and the European Commission is responsible for overseeing the development of SIS II by a consortium led by the Steria Group (headquartered in France), co-contracting with Hewlett Packard, Belgium. The current SIS is administered in Strasbourg by France for the European Commission but it is not yet clear who will administer SIS II once it is developed. The current arrangement with France may be continued, or alternatively, the system may be administered by Europol or FRONTEX.

Europol's Information System (EIS) can transmit images as well as text. The system can be accessed by Europol's Director, its national units and other authorised officials. As part of Europol Convention revisions, the Danish Presidency of the EU proposed to give access to the system to national police officers as well (European Report 2002a). In the other direction, the European Council approved, in principle, a Spanish initiative to give Europol and members of the prosecuting unit, Eurojust, access to SIS. Working groups now must decide what parts of the database will be made accessible.

Police from EU member states may also utilise Interpol, which enables information sharing and co-ordination among its 181 member states. One of the primary means is the International Notice System used to help the National Central Bureaus (NCBs) of its member states exchange information about missing persons, unidentified bodies, persons who are wanted for committing serious crimes, and criminal 'modus operandi' (Interpol 2003). Interpol's email system can handle information in the form of typed texts, graphs and images of counterfeit notes, fingerprints or photographs. Member state police agencies send information to Interpol's central database daily and they can search this database for aliases, passports or identity documents (European Report 2002a).

EURODAC is a fingerprint database to be used to facilitate enforcement of the 1990 Dublin Convention (ratified and went into effect in 1997) that provided rules for determining which member state had jurisdiction in asylum applications governed by the principle that the state of entry would be responsible for any given application. If that state rejected the application, the asylum-seeker could not then apply in other member states. The objective was to eliminate abuse of member state asylum application processes through multiple application (so-called 'asylum shopping'). Since the system can be used to track non-nationals who enter the EU, it has also been viewed as a counter-terrorism tool that has received higher priority from the European Council in the wake of 11 September. At an initial implementation cost of 6.5 million Euro, the EURODAC system went live on 15 January 2003. Asylum-seekers now have their fingerprints taken and transmitted electronically to the central unit housed in the European Commission, and if a check shows that they have already applied in another member state, they will be sent back to that country. Member states are obliged to fingerprint asylum-seekers over the age of 14 and these fingerprints may be stored for up to 10 years. Authorities may also fingerprint illegal migrants to check if they have applied for asylum, however, illegal migrants' fingerprints will not be stored (European Report 2003a).

The 11 September terrorist attacks spurred proposals for the development of a European visa identification system as they raised concerns about the growing illegal migrant population living in Europe and the prospect of terrorists being smuggled into the EU or entering by visa fraud. The European Commission proposed a system featuring a common online database that would complement secure identity documents. A digital photo would be stored in addition to data that are already gathered in visa applications. Travel documents, such as passports, would also be scanned in order to detect any subsequent alterations. Stored images could also be used to get new travel documents should an individual try to resist deportation by attempting to hide his or her identity and nationality by destroying travel documents that had been used to enter the country (European Commission 2001). In June 2002, the Spanish Presidency put forward a proposal to the Council for creating a 'Visa Information System' (European Report 2002b). Subsequently, Germany and the Benelux countries also proposed a uniform format visa incorporating anti-counterfeit features and biometric data such as fingerprints or iris scans stored on a microchip embedded in the document (European Report 2003a) which would thereby provide more precise data to be shared through the emerging visa information system. In February 2004, the European Commission put forward a legislative proposal to create a visa information system and asked for 30 million Euro to do it (European Council 2004a). In June of 2004, the Council established the Visa Information System (European Council 2004b) and the European Commission received authority to oversee its development. The VIS will be on the same technical platform as the SIS and will likewise be developed by a consortium led by Steria, co-contracting with HP Belgium.

Conclusion

The EU is increasingly using information technology to strengthen border controls and post-11 September US security requirements are helping to drive this trend forward. The border control authorities of the EU and its member states collectively have more staff, resources and, in some ways, more 'proactive' border control policies than US border control authorities within the Department of Homeland Security. Nevertheless, European border guards are still primarily organised on a national basis, reflecting the legacy of controlling borders between EU member states—border controls that have largely been lifted with the implementation of the 1990 Schengen Convention. Should further bilateral and European-wide agreements be reached, tens of thousands of EU member state border guards on the current common external border (e.g., a large portion of the German border guards) may be redeployed to the EU's common external borders to the east as internal border controls with the EU's new member states are lifted. While such redeployments may make sense from a financial and security perspective, managing them would require a very robust integrated border management at the European level which itself would be highly dependent on successful implementation of the SIS II and other supportive information technology infrastructures.

References

ANNAN, KOFI. 2004. 'Address to the European Parliament upon receipt of the Andrei Sakharov Prize for Freedom of Thought'. United Nations press release SG/SM/9134. Brussels, 29 January 2004.

BGS. 1996/97. *Bundesgrenzschutz Jahresbericht 1996/1997*. Available at URL: <http://www.bundesgrenzschutz.de>

_____ 1998. *Bundesgrenzschutz Jahresbericht 1998*. Available at URL: <http://www.bundesgrenzschutz.de/start.htm>

_____ 1999. *Bundesgrenzschutz Jahresbericht 1999*. Available at URL: <http://www.bundesgrenzschutz.de/start.htm>

_____ 2000/01. *Bundesgrenzschutz Jahresbericht 2000/2001*. Available at URL: <http://www.bundesgrenzschutz.de/start.htm>

BUNDESREGIERUNG. 2002. 'Erstes Anti-Terror-Paket' Innenpolitik, Presse- und Informationsamt der Bundesregierung, 1 September 2002. Available at URL: <http://www.bundesregierung.de/Themen-A-Z/Innenpolitik-7418/Erstes-Anti-Terrorpaket.htm> (Accessed 1 February 2003)

_____ 2002a. 'Zweites Anti-Terror-Paket in Kraft getreten'. Innenpolitik, Presse- und Informationsamt der Bundesregierung, 1 January 2002. Available at URL: <http://www.bundesregierung.de/Themen-A-Z/Innenpolitik-,7419/6> (Accessed 1 February 2003)

BUSINESS WIRE. 2003. 'Drexler Technology, a Supplier of Digital Governance Products Worldwide, Will Present at Roth Capital Partners Growth Stock Conference on March 17'. Business Wire, 19 February 2003.

DE QUEIROZ, MARIO. 2003. 'Portugal: Weak Border Controls Seen Attracting Illegals'. *Inter Press Service*, 8 January 2003.

DEPARTMENT OF HOMELAND SECURITY. 2005. 'Budget in Brief, Fiscal Year 2006'. Department of Homeland Security.

EUROPEAN COMMISSION. 2000. 'Communication from the Commission to the Council and the European Parliament on a Community Immigration Policy'. COM(2000) 757 final. Brussels, 22.11.2000.

_____ 2001. 'Communication From the Commission to the Council and the European Parliament on A Common Policy on Illegal Immigration'. COM(2001) 672 final. Brussels, 15 November 2001.

_____ 2001a. 'Biannual Update on the Scoreboard to Review Progress on the Creation of an Area of Freedom, Security and Justice' in the European Union (First half of 2001)'. COM (2001) 278 final. Brussels, 23.05.2001.

_____ 2001b. 'EU Enlargement Hungary Regular 2001 Report'. Available at URL:
<http://europa.eu.int/comm/enlargement/report2001/>

_____ 2003. 'Establishing a European Agency for the Management of the Operational Co-Operation at External Borders'. RAPID Press Release IP: 03/1519, 11 November 2003

_____ 2005. 'Proposal for a Regulation of the European Parliament and of the Council on the Establishment, Operation and Use of the Second Generation Schengen Information System (SIS II)'. COM(2005) 236 final/2. Brussels, 23.8.2005.

EUROPEAN COUNCIL. 2001. 'Conclusions and Plan of Action of the Extraordinary European Council Meeting on 21 September, 2001'.

_____ 2001a. 'Presidency Conclusions: European Council Meeting in Laeken 14 and 15 December.'

_____ 2002. 'Note on Centre of Excellence at Dover - Mobile Detection Unit'. September 2002.

_____ 2004. 'Council Regulation (EC) No 2007/2004 of 26 October 2004 Establishing a European Agency for the Management of Operational Co-operation at the External Borders of the Member States of the European Union'. *Official Journal of the European Union*, L 349/1 (25 November 2004).

_____ 2004a. 'Council Conclusions on the development of the Visa Information System (VIS)'. 19 February 2004.

_____ 2004b. 'Council Decision of 8 June 2004 Establishing the Visa Information System (VIS)'. 2004/512/EC

European Insight. 1995. 'EU Makes Protection of Refugees Less Secure'. *European Insight, European Information Service*, Dec. 1, 1995.

European Report. 2001. 'Schengen Information System Cost Euro 5 Million in 2000'. *European Report*, 25 July 2001.

_____ 2002. 'Justice and Home Affairs: Council Moves to Add Al-Qaeda Members to Schengen Information System'. *European Report*, 26 June 2002.

_____ 2002a. 'Danish Presidency Proposes Intra-Police E-mail System'. *European Report*, 24 July 2002.

_____ 2002b. 'EU Visa Database Takes Shape'. *European Report*, 5 June 2002.

_____ 2003. 'Commission Wants New Schengen Data Base to Store Biometrics'. *European Report*, No. 2828, Dec. 13, 2003.

_____ 2003a. 'EURODAC Data Base of Asylum-Seekers' Fingerprints is Launched'. *European Report*, 15 January 2003.

_____ 2003b. 'Council Moves to Make Visas More Forgery Proof'. *European Report*, 18 January 2003.

FAZ. 2001. 'Cabinet Approves Emergency Laws'. *Frankfurter Allgemeine Zeitung*, 19 September 2001. Available at URL: <http://www.faz.com/IN/INtemplates/eFAZ/default.asp>

_____ 2001a. 'Terrorist 'Profiling on the Increase in Germany'. *Frankfurter Allgemeine Zeitung*, 25 September 2001. Available at URL: <http://www.faz.com/IN/INtemplates/eFAZ/default.asp>

_____ 2001b. 'Coalition Experts Approve Schily's Anti-Terror Package'. *Frankfurter Allgemeine Zeitung*, 26 October 2001. Available at URL: <http://www.faz.com/IN/INtemplates/eFAZ/default.asp>

_____ 2001c. 'Coalition Partners Reach Consensus on Anti-Terror Package'. *Frankfurter Allgemeine Zeitung*, 26 October 2001. Available at URL: <http://www.faz.com/IN/INtemplates/eFAZ/default.asp>

FRONTEX. 2005. 'Activities of European Agency for the Management of Operational Co-Operation at the External Borders of the European Union'. Letter of FRONTEX Executive Director to the European Parliament Committee on civil liberties, justice and home affairs, Brussels, October 5, 2005.

GHOSH, BIMAL. ed. 2000. *Managing Migration: Time for a New International Regime*. Oxford: Oxford University Press.

HOBBING, PETER. 2005. 'Integrated Border Management at the EU Level'. Centre for European Policy Studies (CEPS) Working Document, No. 227/August 2005.

HOLLIFIELD, JAMES F. 1992. 'Migration and International Relations: Cooperation and Control in the European Community'. *International Migration Review*, 26 (2).

HOME OFFICE. 2001. 'Consultation Report on Justification for the Use of X/gamma Radiation Scanners by the Immigration Service for Detecting People Seeking to Enter the UK Illegally in Vehicles and/or Freight, by Clandestine Means'. Home Office, 3 September 2001. Available at URL: <http://194.203.40.90/default.asp?pageID=1435>

_____ 2002. 'UK borders extended - Sangatte to close on 30 December'. Immigration and Nationality Directorate of the Home Office (30 December 2002). Available at URL: <http://194.203.40.90/news.asp?NewsId=211&SectionId=1>

_____ 2002a. 'Trust and Confidence in our Nationality, Immigration and Asylum System - Bill published'. 12 April 2002. Available at URL: <http://194.203.40.90/news.asp?NewsId=132&SectionId=1>

_____ 2002b. 'Home Secretary sees operation of new high-tech border controls at Dover'. Nationality Directorate of the Home Office, 17 June 2002. Available at URL: <http://194.203.40.90/news.asp?NewsId=159&SectionId=1>

_____ 2003. 'EU Asylum Fingerprint Database Begins Operating Today'. Immigration and Nationality Directorate of the Home Office, 15 January 2003. Available at URL: <http://194.203.40.90/news.asp?NewsId=226&SectionId=1>

_____ 2005. *e-Borders: Creating an Integrated, Secure Border for the 21st Century*, e-Borders Programme, Home Office, November 2005.

_____ n.d. 'Controlling Admissions'. Available at URL: <http://194.203.40.90/default.asp?pageID=1205> (Accessed 17 February 2003)

INTERPOL. 2003. Fact Sheet: Interpol's International Notices System'. Available at URL: <http://www.interpol.int/Public/ICPO/FactSheets/FS200105.asp> (Accessed 20 February 2003)

INTERNATIONAL ORGANIZATION FOR MIGRATION. 2002. 'International Comparative Study of Migration Legislation and Practice'. International Organization for Migration, April 2002.

JONES, GEORGE. 2003. 'Falconer Signals Retreat on ID Cards'. *The Daily Telegraph*, 25 January 2003.

KABERA KARANJA, STEPHEN. 2002. 'The Schengen Information System in Austria: An Essential Tool in Day to Day Police and Border Control Work?'. Commentary, *The Journal of Information, Law and Technology* (JILT), March 2002 (1). Available at URL: <http://elj.warwick.ac.uk/jilt/02-1/karanja.html>

KOLE, WILLIAM J. 2004. 'EU Expansion to Isolate Poor Neighbors'.
Seattle Times, 11 April 2004.

KOSLOWSKI, REY. 2005. 'Smart Borders, Virtual Borders or No Borders: Homeland Security Choices for the United States and Canada.' *Law and Business Review of the America*, (Summer/Fall).

Migration News Sheet. 2001. 'Candidate Countries Urged To Step Up Border Checks and Internal Security'. *Migration News Sheet*, No. 224/2001-11 (November 2001): 2.

_____ 2001a. 'Family Reunion Directive Likely Outcome to Result in More Disharmony than Harmony'. *Migration News Sheet*, No. 224/2001-11 (November 2001): 2.

_____ 2001b. 'Processing of Asylum Claims By Afghans Has Been Suspended - No Longer Possible to Lodge Asylum Applications at Austrian Diplomatic Missions Abroad'. *Migration News Sheet*, No. 224/2001-11 (November 2001): 12.

_____ 2001c. 'Irregular Migration Will be Government's Main Issue At EU Summit in December'. *Migration News Sheet*, No. 225/2001-12 (December 2001): 7.

_____ 2002. 'No Significant Progress on the Dossiers Concerning Immigration and Asylum - Proposal to Create Border Guard Blocked'. *Migration News Sheet*, No. 226/2002-01 (January 2002): 1-2.

NIEMENKARI, ARTO. 2002. 'The Finnish Border Security Concept'. Geneva Centre For The Democratic Control Of Armed Forces (DCAF), March 2002.

STRABHAAR, THOMAS. 2000. 'Why do we Need a General Agreement on Movments of People (GAMP)?' In Bimal Ghosh ed., *Managing Migration: Time for a New International Regime*. Oxford: Oxford University Press.

UNITED NATIONS DEVELOPMENT PROGRAM. 1992. *Human Development Report*, United Nations Development Program, New York: Oxford University Press.

ZOLBERG, ARISTIDE. 1991. 'Bounded States in a Global Market: The Uses of International Migration Regimes'. In P.B. and J.S. Coleman, eds., *Social Theory for a Changing Society*, Boulder, Colorado: Westview Press

_____ 1992. 'Labour Migration and International Economic Regimes: Bretton Woods and After'. In *International Migration Systems: A Global Approach*, eds., M.M. Kritz, L. Lean Lim, H. Zlotnik. Oxford: Clarendon Press.

Chapter 5

Enlisting Third Parties in Border Control: a Comparative Study of its Causes and Consequences

Virginie Guiraudon

Borders in today's Europe are no longer lines that one crosses. First, physical borders are often construed as 'areas' or 'zones' from safe havens to the frontier zone in the EU with the 20km rule for border mobile units and 'waiting zones' in airports. EU Justice and Home Affairs documents significantly speak of 'surveillance of frontier areas' rather than border control. Moreover, the border that an individual first crosses lies far from her destination: the physical border is a consulate official or airline employee, or— if she resorts to illegal entry—a smuggler. In other words, 'inter-agency co-operation at the border' for the past twenty years has consisted of private-public arrangements in source countries. Those who wish to visit EU countries even for a short tourist or family visit will come into contact with travel agents, domestic authorities, foreign officials, and transport staff to comply with entry requirements. To obtain the required documents even for a short-term visa, they will have to involve additional individuals and institutions: sponsors, financial guarantors, domestic bank personnel, and the family members or tourism agents in the countries that they are visiting.

Given this reality on the ground, this paper analyses the ways one type of actor (carriers) has been co-opted in controlling the movement of people across borders. Based on archival, interview and ethnographic research conducted over five years on this issue in Europe and North America, I discuss the logic and practice of involving private actors in border management. My main focus here is the European Union (EU) as it has acquired competence and legislation in this area that deserve attention, although I will also make reference to developments in the United States.

My aim is first to contextualise and conceptualise the co-optation of private actors in border management. I will then turn to the implementation of carriers' sanctions to highlight the practical consequences of involving third parties in border control. Given the current context, I will then pay particular attention to the consequences of 11 September 2001 in this policy area to the extent that they underscore certain problems of 'democratic control'.

The Logic of Delegation to Third Parties

There are inherent tensions between some constitutive principles of liberal democratic states that overarch capitalist economies. First, democracies seek to simultaneously satisfy public and private interests. Democratically elected governments have an electoral incentive to appease public anxieties over immigration, which public opinion polls have revealed since the late 1970s.[1] Populist politics is a recurring feature in the history of immigration. One such period started in Europe in the late 1970s when parties across the ideological spectrum resorted to a blame-avoiding strategy in the face of rising unemployment by calling for tighter migration controls, although they disagreed over integration policy (Money 1995).

At the same time, governments also have to respond to business demands. This includes traditional sectors like textile, agriculture and related industries such as the packing business that rely on cheap foreign unskilled labour. It also concerns the new demands for importing highly skilled workers in the new IT industries and for facilitating cross-border intra-company transfers in the service sector. Furthermore, governments in a 'globalising' era engage in free trade policies that contradict calls for closing the borders and that affect the movement of people. This had already been the case in the nineteenth century when the partisans of free trade also called for the abolition of passports, leading an Italian advocate to call such a measure, 'of great importance for economic relations, favouring commerce, industry, and progress (...) and liberating travellers from harassment and hindrances' (Torpey 2000, p.92).

The tensions between economics and politics are not new while those between law and politics are much more recent. Post-war liberal democracies are marked by a tension between popular sovereignty and liberal norms that may restrict the discretion of majority governments to enact policies. Since the 1970s, constitutional guarantees and activist high courts significantly circumscribed both the authority and the capacity of states to prevent family reunion or to dispose of migrants at will (Neuman 1990; Guendelsberger 1988; Joppke 1999; Guiraudon 2000a; Groenendijk 2001). The post-war liberal era that allowed humanitarian migration (family reunion and asylum) alongside traditional labour recruitment contrasts sharply with the preceding period.[2] One only needs to recall the expulsion of 400,000 Poles from Imperial Germany in 1885–6 (Herbert 1990) or the mass expulsions of German-speaking Russian war prisoners after the Second World War to grasp the normative evolution that has taken place. Currently, constitutionally guaranteed fundamental

---

[1] On European public opinion, see Commission of the European Communities 1989 and sequentia.

[2] Jim Hollifield (1992) has argued that post-war migration has taken place within a context of 'embedded liberalism' (Ruggie 1982) where notions of liberal rights and norms are partly institutionalised.

freedoms invoked by independent courts significantly circumscribe the ability of democratic governments to control the entry and stay of people on their national territory. The jurisprudence of the European courts in Strasbourg and Luxembourg has also pressed and legitimised activism by national courts (Guiraudon 2000b).

The current situation in European states can be understood as a triangular relationship between populist politics, liberal legal norms and a global economy. Of course, the impact of the economic, legal and political factors varies cross-nationally, depending on the institutional make-up of receiving states. For instance, the need to enact strict migration controls in the face of hostile public opinion is urgently felt in Great Britain, whose parliamentary system is quick to absorb local constituency pressure (Money 1999). In Germany, an autonomous judiciary with broad review powers has helped to consolidate the status of foreigners (Joppke 1999). Immigration policy therefore seeks to resolve conflicting goals (open trade, tourism, highly skilled workers recruitment, seasonal labour recruitment, and restricted family and asylum migration) and contradictory pressures (electoral populism and business lobbying).

Policy instruments often only address part of the pressures that governments are under. Such is the case of highly visible border management. The new immigration countries in Southern Europe have diligently shown their will to be 'good citizens' of Europe by raising fences at the border such as the 8.3 kilometre-long one separating Morocco and the Spanish enclave city of Ceuta (Migration News Sheet 1999, p.5). The visibility of the fence restores the appearance of control yet it only serves to redirect migration flows. More importantly, this strategy is not easily reconciled with the opposite objective of facilitating the movement of welcome people and goods.

'Remote control' however is a strategy that seeks to achieve all goals at once, that is, to circumvent constraints in cost-effective ways, simultaneously appealing to public anxieties over migration, short-circuiting judicial constraints on migration control, while allowing wanted trade, labour, and tourist flows. In practice, this means ensuring that aspiring migrants or asylum-seekers do not reach the territory of the receiving countries. It has taken various forms: visa regimes, carrier sanctions, as well as co-operation with transit and sending countries, with the goal of erecting 'buffer zones' around post-industrial liberal democracies.

Whether remote control consists of forcing airline companies to scrutinise their passengers' passports and visas for their validity, enticing neighbouring countries to guard their own 'frontiers of poverty' (Freudenstein 2000, pp.172–3) or establishing 'anomalous zones' (Neuman 1996) such as extraterritorial waiting zones in airports or offshore 'safe havens', the goal is the same. These measures aim at preventing unwanted migrants from accessing the system of legal protection and the asylum process, thereby avoiding the domestic and international legal norms that stand in the way of restricting migration flows. This strategy, which operates *before* the border, also allows for less control at the point of entry itself, thus facilitating the movement of inhabitants of the first world, tourists and businessmen.

This response to the current control dilemma re-enacts old policy instruments. In fact, the idea that visitors and immigrants should be processed before arriving at port was written into law in the US in the first part of the last century: the 1902 Passenger Act forced steamship companies to re-transport at their own cost inadmissible passengers and the 1924 Immigration Act charged American consuls abroad with managing quotas and delivering visas (Zolberg 1997). In the Ellis Island era, agencies in the sending countries along with steamship companies took measures to ensure that would-be emigrants would pass muster when arriving at US ports (Torpey 2000).

What is novel is that these old instruments are now deployed to circumvent legal constraints absent in the early twentieth century, and that they have now been shifted to the EU level. Indeed, migration control agencies participating in trans-governmental forums are not under the same judicial constraints as at the national level. Regarding the limits of judicial intervention in the European context, it suffices to recall that the European Court of Justice (ECJ) did not have a role to play in the Maastricht 'third pillar' framework. In the post-Amsterdam era, the application of preliminary rulings in areas covered by Title IV is restricted. Furthermore, the ECJ will not have jurisdiction with regard to national measures relating to the maintenance of law and order and the safeguarding of internal security adopted regarding the crossing of the internal borders. Finally, the ECJ may be asked for a ruling on the interpretation of the new Title IV or measures based on it, yet it will not apply to national judgments that have already become *res judicata*. By far the most important restriction of the ECJ competence with regard to Title IV lies in Article 68(1). It stipulates that only the highest national courts may refer a case to the ECJ.

The internationalisation of migration policy-making has also disempowered certain national actors. Most of the national ministries concerned with migration do not attend international negotiations and working groups. Ministries of Justice and Interior ousted other ministries such as Foreign Affairs, and in Germany the Chancellery, during the 1985–1990 drafting of the Schengen implementation agreement (Hreblay 1998, p.28) and the situation endures. The legislative branch has been bypassed as well since national parliaments have been presented with the *fait accompli*, with only a few weeks to examine and ratify without amendments agreements such as Schengen and Dublin. This is not compensated by the role of the European Parliament at the EU level, which had no role in the Schengen 1985 and 1990 agreements. The European Parliament only needs to be consulted. After 2004, co-decision, which gives the EP more weight and an ultimate veto power, may be extended to cover all or part of the areas covered by Title IV only after a unanimous vote by Council members.

The development of common instruments need not imply that they are to be uniformly implemented. In the emerging regime on immigration and asylum, 'co-operation' is often preferred to 'harmonisation' and 'discretion' in implementation is upheld as desirable. This is hardly surprising since Europeanisation aims in large part at regaining bureaucratic autonomy over domestic legal constraints.

Delegation to Private Actors in Practice: Carrier Sanctions

In the case of visas, control is taking place before reaching the border and is performed by civil servants. With laws on carrier sanctions, private actors perform checks before the border and away from the state. In fact, airline companies such as British Airways have argued that transferring migration control functions is not only an illegitimate transfer of competence from the state to the private sector but also that, unlike consular personnel, airline staff do not enjoy the same protection as consular personnel in cases of intimidation (Forster 1997).

As Janet Gilboy (1997) notes, states have traditionally used a variety of private parties and contexts as de facto 'cops on the beat'. Nonetheless, while third-party liability systems are in part decades old, she notes that they have become strikingly popular for law enforcement use. In particular, the recent period has seen a stricter application of the international standards laid down in the 1944 Convention on International Civil Aviation (ICAO), such as standards 3.35 and 3.38 on the responsibility of airlines for the travelling documentation of their passengers.[3]

European states started imitating the US[4] by passing carrier sanctions laws in the late 1980s and, as previously stated, it is now EU policy after the incorporation of the Schengen *acquis*. The recommendations of the 1993 Budapest conference to prevent uncontrolled migration which brought together Western and Eastern and Central European immigration ministers dedicate a full section to 'the obligation of transport operators to prevent illegal migration' [section 8] and called for the training of check-in airline personnel and the imposition of sanctions for airlines, sea and land carriers which transport aliens without the requisite documents (see Bunyan 1997, p.87).[5]

---

[3] This has been secured since the Paris Conference in 1919, which in effect put airspace, the domain through which airlines must travel, under the sovereign control of states. This allowed the resources of private actors to be deployed to the benefit of the state and cooperation is now secured through sanctions and penalties.

[4] In the US, the Immigration and Nationality Act (8 U.S.C) penalises international air carriers with a $3,000 assessment for each infraction, and the cost for removal for each inadmissible individual (8 U.S.C., 1323).

[5] With the signing of the 'Pre-Accession Pact on Organised Crime' at the Justice and Home Affairs Council of 28–29 May 1998, applicant states agreed to constrain their freedom of action in migration policy-making and adapt their relevant administrative structures that implement migration policies, see European Report 1998. Shortly thereafter, Germany initiated a special multilateral meeting within the 'Budapest process' that was dedicated to reducing illegal migration through southeast Europe. Most of the other Central and East European states aspiring to EU mem-

Similarly, in the 1993 Berlin declaration, Eastern and Central European states pledged to pass carrier sanctions laws.

In the logic of remote control, carrier sanctions complement visas to the extent that persons who would not be granted a visa if they declared that they wanted to seek asylum could still in the absence of pre-boarding checks hope to travel to a European country and apply for asylum upon entry. Carrier sanctions are thus targeted specifically at asylum-seekers, whereas visa policy seems to concentrate on the poor as prospective migrants.

Throughout the last ten years, a number of international organisations, namely the UN High Commissioner for Refugees (1995) and the Council of Europe,[6] international NGOs such as the ECRE (1988, 1999) and the European Parliament[7] have denounced the fact that the implementation of article 26 of the Schengen Agreement on carrier sanctions prevented the exercise of the right of asylum. James Forster of British Airways has stated that since the 1987 Carriers sanctions Act came into force in the UK in part to stem the number of Sri-Lankans seeking asylum, four hundred passengers who boarded BA planes 'with apparently correct documentation and yet arrived in the UK without valid documents have been granted asylum status'.[8] One consequence of carrier sanctions has been to criminalise the entry of asylum-seekers since they need either to acquire forged documents to board planes to later discard them or to seek entry through overland routes with the help of smugglers. Yet, this has prompted EU member states such as France to justify calls for a reinforcement of carrier sanctions precisely by the need to 'fight against illegal migration.'

National parliamentary commissions of the House of Lords or the French Senate further warned that carriers should not become immigration officers (Villepin 1991, p.44; House of Lords 1994). Not only has the adoption of carrier sanctions laws continued unabated but also it has indeed obliged airlines to perform control functions. The level of expertise that is required from airline staff by regulations is tantamount to that of an immigration officer: the French Ministry of Interior stipulates, for instance, that the irregularities that they need to detect are, 'not only a *flaw* in the document but also *usurpation*,

---

bership participated and agreed to a set of measures to be taken by sending and transit states including introducing sanctions against carriers.

[6] Recommendation 1163/1991 of the Parliamentary Assembly of the Council of Europe on the arrival of asylum-seekers at European airports adopted on 23 September 1991 (Doc. 6490).

[7] 'Résolution du Parlement européen sur l'incompatibilité des contrôles de passeports effectués par certaines compagnies aériennes avec l'article 7 A du traité CE', adopted 11 March 1994 (Doc A3-0081/94).

[8] Quoted in Migration News Sheet, December 2000, p.10. These figures are available since, according to British legislation, fines will not be levied if the passenger is granted asylum status. To evaluate how many passengers were not allowed on board, British Airways denied flight to 5,568 passengers in 1995 (Nicholson 1997, p.598).

falsification, counterfeiting or *expiration*' (Ministère de l'Intérieur 1996, p.10, italics in original). Similarly, a training program carried out the British Carriers' Liaison Unit has been criticised by airline officials and BARUK (the Board of Airlines Representatives in the UK) as 'more appropriate to an immigration officer' requiring such things as 'a detailed knowledge of forgeries' (Nicholson 1997, p.592).

Measuring the effect of carrier sanctions is not an easy task for several reasons: companies are reluctant to give out information, government bodies rarely and parsimoniously release data on sanctions and seldom evaluate the implementation of the policy, even when required by law as in France.[9] It is even impossible to see the penalties appear either as a credit in the state budget or as a debit in the companies' financial statements. The data that we have managed to obtain reveals some similarities with about 4000–5000 persons each year not allowed to embark per company.[10] In 1995, British Airways released a figure of 5568 passengers that they did not allow to board (Nicholson 1997, p.598). KLM refuses about 4,000 passengers a year, and Air France personnel speak of several hundred per month. For instance, in August 2001 Air France said that they refused to allow the boarding of 813 passengers while eighty-nine passengers who did board were not admitted in the country of destination. 350 of the 813 refused passengers were to fly out of African airports to travel to Roissy (sixty passengers from Africa boarded but were not admitted).[11]

The first European Union operation to assess the presence of persons with invalid documentation attempting to fly to EU destinations or candidate countries took place in 2002 and was called 'Operation RIO II—The struggle against illegal immigration and organised networks trafficking in human beings by air'. Its results were released in May 2002 during the Spanish Presidency.

As the report of the Spanish Presidency to the General Affairs Council on 'advances made in combating illegal migration' makes clear, the operative plan of Europol in combating the trade and trafficking in human beings includes, 'Obliging carriers to pay the repatriation costs of foreigners who do not meet the requirements for legal entry'(Council of the European Union 2002.).

The possibility that an individual is prevented from reaching his/her final destination remains even after boarding the plane and s/he enters a sort of

---

[9] The French Ministry of Interior has stated that in 1998 2175 files for non-compliance had been delivered and 1603 fines levied, and for the first nine months of 1999, 2192 files et 1172 fines levied. Between 1993 et 1995, there were 3444 fines (Ministère de l'Intérieur 1996).
[10] Interviews with personnel from KLM, Air France and British Airways.
[11] From Roissy airport to the UK and Ireland in August 2001, 150 persons were denied boarding, 187 were denied boarding to the US, and 100 to Canada. Figures provided by François Cabrera, CFDT Air France, at the conference 'Frontières et zones d'attente', French senate, 19–20 October 2001.

legal void.¹² In cases known as 'interrupted transit', airline personnel prevent passengers from travelling to their final destination. In France, Article 35, paragraph VII of the *Ordinance of 2 November 1945* states that a 'foreigner transiting in a train station, port or airport whom the carrier refuses to transport to his ultimate destination' can be detained in a waiting zone.¹³ As François Julien-Laferrière notes, the circular of 9 July 1992 that describes how the article should be implemented underlines that these foreigners will not be declared inadmissible and they are thus placed by airlines in a precarious and blurred legal position: 'they do not enjoy any legal protection and can be sent back without delay or procedure, without leaving any trace. No decision has been notified to them since none has been issued' (Julien-Laferrière 1996, p.7). Aside from French waiting zones, passengers suspected by airline staff have also been held in Russian airport transit zones. As Frances Nicholson notes, since 1992 the transit zone at Moscow airport Sheremetyevo 2 'has held up to 20 passengers at any one time, including refugees who have been denied flights to Western European states [...] who are not permitted to fly by airlines seeking to avoid the imposition of fines' (1997, pp.598–9). Nor can they apply for asylum at Sheremetyevo 2. In the end, airlines also participate in the bouncing of asylum-seekers to 'safe third countries'.¹⁴

There are numerous reasons why airline companies collaborate with authorities. First, the amount of fines that they face is not negligible. In the UK, more than £120 million have been levied since the 1987 Carriers Liability Act came into force and British Airways pays about £5 million a year. KLM had to pay millions in a court settlement that they lost against the Ministry of Justice in July 2000.¹⁵ After using the stick of fines, governments generally propose a

---

12 In some cases, passengers have been 'kidnapped' by on-board personnel (*Daily Telegraph*, 7 July 1990).

13 In the original, 'un étranger qui se trouve en transit dans une gare, un port ou un aéroport si l'entreprise de transport qui devait l'acheminer dans le pays de destination ultérieure refuse de l'embarque'.

14 Moreover, airline cooperation on matters of same-day removals of inadmissible foreigners on the 'carrier's next regularly scheduled departure', while somewhat flexible, is critical. It allows the state to avoid the costs of detention, and to prevent the access to lawyers that one night's detention may present. Such a costly exclusion process could be avoided by same-day removal, and airlines are key facilitators (Gilboy 1994).

15 Aside from paying fines, carriers have to invest in hiring and training personnel. At Schipol airport alone, KLM has a staff of 16 full-time employees who work on verifying passports and visas and in Roissy, about 30 employees are in charge of passport and visa control for Air France. The price of control is also high for train companies and ferries. The English Welsh and Scottish Railways (EWS) spent three million pounds for security at Dollands Moor, the first entry point for freight trains coming from the Channel tunnel and Eurotunnel spent two million pounds on reinforced security at Calais including fences, cameras, and the hiring of 160 guards (*Guardian*, Europe Edition, 22 May 2001, p.4).

carrot: exempting carriers from fines if they participate in the 'Approved Gate Check system' or, in Belgium and Germany, if they sign a *Memorandum of Understanding* with immigration authorities. The end result is a multiplication of pre-boarding checks at airports in countries identified as presenting a 'migration risk'. This is where the public/private divide becomes blurred since immigration officers are sent to airports to help companies.[16]

Furthermore, the security agents hired by companies have either been trained by public agencies or are themselves former civil servants from the police forces, intelligence services or border police. The security chief at KLM, Teun Platenkamp worked for the Amsterdam police before joining an anti-terrorism intelligence unit and being trained by the FBI in the US. The Air France director of security was on leave from the French border police (*Police de l'air et des frontières*). He was posted in Pau close to the French–Spanish border before becoming a *commissaire* in Roissy. The head of the security company (AVS) hired by Lufthansa to check documents was a member of the German border guards (BGS) and hired many former border guards. In July 2001, Channel Tunnel operator Eurotunnel appointed a senior British Army officer, General Sir Roger Wheeler, who commanded British land forces, to improve security so as to prevent foreigners from entering the UK illegally.[17]

Yet, in spite of this blurred line between immigration and carrier personnel, in this system of 'shifting liabilities' airlines not only bear the costs of control but also the legal responsibility. There are a few precedents of plaintiffs accusing airline companies of discrimination on the basis of race and

---

[16] In October 1996, JHA ministers agreed to organise joint training assignments for officers including airline staff locally responsible for documentation checks Joint Position on pre-frontier assistance and training requirements, OJ L281/1, 25.10.1996].

[17] The Channel tunnel epitomises some of the issues raised by carrier sanctions. Airlines, ferry companies, lorry and coach drivers face a £2,000 per head fine if it is found that they have carried illegal entrants across the Channel. The British government maintained that this policy is efficient since the number of persons found in lorries had diminished, but failed to mention that foreigners use other means to cross the tunnel. In the end, public forces were reintroduced since fifty British immigration officers were sent to the French side of the tunnel to help stop illegal migrants from using cross-channel trains to get into Britain. Eurotunnel and road hauling companies threatened not to pay fines and have launched high court action to challenge the imposition of civil fines. They point to the commercial losses that they have suffered, which also shows that carrier sanctions change the terms of the debate on immigration and asylum. When Eurotunnel went to a Lille administrative court in September 2001 to ask for immediate closure of the makeshift camp at Sangatte where refugees on their way to the UK are detained, they argued that the camp was costing them millions in disrupted business (Reuters, 11 September 2001). Carrier sanctions have forced transport companies to become policy players in the immigration field, yet so far it has only reframed the debate on control in cost/benefit terms.

nationality, for instance against the Portuguese airline TAP (Cruz 1995). There are also civil cases filed by Kenyans and Sri Lankans against airline companies that refused to fly them to the UK (Nicholson 1997). In a case involving photocopying the documents of a British-born black passenger and his family, British Airways settled out of court after being accused of racial bias (*Financial Times*, 11 November 1995; *Guardian*, 9 October 1996). Although it is the company that is accused of racial discrimination, the laws on carrier sanctions can be said to foster this attitude.[18]

There are reasons to believe that carrier sanctions will result in discriminatory practices. The competition between airlines (and airport authorities) is ferocious and they are keen to save time on passenger processing and speed transfers. Airline security personnel have therefore spoken in favour of 'profiling', i.e., selecting a few individuals for additional checks rather than delaying boarding time by submitting everybody to the same treatment. The Senior Vice President of KLM in charge of security, Teun Platenkamp, spoke in favour of 'focused security strategies' at airports over 'blanket approaches' by arguing that a new blanket security measure that adds only thirty seconds more processing time per passenger' means '3 1/3 hours more processing time per flight', which he finds extremely wasteful of resources (1997, p.1). While profiling was developed in the 1970s in the context of the fight against terrorism at airports, there is no reason to believe that the criteria to choose 'selectees' would be much different in the search for 'migration risk'. In the case of sanctions for instance, airlines may be required to provide photocopies of passports to immigration authorities should a passenger destroy his documents on board (e.g., in the French case). To save time, only a few passengers will have their passport photocopied. The guidelines transmitted to local personnel and techniques taught during training in fact suggest that profiling is

---

18 If we examine the European human rights jurisprudence on the subject of third parties acting beyond a State border yet in compliance with the laws of that State, it appears that the state, and not only the third party, can be held legally responsible. First, in Amuur v. France (ECHR 25 June 1996 [17/1995/523/609], paragraph 52), the European Court of Human Rights asserted that the plaintiffs, although detained in an international transit zone in a Paris airport, according to the French immigration law, were not in France, yet they were subject to French law and France had to respect the Convention. Second, In Mussele versus Belgium (Series A, number 70 (1983, paragraph 29), the Court had found that a State could not escape its responsibilities under the Convention (in the case at hand providing legal aid) by delegating to others. Evert A. Alkema, a former member of the European Commission of Human Rights, has argued that, although a complaint against an individual including a carrier is incompatible with the Convention ratione personae under article 25 of the Convention, the concept of Drittwirkung allows a complaint to be brought indirectly if a Contracting state can be held responsible for the violation. In his view it is 'particularly relevant at a time when several governments are seeking to transfer to private corporations tasks formerly entrusted to public bodies' (1988, p.40).

widespread. Airport airline employees are asked to spot certain behaviours such as nervousness, or to select passengers who appear to be looking for someone in the airport.

By establishing carriers' sanctions, EU states have delegated migration control functions to private actors in the countries of origin and transit yet, in principal–agent terms, as principals, they have ensured that they could closely monitor the behaviour of the agents. One such way has consisted in sending liaison officers to help the security personnel who have been contracted to perform document checks at airports abroad, especially in what are known as immigration 'hot spots'. Originally, this method was amateurish. In 1990, for instance, German border guards were disguised as company employees to check passports and visas in these hot spots in the absence of bilateral agreements with countries of origin (*Frankfurter Rundshau*, 5 September 1990).

This technique has now become institutionalised and is an official European policy, at least since an October 1996 Justice and Home Affairs Council of Ministers joint decision. Interior ministers then agreed to organise joint training assignments for liaison officers including for airline staff locally responsible for documentation checks(see Joint Position of 25 October 1996). The 2000 French Presidency action plan on migration control recommended that the questionnaire centralised by the Centre for Information Discussion and Exchange on the crossing of frontiers and immigration (CIREFI) be adapted to include information on 'non-compliance by carriers'. The French plan also recommended the enhancement of co-operation between liaison officers assigned to airline companies, a task which was described in the document as a 'permanent system'. Furthermore, the plan suggested that, in order to efficiently pool resources, depending on the air connections with destination countries, a liaison officer from one of the member states be solely devoted to 'controls on embarkation' for passengers travelling to any of the EU states.[19]

In brief, EU carriers' sanctions show that the fact that law and order officials delegate to private agents does not mean that they 'lose control'. It helps them act beyond their state borders. Nor does the fact that decisions are now 'European' imply that they have also delegated decision-making. They merely use an intergovernmental setting to institutionalise and render permanent control systems.

---

[19] French 'Action plan to improve the control of immigration' of 4 July 2000, Conseil de l'Union, Bruxelles, DOC 10017/00. After the carriers directive was adopted, the French interior minister declared that one needed to ' renforcer, sur place, la coopération policière avec le pays d'origine ou de transit. Malgré les actions et les efforts entrepris, force est pourtant de constater que les contrôles effectués par les compagnies aériennes et les services de police aux aéroports demeurent insuffisants, particulièrement en Afrique subsaharienne' ('Conclusions orales tirées par Daniel Vaillant', neuvième conférence des ambassadeurs, problématique sécurité et immigration, Paris, 28 August 2001.)

In the Name of the 'War on Terrorism': Post September 11 Pressures

After the attacks on New York and Washington on 11 September 2001, both airlines and the EU have faced tremendous pressure from the US government to increase security checks as part of their co-operation in the 'war on terrorism'. This section retraces major developments in the control of persons demanded of private carriers since the terrorist attacks.

On 4 January 2002, the US Department of Justice, Immigration and Naturalization Service, published a new rule on *Manifest Requirements Under Section 231* of The Immigration and Nationality Act (INA) amended by Section 402 of the Enhanced Border Security and Visa Entry Act of 2002. This 'requires the submission of arrival and departure manifests electronically in advance of an aircraft or vessel's arrival in or departure from the United States.' The list should include crew members and 'any other occupants transported' and must be sent to the US authorities 'no later than 15 minutes after the flight departs... this will allow the Service to check the manifest against the appropriate security databases prior to arrival.' Failure to deliver the list of crew members and other occupants transported will result in fines of '$1,000 per violation on a carrier for each person for whom an accurate and full manifest is not submitted.' The model for this system is that of APIS (Advance Passenger Information System) operated by Australia and New Zealand. The information to be supplied includes name, date of birth, citizenship, sex, passport number and country of issuance, country of residence, alien registration, address while in the US, and 'other such information as the Attorney General determines is necessary for the identification of persons transported, for the enforcement of immigration laws, and to protect public safety and national security.' Personal data on passengers will be exchanged in a standard format known as the UN Electronic Data Interchange for Administration (EDIFACT).

The US had first informed their EU partners soon after 11 September at a closed meeting of the EU Strategic Committee on Immigration, Frontiers and Asylum on 26 October 2001 (Council of the EU 2001). The US delegates wanted data exchange between the US and the EU to include 'intelligence driven data (review of passenger lists), data on persons known to be inadmissible due to involvement in criminal activity (trafficking, dealing in false documents etc)' so as to prevent all inadmissible persons from entering the US and the EU by introducing the APIS system.

The first government to support the US measure was the UK (soon followed by Spain).[20] On 6 July 2002, The *Guardian* newspaper reported that

---

[20] In January 2003, the Spanish Presidency proposed that data on passengers be 'conveyed immediately to the border control authorities in the Member State of destination, this would ensure that a period of time is available to perform a detailed analysis, on the basis of each specific situation or of each passenger's country of departure.' (Council of the European Union 2003).

British Air Transport Association objected to Home Office plans to pass through parliament a Statutory Instrument under the 2001 Anti-Terrorism, Crime and Security Act 2001 (Clark 2002). The latter would require airlines to record many pieces of information on passengers before each plane could take off. British Airways, Virgin and British Midland were opposed to the requirement because of the costs and delays they would entail. The airlines expressed the same criticism as when carriers' sanctions were introduced: 'we have been lumbered with both the task and the cost for something which is really the government's responsibility' (Clark 2002). Tour operators also contested the planned measure as they feared that airlines would use the information to directly contact passengers.

It should be underlined that, until then, airlines had clearly cooperated to implement post 9/11 bans on metal cutlery, sharp objects in hand luggage, and had installed reinforced cockpit doors. Yet providing extensive data on all passengers did not seem a direct response to the 11 September events. In fact, the 'intuition' of the British airline industry was warranted. The minutes of the aforementioned secret meeting between the US and the EU made it clear that 'the US delegation indicated that since the events of 11 September 2001, the whole system of visas, border controls, management of legal migration, etc. had come under close scrutiny and there was a consensus in the US on the need for an effective system across the board, not targeted specifically at terrorism, but taking the events of 11 September as the trigger for developing a new approach' (Council of the EU 2001). In other words, terrorism and 11 September were to be used as a frame for the justification of new measures on immigration and border controls, a 'trigger'—or 'focus event' in the lexicon of political science (Baumgartner and Jones 1993)—that could change policy 'across the board'. In fact, most of the measures discussed at that meeting related to the deportation of foreigners, visa policy and other issues related to migration control. Although several member-state delegates pointed out their commitment to international legal instruments (the principle of *non-refoulement* of the *Geneva Convention on Refugees* and the *European Convention on Human Rights*), the pressure to cooperate was nonetheless obvious.

Beyond these international human rights instruments, US demands seemed incompatible with existing single market rules[21] and EU directives. The US had no data protection legislation and there were no guarantee as to the use of the data provided by airlines, which stood in contradistinction with the 1995 EU data protection directive. On 17–18 February 2003, Senior officials of the European Commission and the US Administration (Director General for External Relations Guy Legras and Deputy US Customs Commissioner

---

[21] The European Commission took legal action against Germany, France, the Netherlands and Belgium because they have signed individual bilateral agreements giving US Customs agents powers to search all containers leaving EU ports for the US under its Container Security Initiative. The UK, Spain and Italy have also signed agreements.

Douglas Browning) met in Brussels and issued a joint statement on reconciling the new Passenger Name Record (PNR) transmission requirements contained in the 2001 US Aviation and Transportation Security Act with the requirements of data protection law in the EU. In fact, it did not take into account the opinion of the Article 29 Data Protection Working Party adopted on 24 October 2002, which had questioned whether it would be legal to transfer passenger data not required for the purpose of booking a plane ticket, where there are no limits on the use of the data nor any guarantees that it will not be amended for other purposes nor who it may be passed on to. In other words, in spite of the nominal existence of a EU independent advisory body mandated by the EU directive to give opinions on data protection, the European Commission agreed to cooperate with U.S. customs and meet the deadline fixed by US authorities of 3 March 2003, at which point US Customs gained direct access to EU airline reservation databases to download personal data on all passengers and crew. The only action that the Working Party could undertake at that point was to alert the European Parliament Committee on Citizens' Freedoms and Rights and ask for a postponement of the measure.

What are the lessons that can be drawn from this unfolding story? First, it is obvious that the 11 September 2001 events have been instrumentalised to reinforce immigration controls and demands on third parties. Second, the secretive and intergovernmental nature of JHA co-operation has made it easier for EU institutions and member-states to cater to US demands. It is a story of policy made behind closed doors except for one article in a British daily and a letter by the chair of the Data Protection Working Party, Mr. Rodota, with little echo in the press. The irony is that decisions taken by government authorities which bypass interest group consultation (the airlines) are aimed precisely at shifting liabilities to these private actors. Third, the fact that the EU, as a 'regulatory state' (Majone 1997), has set up a certain number of advisory boards supposed to act as 'watchdogs' to ensure the respect of EU rules, does not preclude that these are ignored by Commission and Council policy-makers and are unknown to EU citizens. In other words, they cannot be equated with the institutions of 'democratic control' in the member states.

Conclusion

The first obstacle that an individual must overcome before arriving on EU territory could be at a consulate or at an airport. In Europe, the decision to let in a third country national now involves a great number of public agencies and private actors: diplomatic personnel, aliens' police posted abroad, and security agents of transport companies. On the one hand, databases such as the SIS automatically exclude a number of aliens from entry; on the other hand, administrative discretion still plays an important role in consulates, and security agencies use 'profiling' to screen passengers from airports in 'hot spots'. It is therefore often difficult to trace the origin of the decision and also to appeal it.

There has been no plan to harmonise appeal procedures. The legal recourse of persons turned away at the airport is unclear. Remote control instruments diminish third country nationals' access to the legal system of EU receiving states. In this respect, they mirror the dynamics of trans-governmental co-operation at the EU level where the role of the ECJ is circumscribed.

Carrier sanctions increase the criminalisation of migration and encourage the industry of false documents. A Reflection Group set up by the European Commission came to the same conclusion: 'tighter border controls will likely only drive up the price, and thus the profits, of this criminal trade' (Amato and Batt 1999, p.57). Yet, illegal migration is used as a reason to promote the strengthening of the same kind of measures.

As the Seville summit showed, shifting responsibility to the EU does not seem a viable means of stemming anti-immigrant populism and does not call into question the agenda of the extreme right. Nor does the policy toolbox of 'remote control' (visas, carrier sanctions and buffer zones) seem to stem migration flows. Therefore, it would appear that this widespread trend of preventing potential migrants' access to the judicial arsenal of liberal democracies has only exacerbated anti-immigrant rhetoric.

References

ALKEMA, E. A. 1988. 'The Third Party Applicability of *Drittwirkung* of the European Convention of Human Rights'. In *Protecting Human Rights: The European Dimension. Studies in Honour of Gérard J. Wiarda*, eds., F. Matscher and H. Petzold. Köln: Carl Heymanns Verlaag KG.

AMATO, G. and J. BATT, 1999. *Final Report of the Reflection Group on the Long-Term Implications of EU Enlargement: The Nature of the New Border.* Florence.

ANDREAS, P. and T. SNYDER. (eds). 2000. *The Wall around the West: State Borders and Immigration Control in North America and Europe.* New York: Rowman & Littlefield Publishers.

BAUMGARTNER, B. and B. JONES. 1993. *Agendas And Instability In American Politics.* Chicago: University Of Chicago Press.

BIGO, D. 1996. *Polices en réseaux. L'expérience européenne.* Paris: Presses de Science Po.

BUNYAN, T. (ed.). 1997. *Key Texts on Justice and Home Affairs in the European Union. Volume 1 From Trevi to Maastricht (1976–1993).* London: Statewatch.

CLARK, ANDREW. 2002. 'Airlines Warn of Delays over Blunkett Security Plan'. *Guardian*, 6 July 2002.

COMMISSION OF THE EUROPEAN COMMUNITIES. 1989. 'Eurobarometer. Public Opinion in the European Community'. No. 31. Available at URL:

CORNELIUS, W, P. MARTIN and J. HOLLIFIELD, (eds). 1994. *Controlling immigration*. Stanford: Stanford University Press.

COUNCIL OF THE EUROPEAN UNION. 2001. 'Outcome of proceedings of the Strategic Committee on Immigration, Frontiers and Asylum meeting with the United States dated 26 October 2001'. Doc. 13803/01 ASIM 21 USA. 24 Brussels, 12 November 2001.

―――――― 2002. 'Advances Made in Combating Illegal Immigration'. Doc. 10009/02 JAI 141 MIGR 56, 14 June 2002 (Brussels).

―――――― 2003. 'Completing the provisions of article 26 of the Schengen Implementing Convention and of the Council Directive 2001/51/CE of 28 June 2001'. Doc 5174/03, 9 January 2003 (Brussels).

CRUZ, A. 1995. *Carrier Liability in the Member States of the European Union*. Brussels: CCME Briefing Paper 17.

DIMINESCU, D. 2001. 'Le 'système D' contre les frontières informatiques', in *Hommes et migrations* 1230 (March- April issue).

ECRE. 1988. *The Role of Airline Companies in the Asylum Procedure*. Copenhagen.

―――――― 1999. 'Country Up-Date on the Application of Carriers' Liability in European States', February 1999 research paper. London.

Enhanced Border Security and Visa Entry Act of 2002. H.R. 3525. Available at URL: <http://frwebgate.access.gpo.gov/cgi-bin/getdoc.cgi?dbname=107_cong_bills&docid=f:h3525enr.txt.pdf>

European Report. 1998. 'Justice and Home Affairs: Crime-Fighting Cooperation pact Signed up to by 25 States'. No. 2319, 30 May 1998.

Financial Times. 'BA Chief apologizes for copying of "ethnic passport"', 11 November 1995

FORSTER, J. 1997. 'Internal and Devolved Responsibility for Controlling Illegal Immigration: How Effective?'. 497th Wilton Park Conference 'Migration: Prevention, Control and Management', 7-11 April 1997.

Frankfurter Rundshau, 5 September 1990.

FREUDENSTEIN, R. 2000. 'Rio Odra, Rio Buh: Poland, Germany, and the Borders of Twenty-First-Century Europe'. In *The Wall around the West: State Borders and Immigration Control in North America and Europe*, eds., P. Andreas and T. Snyder. New York: Rowman & Littlefield Publishers.

GERMAN FOREIGN OFFICE. 2001. 'New Visa Practice of the German Foreign Office' and 'Visas'. *Auswärtiges Amt* official site: <http://www.auswaertiges-amt.de>

GILBOY, J. 1997. 'Implications of "Third-Party" Involvement in Enforcement: The INS, Illegal Travelers, and International Airlines'. *Law and Society Review*, 31 (3).

GRABBE, H. 2001. 'Les dilemmes engendrés par les politiques frontalières de l'Union: l'exemple des minorités hongroises'. *Hommes et migrations* 1230 (March–April issue).

Guardian. 'BA Pays Tens of Thousands in Racism Claim', 9 October 1996.

GROENENDIJK, K. 2001. 'Security of Residence and Access to Free Movement for Settled Third Country Nationals under Community Law'. In *Implementing Amsterdam: Immigration and Asylum Rights in EC Law*, eds., E. Guild and C. Harlow. Oxford: Hart.

GUENDELSBERGER, J. 1988. 'The Right to Family Unification in French and United States Immigration Law'. *Cornell International Law Journal*, 21.

GUILD, E. 2000. 'Adjudicating Schengen: National Judicial Control in France'. *European Journal of Migration and Law*,1.

_____ 2001. 'Globalizing Europe: Poverty and the Messages of EU immigration and Asylum Laws' Paper presented at the International Studies Association conference in Chicago, February 2001.

GUIRAUDON, V. 1999. 'European Integration and Migration Policy: Vertical Policy-making as Venue Shopping'. *Journal of Common Market Studies*, 38 (2).

_____ 2000a. *Les politiques d'immigration en Europe. Allemagne, France, Pays-Bas*. Paris: L'Haramattan.

_____ 2000b. 'European Courts and Foreigners' Rights: A Comparative Study of Norms Diffusion'. *International Migration Review*, 34 (4).

GUIRAUDON, V. and L. GALLYA. 2000. 'The State Sovereignty Debate Revisited: The Case of Migration Control'. *Comparative Political Studies*, 33 (2).

HAAS, E. 1958. *The Uniting of Europe: Political, Social, and Economic Factors*. London.

HERBERT, U. 1990. *A History of Foreign Labor in Germany*. Ann Arbor.

HIRST, P. and G. THOMPSON. 1995. 'Globalization and the Future of the Nation-State'. *Economy and Society*, 24.

HOLLIFIELD, J. 1992. *Immigrants, Markets, and States: The Political Economy of Postwar Europe*. Cambridge, Massachusetts .

HOUSE OF LORDS SELECT COMMITTEE ON THE EUROPEAN COMMUNITIES. 1994. *Fourteenth Report on visas and Control of External Borders of the Member States*. London. (Published 19 July 1994)

_____ 2000. *Seventeenth Report on Enlargement and EU External Frontier Controls*. London. (Published 24 October 2000)

HREBLAY, V. 1998. *Les accords de Schengen. Origine, fonctionnement, avenir*. Brussels.

Immigration and Nationality Act (8 U.S.C. 1221(a)) § 231 - Lists of Alien and Citizen Passengers Arriving or Departing; Record of Resident Aliens and Citizens Leaving Permanently for Foreign Country'.

IOM. 1997. *The Baltic Route: The Trafficking of Migrants Through Lithuania.* Budapest.

JILEVA, E. 2001. 'Insiders and Outsiders in Central and Eastern Europe: The Case of Bulgaria'. Paper presented at the conference 'Nationality and Citizenship in Post-Communist Europe', Institute of Political Science, Paris, France, 9–10 July.

'Joint Position of 25 October 1996 defined by the Council on the basis of Article K.3 (2) (a) of the Treaty on European Union, on pre-frontier assistance and training assignments'. 96/622/JHA.*Official Journal of the European Union,* L 281/1, 31 November 1996.

JULIEN-LAFERRIÈRE, F. 1996. 'La situation des demandeurs d'asile dans les zones d'attente et les lieux de rétention administrative'. *Cultures et Conflits* 23 (Fall).

KOSLOWSKI, R. 2001. 'Personal Security, State Sovereignty and the Deepening and Widening of European Co-operation in Justice and Home Affairs'. In *Controlling a New Migration World,* eds. V. Guiraudon and C. Joppke. London: Routledge.

IND. 2000. 'Visa for Short stay in the Netherlands'. Ministry of Justice. The Hague.

JOPPKE, C. 1999. *Immigration and the Nation-State: the United States, Germany, and Great Britain.* Oxford: Oxford University Press.

MANIG, W. 1999. 'The modalities of issuing temporary residence permits by German missions abroad – interaction with other agencies'. Paper presented at the Odysseus program seminar on consular issues in the Baltic countries, Vilnius, Lithuania, 26 November 1999.

Migration News Sheet. 1999. No. 192/99-03 (March).

MITCHELL, C. 2000. 'The Political Costs of State Power: US Border Control in South Florida'. In *The Wall around the West: State Borders and Immigration Controls in North America and Europe,* eds., P. Andreas and T. Snyder. New York: Rowman & Littlefield Publishers.

MONEY, J. 1995. Two-Dimensional Aliens: Immigration Policy as a Two-Dimensional Issue Space'. Unpublished manuscript.

―――――― 1999. *Fences and Neighbors. The Political Geography of Immigration Control.* Ithaca, NY.

MORAWSKA, E. 2001. 'Gappy Immigration Controls, Resourceful Migrants, and *Pendel* Communities: East-West European Travellers'. In *Controlling a New Migration World,* eds., V. Guiraudon and C. Joppke. London: Routledge.

MORAVCSIK, A. 1998. *The Choice for Europe.* Ithaca: Cornell University Press.

NEUMAN, G. 1990. 'Immigration and Judicial Review in the Federal Republic of Germany'. *New York University Journal of International Law and Politics,* 23 (1).

_____ 1996. 'Anomalous Zones'. *Stanford Law Review*, 48.

NICHOLSON, F. 1997. 'Implementation of the Immigration (Carriers' Liability) Act 1987: Privatising Immigration Functions at the Expense of International Obligations?'. *International and Comparative Law Quarterly*, 46 (3).

PLATENKAMP, T. 1997. 'The Benefits of Focused Security strategies over Blanket Security Policies'. Paper presented on January 14th, 1997 at the international conference on aviation safety and security. George Washington University, Washington, DC.

RUGGIE, J. 1982. 'International Regimes, Transactions, and Change: Embedded Liberalism in the Postwar Economic Order'. *International Organization*, 36 (2).

STEENBERGEN, JDM. 1992. 'Schengen and the Movement of Persons'. In *Schengen: Internalionalization of Central Chapters of the Law on Aliens, Refugees, Privacy, Security and the Police*, 2nd edition, eds., H. Meijers et al. Stichling: Boekerij.

STRELTSOVA, I. 2001. 'Le coût de la nouvelle frontière Schengen pour la Russie et l'Ukraine'. *Hommes et Migrations* 1230 (March–April issue).

TANDONNET, M. 2001. 'La politique d'européenne d'immigration à la croisée des chemins'. *Hommes et Migrations* 1230 (March–April issue).

TORPEY, J. 1998. 'Coming and Going: On the State Monopolization of the "Legitimate Means of Movement"'. *Sociological Theory*, 16 (3).

_____ 2000. *The Invention of the Passport. Surveillance, Citizenship and the State*. Cambridge: Cambridge University Press.

UNHCR Regional Bureau for Europe. 1995. *An Overview of Protection Issues in Western Legislative Trends and Positions Taken by the UNHCR*, European Series vol. 1, no. 3, Geneva.

VACHUDOVA, M. 2000. 'Eastern Europe as Gatekeeper: The Immigration and Asylum Policies of an Enlarging European Union', in Andreas, P. and Snyder, T., eds. *The Wall around the West: State Borders and Immigration Control in North America and Europe*. New York: Rowman & Littlefield Publishers.

de VILLEPIN, X. 1991. *Rapport 406, seconde session ordinaire 1990–1991*. Paris: Sénat Français.

WEIL, P. 1997. *Mission d'étude de la législation de la nationalité et de l'immigration. Rapports au Premier Ministre*. Paris: La Documentation Française.

ZOLBERG, A. 1997. 'The Great Wall against China: Responses to the first Immigration Crisis, 1885–1925'. In *Migration, Migration History, History: Old Paradigms and New Perspectives*, eds., Jan Lucassen and Leo Lucassen. New York: Peter Lang Publisher.

PART III

EUROPEAN UNION

Chapter 6

Towards a European Approach on Border Management: Aspects Related to the Movement of Persons

Daphné Gogou

The development of a common approach on border management in the European Union is a recent and ongoing process. The elaboration of the new concept at community level is related to the political dynamic in favour of the free movement of persons within the European Union. This dynamic is a direct consequence of the development of the European citizenship.

Historical Development: From the Free Movement of Workers, Via the Schengen Experience, to the Creation of the Common Area of Freedom, Security and Justice

Free movement of workers: the first step towards 'Europe of the citizens'

The creation of an area of freedom, security and justice (AFSJ) could be seen as the outcome of a long process of European integration. Indeed, none of the three founding treaties of the European Communities attributed any competence to the Community institutions in these areas. Justice and home affairs issues were considered closely linked to the national sovereignty—a highly sensitive field—and for this reason the founding countries opted for a more concrete economic and social approach, and thus agreed to include the measures aimed at facilitating the free movement for workers as one of the four freedoms of the common market into the Treaties. Without doubt this choice reflected at that time the stage of maturity of the European construction, which was limited to exclusively economic matters.

Although some important pieces of legislation were adopted during the 1960s—regulation 1612/68/EEC and Directives 64/221/EEC and 68/360/EEC (Council of the European Union 1964; 1968; 1998)—these measures focused mainly on nationals of Member States and the members of their family. The EU had to wait until the mid-1980s for a more global movement in favour of a 'Europe of the citizens' to emerge. The adoption of the 'Single European Act' in 1986 defined for the first time the freedom of movement for persons as an objective to achieve at a Community level. In concrete terms this meant that citizens of the Member States would be able to travel freely crossing the borders without being checked systematically.

Very early it was felt necessary to tackle simultaneously both aspects of the border management problem; the abolition of the borders between Member States, the so-called 'internal borders', was thus coupled to the reinforcement of the external borders (borders with third, non-EU countries).

Despite the fact that the abolition of controls on persons at the borders between the EU Member States was by the late 1980s a central element of the European integration process, the process was fraught with difficulties. A key concern expressed in relation to the abolition of internal border controls concerned the enormous practical difficulties faced by member states in defining a common approach to measures offsetting the possible negative effects of the complete lifting of internal border controls. The internal security dimension was the key preoccupation of national governments, which were keen to control any initiative that could anticipate the lifting of controls between the member states. This reaction was understandable as the protection of the individual has been a central element of a state's legitimacy ever since the creation of modern states in Europe. Hence, several fundamentally diverging opinions were formed among the member states regarding the definition of the minimum internal security level. This was due mainly to their different attitudes and sensitivities on the issue of border controls concerning persons. It was obvious at that time that Member States were not ready to work towards a harmonisation of the procedures for carrying out border controls on persons or for collecting and handling personal data for citizens.

In the absence of a well defined political project and faced with a lack of instruments that could translate such a project into concrete actions, the member states opted for the development of two parallel and competing methods for achieving the free movement of persons: the intergovernmental co-operation and the community approach.

On the basis of the community approach, a number of new legal texts were adopted facilitating the mobility of specific categories of persons such as pensioners and students. Examples of such instruments are the Directives 90/364/EEC, 90/365/EEC and 93/96/EEC (Council of the European Union 1990a; 1990b; 1993). However, other initiatives proposed by the Commission during the 1990s have not been adopted due to the complexity of the exercise and the difficulties to achieve political consensus. This has been the case, for instance, with the Commission initiatives known as the 'Monti package' (European Commission 1995a; 1995b; 1995c).

Intergovernmental approach: the Schengen laboratory

On the basis of intergovernmental co-operation mechanisms, Member States were able to introduce since the mid-1970s informal regular structures, outside the Community structure, for the exchange of information on internal security problems. The expansion of threats like drugs, terrorism, transnational organised crime and the new (and increasing since the beginning of the 1990s) migratory pressures, convinced several governments that problems were rapidly acquiring a global dimension and it was considered necessary to fight more effectively against these phenomena by acting in concert. More co-operation was clearly needed as the national scheduled measures for the internal security were not considered an adequate response to the new increasing transnational challenges. As a first step, the member states developed the structure of 'TREVI' (which existed in embryonic form since 1976) for meetings between Ministers of Justice and Home Affairs covering co-operation in areas of general police matters as well as issues of public order, terrorism, drugs and organised crime.

Within this framework some of the Member States expressed the political will to implement in practice the free movement of persons and to commit themselves to the abolition of internal border controls despite the reluctance of other member states to follow them in this direction. On 14 June 1985 the Benelux countries, France and Germany signed the Schengen Agreement, which foresaw the gradual abolition of controls and was accompanied by a broad range of compensatory measures in several Justice and Home Affairs issues. Five years later, on 19 June 1990, the same countries signed the Convention Implementing the Schengen Agreement which sets up (in 142 Articles) precise provisions on, *inter alia*, the abolition of internal border controls, the management of external borders, the issuing of visas, the movement of third country nationals within the common area and the responsibility for the processing of applications for asylum. The Convention also included more general provisions on police co-operation, extradition, other issues of criminal justice co-operation, on narcotic drugs, firearms and the Schengen Information System (SIS). SIS, which started to function in 1995 with the entry into force of the whole Schengen system, soon became the core operational element.

As has been noted by several analysts, Schengen would never have been created in the absence of the political objective of promoting the free movement of persons at the community level. In the spirit of the founding Schengen partners, Schengen was a 'laboratory' of free movement which would be integrated into the Community structure as rapidly as possible. For this reason all Schengen provisions are applicable if they are compatible with Community law (*Schengen Convention*, Article 142). From such a perspective it is obvious why the founding States did not provide Schengen with any permanent organisational structure and did not endow it with an autonomous legal personality. Similarly, accession to the Schengen agreement was limited to the states that were full members of the European Union. Nevertheless, there were exceptions. An agreement was concluded in December 1996 for the accession of Norway and Iceland to the Schengen Convention.

For the member states, the advantages of an intergovernmental approach like Schengen compared to the traditional community method were mainly understood in terms of national sovereignty. Indeed, as a typical intergovernmental initiative, the Schengen approach escapes any form of political control by the European Parliament. It is also outside the jurisdictional control of the European Court of Justice. As regards in particular the legislative process, the Schengen framework deviates from the exclusive prerogative of the European Commission in initiating legislative proposals.

Although many authors deplored the lack of democratic accountability, judicial control and transparency of the Schengen decision-making framework, the majority of the Schengen provisions, based on an executive culture and carefully worded to apply to practical situations, have been effectively implemented.

Communitarisation of the Schengen acquis: a complex exercise

The reform introduced by the Amsterdam Treaty put an end to the competition between the two approaches for the implementation of the Schengen rules. As a result of the development of the EU towards an area of freedom, security and justice, the free movement of persons is ensured by means of concrete and appropriate measures, and figures prominently in the list of the main objectives of the European Union (Article 2).

Among the areas in which 'appropriate measures' (flanking measures) had to be taken in order to ensure internal security, explicit reference was made to external border controls. The introduction of a new Title IV creating this area (Articles 61–69) completed the Title III provisions related to the free movement of workers.

The management of the borders was defined within Title IV. In particular Article 62 of the Treaty provides that the following objectives should be achieved progressively within five years of the entry into force of the Treaty (since 1 May 1999):

- Removal of any controls on person who are citizens of the European Union or nationals of third countries when they cross the internal borders from any EU member state to another;
- Establishment of rules concerning visas, as well as standards and methods for the control of persons crossing the external borders of the member states (for example when they come into the EU).

Linked to these provisions, other measures aimed at ensuring internal security have been added mostly in Title VI of TEU. This exercise listed actions to be carried out within an intergovernmental framework (Third Pillar).

The rules for the integration of the Schengen *acquis* were laid down in a protocol annexed to the Final Act. The principal role of this Protocol was to facilitate the transposition of all existing commitments between the Schengen states into the European Union legal structure. The integration of Schengen rules into the 'community *acquis*' was not limited to the Schengen Convention, but also included about 200 decisions, mostly unpublished, issued by the Schengen institutions. Due to the different methodology followed, the integration of the Schengen provisions into the Treaty on the European Union gave rise to some serious legal and administrative difficulties such as the definition of the legal basis for the main rules, the determination of the status of some Member States, and the incorporation of the Schengen temporary institutional structures. The Schengen rules were defined by two Council Decisions of May 1999 (Council of the European Union 1999a; 1999b), which defined the *acquis* and allocated legal bases to those Schengen provisions which were evaluated as active and functioning in the Community framework (the so-called 'ventilation' of the Schengen *acquis*).

The Dimension of Border Management

Abolition of internal borders

The specific rules for the creation of a common area of freedom, security and justice in the TEU contain a reference to the four freedoms of the common market. Article 62 of the Treaty requires the adoption of directly related flanking measures as a pre-condition for the abolition of any controls for the persons when they cross the internal borders from one EU Member State to another. Such flanking measures in respect to the controls at the external border and the conditions of travel of third country nationals, as well as measures concerning asylum requests and immigration have thus to be adopted on the basis of Articles 62 and 63 of the Treaty.

Citizens of the member states and members of their family, as well as citizens of third countries who hold residence permits issued by a Schengen state (*Schengen Convention*, Article 21) may benefit from the measures related to the freedom of movement of persons. It should be mentioned here that these measures are of benefit also to aliens who have been granted an 'authorisation of short stay' (not exceeding three months). These categories of persons can also benefit from the abolition of checks at the internal borders and can circulate freely within the common area.

Article 2(2) of the Schengen Convention introduces a safeguard clause allowing the reintroduction of checks at the internal borders by a Member State in specific circumstances. Thus, by derogation from paragraph 2(1), which provides for the abolition of controls on persons at the internal borders, a member state may introduce for a limited period of time at its internal borders checks and controls appropriate to the situation, provided that such a measure is necessary on the basis of public policy or national security considerations and after consulting other Member States. If public policy or national security imperatives require immediate action, the Member State concerned takes the necessary measures and informs the other Member States accordingly at the earliest opportunity. The wording of this provision is such that the authorisation of a reintroduction of checks has until now remained an exceptional measure. Internal border controls are reintroduced on grounds of public policy, for a predetermined duration and for specific and prescheduled events. A Member State may also reintroduce checks at the internal borders in cases where there is a need of immediate decision based on public policy or national security reasons and specify if it requests assistance or co-operation from other Schengen members (Schengen Executive Committee 1995).

The implementation of this safeguard clause is excluded from the jurisdictional control of the European Court of Justice. According to Article 68(2) of the Treaty, the Court of Justice has no jurisdiction to rule on any measure or decision taken pursuant to Article 62(1) relating to the maintenance of law and order and the safeguarding of internal security. Nevertheless, the Court retains a residual jurisdiction to determine the limits of its jurisdiction by assessing itself what it may legitimately review and what it may not.[1]

In practice, the member states have made use of this safeguard clause in a disparate manner, for instance when faced with risks related to the organisation of sporting events or demonstrations, or in order to protest against policies pursued by other member states for the liberalisation of the use of certain narcotic substances and drugs.

In view of the disparate experiences with implementation, there is a need to clarify and define in a more precise manner the scope of this provision. There is also an interest to enhance the possibilities of co-ordinated use of the safeguard clause by more than one member state. It could be desirable, furthermore, to provide a harmonised mechanism at the Community level for a co-ordinated reinstatement of internal border checks in the event of a major security threat potentially affecting the public order of a number of Member States, reflecting the shared sense of European responsibility based on common values and the respect for fundamental rights.

Participation in the common area: differentiated structure and membership

The Treaty provisions organising the decision-making process in the new area reflect a certain political compromise which has led to the recognition of a different status for some Member States.

Keeping in mind the past experiences with multiple decision-making structures which weakened the Union's political role, Member States opted for the preservation of the integrity of the Schengen rules. They agreed, however, to introduce flexible arrangements for the member states who did not participate in the new common area and/or did not wish to be involved in the new decision-making structure. This arrangement authorised 13 Member States to establish among themselves closer co-operation in the area covered by the new Title of the Treaty (the five founding Schengen states, plus Spain, Portugal, Italy, Greece, Austria, Denmark, Finland and Sweden).

The United Kingdom, Ireland and Denmark negotiated special protocols. A new protocol explicitly excluded the United Kingdom and Ireland

---

[1] See in this sense the Court Judgement given in Commission v. Council, Case C-170/96, 1998 I-2763.

from the obligation to implement measures under Title IV of the TEU and incorporated Schengen provisions. The protocol authorises these countries to derogate from the freedom of movement provisions in Title IV and provides for these Member States a guarantee that they can continue to impose border controls on persons at their borders with other Member States. Further, it maintains the 'common travel area' between these Member States. The specific rules included in this protocol recognise for these countries the possibility to opt-in at a later stage, adopt and implement certain or all of the Schengen clauses at any time on the basis of an enabling Council Decision. Pursuant to these provisions the UK and Ireland can maintain their border controls. Decisions enabling the UK and Ireland to participate in an action under Title IV must be adopted unanimously by the Schengen states on the basis of a Commission opinion. A representative of the country concerned takes part (and votes) in the adoption of such decisions. It should be noted that the UK is participating in 95 percent of the security-related measures under the Third pillar. This is due to the possibility foreseen in the Treaty to establish a new framework of co-operation for such actions under different conditions. At the same time the UK and Ireland participate in compensatory security measures and most of the Schengen aspects that are not related to border control, such as the SIS (Council of the European Union 2000; 2002).

A specific protocol was adopted concerning Denmark whose situation is more complex. Although Denmark has been a Schengen state since 1996, it was granted an opt-in regime for all Council decisions building on the Schengen *acquis*. According to the protocol, once the Council has taken such a decision, Denmark has a period of six months to decide whether it will implement the new rules or not. If Denmark decides to implement a new measure that develops the Schengen *acquis*, its decision creates for Denmark an obligation under public international law, and not within the framework of community law. The effect of this regime is clearly to bypass the jurisdictional control of the European Court of Justice, and has an impact on community law in the area of the implementation of the Danish decision to opt-in. This complex situation is due to the fact that Denmark refused to follow the traditional community method of co-operation in the areas covered by Title IV and preferred participating on the basis of an intergovernmental co-operation mechanism. In this sense, the Danish situation is different from the British and Irish one, as it is largely explained in terms of a diverging approach regarding the methodology for a closer co-operation in the area of the free movement rather than any fundamental political concerns. In this way Denmark is able to participate in Third Pillar measures, whether they are Schengen-related or not, as well as in measures related to the visa policy in relation to third country nationals.

The situation of Norway and Iceland is different. In fact these countries participated since the mid-1950s in the Nordic Passport Union (NPU), which aimed to facilitate travel without passport controls of Nordic citizens between the Nordic countries. At the time of the accession of Denmark, Finland and Sweden to the Schengen Agreement, the Schengen states demonstrated their openness towards the NPU by accepting the accession of Norway and Iceland as well. Despite the fact that they did not belong to the EU, the two countries became Schengen states pursuant to a specific agreement signed in 1996. With the incorporation of the Schengen *acquis* in the Treaties, it became necessary to reassess the situation. It was agreed that Norway and Iceland should be able to participate in the compensatory measures needed to realise the common area without frontier controls on the basis of an Association Agreement (Council of the European Union 1999c). In contrast to the Danish situation, as far as Norway and Iceland are concerned, the Schengen *acquis* covers not only the Schengen provisions at the time of the signature of the Association Agreement, but also new community provisions building on the Schengen *acquis*.

In May 2004 the Union was enlarged to include ten new Member States. This was the first enlargement after the integration of the Schengen *acquis* to the Treaties. In order to avoid any further opt-outs in respect to the Schengen *acquis*, the Schengen Protocol stated that candidate countries would have to accept both the Schengen *acquis* as well as measures building upon it as a whole (Article 8).

Under this approach, Article 3 of the Accession Treaty states that 'the provisions of the Schengen *acquis*, as integrated into the framework of the European Union by the Protocol annexed to the Treaty on European Union and to the Treaty establishing the European Community ... and acts building upon it or otherwise related to it, listed in Annex I of this Act, as well as any further such acts which may be adopted before the date of accession, shall be binding on and applicable in the new Member States from the date of accession' (that is before the lifting of the internal borders). This provision clearly differentiates the position of the new Member States from the position of the United Kingdom and Ireland.

For the provisions of the Schengen *acquis* which are not included in the above mentioned Annex 1, the second paragraph of Article 3 states that, while binding on the new Member States from the date of accession, such provisions will only be implemented at a later stage (that is after the lifting of the internal border controls).

In fact the wording of Article 3 of the Accession Treaty reflects the two-step approach chosen for the implementation of the Schengen *acquis* by the new Member States. Despite the maintenance of controls at the 'provisional external borders' from 1 May 2004 (date of accession), the new member states will fully participate in the adoption by the Council of all measures building upon the Schengen *acquis*, including measures necessitating a Council Decision pursuant to Article 3 of the Accession Treaty for their full application.

For technical and operational reasons it was not possible to fully implement the Schengen *acquis* upon accession. For example a functioning Schengen information System (SIS) is a key precondition for such a decision. Considering that the second generation of SIS, which will render the accession of new Member States in the Schengen system technically feasible, is (on the basis of current estimates) not expected to be operational before the end of

2006 at the earliest, it is not possible to take any decision concerning the lifting of controls at the 'new' internal borders before that time.

Reinforcement of the management of the external border (control and surveillance)

Article 1 of the Schengen Convention departs from the concept of a complementarity between internal and external borders. Indeed Article 1 confirms that the definition of the external border covers land, sea borders, airports and sea ports provided that such borders are not internal border. The reinforcement of policies for the management of external borders and the development of common and coherent standards was a precondition for the lifting of internal border controls and the creation of an area of freedom, security and justice.

Once internal border checks are abolished, it is essential to create a relationship of mutual trust between the Member States involved before an effective policy of external border controls can be implemented with success. The external border management policy has to respond to new and increasing challenges: for instance it is necessary to be effective in the fight against illegal immigration while respecting the principles of the right to asylum. Adequate measures are also necessary to counter trafficking in human beings and trafficking of all kinds connected with organised crime and narcotics.

After the events of the 11 September 2001, border management had to face new external and transnational threats to the security of persons. At the European level, the current enlargement with ten new Member States is viewed as an additional challenge given the dimension of the new external borders. The main objective of the new policy is to ensure that the external borders of the Members States of the European Union constitute a reliable filter against all potential threats to the common area and to its internal security, with the exception of military and defence-related threats to the external borders.

The main task of the public authorities in charge of the management of the external borders is to carry out checks and surveillance in conformity with the current rules, to exchange intelligence information related to the person crossing the borders, to analyse the threats linked to security, and to anticipate logistic and support requirements.

Common Corpus of Legislation

The development of a common corpus of legislation was the first step towards the creation of a common model of management for the external borders of the EU.

The main rules of the external border management are described in the Schengen Convention:

- Article 3 provides that 'External borders may in principle only be crossed at border crossing points and during the fixed opening hours'.

- Article 5 lays down the entry conditions to the Schengen area for a 3-month stay.
- Article 6 refers to the obligation of checks. Pursuant to this provision all persons crossing the external borders are checked in a systematic way. The same Article introduces an obligation of surveillance. It is indeed compulsory to ensure effective border surveillance between authorised border crossing points in order to discourage persons from crossing the external border illegally.
- Other provisions of the Schengen Convention are also linked to the management of external borders, such as Article 26 concerning the carriers' liability and the horizontal provisions on SIS (*Schengen Convention*, Articles 92–101).

In the Common Manual are laid down detailed rules for the implementation of the principles defined by the Schengen Convention. It is divided in two main parts: one dedicated to the conditions for entering and residing in the territory of the Schengen States and one on border checks on persons. The Common Manual includes some twenty annexes containing detailed information and technical specifications for use by border guards. It must be noted here that the Manual serves also as a 'handbook' for them. The coexistence in the same Manual of different types of rules (regulatory, implementation measures and lists of information) make it a difficult text to read and can create a certain ambiguity as regards the legal status of its provisions.

Before the incorporation of the Schengen *acquis* into the Treaty, a specific monitoring mechanism was established. This mechanism is used to carry out evaluations of the implementation of the Schengen rules by the Member States. It is the so-called Standing Committee on the Evaluation and Implementation of Schengen (Schengen Executive Committee 1998). The main task of this group is to evaluate how Member States implement the Schengen *acquis* and, in particular, to check if candidate countries comply with the Schengen *acquis*. This exercise is necessary in view of the preparation of a Council Decision which will enable them to integrate the Schengen area. The evaluation process covers areas such as the lifting of internal borders, checks and surveillance are carried out at external borders, practices for the issuing of visas, police and judicial co-operation, use of the SIS. After the integration of the Schengen *acquis* into the European Union, it was clarified that this monitoring mechanism does not effect the Commission powers as guardian of the Treaties to initiate infringements procedures against Members States who do not apply correctly the current rules (Council of the European Union 1999d).

After four years of integration of the Schengen *acquis* into the Treaties, several gaps of the current rules have been identified. In this context, the Commission has announced the recasting of the Common Manual before the end of 2004 (European Commission 2003f). The objective is to go further than a simple 'clean-up' exercise updating, deleting obsolete and redundant provisions or clarifying some current rules. It is seen as an opportunity to insert additional provisions to fill gaps that have been identified. However the revision of the Common Manual remains a complex and complicated exercise taking into account the double nature of the Common Manual (regulatory instrument and 'handbook') and the different types of provisions and procedures for its amendment.

Definition of Additional Operational Components

The adoption of a common corpus of legislation was not as such sufficient for ensuring the internal security of the common area and a common effective management of the external borders. Member States expressed the political will to reinforce their policy in particular for the management of external borders. Consequently, the European Council in Laeken in December 2001 (European Council 2001). highlighted the need for a better management of the Union's external border controls in order to fight effectively against terrorism, illegal immigration and traffic in human beings. The Laeken conclusions called for further development of the co-operation mechanisms between the services responsible for external borders and for an examination of the possibilities to create a common mechanism or common service to control external borders of the Members States.

On the basis of the Council conclusions and in order to respond to the new challenge of the enlargement, a 'Catalogue of recommendations for the correct application of the Schengen *acquis* and best practices for external border controls, removal and readmission' was elaborated by the Council on February 2002. It is a practical instrument listing a series of measures for the correct implementation of the Schengen rules and dressing up a non exhaustive set of working methods for its optimal application.

In the Commission's 'Communication towards integrated management of the External borders of the Member States of the European Union' presented in May 2002 (European Commission 2002) are consigned the five core components on the basis of which the European concept of the management of the external borders is to be developed. The objective was to propose a working mechanism for co-operation at a Union level to allow practitioners of the border management to co-ordinate their operational actions.

In effect, in addition to the common corpus of legislation, the Communication suggests developing the following four new elements:

1. A common co-ordination and operational mechanism

As concerns the common co-ordination and operational mechanism, the Commission's Communication foresaw the creation of a Common Unit of External Border Practitioners. Some weeks later the Action Plan adopted by the

Council in June 2002 (European Council 2002) called for an immediate establishment of this body. Despite the discussions concerning the legal basis for the creation of this new body, it was decided to set up a group under the aegis of the Strategic Committee for Immigration, Frontiers and Asylum Working group (SCIFA) at the Council, but without any implication to legal work.

SCIFA stands for Strategic Committee for Immigration, Frontiers and Asylum. In fact SCIFA normally examines draft legislation, whereas the members of this new formation of SCIFA (external border practitioners) would be devoted to operational questions related to concrete actions. The Common Unit would be characterised by a highly multidisciplinary and horizontal approach. It would be assisted in its tasks by experts from other Council working groups such as Frontiers, Visa, Schengen, Sch-eval, as well as the High Level working group on Asylum and Migration.

The Common Unit, composed of the Heads of the national service in charge of border control and surveillance, has met for the first time last July 2002 in Denmark. The introduction some weeks after Seville of this Common Unit confirmed the will of Member States to continue and deepen the progress already made during a couple of months.

During the first year of its creation the Scifa+/Common unit of external borders practitioners launched pilot projects and started developing specialised centres dedicated to specific issues as common training and common risk analysis. In particular, a centre of land borders with Germany as the leading country was created for promoting exchanges of personnel and implementing common operations in selected points of the external land borders, aimed to harmonise and improve the practices of the component national units.

Pilot projects and common operations have been launched by several Member states, for instance the operations in the Mediterranean sea borders (operation Ulysses with Spain as leading country and operation Triton with Greece as a leading country) or in the airports (Operation RIO III with Denmark as leading country).

The first evaluation of the results was presented in June 2003. This evaluation brought to the surface the structural limits of the current situation and demonstrated, *inter alia*, the problems in implementation of the common monitoring mechanism. At the same time it has identified some specific legal gaps for the participation in joint actions as well as difficulties on operational matters. Taking note of the evaluation, the European Council in Thessaloniki in June 2003 agreed to reinforce the Common Unit of Practitioners and invited the Commission 'to examine in due time course, drawing on experience by the Common Unit activities, the necessity of creating new institutional mechanisms, including the possible creation of a Community operational structure, in order to enhance operational co-operation for the management of the external borders' (European Council 2003).

2. A common integrated risk analysis

The development of a common risk analysis mechanism can be seen as a tool for the optimisation of border control. Risk analysis is expected to assist in organising border checks in a way that could save time and enhance co-operation. In practice this refers to the evaluation of persons, vehicles, vessels or aeroplanes to be checked. This evaluation is carried out in the context of a real time tactical situation, and thus, the methods can be called tactical risk analysis methods.

At the external border all persons must be checked according to the Common Manual. To uncover border crossing crime, extra emphasis must be put on the procedures for checking risky objects. Personnel should be provided with knowledge of risk indicators, risk profiles and typical *modi operandi* of border crime. It is essential to monitor risk indicators on an ongoing basis. The information collected should be backed up by organised intelligence gathering and analysis.

To fulfil the demands set out in Article 6 of the Convention, one should operate under the assumption of permanent risk of irregular border crossing at all parts of the external border at all times. A thorough and constant analysis of the control system is required to discover gaps in border security and should always be part of the risk analysis. New instruments of technological surveillance can also be very useful.

Following the request of the European Council in Seville in 2002 to set up a common model of risk analysis, a project for the creation of a common risk analysis model was led by Finland with the participation of several other Member States. A Common Integrated Risk Analysis Model was to be defined along the lines of a systematic and continuous process including the content, the matrix structure, the systemic measures to process relevant information as well as the body responsible of it. The Common Integrated Risk Analysis Model would pave the way for more cost-effective and timely border management, improving the effectiveness of the actions against cross border threats.

3. A common approach on staff training and infrastructure

Harmonising issues related to personnel used for border management is still a very complex exercise. Due to the lack of a harmonised common concept concerning the organisation of the body or bodies in charge of the border management in the member states, the European approach is limited to the basic principle that the external border control shall be conducted by professional staff, well trained for that purpose.

Staff could be police officers (as is the case in Belgium) or officers of an independent body (as in Finland). In some countries the border controls are carried out by military personnel under the control of civil authorities (like the *gendarmerie* in France or the *Limeniko* in Greece, a body tasked with the control of the blue borders). The staff management is linked to the member state concerned taking also into account other particularities related to the specific crossing point (e.g., its geographical position, the type of border or the volume of border traffic). The training of staff is a main factor for achieving high security and good quality of service at the borders. The profile for staff whose duties require access and use of personal data, research in confidential registers and interference with the freedom or physical integrity of persons is an extremely complex and demanding one.

Efforts at the European level were focused on the development of a common syllabus for border guards, familiarisation with foreign languages and knowledge of history and culture of other member states. To this basic common training one could add specific courses dedicated to immigration (new regulations, circulars, practical and operational aspects), falsification techniques and methods of intelligence and investigation.

As requested by the European Council in June 2002, a Common Curriculum Programme for the training of border guards and the scheduling of regular training sessions was established in 2003. The Programme was based on the network of national training institutes and aimed at formulating recommendations, standards of training, and rules which would be implemented by the member states on national level.

Concerning the matter of infrastructure and equipment, the member states agreed to converge their relevant policies, including mobile telecommunications services, and to promote the development of new technologies facilitating the management of their external borders. In the Catalogue of Best Practices published in February 2002 there are specific references to the recommended types of equipment covering different needs.

4. Burden-sharing between Member States

With regard to the last of the components of the common model for the management of the external borders—the burden-sharing mechanism between Member States—the Commission (as requested by the European Council in Seville) launched a questionnaire in order to develop criteria and a typology of actions towards this principle of solidarity. All member states do not face the same situation or the same intensity of problems at the borders. One could think of several examples to illustrate the different situations of some Member States having few external borders and others with long and varied types of borders and intensive traffic: for instance Luxembourg only guards its airport as an external border; Germany and Austria control lengthy land borders; Greece surveys both external land borders and very important sea borders; Italy also carries out a huge task in surveying its sea borders.

The geographical situation of the Member States, the nature of their borders, the number of authorised border crossing points, the number of checks carried out on persons entering and leaving the common area, the quality standard of controls and surveillance at the external borders, and the cost of reception of asylum seekers or of return measures have been identified as the main criteria for the implementation of the burden-sharing mechanism.

For the determination of the Community's financial support, it was agreed that only operations having a clear added value for the Community could be financed by the Community budget. The Community dimension of the actions selected (such as the costs from the organisation of joint operations, improvement of standards or control of monitoring and implementation) is a determining factor for the eligibility of the measure.

The implementation of the solidarity principle in concrete terms was one of the key points in the European Council in Thessaloniki, which recognised the need to reflect upon the financial perspectives (post-2006) of this political priority issue. In the meantime, during the period 2004–2006, the Commission has been invited to address the most pressing structural needs. In the short term, the Commission put forward the framework of the ARGO programme of financial support to national projects in areas of management of the external borders, which have been selected on the basis of objective criteria. It is questionable whether a programme like the ARGO programme, aimed at promoting administrative co-operation, is sufficient for addressing the huge structural dimension of the formulated financial requirements (European Commission 2003e).

Activities in Third Countries (visa/liaison officers network)

Part of the measures foreseen in the European model of Integrated Border Management is related to actions and activities to be taken in third countries. We are referring to measures aimed at safeguarding internal security and in particular preventing illegal immigration. These activities are carried out on the territory of third countries and especially in countries of origin and transit,[2] and include in particular the collection of information by liaison officers and the work of consular posts in the process of issuing visas. The activities of liaison officers or consular offices abroad have an important role to play in the selection of third country nationals who would be authorised to enter into the common area. In this sense, they can be seen as facilitating the control activities at the external borders of the Member States. These actions can been seen as a pre-frontiers measures in addition to the bilateral co-operation agreements and the specific rules on carrier liability (*Schengen Convention*, Article 26).

---

[2] As a concrete follow-up of the Seville conclusions, the Council identified in November 2002 the following nine countries with which co-operation on the management of migration flows would need to be intensified in the first instance : Albania, China, the former Republic of Serbia and Montenegro, Morocco, Russia, Tunisia, Ukraine, Libya and Turkey.

1. Liaison officers network abroad

In the Schengen Convention, Articles 7, 47 and 125 provide for the possibility of Schengen states to send liaison officers to other Schengen states. Based on bilateral agreements, co-operation has been developed at the operational level between Member States. It relates to advice and assistance work by liaison officers at the external borders (Schengen Executive Committee 1999). On the basis of positive results of the work done by the liaison officers within the Schengen states, some Member States extended the network to third countries drawing on experiences gained from ongoing projects.

The liaison officers abroad proved to be playing a very important role in particular in combating illegal immigration. In this area they provide useful information on illegal migration flows, clandestine immigration networks, operating methods, use of false documents, transit and final destination countries. The work done by the liaison officers in the Western Balkans can be mentioned as a good example in this context.

Since 2001, the Member States have recognised the important role that liaison officers carry out in the prevention and fight against illegal immigration in the countries of origin or transit and intensified their efforts to formalise co-operation among their liaison officers, to streamline their tasks and to define the scope of their activities (Council of the European Union 2003c). However, different concepts were formulated as concerns the dimension of the liaison officers' duties and their co-operation with host third countries. In the research for a common approach, the Nordic experience of co-operation in this area could be used as a model (Council of the European Union 2003a).

The need to harmonise the framework for the activities of liaison officers abroad was stressed in the plan for the management of the external borders of the Member States of the European Union, agreed by the Council at its meeting of 13 June 2003. It envisaged setting up networks of immigration liaison officers posted in third countries. In more concrete terms, the draft Regulation initiated by the Greek presidency proposed to specify the framework for the Immigration Liaison Officers Network defining, *inter alia* their tasks, the modalities of the contacts between them (regular meetings), the obligation of exchanging information at local or regional level, and the establishment of a common liaison office (Council of the European Union 2003a).

2. Issuing visas

According to the Schengen Convention (Article 5) one of the conditions for allowing a third country national to enter into the territory of the Schengen states is the possession of a valid visa.

After the entry into force of the Amsterdam Treaty, the European short stay visa policy (Article 62.2.b) covers the following areas:

- List of third countries whose nationals must be in possession of visas when crossing the external borders and those whose nationals are exempt from that requirement.
- Procedures and conditions for issuing Schengen visas by Members States.
- Uniform format for visas.
- Rules on a uniform visa.

The Council Regulation 539/2001 (Council of the European Union 2001) lays down a list of third countries whose nationals must be in a possession of visa when crossing the external borders of the Member States and a list of third countries whose nationals are exempted from such a requirement. Referring to the criteria that should apply when drawing up the list of countries defined in Annexes I and II, the fifth recital of the Regulation mentions 'a considered, case by case assessment of a variety of criteria relating *inter alia* to illegal immigration, public policy and security and to the European Union's external relations with third countries, consideration also being given to the implications of regional coherence and reciprocity'.

However, despite the fact that the Regulation defines the aforementioned five basic criteria for the purpose of establishing the entry regime (visa obligation or visa free), it is considered that these criteria should be applied flexibly and with differentiation as regards each specific situation.

Until now these criteria, formulated in general terms, have been implemented in a flexible way in order to preserve a margin of political discretion by the Council. The decisions to lift the visa obligation for Bulgaria and Romania, could be mentioned as examples in this respect, as the evaluation reports presented by the Commission before removing these countries from the negative list considered the concrete improvements made by the governments of these countries, in particular in the areas of illegal immigration, border management, document security and readmission issues.

The procedures and conditions to be followed for the issuing of Schengen visas are defined in the Common Consular Instructions (CCI) (Council of the European Union 2002c), which lay down the details in respect of each type of visa, initiation, examination and decision on a visa application. As a general rule the visas are issued by the Consular Offices of the Member States. Only in exceptional circumstances may the authorities of a Member State issue a Schengen visa at the border (Common Manual, Part II, point 5). In practice, on the basis of the common rules, the consular offices of the member states evaluate the applications of visa submitted and decide after examination of each individual case.

In the framework of reinforcement of the existing common visa rules in recent years, specific attention is drawn to the document security aspects. Regulation 1683/95 (Council of the European Union. 2002b) provides the security features of a short-term visa and establishes a reliable link between the document issued and its holder.

In the broader context, the verification and identification of travellers and the vulnerability of current travel documents have been on the agenda of the European Council since Seville in June 2002. A year later, the Thessaloniki European Council called for a coherent approach of the European Union to the introduction of biometric identifiers or biometric data which would result in harmonised solutions for documents for third country nationals, EU citizens' passports and information systems, and invited the Commission to prepare appropriate measures, starting with the visa. The introduction of the new advanced security technology based on biometrics is subject to political considerations as well as technical problems. In this context, in September 2003, the Commission presented a new proposal foreseeing the mandatory storage of the facial image as the primary biometric identifier to integrate into the visa (European Commission 2003a). The proposal foresees also that the additional storage of a second biometric identifier, the fingerprints, will ensure the highest matching rate and enable searches in databases.

As requested by the Council, in May 2003 the Commission presented the results of the feasibility study aimed at establishing a Common Visa Information System. The objective was to develop a common instrument facilitating the fight against fraud, border and police controls, contributing to the improvement of consular co-operation, and preventing 'visa shopping'. The Council decided in 2004 on the basic elements to be selected for the new system as well as on the timetable for its implementation.

Conclusions

Four years after the incorporation of the Schengen *acquis* into the European Treaties, we can evaluate the progress made in the establishment of an area of free movement of persons and the effective implementation of flanking measures. In particular, the development during this period of new parameters translating in operational terms the concept of external border management and the elaboration of a European common model could be seen as important steps towards the 'common secure area'. At the same time, serious efforts were made towards defining and clarifying the rules in view of the 1 May 2004 enlargement of the European Union.

In the beginning of the new post-accession period, the enlarged Union is facing a host of new challenges: first of all the evaluation of the new Member States and the assessment of their record in implementing the *acquis* in view of the preparation of the Council Decision on the lifting of the controls at the 'provisional external borders'. The passage of these countries from the legislative alignment to the effective implementation of the *acquis* has to be considered with particular attention. In order to achieve this objective, the new Member States will have to make use of the temporary financial instrument foreseen in Article 35 of the Accession Treaty, the Schengen Facility. In particular, on the basis of defined criteria, the selection of actions aimed at improving the infrastructure and equipment as well as other initiatives reinforcing border management capacity could be identified and financed by the Schengen Facility Instrument, thus assisting the new Member States that are most affected by this exercise.

It is obvious, however, that the creation of the common area of freedom, security and justice and the implementation of flanking measures at the borders has inevitably produced an effect on states neighbouring the enlarged European Union. The reinforcement of external borders of the Union should not be seen as a rigid barrier dividing a 'safe inside' from an 'unsafe outside'. If the European Union is to provide security for European citizens (*Charter of Fundamental Rights of the European Union* 2000), it should be done by promoting institutionalised economic, cultural and security co-operation with third countries, and in particular with its neighbours. In this perspective the European Union supports the dialogue with Western Balkan countries in the framework of the Stabilisation and Association process and provides assistance in specific areas via the CARDS instrument (Council of the European Union. 2003b) In this context, the Commission presented in March 2003 its Communication on the 'Wider Europe Neighbourhood' (European Commission 2003b) which aimed at strengthening in the next decade the relations of the enlarged Union with its Eastern neighbours (namely Russia, Ukraine, Moldova and Belarus) as well as with the Southern Mediterranean countries. The objective is to export stability and develop a zone of prosperity around the enlarged European Union, enhancing co-operation on the basis of shared values. Among other areas, a specific reference is included in the Communication to the perspectives for lawful migration and movement of persons. On the basis of these perspectives, and striving to develop further concrete actions, in August 2003 the Commission proposed the establishment of a regime of local border traffic at the current and temporary external borders of the member states (European Commission 2003c). Others initiatives should be developed in the future promoting the cross-border co-operation and facilitating its implementation by using the new Financial Neighbourhood Instrument from 2007 (European Commission 2003d). The recent initiatives demonstrate the political will of the European Union to establish a confidence-building dialogue with the new neighbours of the enlarged Europe which will act as a bridge between different nations and cultures.

References

ANDERSON, MALCOLM and EBERHARD BORT (eds). 2001. *The Frontiers of the European Union*. Palgrave, 2001.

BORT, EBERHARD. 2003. 'EU Enlargement—Policing the New Borders'. *The International Spectator*, 38 (1): 51–68.

CHARTER OF FUNDAMENTAL RIGHTS OF THE EUROPEAN UNION. 2000. 'Article 6'. *Official Journal of the European Union*, C 364/1.

COUNCIL OF THE EUROPEAN UNION. 1964. 'Council Directive 64/221/EEC of 25 February 1964 on the Coordination of special measures concerning the movement and residence of foreign nationals which are justified on grounds of public policy, public security or public health. *Official Journal of the European Union* L 56/850.

_____ 1968. 'Council Directive 68/360/EEC of 15 October 1968 on the abolition of restrictions on movement and residence within the Community for workers of Member States and their families'. *Official Journal of the European Union*, L 257/13.

_____. 1990a. 'Council Directive 90/364/EEC of 28 June 1990 on the right of residence'. *Official Journal of the European Union*, L 180/26.

_____ 1990b. 'Council Directive 90/365/EEC of 28 June 1990 on the right of residence for employees and self-employees who have ceased their occupational activity'. *Official Journal of the European Union*, L180/28.

_____1993. 'Council Directive 93/96/EEC of October 1993 on the right of residence for students. *Official Journal of the European Union*, L 317/59.

_____. 1998. 'Council Regulation n° 1612/88 of 15 October 1998 on freedom of movement for workers within the Community. *Official Journal of the European Union*, L 257/2.

_____ 1999a. 'Council Decision 1999/435/EC of 20 May 1999'. *Official Journal of the European Union*, L 176/1.

_____ 1999b. 'Council Decision 1999/436/EC of 20 May 1999'. *Official Journal of the European Union*, L 176/17.

_____. 1999c. 'Council Decision 1999/439/EC of 17 May 1999'. *Official Journal of the European Union*, L 176/35.

_____ 1999d. 'Council Decision 1999/435/EC'. *Official Journal of the European Union*, L 176.

_____ 2000. 'Council Decision 2000/365/EC of 28 February 2000 concerning the UK request to take part in some of the provisions of the Schengen acquis'. *Official Journal of the European Union*, L 131/43.

_____. 2001. 'Regulation 2414/2001/EC of 7 December 2001'. *Official Journal of the European Union*, L 327/1.

_____ 2002a. 'Council Decision 2002/192 of 28 February 2002 concerning Ireland's request to take part in some of the provisions of the Schengen acquis'. *Official Journal of the European Union*, L 64.

_____ 2002b. 'Regulation 334/2002 of 18 February 2002.' *Official Journal of the European Union*, L 53/7

_____ 2002c. 'Common Consular Instructions on Visas for the Diplomatic Missions and Consular Posts'. *Official Journal of the European Union*. 2002, C 313/1.

_____ 2003a. 'Draft Council Regulation on the creation of an immigration liaison officers networks (2003/C, 140/10)'. *Official Journal of the European Union*, C 140/12.

_____ 2003b. 'Regulation 453/2003/EC of 6 March 2003'. *Official Journal of the European Union*, L 69/10.

_____ 2003c. 'Council Decision 2003/170/JHA of 27.2.2003'. *Official Journal of the European Union*, L 67/27.

DE LOBKOWICZ, WENCESLAS. 2001. *L'Europe de la sécurité intérieure: une élaboration par étapes*. Paris: Ed. Documentation française, 2001.

DEN BOER, MONIKA. 1997. 'Justice and Home Affairs Cooperation in the Treaty on European Union: More Complexity Despite Communautarisation'. *Maastricht Journal of European and Comparative Law*, 4(3).

_____ 1999. 'An area of Freedom, Security and Justice: Bogged Down by Compromise'. In *Legal Issues of the Amsterdam Treaty*, eds., Patrick Twoney and David O'Keeffe, 303–321. Oxford: Hart Publishing.

EU Schengen Catalogue. 2002. 'Volume 2, Schengen Information System'. Sirene, December 2002.

_____ 2003.'Volume 3, Issuing visa'. March 2003.

EUROPEAN COMMISSION. 1995a. 'Proposal for a Council Directive on the Right of Third- Country Nationals to Travel in the Community'. COM(95) 346 final. *Official Journal of the European Union*, C 306/5.

_____ 1995b. 'Proposal for a Council Directive on the Elimination of Controls on Persons Crossing Internal Frontiers'. COM(95)347 final. *Official Journal of the European Union*, C 289/16.

_____ 1995c. 'Proposal for a COUNCIL REGULATION (EC) amending Regulation No. 79/65/EEC setting up a network for the collection of accountancy data on the incomes and business operation of agricultural holdings in the European Economic Community'. COM(95)348 final. *Official Journal of the European Union*, C 307/18.

_____ 2002. COM(2002)233 final (7 May 2002).

_____ 2003a. COM(2003)558 final (24 September 2003).

_____ 2003b. COM(2003)104final (11 March 2003).

_____ 2003c. COM (2003)502 final (14 August 2003).

_____ 2003d. COM(2003)393final (1 July 2003).

_____ 2003e. COM(2003)323 final (3 June 2003).

_____ 2003f. 'Commission Staff Working Document on the recasting of the Common Manual: towards a "Community Borders Code as regards Movement of Persons"?' SEC(2003)736 (20 June 2003).

EUROPEAN COUNCIL. 2001. Laeken Council, Presidency Conclusions.

_____ 2002a. Seville Council, Presidency Conclusions.

_____ 2003. Thessaloniki Council, Presidency Conclusions.

HEBERMANN-ROBINSON, MARTIN. 1999. 'The Area of Freedom, Security and Justice with regard to the UK, Ireland and Denmark : The "opt-in opt-outs" under the treaty of Amsterdam'. In *Legal Issues of the Amsterdam Treaty*, eds., Patrick Twoney and David O'Keeffe, 289–302. Oxford: Hart Publishing.

LABAYLE, HENRI. 1997. 'La libre circulation des personnes dans l'Union Européenne, de Schengen à Amsterdam'. *AJDA – L'actualité juridique-droit administratif*, n°12, 20 décembre 1997: 923–935.

_____ 1997. *Un espace de liberté, de sécurité et de justice*, RTDE.

MONAR, JÖRG. 1998. 'Justice and Home Affairs in the Treaty of Amsterdam: Reform at the Price of Fragmentation'. *European Law Review*, 23: 320–326.

_____ 2001. 'The Justice and Home Affairs Dimension of EU Enlargement'. *The International Spectator*, 36 (3): 37–46.

MONAR, JÖRG and WOLFGANG WESSELS (eds). 1999. *The Treaty of Amsterdam: Challenges and Opportunities for the European Union*. London: Cassel/Pinter.

_____ 2001. *The European Union after the Treaty of Amsterdam*. London: Continuum.

MONAR, JÖRG, VALSAMIS MITSILEGAS and WYN REES. (eds). 2003. *The European Union and Internal Security: Guardian of the People?* Palgrave-Macmillan.

O' KEEFFE, DAVID. 1995. 'Recasting the Third Pillar'. *Common Market Law Review*, 38: 893–920.

_____ 1999. 'Can the Leopard Change its Spots? Visas, Immigration and Asylum-Following Amsterdam'. In *Legal Issues of the Amsterdam Treaty*, eds., Patrick Twoney and David O'Keeffe, 271–287 Oxford: Hart Publishing.

SCHENGEN EXECUTIVE COMMITTEE. 1995. 'SCH-COM-ex(95)20 rev.2'. *Official Journal of the European Union*, L 239, p.133 (22 September 2000).

_____ 1998. 'Decision SCH/COM-ex (98)26 def. of 16 September 1998'. *Official Journal of the European Union*, L 239/138 (22 September 2000).

_____ 1999. 'Decision on liaison officers, SCH/Com-ex(99)7 rev2'. *Official Journal of the European Union*, L 239, p.411 (22 September 2000).

Schengen's Final Days? Incorporation into the new TEU, External Borders and Information Systems. 1998. Maastricht: European Institute of Public Administration.

TWOMEY, PATRICK. 1999 'Constructing a Secure Space: The area of Freedom, Security and Justice'. In *Legal Issues of the Amsterdam Treaty*, eds., Patrick Twoney and David O'Keeffe, 351–374. Oxford: Hart Publishing.

YLI-VAKKURI, LAURA. 2001. 'Building upon the Schengen Acquis' *ERA – Forum*, (2): 53–56.

Chapter 7

Enlarging and Deepening the EU/Schengen Regime on Border Controls

Monika Sie Dhian Ho

The European Union (EU) is simultaneously facing two major challenges in the field of border controls: enlarging and deepening the EU/Schengen regime.[1] As part of the process of enlargement of the EU, candidate countries that want to become EU members must adopt and implement the Schengen regime on border controls. After their ability to fully implement these rules has been confirmed through the Schengen evaluation process, border controls between the incumbent and the new Member States will be lifted and several of the new Member States will become the main actors responsible for controlling the EU's external frontier. Enlargement will move the EU's external land frontier eastwards, to border states of the former Soviet Union, and will add a large part of the Baltic Sea and (after the expected accession of Bulgaria and Romania) the Black Sea to the EU's external maritime frontier. The EU's external border will thus increase significantly in length whereas controls will take place in a regional environment that is often likely to be more difficult.

At the same time the process of 'deepening' EU co-operation in the field of border controls is gathering momentum. The import of the Schengen *acquis* into the EU framework by the Treaty of Amsterdam (which entered into force on 1 May 1999) has been a major step towards the abolition of internal border controls within the EU. Initially the ambition to remove internal border controls was primarily economically motivated (e.g., removing all barriers to trade within the Internal Market). More and more, however, it is also being presented as a political project (e.g., removing all barriers to free movement of persons in a 'Union of the citizens'). While controls on internal borders are thus being dismantled, co-operation in the field of external border controls is deemed necessary as a 'compensatory measure'. Since the Treaty of Amsterdam, external border controls co-operation has been high on the EU agenda, with successive European Council meetings emphasising its role in the fight against illegal immigration networks and trafficking in human beings,

---

[1] Editors' note: This article was written shortly before the May 2004 enlargement of the European Union.

cross-border crime and terrorism. Moreover, EU policy makers are waking up to the fact that new policies have to be developed in order to prevent negative side effects of intensified EU external border controls on relations with third countries.

The objective of this chapter is to analyse the special character of the processes of enlargement and deepening in the field of border controls, and to identify the challenges to be expected post-enlargement. It then discusses various directions for border controls policy in an enlarged European Union.

The Special Character of Enlarging the EU Regime on Border Controls

The European Union envisages a process of enlargement that might more than double its membership. More than a decade of accession preparations has resulted in the signature of an Accession Treaty between the EU Member States and a first group of ten candidate countries in April 2003. Accession negotiations between the EU Member States and candidates Bulgaria and Romania are still going on, while negotiations with Turkey are expected to start in 2005, provided that the European Council in December 2004 decides that Turkey fulfils the Copenhagen political criteria (Presidency Conclusions – Copenhagen European Council 2002).[2] The list of prospective members goes well beyond these thirteen candidates, with several of the aspirant countries already having received explicit or implicit EU recognition of their membership ambitions.[3]

Part of the conditions for EU membership is that candidates adopt and implement the entire EU *acquis*, which includes the EU/Schengen border controls regime. The strategy the EU has pursued in the accession negotiations can be described as 'take-it-or-leave-it': applicants must adopt the entire EU *acquis* and are not eligible for any permanent exemptions from it (temporary ones are granted in exceptional cases). Whether incumbent Member States have managed to negotiate 'opt-outs' (permanent exemptions) from the *acquis* has no influence on the enlargement strategy (Philippart and Sie Dhian Ho 2001,

---

[2] According to the political criteria decided by the European Council of Copenhagen (1993), membership requires that a candidate country has achieved stability of institutions guaranteeing democracy, the rule of law, human rights and respect for and protection of minorities.

[3] E.g., the countries of the Stability Pact for South Eastern Europe (including Bosnia and Herzegovina, Croatia, the Federal Republic of Yugoslavia, the Former Yugoslav Republic of Macedonia, and Albania) have been promised that 'the EU will draw the region closer to the perspective of full integration of these countries into its structure ... through a new kind of contractual relationship taking fully into account the individual situations of each country with the perspective of EU membership' (Stability Pact 1999, para.20), and the European Council of Göteborg (June 2001) has recognised the 'European aspirations' of Ukraine (Presidency Conclusions - Göteborg European Council 2001, para.14).

Chapter 4). The same holds true for the EU border controls regime. A large part of this regime has been developed in the context of 'Schengen' co-operation among a limited number of EU Member States, and has been imported into the EU framework by the Treaty of Amsterdam (which entered into force in May 1999) (Council of the European Union 2001b).[4] Article 8 of the protocol integrating the Schengen *acquis* into the framework of the EU says that 'For the purposes of the negotiations for the admission of new Member States into the European Union, the Schengen *acquis* and further measures taken by the institutions within its scope shall be regarded as an *acquis* which must be accepted in full by all State candidates for admission.'[5] The fact that several Member States (the United Kingdom, Ireland and Denmark) negotiated permanent exemptions from parts of this regime, in exchange for their consent to the incorporation of the Schengen *acquis* into the EU framework, has had no influence on the 'take-it-or-leave-it' strategy adopted by the EU vis-à-vis the candidate countries.

There are several reasons why the enlargement of the EU regime on border controls is a special case within the wider process of EU enlargement. First, accession preparations of the new Member States have started relatively late in this sphere (Monar 2000, p.27). Border controls are one of the newest areas of co-operation within the European Union. Until the Amsterdam Treaty there were hardly any measures on border controls in the EU and the integral import of the Schengen *acquis* has taken the candidates more or less by surprise. Whereas candidates have started to prepare for implementing the EU internal market *acquis* since the early 1990s, capacity building in the field of border controls only gathered momentum around the turn of the century. Also on the side of the EU, instructions and assistance to candidates got going only relatively late. Whereas the European Commission already published a White Paper (European Commission 1995) instructing candidates how to adopt the Internal Market *acquis* in 1995, it took the Union until 1998 to define the Justice and Home Affairs *acquis* and until 1999 to allocate the Schengen *acquis* among

---

[4] The Schengen *acquis* that has been incorporated in the EU Treaties by the Treaty of Amsterdam consists of the 1985 Schengen Agreement and associated implementing acts. The objective of the Schengen cooperation is the gradual abolition of checks at common borders of its Member States. To compensate for the loss of internal border controls, a set of measures has been agreed among the Schengen Member States in the fields of external border controls, visa, asylum, immigration, police, customs and judicial cooperation, data-exchange (the Schengen Information System, SIS) and data-protection. All these measures are now part of the EU *acquis*, allowing for free movement of persons within the EU, with the exception of the UK and Ireland.

[5] Protocol integrating the Schengen *acquis* into the framework of the European Union, protocols annexed to the Treaty on European Union and to the Treaty establishing the European Community, Treaty of Amsterdam amending the Treaty on European Union, the Treaties establishing the European Communities and related acts (*The Treaty of Amsterdam* 1997).

its pillars. EU financial assistance in the sphere of JHA has also long been focussed on internal market related strengthening of the administrative and judicial systems (Monar 2000, p. 54).

A second distinguishing characteristic is that the accession process in the field of border controls takes place in two steps. This two-stage procedure entails that a new Member State after accession to the EU does not immediately participate in full in the 'Schengen' part of the EU *acquis*. The first stage commences after the signature of the Accession Treaty with the EU and involves a period of close monitoring of the new Member State's implementation of Schengen obligations (the Schengen evaluation process). The second stage, which comprises full participation of the new Member State in the Schengen co-operation and most notably the lifting of internal border controls, only enters into force after a separate and unanimous decision of the JHA Council (Council of the European Union 2001a). Since several Schengen provisions are closely related to the lifting of internal border controls, not the entire Schengen *acquis* has to be implemented upon accession. The Council of the EU has published an 'Information note' on Schengen and Enlargement, making a distinction between the requirements that have to be implemented upon accession to the EU and the ones that are to be implemented upon the lifting of internal border controls at the latest (Council of the European Union 2001a). As regards the border control measures, there are not many that can be postponed until after accession (one of the few being the separation of extra- and intra-Schengen passenger flows at the international ports and airports). In the same document on Schengen and Enlargement the Council announced that there is no predetermined timetable for the elimination of checks on internal borders after accession to the EU. Even if a new Member State were capable of implementing the Schengen *acquis* in full upon accession, checks on internal borders would not be lifted instantly, since the Schengen evaluation process takes some time. Moreover, the EU itself is not ready for abolishing checks on borders with new Member States, since an important precondition—the completion of the second generation Schengen Information System (SIS II)—is only foreseen for the end of 2005 (Council of the European Union 2001a). However, considering the magnitude of the implementation tasks it is anyway unlikely that internal border controls with new Member States will be lifted in the beginning of 2006. By way of comparison, it took other countries (e.g., Italy and Greece) up to eight years after signature of the Schengen accession agreement before the decision to abolish internal border controls was taken..[6]

---

[6] These cases are not fully comparable though, since at that time the Schengen *acquis* was not integrated into the EU framework. Moreover, new Schengen Members at the time of their accession to Schengen had not started implementing the Schengen *acquis* to such an extent as the new EU Member States have done at the time of their accession to the EU, since a large part of the Schengen obligations is now a condition for accession to the EU.

A third reason why enlarging the EU border controls regime deserves special attention is the high cost of implementation for the new Member States and the heavy burden these expenses imply for their budgets. Several new Member States will eventually become the main actors responsible for controlling the EU's external frontier. A striking example is Poland, which will become responsible for the control of the EU border with Russia, Belarus and Ukraine—one of the longest stretches of external land border to be guarded by a single Member State (over 1,150 km) (Piorko and Sie Dhian Ho 2003). Fulfilling the EU requirements regarding border controls entails big investments in staffing, training and equipment. It is estimated that a modern Polish border control system will require 18,000 officers (Poland Ministry of Interior and Administration 2000, p.142). Bringing the Border Guard to full strength means hiring new officers, replacing conscripts by professionals and training all personnel. Moreover, massive investments are needed in infrastructure and equipment. Total costs for Poland of enhancing border controls in the three years to come are estimated at around Euro 257 million (Poland Ministry of Interior and Administration 2002, p.108). These expenses are a considerable burden for the budgets of the new Member States in times of economic transformation.

A fourth complicating factor is the impact that EU enlargement in the field of border controls will have on the relations between the new EU Members and adjacent countries that will remain outside the EU. Part of the EU membership obligations is the introduction of visa for citizens of countries that are on the EU visa list (Council of the European Union 2001c; 2001d)—the most difficult cases being neighbouring countries like Ukraine, Russia and Belarus. Besides, existing bilateral agreements on simplified border crossings with neighbouring countries have to be terminated. The implementation of the Schengen *acquis* by the new Member States will significantly alter the post-1989 situation that was characterised by rather open borders in Central and Eastern Europe and liberalised (e.g., visa-free) movement of people between them (Apap et al. 2001). The introduction of visas may disturb social relations and historical ties with neighbouring countries and minorities that live there. By way of example, the Slovak introduction of visa for Ukrainian citizens in June 2000—as part of the implementation of the Schengen *acquis*—was followed by a significant drop in border crossings (Duleba 2002, p.2).[7] Not surprisingly, the introduction of visa requirements is getting a frosty reception in neighbouring countries and their societies, having triggered Ukraine's President Kuchma for instance to comment that the EU is replacing the Iron Curtain with a paper one. The adoption of the EU visa regime also implies economic costs for the new Member States related to a decrease in non-registered trade with neighbouring countries. Although at macro-level these economic effects are

---

[7] This concerned especially Ukrainians coming to Slovakia: their number dropped from 1.7 million persons in 1998 to 0.3 million in 2001.

expected to be limited, specific regions and sectors will suffer seriously from the drying up of this petty trade.[8]

A fifth important characteristic is the lack of clear-cut technical criteria for assessing border control performance of new Member States. In the accession negotiations, the EU has taken the position that candidates should have upon accession a 'high level of external border control'. But what does a 'high level of external border control' require exactly? The EU is still in the process of establishing standards that define the minimum application of the Schengen *acquis*. Only recently the Working Party on Schengen Evaluation has drawn up a Catalogue of recommendations for the correct application of the Schengen *acquis* and best practices, including an outline of the so-called Schengen integrated border management strategy (Council of the European Union, General Secretariat DG H).[9] Interesting to note is that even the Council has stated that the notion of a 'high level of external border control' is partly a political one, (Council of the European Union 2001a) acknowledging that it is not only a matter of technical standards, but unavoidably also a question of perception, politics and trust.

The last distinguishing characteristic is the political sensitivity—both in incumbent and new Member States—of border control issues in the context of EU enlargement (Monar 2000, p.29). In the current Member States politicians are particularly wary of a potential decrease in internal security following enlargement and/or the abolition of internal border controls with the new Member States. Political decisions perceived by the public as 'imprudent' in this sphere could be very costly politically, both in the domestic and EU context. This heated political climate has led to intensive EU monitoring,[10] to a relatively uncompromising attitude taken by the EU in the accession negotiations concerning this field, and the expectation of a thorough Schengen evaluation process for the new Member States after accession. At the same time the abolition of internal border controls is a sensitive issue in the new Member States. Considerable public pressure is likely to develop following accession for rapid lifting of internal borders. The feeling of being treated as second-class European citizens who have to make considerable sacrifices for EU

---

[8] For a more elaborate analysis of the effects of the introduction of the EU visa regime on cross-border trade of the new Member States with neighbouring non Member States, see I. Piorko and M. Sie Dhian Ho 2003b; Duleba 2002; and Orlowski 2001.

[9] The Schengen Integrated Border Security Model consists of four complementary tiers: activities in third countries, countries of origin and transit; bilateral and international cooperation; measures at the external borders; and further activities inside the territory.

[10] E.g., the Council has introduced in 1999 its own confidential 'Collective Evaluations' on progress made in the Justice and Home Affairs sphere by the acceding countries (produced by the Council Collective Evaluation Working Party), in addition to the existing annual Progress Reports made by the European Commission.

membership (having to implement the EU visa regime) while being withheld the main benefits thereof (free movement of persons) could undermine support for EU membership in the new Member States.

The Special Character of Deepening the EU Regime on Border Controls

The pressure on EU decision-makers to deepen the EU regime on border controls is high. Policy problems like organised crime, drugs trafficking and illegal immigration are increasingly defined as external threats and tightened external borders as an adequate means of defence against them (Andreas 2000, p.145). Moreover, the very prospect of EU enlargement has been an important driving factor for the deepening of EU border controls co-operation. It was feared in incumbent Member States that EU free movement rules would become applicable to the new Member States after EU enlargement, while these states would probably not meet internal security standards considered necessary to compensate for diminished border controls. Incorporation and development of the Schengen *acquis* within the EU framework before enlargement seemed the most effective way to avoid this situation (Mitsilegas et al. 2003, p.34). Persuading candidates eager to join the EU to accept an existing EU border controls regime as a condition for accession was definitely going to be easier than having to negotiate such a regime in a EU of 25 members. Apart from thus speeding up the codification of rules and standards, the prospect of enlargement has stimulated the development of ideas about forms of co-operation that could partially compensate for the implementation deficits of individual Member States.

Against this background the European Council of Laeken has asked the Council and the Commission '...to work out arrangements for co-operation between the services responsible for external border control and to examine the conditions in which a mechanism or common services to control external borders could be created' (Presidency Conclusions – Laeken European Council 2001, Conclusion n. 42). Laeken and the subsequent European Councils (i.e., Seville and Thessaloniki) have put considerable pressure on the European institutions and Member States to deepen border controls co-operation, which among others resulted in several European Commission Communications to the Council and European Parliament on the subject, (Commission of the European Communities 2001; 2002a; 2002b; 2003) as well as a Council Plan for the management of the external borders of the Member States of the European Union (Council of the European Union 2002). Since the European Council of Seville the Council Presidency has regularly published a 'Road Map' including precise delegation of and deadlines for measures to be taken, as well as progress reports (Council of the European Union 2003b). All these initiatives to deepen the EU border controls regime run into three distinguishing characteristics of this issue area: the high level of diversity among Member States; the political salience of border controls in the domestic context; and the fact that harmonisation of legislation is not enough to guarantee effective border controls policy.

Diversity among EU Member States in the sphere of border controls has many faces. The EU in fact consists of a number of functional and regional sub-systems when it comes to border controls. Functionally, the EU is divisible into three subsystems of Member States that have to deal with land borders, sea borders and air borders respectively (with several Member States being part of various of these functional subsystems). Within this functional map, regional sub-systems can be identified, e.g., the northern Mediterranean, the eastern Mediterranean, the North Sea, or the eastern external land border. The border control situation differs markedly among these functional and regional sub-systems (e.g., in terms of migration pressure, level of internal security risks and border control instruments to be deployed).

Moreover, national policy approaches to internal security vary considerably among the Member States, with the United Kingdom (and Ireland) clearly taking a separate position concerning border controls as an instrument of internal security. The continental Member States have all decided to lift internal border controls and to compensate for their abolition by tightening external border controls and surveillance. Besides, several mainland Members have seen a gradual 'thickening' of the border function, including extensive internal controls (e.g., mandatory resident registration systems and national identification cards, and work place regulations and controls) and selective targeting by the police of 'foreign looking' persons (Andreas 2000). Successive United Kingdom governments have argued that this continental approach to internal security does not fit the UK geographical situation and internal security tradition. The main focus of UK immigration control has traditionally been at the point of entry, since the island geography of the UK, with arrivals 'funnelled' through ports and airports (UK House of Lords 1999, para 20), is claimed to make possible effective frontier controls (in contrast with the continental EU situation with long external land borders that are allegedly more difficult to control) (UK 1998, para. 2.9). Moreover, extensive identity documentation and identity checks that are relatively non-controversial in several mainland Member States are likely to be perceived as violations of civic liberties in the UK and expected to have harmful effects on race relations (UK House of Lords 1999, para. 20).

Apart from geographic heterogeneity and divergent approaches to internal security, Member States' border controls systems differ substantially. Border controls—although subject to several common EU principles and rules—are a national responsibility (Mueller-Graff 1998); they are supposed to be carried out 'within the scope of national powers and national law' (The Schengen Acquis 2000, Article 6). Each Member State is thus free to entrust checks and surveillance tasks at external borders to the authorities of its choice, according to its own national administrative structures. As a consequence considerable diversity remains in terms of type of authorities present at external borders, their tasks, and powers of enforcement, prevention and investigation (Commission of the European Communities 2002a).

Lastly, Member States differ in their level of economic development, which affects implementation capacity and potentially also standpoints vis-à-vis initiatives to deepen the border controls regime. Implementation capacity might suffer from lack of public funds to staff, train and equip the border guard, and inadequate salaries for law enforcement officials might increase the susceptibility to corruption. Diverging levels of economic development are also likely to influence standpoints as regards initiatives to deepen the border controls regime, for instance if they are costly and/or if they concern the funding of border controls initiatives.

Apart from high diversity, efforts to deepen the EU regime on border controls are likely to encounter political sensitivity due to the high political salience of the issues involved (e.g., illegal immigration and organised crime) and the symbolic value of state control over national frontiers. By emphasising the role of border controls in the fight against organised crime and illegal immigration, they have been upgraded from the status of 'low politics' to 'high politics' (Andreas 2000, p.3). National politicians are relatively reluctant to transfer sovereignty here, since they fear being held responsible for a possible drop in internal security (or perceptions thereof). Moreover, border controls are still seen as an integral part of the identity of the state. Several authors have emphasised that especially in the new Member States, closer European integration in the field of border controls is perceived as a threat to territorial sovereignty, and national and cultural identity (Anderson and Bort 2001, p.166).

A last important characteristic of this field of EU activity is that effective external border control policy and the maintenance of a zone of free movement of persons require more than approximation of national border control legislation. First, a homogeneous implementation of the common principles and rules is as important as their incorporation into national legislation. Differences in implementation culture and capacity can generate security discrepancies between sections of external borders controlled by different Member States (Council of the European Union 2002). Secondly, legislation on border controls needs to be complemented by cross-border operational co-operation and information exchange. And finally, mutual understanding and trust are crucial for effective external border control policy and the continued willingness of Member States to be part of the zone of free movement of persons. Trust among law enforcement and judicial authorities is required among others as a condition for the exchange of sensitive information and participation in joint operations. And trust of the public of one Member State in the border controls performance of other Member States is necessary for their continued tolerance of the interdependence and vulnerability that accompany an open internal border policy. Borders are always permeable to a certain extent and technical criteria for obtaining effective border controls can always be questioned. Therefore, the perception of effectiveness and mutual trust in each other's implementation practices are at least as important.

Challenges of Border Control Co-operation in an Enlarged EU

An analysis of the special character of the enlargement and deepening processes highlights several challenges for EU border controls co-operation in the near future. A direct challenge after EU enlargement is to realise a smooth and swift passage of the new Member States to the stage of full participation in Schengen co-operation (as integrated into the EU framework). The strengthening of the implementation capacity of the new Member States, and the trust among Member States that this passage requires, brings us to the more general challenge of stimulating a more homogeneous implementation culture and mutual understanding and trust among all Member States. Furthermore, the issue of burden-sharing is likely to move up the agenda, as well as the effects of the EU regime on relations with neighbouring countries. In terms of decision-making, the main challenges will be to avoid frequent and prolonged decision-making deadlock, as well as to strengthen the democratic and judicial control of the structures for border controls co-operation.

The political salience for the new Member States of the decision to let them participate in full in Schengen co-operation and to lift internal border controls has been outlined above, as well as the preoccupation of incumbent Member States that this does not result in increased internal security risks. The passage to full participation in Schengen co-operation requires still considerable strengthening of the new Member States' implementation capacity after their accession. Monitoring reports by the European Commission and Council point at several remaining implementation deficits. These concern, for instance, the organisation and means of the border guard. Some new Member States do not have a specialised separate unit that is responsible for border controls with an independent budget. Administrative capacity is likely to suffer from fragmented organisational structures and lack of financial priority in these cases. In general, the financial means for the implementation of the costly *acquis* on border controls are lacking in all new Member States. Partially related to insufficient funds, staffing, training and equipment will remain points of concern. In many new Member States the transformation from the old Soviet-type system (with conscripts performing border control tasks) to a professional and specialised organisation is still underway. Recruitment of staff is often difficult considering relatively low salaries. Several new Member States still need to recruit thousands of border guards before they are at 'target strength'. Moreover, all new staff needs to be trained within a short time frame. Lack of equipment is especially a problem for surveillance tasks at sea and green borders.

Monitoring reports further point out that co-operation among different law enforcement authorities within the new Member States is often still not optimal. In some cases the units responsible for green border surveillance and units carrying out border checks do not cooperate effectively. In other cases the organisations responsible for border controls and customs do not get along very well. International co-operation is also a point of concern. Many practical problems with border authorities of neighbouring countries exist, and sometimes corruption plays a role as well (Anderson and Bort 2001, p.163). The implementation of the Schengen Integrated Border Security Model, as set out in the Schengen Catalogue, has also in many cases only existed on paper up until now. National and regional risk assessment capacity are for instance still rather weak and statistics are not reliable.

One complication for a smooth and swift passage might be that criteria for implementation performance in this field are often vague or difficult to quantify (what does it take to have 'proper interagency co-ordination' or 'effective international co-operation') and if quantitative targets are stated at all (e.g., number of border guards to be recruited in the short term) their sufficiency can be called into question quite easily. Perceptions and politics unavoidably play a role in decision-making. Awareness of the uncompromising attitude in the incumbent Member States in combination with uncertainty concerning the exact interpretation of criteria may have contributed in some cases to 'overshooting' by new Member States, for instance by providing the border guard with extensive competences (Piorko 2003).

The specific concern with the new Member States' implementation capacity touches on what is in general more a challenge for border controls co-operation in the enlarged European Union: how to organise more homogeneous implementation of the EU *acquis* by all national border control units with a view to a more uniform level of security at the Union's external borders, and how to enhance mutual trust between the Member States that have abolished checks on persons at their internal borders (Commission of the European Communities 2002a)?

Another issue that will become more urgent after enlargement concerns the sharing of the burden of controlling the Union's external borders. Whereas all Member States profit from the abolition of internal border controls, the burden of the 'compensating measures' at the external border is not shared in a fair way. Some Member States are responsible for the surveillance of very long external maritime or land borders, whereas others no longer have external borders and only have to perform checks on persons at their airports. Moreover, migratory pressure differs substantially along the external border of the European Union. This uneven situation will become even more untenable when—after the abolition of internal border controls with the new Member States—some of the least affluent Member States of the Union will become responsible for the financing of long sections of external borders of the European Union. A more structural system of financial burden sharing will be necessary to ensure continued commitment of the countries that bear the heaviest load. The Commission in its Communication of May 2002, although emphasising that national budgets should remain the principal resources for border controls expenses, suggested that the Community budget could be used to establish a mechanism for financial burden-sharing between the Member States as well as to finance in the longer term the acquisition of common equipment (Commission of the European Communities 2002a, pp.19–20). In its ensuing plan for the management of the external borders of the Member States, the Council took up the idea of financial redistribution, and asked for an assessment of the different options for burden-sharing (Council of the European Union 2002).

Furthermore, an important challenge will be to avoid a situation in which the introduction of the EU external border and visa regime by the new Member States has adverse effects on trade, social and cultural exchange and regional co-operation with adjacent countries (e.g., Russia, Ukraine, Belarus and Moldova). The new borders of the Union should be 'managed' in such a way that *bona fide* border crossings do not suffer from EU efforts to prevent illegal immigration and counteract crime. The Union has declared at several occasions its commitment to building bridges in stead of putting up barriers, pointing at the importance of good relationships with 'Wider Europe' for reasons of regional stability, economic specialisation in times of globalisation, and the possible need for immigration of workers in times of demographic decline (Commission of the European Communities 2003). More specifically in relation to border controls, several experts have stressed that effective border management itself requires a context of good relationships and trust with neighbouring countries (UK House of Lords 1999, p.17).[11]

Considering the increased number of actors after EU enlargement, their diversity, and the political salience of border issues, avoiding decision-making deadlock will be another challenge. Decisions on border control initiatives still require unanimous support from the Member States, despite the transfer of the legal basis from the intergovernmental third pillar to the communitarian first pillar in the Treaty of Amsterdam.[12] Moreover, reading the Protocol integrating the Schengen *acquis* into the framework of the European Union, it seems that the new Member States will have full decision-making rights upon accession as regards proposals to build upon the Schengen *acquis*, even though they will not participate in full in all Schengen co-operation upon accession to the EU (*The Treaty of Amsterdam* 1997, p.93). Although unanimity should not be equated with blockage, the combination of high diversity and political salience could lead to frequent decision-making deadlock and/or linkage politics between, on the one hand, decisions on new Member States' passage to full participation in Schengen, and on the other hand, decisions to deepen the border control *acquis*.

Last but not least, the issue of democratic scrutiny and legal control should be addressed more thoroughly, especially since joint border control operations and data-exchange between Member States are proliferating. Which

---

[11] See the evidence Pekka Jarvio gave to the House of Lords Select Committee on the European Union

[12] Border controls cooperation is currently based on Article 62 in Title IV of the Treaty establishing the European Community (TEC). After a transitional period of five years following the entry into force of the Treaty of Amsterdam (that is, in May 2004) the Council, acting unanimously after consulting the European Parliament, can take a decision to introduce the co-decision procedure for all or parts of the areas covered by Title IV (including border controls cooperation).

European body makes operational decisions could be more transparent, and these decisions should be subject to scrutiny by national parliaments and the European Parliament. Multinational teams performing joint controls are too much operating in a legal void when it comes to their powers and accountability. The same holds true for the exchange of information in support of these joint operations. Specific data protection rules are required here (House of Lords 1999, p.19). It is remarkable that neither the Commission Communication nor the Council Plan has made concrete suggestions to enhance democratic and legal control.

Directions for Border Policy in an Enlarged EU

Against the background of these challenges, several directions for policy in an enlarged EU come to the fore. First, all incumbent Member States seem convinced of the fact that a swift passage of the new Member States to full participation in the Schengen co-operation requires continuation of financial assistance after enlargement. During the last few years financial support in the field of migration policy and border management has already seen a steady increase. For instance, between 1997 and 2001 the ten candidate countries received a total amount of 356 million Euro for projects in this sphere. In addition to that a Phare Multi-Country programme on 'Migration, Visa, External Border Control Management' started in January 2001 (Commission of the European Communities 2002b). A large part of these funds were focused on the transfer of expertise and training, neglecting to a certain extent the upgrading of technical equipment and infrastructure (Monar 2000, p.54). At the European Council of Copenhagen the Member States agreed to reserve additional funds for financial assistance beyond their accession. The 'Schengen Facility' will assist the new Member States between the date of accession and the end of 2006 to finance 'actions at the new external borders of the Union for the implementation of the Schengen *acquis* and external border control'. More generally, the Union will between the date of accession and the end of 2006 provide temporary financial assistance under the so-called 'Transition Facility' to develop and strengthen the new Member States' administrative capacity to implement and enforce Community legislation and to foster exchange of best practices among peers. The types of intended action in the context of these facilities suggest a more balanced attention for investment in infrastructure (construction, renovation and upgrading of border crossing points and related buildings) and operating equipment (e.g., detection tools, SIS hardware and software, means of transportation), training of border guards, and support for logistics and operations.[13]

To stimulate more homogenous implementation practices and mutual trust among all Member States, a series of activities can be developed, including a common curriculum for border guards, joint operations and monitoring of

---

[13]   See Article 35 of Treaty of Accession 2003

implementation performance. The value of determining minimum adequate standards for training of border guards has been identified already in the 2002 Council Plan and has been followed up by an initiative led by Austria and Sweden to create a common curriculum. Joint operations at the external borders can further contribute to mutual understanding and trust. Since the European Council of Seville a series of joint operations have taken place (e.g., 'Ulysses' for sea border controls of the coasts of the northern Mediterranean and the Canary Islands; 'Triton' in the South-eastern Mediterranean; 'ORCA' for the prevention of illegal immigration, trans-border crime and illegal use of visas and documents issued to seamen; 'RIO III' for the detection at airports of the use of visas for illegal immigration; and RIO IV to improve border control systems and practices in ports in candidate countries). Experience with these joint operations underscores that in order for them to be successful, better planning, preparation and operational co-ordination are required, as well as feedback and learning from the difficulties which arose during their implementation (apart from commitment of participating countries to meet their obligations, which was in several cases still lacking) (Council of the European Union 2003a). Apart from common training and joint operations, more homogeneous implementation practices and mutual trust can be stimulated by regular monitoring and evaluation of implementation performance of all Member States. For this purpose, the existing Schengen evaluation mechanism could be developed further. Such regular monitoring could contribute both to the identification of implementation deficits and their rectification (through a process of 'naming and shaming'), as to the identification of best practices and a process of mutual understanding and learning.

As outlined above, the issue of burden sharing will move up the agenda after EU enlargement. Until now, the financing of border controls has been a national responsibility. This situation differs significantly from the customs field, where Member Sates can keep 25 percent of resources derived from customs duties to pay for infrastructure at the external customs border (Commission of the European Communities 2002a, paragraph 14). In 2002, the financial instruments in support of Community policy on asylum, immigration and management of external borders represented less than 60 million Euro, that is less than 1 percent of total expenditure for Community internal policies (Commission of the European Communities 2003). The only EU financing available involves instruments to strengthen administrative co-operation, like the Odysseus and Argo programmes. A structural EU burden-sharing instrument for the field of border controls—comparable to the European Refugee Fund for asylum policy—does not exist. The Commission has on several occasions drawn attention to the clear disparity between the political importance given in the EU to JHA policies and the financial resources of the Community budget allocated to them.

Against this background the Commission has suggested introducing a more structural mechanism for burden-sharing in the field of border controls. Initially, Member States not responsible for long sections of the external border perceived such proposals solely as financial redistribution measures. Recently however, there has been a remarkable shift in opinion among the majority of the Member States. Controls at the external border, reception of asylum seekers and return measures are increasingly understood to be strongly interconnected European problems. Considerable acclimatisation has taken place to the idea that, in order to be effective, these problems should be addressed jointly and their financing should not fall disproportionately on those Member States that happen to be responsible for the longest sections of external border, for processing the largest number of asylum requests, or for implementing a large share of the return measures. There is a consensus developing within the EU that more structural burden-sharing is unavoidable, although some governments still define this solidarity in rather narrow terms (UK House of Lords 1999, p.22).[14] An indication of this growing consensus is the specific provision made for the principle of solidarity and fair sharing of responsibility (including its financial implications) between the Member States in the Draft Treaty establishing a Constitution for Europe (Draft Treaty 2003).

Concretely, in its December 2002 Communication, the Commission has proposed four criteria to be taken into account when assessing the burden of each Member State in the field of border controls: (1) the geographical situation of a Member State and the nature of the borders; (2) the migratory pressure at the different types of border (land, sea and airport); (3) the number of checks carried out on persons entering and leaving the Schengen area; and (4) the quality standard of controls and surveillance at external borders, as measured by a common risk analysis method applied to each type of border (Commission of the European Communities 2002b, p.43). The Commission added that '...it has to be recognised that the mechanism for financial solidarity between Member States will have to be on a substantial scale if it is to tackle structural problems', and suggested that the issue of structural burden-sharing should be taken up in the preparation of the next multi-annual financial perspective (Commission of the European Communities 2002b, p.43).

As outlined in the previous section, one of the main post-enlargement challenges will be the realisation of an EU border controls regime that functions as a barrier for illegal crossings and activities, while at the same time working as a bridge for lawful cross-border relations and co-operation, especially with neighbouring countries of the new Member States. Unlike the present situation, most of the third countries neighbouring the new EU Member States are countries whose nationals must be in possession of a visa when entering the EU. Over the last decade border crossings between the new Member States and their neighbours have grown significantly and were facilitated by bilateral arrangements on 'local border traffic' (these arrangements were terminated recently as part of the conditions for EU membership) (Piorko and Sie Dhian Ho 2003, p.195). The EU border control regime does not

---

[14] See for instance the statements of Peter Hain on behalf of the British government.

provide for such special arrangements with neighbouring countries. However, Article 3(1) of the Schengen Implementing Convention (that has been integrated into the EU *acquis*) states that the 'Schengen Executive Committee' (now replaced by the Council of the European Union) can adopt special arrangements on local border traffic. Such development of the EU *acquis* on local border traffic could make *bona fide* crossings of residents in border regions considerably easier and thus mitigate the negative effects of EU enlargement on relations with adjacent countries.

Minimum rules on local border traffic are only one aspect of the common corpus of legislation that needs to be developed in the short term. One of the challenges identified above is to avoid that decision-making around such development of legislation will be blocked because of high diversity among Member States and the political salience of the issues involved. One obvious remedy would be the introduction of qualified majority voting (QMV). The Treaty of Amsterdam allows the Council, after a transitional period of five years following the entry into force of the Treaty of Amsterdam, acting unanimously after consulting the European Parliament, to take a decision to introduce the co-decision procedure for all or parts of the areas covered by Title IV (including border controls co-operation). The introduction of QMV would thus not require treaty change (i.e., insertion in the Draft Treaty establishing a Constitution for Europe) and could be decided already in May 2004 (instead of being dependent on and delayed by lengthy ratification procedures of the new treaty).

Although QMV is certainly in the short run an effective solution to decision-making deadlock, it may not always be the most functional one because of its potential divisiveness (this holds true especially for issues that feature prominently on domestic political agendas like illegal immigration, organised crime and border controls). The repetitive use of QMV can indeed be experienced by the outvoted Member States as 'traumatic', in comparison with the slow but comforting consensus-building approach, *a fortiori* if the latter combines concessions and package-deals, side-payments or acknowledgement of diversity. Being repeatedly outvoted might be particularly sensitive for new members from Central and Eastern European countries, considering the special symbolic value of a recently recaptured sovereignty. Such an approach could therefore produce backlashes at decision-making level (multiplication of vetoes on other issues), as well as at the level of implementation and enforcement. Surely, QMV does not need to be actually used to exert its effect on decision-making. In the words of Weiler, 'reaching consensus under the shadow of the vote is altogether different from reaching it under the shadow of the veto' (Weiler 1999, p.72).

A useful addition to the EU toolbox of diversity management are the provisions on 'enhanced co-operation' which allow a limited group of Member States willing and able to further co-operation among themselves to use the Union's institutions, procedures and mechanisms. These provisions for enhanced co-operation have been introduced by the Treaty of Amsterdam and made more flexible by the Treaty of Nice. They could be used for instance by a sub-system of Member States within the Union (e.g., Member States responsible for the control of long external sea borders) to deepen border control co-operation that is functional for them, while being unnecessary for other Member States. Moreover, Member States could also use these provisions to experiment with new policies (e.g., in the sphere of information exchange or hot pursuit) and generate trust among a limited group of willing and able Member States. Such usage of enhanced co-operation as a 'policy laboratory' offers a better alternative to co-operation by a limited number of Member States outside the EU framework (e.g., a 'Schengen-II' formula). Such extra-EU co-operation could lead to the multiplication of parallel and competing regimes, duplicating and emptying out of existing EU policies, and contributing to the disintegration of the EU legal order. Moreover, extra-EU co-operation suffers from a lack of transparency, limited democratic control and absence of independent judicial review. Since it is open to all Member States, enhanced co-operation inside the EU is also expected to be more cohesive—contrary to some extra-EU *directoires* (Philippart and Sie Dhian Ho 2000).

Using the provisions for 'enhanced co-operation' to embed more structural joint endeavours among a limited number of Member States in the Union institutions and procedures would be one way to strengthen democratic and judicial control in this field. More generally, institutionalisation and democratic and judicial control have lagged behind during recent years that have seen quite some activity in terms of 'joint operations', 'pilot projects' and 'ad hoc centres'. The light network structure connecting all these projects and centres has facilitated the quick development of new initiatives, but its accountability is questionable. It is therefore time to create an EU institutional structure to prepare, coordinate, monitor and evaluate all these activities, in order for these functions to become more transparent and subject to legal rules and parliamentary scrutiny.

The Commission in its May 2002 Communication recommended the establishment of a Common Unit of external border practitioners, to be developed from the Strategic Committee for Immigration, Frontiers and Asylum (SCIFA) that operates within the Council framework. First experiences with this Common Unit—which was created in the autumn of 2002—are not very positive because of too large a membership and too diverse an agenda (including both legal and operational matters). Moreover, its competences and accountability are not formally defined and its information exchange activities are not subject to specific data protection rules. Against this background, the European Council at Thessaloniki in June 2003 called for the Commission to examine the necessity of creating new institutional mechanisms, including the possible creation of a Community operational structure. The drafting of the new European Union treaty provides a good opportunity to embed such a new institution in the democratic and judicial control structures of the European Union, and to install a proper data protection regime for its activities.

References

ANDERSON, M. and E. BORT. 2001. *The Frontiers of the European Union*. Houndmills, Basingstoke, Hampshire and New York: Palgrave.

ANDREAS, P. 2000. *Border Games. Policing the U.S.–Mexico Divide*. New York: Cornell University Press.

APAP, J., J. BORATYNSKI, M. EMERSON, G. GROMADZKI, M. VAHL and N. WHITE. 2001. 'Friendly Schengen borderland policy on the new borders of an enlarged EU and its neighbours'. Collective CEPS-Batory Foundation Paper. Brussels: CEPS.

COMMISSION OF THE EUROPEAN COMMUNITIES. 2001. 'Development of the Schengen Information System II'. COM(2001) 720 final. Brussels, 18 December 2001.

_____ 2002a. 'Integrated Management of the External Borders of the Member States of the European Union'. COM(2002) 233 final. Brussels, 7 May 2002.

_____ 2002b. 'Integrating Migration Issues in the European Union's Relations with Third Countries'. COM(2002) 703 final. Brussels, 3 December 2002.

_____ 2003. 'On The Development of a Common Policy on Illegal Immigration, Smuggling and Trafficking of Human Beings, External Borders and the Return of Illegal Residents'. COM(2003) 323 final. Brussels, 3 June 2003.

_____. 2003. 'Wider Europe – Neighbourhood: A New Framework for Relations with our Eastern and Southern Neighbours'. COM(2003) 104 final. Brussels, 11 March 2003.

COUNCIL OF THE EUROPEAN UNION. 2001a. 'Information Note, Schengen and Enlargement; Chapter 24: Cooperation in the Fields of Justice and Home Affairs'. 10876/01 Limite Elarg 172.

_____ 2001b. *The Schengen acquis integrated into the European Union*. Luxembourg: Office for Official Publications of the European Communities. Available at URL: <http://ue.eu.int/jai/default.asp?lang=en>

_____ 2001c. 'Council Regulation (EC) No 539/2001 of 15 March 2001 listing the third countries whose nationals must be in possession of visas when crossing the external borders and those whose nationals are exempt from that requirement'. *Official Journal of the European Union* L 81/1, Volume 44 (21 March 2001)

_____ 2001d. 'Council Regulation (EC) No 2414/2001 of 7 December 2001 amending Regulation (EC) No 539/2001 listing the third countries whose nationals must be in possession of visas when crossing the external borders of Member States and those whose nationals are exempt from that requirement'. *Official Journal of the European Union* L 327/1, Volume 44 (12 December 2001)

_____ 2002. 'Plan for the Management of the External Borders of the Member States of the European Union'. Doc. 10019/02 FRONT 58 COMIX 398. Brussels, 14 June 2002

_____ 2003a. 'Report on the implementation of programmes, ad hoc centres, pilot projects and joint operations'. Doc. 10058/1/03. Brussels, 11 June 2003

_____ 2003b. 'Council Regulation (EC) No 453/2003 of 6 March 2003 amending Regulation (EC) No 539/2001 listing the third countries whose nationals must be in possession of visas when crossing the external borders and those whose nationals are exempt from that requirement'. *Official Journal of the European Union* L 069/10, Volume 46 (13 March 2003)

_____ 2003c. 'Council Regulation (EC) No 453/2003 of 6 March 2003 amending Regulation (EC) No 539/2001 listing the third countries whose nationals must be in possession of visas when crossing the external borders and those whose nationals are exempt from that requirement'. *Official Journal of the European Union* L 069/10, Volume 46 (13 March 2003)

COUNCIL OF THE EUROPEAN UNION, GENERAL SECRETARIAT DG H. 2002. *EU Schengen Catalogue – External border control, Removal and readmission: Recommendations and best practices*, Brussels, 28 February 2002.

'DRAFT TREATY ESTABLISHING A CONSTITUTION FOR EUROPE'. 2003. *Official Journal of the European Union* C 169/01, Volume 46 (18 July 2003)

DULEBA, A.R.S. 2002 'Effects of visa regime on legal and illegal migration through the Slovak–Ukrainian border'. Paper presented at the conference 'EU Governance and the Challenge of Internal Security'. Leicester, 20–21 September 2002.

EUROPEAN COMMISSION. 1995. 'Preparation of the Associated countries of Central and Eastern Europe for integration into the internal market of the Union'. White Paper. COM(95)163. Brussels.

GENERAL SECRETARIAT DG H. 2002. *EU Schengen Catalogue – External border control, Removal and readmission: Recommendations and best practices*. Brussels: Council of the European Union.

MITSILEGAS, V., J. MONAR and W. REES. 2003. *The European Union and Internal Security, Guardian of the People?* Houndmills, Basingstoke, Hampshire and New York: Palgrave Macmillan.

MONAR, J. 2000. *Enlargement-related Diversity in EU Justice and Home Affairs: Challenges, Dimensions and Management Instruments*, The Hague: Scientific Council for Government Policy.

MUELLER-GRAFF, P-C. 1998. 'Whose Responsibility are Frontiers?'. In: M. Anderson and E. Bort (eds.), 11–21. *The Frontiers of Europe*. London: Pinter.

ORLOWSKI, W.M. 2001 'Konsekwencje ekonomiczne Schengen'. In Institute of Public Affairs (ed.), *Polska droga do Schengen – Opinie ekspertow*. Warsaw: Instytut Spraw Publicznych.

PHILIPPART, E. and M. SIE DHIAN HO. 2000. 'Answering EU's need for policy laboratories and sub-systemic schemes: reflections on the reform of 'closer cooperation', in: *Current Politics and Economics of Europe*, Volume 10, Number 1: 51–72.

_____ 2001 *Pedalling against the wind. Strategies to strengthen the EU's capacity to act in the context of enlargement*. The Hague: WRR Working Documents 115.

PIORKO, I. 2003 Speech at the Workshop 'Managing International and Inter-Agency Cooperation at the Border', Geneva, Geneva Centre for the Democratic Control of Armed Forces, 13–15 March 2003.

PIORKO, I. and M. SIE DHIAN HO. 2003a. 'Integrating Poland in the Area of Freedom, Security and Justice'. *European Journal of Migration and Law*, 5: 175–199.

_____ 2003b. 'The Costs and Benefits of Polish Accession to the EU in the Field of Justice and Home Affairs'. In Centrum Europejskie Natolin (ed.), *Costs and Benefits of Poland's Membership in the European Union*, 216–229. Warsaw: Centrum Europejskie Natolin.

POLAND. MINISTRY OF INTERIOR AND ADMINISTRATION. 2000. 'Poland Strategy of Integrated Border Management'. Warsaw: Ministerstwo Spraw Wewnetrznych i Administracji.

_____ 2002. 'Strategia zintegrowanego zarzadzania granica w latach 2003–2005'. Warsaw: Ministerstwo Spraw Wewnetrznych i Administracji.

'Presidency Conclusions - Copenhagen European Council 12 and 13 December 2002'. Council of the European Union, 15917/02, Brussels, 29 January 2003.

'Presidency Conclusions - Göteborg European Council 15 and 16 June 2001'. 2001. SN 200/1/01 REV 1. Available at URL: <http://europa.eu.int/comm/secretariat_general/impact/docs/g%F6teborg.pdf>

'Presidency Conclusions - Laeken European Council 14 and 15 December 2001'. SN 300/1/01 REV. Available at URL: <http://ue.eu.int/ueDocs/cms_Data/docs/pressData/en/ec/68827.pdf>

'The Schengen Acquis'. 2000. *Official Journal of the European Union*, L 239,.Volume 43 (22 September 2000)

'The Schengen Acquis Integrated in the Framework of the European Union'. 2004. Treaty establishing a Constitution for Europe. *Official Journal of the European Union*, C 310/348, Volume 47 (16 December 2004).

'Stability Pact for South Eastern Europe'. 1999. Cologne, 10 June 1999.

"The Treaty of Accession 2003'. 2003. *Official Journal of the European Union* L 236/17, 23 September 2003.

'The Treaty of Amsterdam'. 1997. *Official Journal of the European Union* C 340/01, 10 November 1997.

UNITED KINGDOM. 'Fairer, Faster and Firmer. A Modern Approach to Immigration and Asylum'. 1998 Presented to Parliament by the Secretary of State for the Home Department. The Stationary Office Cm 4018. Available at URL: <http://www.archive.official-documents.co.uk/document/cm40/4018/4018.htm>

UNITED KINGDOM. HOUSE OF LORDS. 1999. 'Schengen and the United Kingdom's Border Controls'. European Communities – Seventh Report. Session 1998–1999. Available at URL: <http://www.publications.parliament.uk/pa/ld199899/ldselect/ldeucom/37/3701.htm>

WEILER, J.H.H. 1999. The Constitution of Europe: Essays on the Ends and Means of European Integration. Cambridge: Cambridge University Press.

Chapter 8

Challenges for Non- (and Not Yet) Schengen Countries

Prof. Dr. Kurt Schelter

'... ohne Sicherheit ist keine Freiheit...' (*Wilhelm von Humboldt*)

Border Security in Europe – the Result of a Long and Difficult Political Process[1]

European Union (EU) / Schengen

At the beginning of this new century, border security is accepted as a top priority in the politics of all the member states of the European Union and the Schengen[2] community. Those communities more and more will have to meet the challenges faced at the common borders. Border security has become an integral aspect of almost all political issues. External border security is key to the enlargement of the EU, not only because a coherent and effective common management of the external borders of the EU member states is needed for the internal security of the EU citizens, but also because it is crucial in the fight against terrorism, illegal immigration networks, and the traffic in human beings.

There is as yet no completely harmonised policy on border security within the EU. This situation exists despite the fact that all legal instruments and operational experience built up in the Schengen *acquis* were integrated into the institutional framework of the European Union by the Treaty of Amsterdam and the Protocol annexed to it. Indeed, the United Kingdom and

---

[1] An excellent overview concerning this issue is provided by the '*Communication from the Commission to the Council and the European Parliament: Towards integrated management of the external borders of the Member States of the European Union*', issued on 7 May 2002, COM (2002) 233 final.

[2] The name 'Schengen' originates from a small town in Luxembourg. In March 1995, seven Member States of the European Union signed a treaty to end internal border checkpoints and controls. More countries have joined the treaty over the years. At present, there are 25 Schengen countries, of which 23 are EU member states and two are non-EU member states, namely Norway and Iceland. This territory without internal borders became known as the 'Schengen area'.

Ireland do not automatically and fully take part in Schengen and Title IV of the EC Treaty. Both Member States, however, have sought to participate in Community actions against carriers, unauthorised entry, transit and residence, readmission agreements with third countries and measures to strengthen visa security, they do co-operate in all fields of Title VI of the EU Treaty, and they have decided to participate in police and judicial co-operation.

Denmark has joined the Convention Implementing the Schengen Agreement, which entered into force for Denmark in March 2001. The Schengen Protocol to the Treaty of Amsterdam of 2 October 1997 incorporated Schengen co-operation into the framework of the EU. The European Community thus acquired competence for large areas of the Schengen *acquis* as well as its further development. At that time, special arrangements had to be made for Denmark. It will decide, on a case by case basis, whether to participate in the further development of the *acquis*, and whether to incorporate Community law, developed without its participation, into its national law.

Looking at this rather positive situation and thinking about the management of international and inter-agency co-operation at the borders, one should bear in mind that the actual status of border security is the result of a long and very difficult political process:

- It was initiated in the 1970s when some member states of the European Community (EC) sought to overcome years of threats and violence caused by terrorists.
- At the end of the 1980s, when the iron curtain in Europe was lifted and the highest possible degree of freedom of movement between the liberated East and the West had become an important political goal, those responsible for border security had to prove again and again that it would have been a great mistake to weaken the standards of external border controls towards the East. This was because an integral part of the idea of Schengen—namely to abolish the internal border regime between the Member States—is the strengthening of external border security.
- During the 1990s, the discussion concerning the enlargement of the European Union had a very strong impact on the philosophy of border security in Europe. The question was: 'Does it make sense to tighten our external borders to our Eastern neighbours at a time when they are preparing themselves to become new members of an "area of freedom, security and justice" established by the Amsterdam Treaty? And what about the attitude of the citizens of the new Member States towards a European Union that continues to build a fortress against its neighbours and friends?' The discussion over the visa regime for Bulgaria, Romania and the Baltic States, especially, was affected very strongly by those questions.
- The new dimension of terror we had to face after 11 September 2001

in the US, and the way it was 'prepared' in Europe, made it more than clear to all respective authorities that effective border security is crucial for successful prevention of this activity. If we wish to be successful in our efforts against international terrorism, our borders must be secure. This naturally applies to entry at the borders, but on 11 September it became evident that we also have to pay more attention to those leaving our countries.

Associated countries

Partly due to the fact that two EU Member States—Sweden and Finland—are still connected with Norway and Iceland by the Nordic Passport Union, these two Nordic Countries have decided to co-operate with the Schengen Community in a most effective way. It was the success and the attractiveness of Schengen co-operation that led Norway and Iceland to sign co-operation agreements and later to become Associate Members of Schengen.

A Schengen co-operation agreement was concluded with the two non-EU members of the Nordic Passport Union in 1996. Norway and Iceland have also fully implemented the Schengen regime since 25 March 2001. The co-operation agreements between the implementing countries, on the one hand, and Norway and Iceland, on the other hand, have been replaced by association agreements with the EU, which are very similar in content and concluded on the basis of the Treaty of Amsterdam. Norway and Iceland continue to participate in the drafting of new legal instruments building on the Schengen acquis. These acts are adopted by the EU Member States, but they apply to Iceland and Norway as well. In practice, this association takes the form of a Joint Committee beyond the EU framework, made up of representatives from the Icelandic and Norwegian governments and members of the EU Council and the Commission. Procedures for notifying and accepting future measures or acts have been laid down. This kind of co-operation cleared the way for similar agreements with other third countries.

Third countries—the Swiss model

From the very beginning of a common border regime at the level of Schengen and the EU, it was more or less accepted among all experts that Switzerland—being an important country in the heart of Europe—should become a partner in close co-operation as soon as possible. As host of a great number of UN agencies, international organisations and multinational companies, as an attractive destination for tourists from all over the world, and situated at the crossroads of international land and air traffic, Switzerland is destined to be an integral part of border security in Europe. Some political resentments of the political class in a couple of EU Member States, against the background of the negative vote of the Swiss citizens on EU membership, have meanwhile been overcome and given way to a real partnership.

Switzerland seeks arrangements which will give it a right of close co-operation with the EU at every level. The 'Bilateral Agreements I' between Switzerland and the EU, signed in June 1999, came into force on 1 June 2002. The agreements comprise, *inter alia*, free movement of persons. On 17 June 2002, the European Council authorised the European Commission and the Presidency of the EU to start negotiations with Switzerland in order to associate it with co-operation under the Schengen Agreement ('Bilateral Negotiations II'). Switzerland seeks access to the SIS[3], co-ordinated visa policies, and closer co-operation between the police and judicial authorities. More generally, the 'Bilateral Negotiations II' in the fields of justice, police, asylum and migration, also include participation in the Dublin Convention on the Country of First Asylum and in EURODAC.

The negotiations had followed the treaty agreed upon with Iceland and Norway and have come to a 'happy end' by the two successful referenda on the association with the Schengen/Dublin area and framework for freedom of movement between Switzerland and the EU. This is a firm basis for the ratification of the Schengen/Dublin Association Agreement by the member states of the EU.

New EU member states—the Polish model

Performing effective border security means: accepting this issue as a permanent challenge; adjusting measures to the changing risks; and taking into account the fact that since the lifting of the iron curtain Europe has also become a common space for criminals and all kinds of organised crime. Against this background it was very important to develop the future design of an effective border regime in a very faithful manner with all new Member States, on bilateral and on the Community levels.

After its reunification, Germany began very close bilateral co-operation with Poland on all aspects of border security. On the basis of a bilateral agreement on police co-operation and asylum in 1992, Poland received about DM 120 million of assistance to implement an effective asylum regime and border security, especially at the eastern border. Both governments and the German Länder agreed upon the exchange of liaison officers, joint border patrols, and police officers at the common border.

Since the 'Third Pillar' of the EC Treaty (dealing with 'Home and Justice Affairs') was implemented by the Maastricht Treaty of 1993, all applicant countries were invited to take part in a 'structured dialogue' on border

---

[3] The Schengen Information System (SIS) is an information system that allows the competent authorities to obtain information on wanted persons and stolen objects (and to introduce relevant data). Participation by an applicant state in the SIS is an essential prerequisite to lifting controls to common frontiers. Authorised checks are so far carried out by the police, border police, customs, and partially by authorities responsible for delivering visa and residence permits.

security and the fight against illegal migration and all kinds of organised crime. Starting with the German Presidency of Schengen in 1998, governments and experts from those countries are permanent and highly welcomed partners in the shaping of border security in a reunified Europe.

According to the 2002 Regular Report, continued progress can be noted regarding the management of the external borders and preparations for entering Schengen. This progress takes place in spite of considerable financial constraints for implementing planned improvements such as tightening the network of border patrol units and strengthening the land border surveillance system. Although the legal framework is broadly in line with the *acquis*, the capacity to implement it has been rather limited. The preparations with regard to the Schengen provisions that are relevant for accession are broadly satisfactory but significant efforts will be needed to achieve the timely lifting of internal borders and full implementation of the Schengen *acquis* after EU accession. The process of the ratification of the co-operation agreement between Poland and EUROPOL was accomplished in July 2002.

New neighbours—the Ukrainian model

After the finalisation of the enlargement process in 2004, the European Union will have to integrate ten new Member States into its daily work. The Union will have to implement border security at new external border. Among experts there is no doubt that this crucial problem can only be tackled successfully in co-operation with our new neighbours, especially in the East. It is obvious, that the close co-operation with Romania and Bulgaria must be developed, and with an accession perspective in mind, which in the meantime has been granted.

From a strategic point of view, co-operation on the new external border with the Ukraine is most important.[4] The preconditions for a fruitful

---

[4] Ukraine is connected with the Republic of Azerbaijan, Georgia, the Republic of Moldova and the Republic of Uzbekistan in the GUUAM Group, which was founded 1996 in Vienna. The Agreement on Co-operation provides for co-operation and interaction both in bilateral and multilateral formats. Participating States have committed themselves to consolidate their efforts in the fight against terrorism, to contribute to the fulfilment of international obligations as enshrined in UNSC Resolutions 1368 and 13777 (2001) and UNGA Resolution 56/1 and to become parties to all UN Conventions and Protocols related to terrorism. At the 2002 GUUAM Summit in Yalta the Presidents of the Participating States reiterated their firm positions on the issue of combating terrorism and organised crime. They identified border and customs control as very important measures to prevent and combat against terrorism and organised crime. In September 1998 and February 2003 meetings of the heads of the Border Control Agencies were held in Tbilsi. The GUUAM-US Framework Program includes the implementation of the following projects: Establishment of the GUUAM Virtual Centre on combating terror-

and open-minded co-operation in the area of border security, migration and visa policy have become much better after the success of the 'Orange Revolution' in the Ukraine. EU relations with Ukraine are to a large extent based on the Partnership and Co-operation Agreement (PCA), which entered into force in 1998. The EU Common Strategy on Ukraine was adopted in 1999. One of its strategic objectives is to enhance co-operation in the field of Justice and Home Affairs (notably within the PCA framework and the Sub-Committee four on customs and cross-border co-operation in Justice and Home Affairs). The first EU Troika meeting in this field took place in Brussels in November 2002. Joint efforts have been agreed upon on a limited number of clearly defined crime areas such as: readmission and migration; border management; money laundering; trafficking in human beings and drugs; corruption; and sexual exploitation of children and child pornography.

Assistance is being provided to Ukraine under the TACIS programme to finance such measures as support for border management etc. Further support is provided by the JHA programmes (STOP, etc.). Both sides have agreed to co-operate on the basis of the EU Action Plan. This plan envisages, inter alia, the strengthening of border management and improvement of the effectiveness of the police. In late 2002, negotiations started on a Readmission Agreement for illegal migrants from Ukraine, but Ukraine has linked signing a readmission commitment with the liberalisation of visa requirements by EU countries.

In August 2005 the European Commission adopted a recommendation to the Council to authorise it to open negotiations between the EU and Ukraine for the conclusion of an agreement on the facilitation of granting 'short-stay visas' for three months. Negotiations on visa facilitation will be launched before the next EU–Ukraine Summit to be held in December 2005 and shall go in parallel with the ongoing negotiations on a EU–Ukraine readmission agreement.

In March 2005 the President of Ukraine had signed the 'Decree on Temporary Introduction of the visa-free regime for citizens of the Member States of the EU and the Swiss Confederation', which was followed by the decree of 9 January 2005 granting a permanent visa-free regime.

Special case—the Western Balkans

The emergence of five new nations from the break-up of the former Yugoslavia has created over 5000 kilometres of new international borders in the region of the Stability and Association process (SAp) which are characterised by the major problems below.

---

ism, organised crime, drug trafficking and other dangerous types of crime; introduction of an unified data exchange system in antiterrorism activities; proposals on implementation of projects on strengthening the co-ordination of and interaction between GUUAM States on border and customs control issues.

Firstly, borders in the region are frequently not marked, and the emergent border control agencies are often inefficient and open to corruption. Border crossing points are not equipped to handle the traffic crossing them and organised crime networks in the region have become well established, highly violent, and increasingly international.

Illegal migration is clearly another major cross-border problem in the region. While the Western Balkans region is in itself a source of illegal immigrants into the EU—largely Albanians and Kosovars—the problem is mainly one of the regions being used by local criminal groups as a transit route for smuggling immigrants, who have come from other regions (e.g., Middle East and Asia), into the EU.

In addition to national problems associated with inadequate laws, enforcement and institutional capacities, there are international weaknesses that limit the SAp countries' capacity to co-operate in combating their justice and home affairs' problems, such as:

- lack of structures and networks within which countries can address shared cross-border problems such as border management and co-operation between national police and judiciary;
- no common regional policies being developed (e.g., visas, access rights, readmission and asylum), leaving loopholes that are exploited by criminal networks; and
- inadequate information systems that are generally not regionally interlinked or Schengen compatible, restraining the countries' capacities to investigate and tackle crime internationally. Hence, the EU Regional Strategy programme—the so-called CARDS Assistance Programme to the Western Balkans—provides specific support for integrated border management. The CARDS programme seeks to foster a more integrated and all encompassing approach to border management, mainly through incentives for inter-agency co-operation, including co-ordinated processing at border crossings, integrated information technology systems, awareness-building and joint responsibilities.

With regard to border control, regional CARDS support programmes have identified two goals for 2002–2003: (1) to build effective border security systems linked with national police structures and migration management authorities that are charged with dealing with illicit activities at border crossings and across the national territory more generally; and (2) the physical demarcation of agreed national borders where agreed by the national governments concerned.

EU support for border control will emphasise equipment and infrastructure but, as a condition, will be complemented by institution-building, technical assistance and twinning type arrangements to ensure coherence, sustainability and the overall enhanced effectiveness of the border control institutions involved.

All border projects in the Western Balkan region are funded by the EC (PHARE, CARDS, TACIS). They all seek to set up integrated border management systems that are in line with EC standards and that are in line with the perspective of future European integration. They all also envisage border demilitarisation in the spirit of an area of freedom, security and justice.

Old and New Challenges

The management of border security in Europe at the beginning of this century has to face a couple of well-known old and new challenges. Even in times of free movement external borders remain a hotspot for all forms of international organised crime, such as smuggling of all kinds of goods including stolen cars, cigarettes, drugs, weapons, and nuclear material, and illegal migration, people smuggling and organised prostitution. External borders promise to be the most important area to prevent and counter/fight organised crime.

In an area without internal border controls, as is the Schengen region, police authorities have to take into account that not just national land borders, but crossroads of international traffic, such as airports, railway stations, trains and service areas on highways, are becoming more and more important as locations for successful investigation.

We have known very well since the 1970s that terrorists do not normally act on a national basis, and we have learnt painfully at the beginning of this new century, that they even act at the global level. Countries of origin, countries of living, countries of conspiracy and countries of action are not the same. On the contrary, it has become the 'modus operandi' of terrorists to split those areas from each other very carefully. This is a new dimension of terrorism, which has to be taken into account in organising border security.

In spite of all the precautions, which already had been taken, 11 September 2001 proved that there are no obvious solutions in the fight against terrorism. What we need is a large number of intertwining measures working together to bring about a global strategy for the fight against terrorism. What approach should be taken at our borders? The key word is 'prevention'. We have to take into consideration that:

- Terrorists need new recruits, drawn largely from among sympathisers in support groups and organisations from abroad. They enter and they leave the country for many purposes.
- Terrorists need money and logistical support. We must dry up the sources. This takes us to areas with close links to organised crime, such as drug trafficking, and it explains why measures to combat money laundering even at the borders are so important for the fight against terrorism.
- Terrorists need weapons, explosives and other substances that can be used in attacks. This is why the arms trade must be placed under more

effective control, arms smuggling must be stopped, and new methods must be developed to better identify the origin of explosives and other substances. This new task of prevention requires very sophisticated technical devices even at the borders.
- If we wish to fight successfully against internationally active terrorists, our borders must be secure. This naturally applies to border entries. But why do we not give more attention to those leaving our countries? We know that terrorists frequently establish resting places between their countries of origin and their destinations. The European states linked in the Schengen Agreement are trying to adjust their systems in line with this idea. Freedom of movement and border security are not mutually exclusive if the necessary measures are taken at the external borders.
- The Achilles' heel in the fight against terrorism is the grotesque fact that in addition to the worldwide networking between terrorist organisations on our planet there are states that not only tolerate terrorism as policy tool, but also support it. Undoubtedly, this attitude affects the efficiency of border security in those countries and the readiness for co-operation on a good faith basis. Seamless solidarity and the closest possible co-operation at a multilateral level are therefore particularly significant as the decisive keys to success.
- The weakest link in the fight against terrorism is still the human factor. Routine—wherever it occurs—leads too quickly to carelessness and negligence. We therefore need to continuously tighten up our awareness of security and to check up on the controls established in order to maintain high security standards, especially at the borders.

We should not draw any hasty conclusions from the fact that a country at present is not a preferred target of international terrorism. The global threat of terrorism is unchanged. We were reminded of it on 11 September in the worst possible way. The history of terrorism tells us that states, which have not been targeted by international terrorism for some time, cannot be certain that this will remain the case. For this reason, it is vital for our security services to carefully observe those groups that are willing to carry out politically motivated acts of violence and terror in order to be able to recognise and react to new developments at an early stage. This is a most important task for inter-agency co-operation, even at our borders.

Co-operation so Far

Bilateral

To improve border security means first of all to perform a permanent and most intensive co-operation border covering all aspects of border management between the direct neighbours on both sides of the border. This requires mutual trust above all, given that it is quite easy to perform close co-operation at the land borders, but more difficult at the sea borders and at the airports. Nevertheless there are many good examples for such an effective and efficient co-operation. Germany's activities in this field are indicative. As the biggest member state of the European Union, situated in the heart of Europe, Germany has borders with nine European States—more than any other member state. This fact has initiated a very intensive, and in the end very successful, policy for common bilateral border management:

- Germany and France, sharing a very long border roughly paralleling the Rhine valley, and suffering from many bloody wars in the past, were the 'founding fathers' of the idea of Schengen in the 1980s and have acted in very close co-operation in border security for half a century. Today, this co-operation at an internal border of Schengen is a model for many other countries: Joint police—and customs—offices and common border patrols have been an integral part of a modern management of border security for the past few years.
- Poland and Germany share a long border mainly following the Oder River. Since 1998 German and Polish border police have performed nearly seven thousand common patrols at this borderline. Since February 2003 a similar kind of co-operation has started with the Czech Republic.
- On trains between Munich and Bolzano (Italy), German, Italian and Austrian border police are jointly on duty.
- Liaison officers of the German 'Bundespolizei' have been located at almost all big international airports for many years now. At the airports of Frankfurt/Main and Munich, border police officers from a couple of partner states are integrated in the daily work.
- Police officers from Romania are hosted at the 'Bundespolizeischule' in Lübeck and trained in all aspects of border security.
- For many years now German Länder have supported the police forces in nearly all Eastern European States by delivering equipment and know-how, adding significant value to border security.

Interregional

In the regions where borderlines intersect in a relatively small space, border security is a task, which cannot be carried out successfully on a bilateral basis. In such border regions regional co-operation is required. From a German perspective, very good examples are the regions of Lindau/Bregenz (Germany/Austria/ Switzerland), Basel (Switzerland/France/Germany), Aachen (Germany/ Belgium/Netherlands) and Passau (Germany/Austria/Czech Republic). This kind of co-operation is based on burden-sharing and synergy in all aspects of managing border security.

Successful regional co-operation on this field is not limited to Western

Europe. The Western Balkans offer a good example of negotiated regional co-operation as well. The CARDS regional strategy approach combines border control with trade facilitation and co-operation among border regions. The aim is to strengthen state identities and ease the life and economy of regions across stable and safe borders, through sustainable and effective professional services addressing criminal cross-border activities. The 2002 JHA (Justice and Homes Affairs) regional co-operation programme has a border control component to define common standards that are in line with those within the EU and to build operational mechanisms. Also customs assistance allows customs services a greater role in border control in the sense of border security. At a regional level, the South Eastern Europe Messaging Services (SEMS) is a valuable instrument of regional co-operation since, even though it was built for customs operations, it can be used for crime fighting activities.

EU/Schengen level

Co-operation in police matters in Europe is a story of success, especially if set against the background of European history. Some politicians and experts in this field complain about the fact that police co-operation for many years was a merely intergovernmental task in the EU, and it is still very difficult to move on under the special conditions of the third pillar of the Maastricht Treaty. But the results in this field provide a good argument against those critics. And, from a wider political point of view, it is more than a miracle that European citizens on the whole do not have substantial objections against close trans-border co-operation of their respective police forces. The co-operation of the border police benefits from this relaxed attitude of the citizens.

The work of the past several years has shown that the Schengen philosophy does not only work in theory, but also can be practically implemented. All member states of the Schengen Community have shown that it is possible, despite differing situations, to create an efficient system for safeguarding the external borders.

The Schengen Agreement also serves as an example of the kinds of results that can be achieved by long-term co-operation. What began as intergovernmental co-operation was then partially included in the third and the first pillars. The Schengen Agreement proves that intergovernmental co-operation is, in fact, a motor for European integration.

The success and attractiveness of Schengen co-operation is based on the dual strategy of freedom of movement and security. Security is guaranteed by a comprehensive and technically well thought-out security package consisting primarily of the following elements:

- Increased border control of passengers by commonly defined criteria. All persons are subject to at least one identity check upon entering a country. Passports and entry requirements, visa and residence permits, and prospective departure dates for third state nationals are verified.

But one would have to avoid profiling according to unacceptable criteria.
- Adaptation of visa standards as a requirement for a uniform entry policy for third country residents. All states that comply with the Schengen Agreement are required to follow a common visa policy for short-term stays of up to three months within a one-half year period. This short-term visa is uniform and valid in all participating states. Criteria for long-term visas, on the other hand, remain within the jurisdiction of individual states.
- Entry of illegal third state nationals is prevented mainly via a policy that requires transportation companies to return third state nationals to the country of origin at their own expense if they are denied entry at their final destination.
- Stipulations which determine the state that implements asylum procedures. The responsible state applies its national rights of asylum. This decision must be accepted by all participating states. The state is then responsible for returning the asylum seeker to his or her country of origin in the event that asylum is denied.
- Establishment of a common tracing system. The Schengen Information System has thousands of terminals at all border crossings at land, air and seaports. It is an important measure for providing security for all participating states. Mainly criminals, third country nationals with prohibited access, missing persons, or persons wanted in connection with criminal proceedings are tracked at these terminals. Moreover, information on stolen vehicles, firearms, blank official documents, personal documents, and banknotes is stored and appropriate controls are implemented.
- Policies for enhanced police and border police co-operation. This consists mostly of transnational observation, cross-border pursuit, and an obligation to report on travelling foreigners.
- Policies on criminal law. Mutual judicial assistance in criminal cases, prohibition of double jeopardy, extradition and transfer of execution of criminal judgments are the most important of these policies. The harmonisation of drug and arms laws, which still vary across different Schengen countries and associated states, such as Switzerland, should also be considered under this heading.
- The close relationship between the Schengen Agreement and co-operation in the area of justice and home affairs is evident in the historical development of European co-operation. The goals of those systems are largely identical in the areas of border policies and the fight against crime. The Schengen Agreement thus served as a pace-setter for the Union. Integration of the Schengen Agreement into the treaty was the only logical course in the end. Moving beyond Schengen is the goal of harmonising asylum rights as a part of the European area of freedom, security and justice. The decisive contributions of the

Schengen system to the European area of freedom, security and justice are freedom of movement of persons between member states and measures to fight organised crime.

These last two points are closely related considering that Europe has become a geographically open sphere for international organised crime. Through numerous regulations, the Schengen Agreement has done much to encourage an efficient fight against organised crime at home despite increased freedom of movement within Europe. This is achieved by protection from 'imported crime', which results from preventative measures taken at external borders and the effective fight against organised crime at home. Thus Schengen is a fundamental basis for the development of the European area of freedom, security and justice.

The Schengen Information System (SIS) is the best example of the progress made by the Schengen States in the area of police co-operation and border security. Only a few years ago it would have been inconceivable that more than six million data files for tracing stolen property and wanted persons from ten European countries would be available online at 1,500 border crossings. With this instrument, border police can take the offensive against organised trafficking of persons and against cross-border organised crime.

Nevertheless, it goes without saying that we cannot stop here. Technological advances require permanent improvement of the Schengen Information System so that it remains technically up to date. Keeping in mind that issues concerning border security are constantly changing, it is also necessary that the measures adopted to deal with changing risks be adjustable. A regional enlargement is also needed. These considerations include Ireland and Great Britain, third states such as Switzerland, and the new Member States. Technical progress and the advancement of police tracing capabilities eventually make the introduction of a new system indispensable.

Apart from the implementation of SIS II we have to work very hard on the further development of Schengen. In this regard the following issues need to be considered:

- Verification and approval procedures for visa applications need to be harmonised so that applicants cannot receive a visa more quickly or more easily in one Schengen State than another, thus avoiding 'visa-shopping'. This includes, for instance, use of uniform, counterfeit-proof forms and harmonisation of regulations concerning health insurance protection. Thus the ultimate goal is to enable the establishment of a common office for visa applications for all Member States.
- It is also necessary to continue the process of widening and deepening the exchange of information and common Schengen Visa Files. Thus, registering, processing and controlling the distribution of visas by national registration systems are no longer necessary within the

Schengen Area. The project of a common diplomatic service of the EU, which is part of the Constitutional Treaty, has to be designed in a way that even the granting of Schengen Visa Files should be a matter of common visa agencies in the embassies of the EU. The European Commission and the Council should control those agencies.

- In the fight against drug abuse, it is inadequate that co-operation between Schengen States stops with police-enforced consequences of cross-border drug trafficking. In close co-operation with third countries, the Schengen States must obtain information on the production, supply and distribution of synthetic drugs. Most importantly, though, it is necessary that drug-related policies and legislation at the national level be harmonised within the European Union. Surveillance by the police should also be possible for crime prevention with regard to potential victims of crime. The lack of common and compatible telecommunication systems constitutes an obstacle for police co-operation between Schengen States. Criminals and terrorists are linked together by an international mobile phone network, and use it at any cost. As this is not possible for national police forces and intelligence services in their cross border activities, we need to have a special communication system for those agencies.

Multilateral

Against the background of globally active organised crime, border security is not just a task for national or supranational authorities. International organisations such as the UN and the OSCE have recognised that they have to be engaged in this field. Freedom, security, justice and peace in Europe and beyond are threatened more by terrorists and criminals than by states. This is not only a consequence of 11 September 2001. But after those brutal attacks, the UN, for the first time in its history, drew a line between global security, and border management and reminded its member states not to allow asylum seekers to abuse their rights for the preparation of terrorist actions (UNSC 2001). The OSCE no longer refuses to recognise that terrorism and organised crime in Europe are a danger for the security of states in Europe, and therefore border security has to be supported at the international level, which is within its ambit.

Problems

An even better management of international and inter-agency co-operation at the borders in Europe requires officials to tackle a couple of problems they face in spite of all the progress already made:

Politics

On various fields one can feel that the salience of common interests among the Member States is beginning to decline. New Member States are carrying a heavy burden due to their common history with former allies, who have now become new neighbours of the EU. The case of Kaliningrad has shown us that it is very difficult for Russia to accept that their citizens living in this exclave need to have visas to cross the territory of a former satellite state, or member of the USSR, for a visit to Moscow. We must not accept any substantial weakening of border security of the EU for such reasons. Border security must remain a first priority in EU politics.

Funding

Priority means above all 'priority in the budgets'. History shows that there is a lack of money on the national and EU levels, especially for prevention, until something extraordinary has happened. To spend more money after terrorist attacks is to a great extent just window dressing. We must pool resources and use them on a basis of financial burden-sharing between member states and the EU (Commission of the European Communities 2002, p.19).

According to the Annual Policy Strategy for 2004 one major strategy was to develop stability at the borders of the EU and beyond. For the internal aspects the Commission has proposed an additional allocation of 175 million Euros. Within the EU there should be emphasis placed on improved border control, establishing an integrated IT system on visa information, and developing a policy of security for telecommunication network. It also included activities such as the fight against bio-terrorism. Stability outside the EU will be supported with an increase in support to the Western Balkans and Mediterranean region.

In February 2004 the European Commission announced its Annual Policy Strategy for 2005. The following key initiatives were selected amongst others:

- Preparation of the second phase of the Common Asylum System (including implementation of European Refugee Fund II).
- Strengthening policy for common visa and security of travel documents (including biometrics): Implementation of VIS (Visa Information System) following adoption of the legal act by the Council and co-ordination of design and development of SIS II.
- Enhancing the role and capabilities of the European Police College (CEPOL) in the training of senior EU police officers, in particular by transforming CEPOL into a body of the European Union.

The appropriations allocated to the development of the Schengen Information System II in 2005, have been proposed to increase to 14.5 million Euros following the feasibility study which indicated a spending profile slightly different from the one originally planned.

Personnel and equipment

Today we have to admit that despite all bilateral and EU efforts there are still remarkable quantitative and qualitative disparities between the border police agencies at the external borders. These disparities will increase after the enlargement of the EU in 2004. The success of border management relies on complementarity, which requires the convergence of national staff policies (Commission of the European Communities 2002, p.18). Compatible systems of telecommunication are a precondition for successful prevention, law enforcement and border management. Organised illegal migration from one shore to another can only be successfully prevented and hindered by monitoring the coast by radar or satellite. Speedboats can help as well.

Education and training

Despite all technical devices at the border, the human factor remains the most important precondition for successful border management. We have to continue developing a common syllabus for the training of border guards and to organise advanced training courses. Bearing in mind that border guards have to communicate with their colleagues across the border and will soon work together in a European Corps of Border Guards, very close attention must be paid to language training (Commission of the European Communities 2002, p.18).

Legislation

The lack of formal legal basis, or the divergence among national legal systems, does hamper the objective of enhancing operational co-operation. While legislation might be in place, it is also necessary to have the institutional capacity to implement that legislation. Enforcing border security in most cases implies the need to strengthen capacity building and to develop the necessary infrastructures, (meaning the availability of financial and technical assistance). Sufficient funding must ensure coherence, sustainability, and the overall effectiveness of the border control institutions involved.

New Forms and New Dimensions of Co-operation

Integrated management of the external borders of the EU

In December 2001, the European Council of Laeken concluded that better management of the EU's external border controls would help in the fight against terrorism, illegal immigration networks and the traffic in human beings.

Hence, the European Council asked the European Commission (EC) to work out arrangements for co-operation between services responsible for external border control, and to examine the conditions in which a mechanism (or common services) to control external borders could be created. Consequently, in 2002 the EC adopted a Communication entitled 'Towards Integrated Management of the External Borders of the Member States of the European Union' (Commission of the European Communities 2002). One of its ambitions is to propose mechanisms for working and co-operation at the EU level, which will permit practitioners at external borders to co-ordinate their operational actions in the framework of an integrated strategy.

Indeed, in order to achieve a better co-ordinated and more homogeneous level of security, operational synergies must be improved in the framework of an integrated strategy. The EC Communication (Commission of the European Communities 2002, p.22) proposes that a common policy could include: a common operational co-ordination and co-operation mechanism (i.e., to set up an external border practitioners' common unit as a co-ordinating steering committee); a common integrated risk assessment; and inter-operational personnel and equipment, such as the development of a common base of training border guards, and the introduction of a common radar or satellite based external border surveillance network.

This would imply burden-sharing between the Member States and the EU. National budgets should remain the principal resources for financing. However, Community budget support could be used to establish a mechanism for financial redistribution between the member states. This financial burden-sharing should, in the long run, be supplemented by operational burden-sharing through the establishment of European Corps of Border Guards. (See Monar and Hobbing, in this volume).

European border police

The Treaty of Amsterdam has defined the protection of the external borders of the EU as a common issue of the Union. It is a natural consequence of this very long and well reflected decision of the Members States that the integration of national border police proceed on a step by step basis.

This does not mean that the national border protection and border police should be abolished completely. Following the principle of subsidiarity, Member States have to continue to make their contributions to provide for the security of their respective part of the external borders of the Union. But there are problems at the borders which can be tackled much better by a multinational team.

This is the reason why some Member States—such as Germany—have pushed very hard since the middle of the 1990s to organise border security on supranational basis, especially against the background of the enlargement of the Union.

The European Commission recommends in its Communication of 7

May 2002 (COM(2002)233 final) 'that the national services of the Member States receive the support of a European Corps of Border Guards' (p.20). The Commission proposes that this Corps should work in accordance with the following elementary principles (p.21):

- initially handling surveillance functions at the external borders of the Member States;
- subsequently, handling checks at the border crossing points;
- staff involved should have the full prerogative of public authority needed to perform these functions, irrespective of their nationality and their place of deployment;
- the Corps should be placed under the operational command of the External Border Practitioners Common Unit; and
- it should be open at all hierarchical levels to any Member State who satisfies the requirements as to qualifications and ethical standing.

The European Commission is very much aware of the difficulties that have to be overcome, such as the method of recruiting staff, staff regulations and status for disciplinary purposes (p.21), and recommended that the staff be empowered to:

- check the identity papers, travel documents and visas of persons crossing the external border legally or illegally;
- question aliens on the reason for their stay... or on the reasons why they have crossed the external border outside the official crossing points;
- board a civilian ship or boat in territorial waters to question the captain as to his route and to verify the passengers' identities;
- notify a person that he (or she) is admitted or refused entry to the common area of freedom of movement; and
- apprehend a person and hand him (or her) over to the competent national authorities to take the appropriate preventive or enforcement measures where necessary (p.22).

The Spanish EU Presidency had initiated the ambitious project of a European Corps of Border Guards at the European Council at Seville, and had asked the Member States to implement new forms of co-operation in border security. Meanwhile, 17 projects are on their way.

Germany, for example, is running a centre for the protection of land borders. The main task of this centre is to evaluate joint services at the external borders. Common offices will be implemented at the borders. The centre has started to perform joint operative actions near Frankfurt/Oder, at the Austrian/ Slovakian and at the Italian/Slovenian borders. A first report will be delivered in the summer of 2003.

In addition, Italy is responsible for the improvement of co-operation at the major international airports in the EU; Austria is working on a union-wide syllabus for the training of border policemen; and Spain is organising a multinational coast guard in the Mediterranean Sea.

There is a lot to be done before a European Corps of Border Guards is really operative. Some obstacles—for instance, provisions in a couple of national Constitutions—have to be overcome. Against the background of the increasing challenge of international terrorism, the protection of national borders should no longer be considered a matter of national sovereignty and should be protected by the Constitution. But in view of the increasing threat at our external borders, there is no alternative but to implement this project without delay. At the first stage, the Corps could exercise real surveillance functions at the external borders by joint multinational teams. The powers conferred on the staff of the European Corps could be confined territorially, for example to a strip a few hundred metres wide at external borders. In the immediate future, a European Corps will not be able to replace the national authorities. The main difficulty to be overcome is connected with conferring the prerogatives of public authority to the staff of the European Corps who do not have the nationality of the Member States where they are working.

Conclusions

In order to respond to the complex challenges of the 21st century in the field of border security, comprehensive solutions are necessary, but these can be based only on enhanced co-operation among all relevant actors, while respecting basic laws and fundamental principles. To this end, the following points must be recognised:

- Border security has become an integral aspect of many political issues.
- External border security is key to the EU enlargement.
- There is no completely harmonised policy on border security within the EU and on the European continent. Performing effective border security, therefore means to accept this issue as a permanent challenge, adjusting measures to the changing risks.
- It remains very important to develop the future design of an effective border regime in a faithful manner with all new Member States, on bilateral and on Community levels.
- Switzerland should become a partner for close co-operation as soon as possible.
- After the finalisation of the enlargement process in 2004, the European Union will have to implement border security at new external borders in close co-operation with our new neighbours, especially in the East.[5]

---

5   Author's postscript: In the ten new Member States continued progress can be

- Close co-operation with Romania and Bulgaria must be attained with a view to accession.
- Co-operation on the new external borderline with the new neighbour Ukraine is most important. Common efforts have to be concentrated especially on readmission and migration, border management, money laundering, trafficking in human beings and drugs, corruption, sexual exploitation of children and child pornography.
- The emergence of five new nations from the break-up of the former Yugoslavia, has created over 5,000 kilometres of new international borders in the region of the Stability and Association process that are characterised by major problems including insufficient border security measures and the growing threat posed by organised crime.
- The management of border security in Europe at the beginning of this century must face a couple of well-known old and new challenges:
  - 11 September 2001 has shown us that we need a large number of intertwining measures working together to bring about a global strategy for the fight against terrorism.
  - To improve border security means to perform a permanent and most intensive co-operation between the direct neighbours on both sides of the border covering all aspects of border management.
  - In regions where borderlines are intersecting in a relatively small space regional co-operation is required.
  - Technological advances require permanent improvement of the Schengen Information System. Technical progress and the advancement of police tracing capabilities eventually make the introduction of a new system indispensable.
  - Verification and approval procedures for visa applications need to be harmonised to avoid 'visa-shopping' and to enable establishment of a common office for visa applications for all Member States.
  - The process of widening and deepening the exchange of information and common Schengen Visa Files is to be continued.
  - In the fight against drug abuse, the Schengen States—in close co-operation with third countries—must obtain information on the production, supply and distribution of synthetic drugs and harmonise drug related policies and legislation.
  - Surveillance by the police should also be possible for crime prevention in relation to persons living in the offenders' sphere and victims of crime.
  - International organisations such as the UN and the OSCE can no

---

noted in relation to the management of the external borders and preparations for Schengen. Although the legal framework is broadly in line with the *acquis*, the capacity to implement has been rather limited. Significant efforts will be needed to achieve the full implementation of the Schengen *acquis*.

longer refuse to recognise that terrorism and organised crime in Europe are a danger for the security of all states in Europe, and therefore border security has to be supported even at the international level.

References

COMMISSION OF THE EUROPEAN COMMUNITIES. 2002. *'Communication from the Commission to the Council and the European Parliament: Towards integrated management of the external borders of the Member States of the European Union'*. Brussels, 7 May 2002, COM(2002) 233 final.

UNITED NATIONS SECURITY COUNCIL (UNSC). 2001. *Resolution 1377*.

Chapter 9

Management of External EU Borders: Enlargement and the European Border Guard Issue

Peter Hobbing

Talking of the possible creation of a European Border Guard, similar to the federal border services of the United States, has until recently been an absolute taboo in official EU fora. Critics underline that European post-World War II history has been that of an economy-driven integration engine with no appropriate back-up in security matters. Or, in other words, it was a case of the 'economic cart put before the security horse'. There are sufficient (and even satisfactory) explanations of why European integration could develop only along that line (and not the other way round); these will be discussed in this paper.

There comes a time when provisional approaches do not work any more or prove too costly: for EU border security, this moment seems to have arrived, some 50 years after the beginnings of European integration. In fact, the Laeken EU Summit in December 2001 already recognised that 'better management of the Union's external border controls will help in the fight against terrorism, illegal immigration networks and the traffic in human beings' (and other counterproductive phenomena) and consequently directed the Commission and Council to look into the possible creation of 'a mechanism or common services to control external borders' (European Council 2001). This represented a revolution, a first breakthrough, in EU-history, of Member States' monopoly in implementing and enforcing EU legislation at the borders.

With the expected accession of ten new Member States in 2004 and possibly three more in the years after, the number of Member States was to almost double, the length of the external border would drastically increase and its location shift further to the east. This implied, according to the Laeken scenario, that a great share of the new border would fall under the responsibility of the new Member States, less experienced and less well-off in financial terms.

Commission and Council reacted quickly and presented their ideas on border management in May (Commission of the European Communities 2002) and June 2002 (Council of the European Union 2002a), respectively: both considered the option of the ECBG as a valid solution. Even the European

Constitution as adopted in December 2004 provides for the 'gradual introduction of an integrated management system for external borders'.[1]

Interestingly enough, the trend to multilateral border services is promoted not only by the EU institutions, but, in a very 'hands-on' way, by various Member States: they created inter-agency, regional 'Co-operation Centres' in which representatives from at least two Member States and various police and customs forces perform day-to-day and border-related enforcement work[2]. Furthermore, individual Member States have launched pilot projects to study specific aspects of joint border management.[3] The present article undertakes to show:

- why, due to EU history, integrated border management is such a delicate matter;
- what the EU and Schengen have done to cope with the matter;
- how the development towards a shared responsibility for the external borders logically led to the concept of multilateral border services, in particular the European Corps of Border Guards.

The Difficulties of Border Management in the EU

EU history appears to many as a continuous and radical abolition of internal frontiers starting in 1968 and continuing until present.
First to go were the customs borders in July 1968, second that of the remaining obstacles to free movement of goods achieved by 1993, to the effect that controls on goods had entirely been abandoned at that date; on 26 April 1995 passport controls were abolished between the original Schengen members France, Germany; Belgium Netherlands and Luxemburg as well as the newcomers Spain and Portugal. Others followed in the years after to the extent that they were able (and willing) to implement the strict Schengen criteria. By March 2003, identity checks were abolished between 15 member states. But surprisingly enough, these 15 members are not identical to those of the customs union. The United Kingdom and Ireland were not willing to renounce on checks at their borders, while Norway and Iceland, normally considered traditional opponents of full EU membership, decided to join this very sensitive part of European integration, due to the existing Nordic Passport Union with Denmark, Finland and Sweden which they did not want to sacrifice.

---

[1] The Constitutional Treaty has been adopted by the Council, but not yet ratified by all Member States (situation as of August 2005).
[2] The first of these centres was the Franco–German Cooperation Centre situated in Kehl close to the Rhine border and created on the basis of the 1997 Mondorf Agreement between Germany and France.
[3] Germany is looking into land borders, Italy into airports, and Spain into maritime cooperation.

However, one border remained and gained increasingly in importance: from that time on, the external EU border represented the only filter between inside and outside the EU and thus the only barrier to protect 'public policy, national security or the international relations of any of the Member States' (Schengen Convention 1990, Art. 5; Convention Implementing the Schengen Agreement 2000).

As regards the external EU border, efficient border management encounters a number of problems, mainly related to the general history of the EU.

The principle of 'economic concerns first'

In the EU, it seems that economic concerns have always been accorded first priority. There were good reasons for this being so: first, one lesson taught by the First and Second World Wars was that pooling the coal and steel resources of, in particular, Germany and France would be the best protection against another European war (Schuman 1950). Second, economic actors in Europe were traditionally much more enthusiastic about opening internal borders than policemen and others responsible for internal security.

This reticence on the part of the security sector is far from being incomprehensible: while commercial interests mainly see an enlarged market as offering new opportunities, justice and home affairs are confronted with the fear of influx of crime and illegal immigration, for which they would be they would be blamed by public opinion. On the other hand, enforcement administrations (customs as well as police) are sometimes being criticised for not having recognised the signs of the new times. Instead of actively participating in the creation of borderless Europe, they frequently remained offside and lost the opportunity to effectively influence the new construction from a law and order point of view.

As a result, politicians developed the European Union mainly on the basis of positive economic approaches and concepts of international understanding. Internal security concerns were considered on a secondary level under the header of 'compensatory measures'.[4]

Diversity of Legal Systems, Administrative Structures, Languages

Until recently, Member States' legal systems in justice and home affairs (JHA) have stayed practically untouched by the integration trend prevailing in the EU in general.

---

4   Compensatory measures are the mechanisms that must be in place before an internal EU border is removed. They relate to the security of new external borders, visa policy, police cooperation, and participation in the Schengen information system. Cf. Glossary Justice and Home Affairs

From Trevi to the third pillar under the Maastricht Treaty of 1992

For a long time, the concept of the European Economic Community was taken literally and no need was seen for action in justice and home affairs matters. When the opening of borders emerged on the horizon under the sign of the Single Market, Member States were roused from their lethargy and started to react, but in the prudent and reserved way that is characteristic of co-operation in JHA (justice and home affairs) matters. Their first joint consideration of security concerns took place in a strictly non-EC/EU context, i.e., the TREVI Group (Peek 1994), to make it absolutely clear that this was of 'no business whatsoever to the Brussels institutions'. JHA always remained separate from the mainstream, even when these matters were finally taken under the EU roof by the Maastricht Treaty of 1992: the strict distinction between first pillar (Community field) and third pillar matters (JHA) has been sustained through the Treaties of Amsterdam and Nice until today.

Elements to demonstrate the primacy of the nation-state and the intergovernmental character of any co-operation in this field were numerous (Fehérváry 2001): such co-operation relied on conventions rather than regulations or directives, unanimity rather than majority vote, the principle of reciprocity rather than unconditional respect of rules.

Schengen co-operation

Schengen co-operation equally grew from intergovernmental beginnings (Schengen Agreement 1985; Convention Implementing the Schengen Agreement 1990), and was integrated into the EU framework only in 1999 on the basis of the Amsterdam Treaty (Commission of the European Communities 2002, paragraph 15)

Under the primacy of the nation-state concept, hardly any harmonisation in the JHA field has taken place. As a result, staff at the Schengen border must, in theory, be familiar with 25 different legal orders in order to determine whether a given foreign national is to 'be considered a threat to public policy, national security or the international relations of any of the Member States' (Article 5, Schengen Convention). In reality, of course, none of the staff has such far-reaching knowledge, and threat assessments are 'performed on national criteria which are not equivalent from one Member State to another' (Commission of the European Communities 2002, paragraph 13).

Administrative structures are definitively diverging in the various Member States: different organisations exist in the police as well as customs field and their respective remits are also diverging. Basic organisations are police, responsible for the control of persons, and customs, responsible for goods. In a number of states, this division of labour is further subdivided into more complicated structures, e.g. customs and the *Guardia di Finanza* in Italy, the *Bundesgrenzschutz* and State border police in certain parts of Germany,

Gendarmerie and *Police nationale* in France. In some cases, such as Germany, it is customs that has also the function of controlling passports.

As a result, national services of one Member State often do not have an exact counterpart in the neighbouring state (Commission of the European Communities 2002, paragraph 13).

Public opinion

One should also not underestimate the weight of public opinion in this area. Many citizens still appear to be afraid of accepting 'foreign elements' in their criminal justice and police system. As one could read recently in the British press, the 'worst case scenario for any UK citizen is to undergo sentencing by a judge from Latvia or an arrest imposed by a policeman from Greece' (the nationality of the judge/policeman is replaceable by most other EU-nationalities). The same would doubtlessly be true for the question as to whether protection of the border with the outside world should be entrusted to an organisation not exclusively under national control.

In view of these sentiments, and with criminal justice and police matters considered to be close to the constitution and 'the heart of a nation', it is comprehensible why Member States have been more hesitant to give up national sovereignty in these matters than they were in the economic field (see Fehervary 2001). The criticism often expressed towards the slow pace and zigzag path of progress in JHA matters should recall these difficulties: the complicated and costly Third Pillar structure, which offered Member States a system of checks and balances to revoke, where necessary, any concession previously made, was often the only way to escape deadlocks.

Diversity of border burdens

During the initial phase of the EEC/EU, things were rather well balanced: every Member State maintained its own border surveillance on internal as well as external borders. With the arrival of the Single Market and free movement of goods by 1993,[5] it was first of all the customs that 'jumped ship'. Suddenly there were Member States without any external land border—Belgium, the Netherlands, Luxembourg and Portugal—and any goods destined for these countries had to be cleared by control staff of other Member States.[6] France's land border shrank from 2,889 km to a mere 630 km, and that of Spain from

---

5 The completion of the Customs Union by 1968 had no such effect yet, as only customs duties *stricto sensu* had been abolished; customs administrations had to maintain their border presence to ensure the respect of other goods-related regulations such as VAT and other taxes, interdictions and restrictions not yet harmonised.

6 This applies unless the goods arrive via sea or air, as seaports and international airports remain external borders.

1,918 km to 80 km (CIA 2002). Practically the same developments occurred with the completion of the first phase of the Schengen abolition of internal borders in 1995.

Nevertheless, given the relatively comparable economic strength of all partners and relatively comparable proficiency of the various customs administrations, no one complained: neither those who had to take over the additional clearing and control tasks,[7] nor those who, although relieved from own control tasks, had to rely on the correctness of controls carried out by others.

This situation changed with the massive enlargement of the Union which took place in 2004. Not only would the burden of control in the greater EU remain on the shoulders of an ever decreasing share of Member States, the shoulders most loaded would in addition be those with the least performing economies and those with an, at the least, 'unconfirmed' experience in border management. Land border protection of the customs territory since 2004 is in the hands of just 15 out of 25 Member States (7 of which are new members), whereby the heaviest load, i.e. the border with ex-USSR and ex-Yugoslav states are on the poorest members: GDP per capita for the Baltic states, Poland, Hungary, Slovakia and Slovenia are at approximately just 40 percent of the current EU average.

As recently as 1995, 98 percent of the 'Schengenland' land border was controlled by the experienced staff of France and Germany; by 2003 this share had shrunk to less than 42 percent and, with the gradual accession of the eastern neighbours, it will soon fall below 20 percent. On the other side, 75 percent of the sensitive eastern/south eastern borders will soon be entrusted to the new members, notably Lithuania, Poland and Slovenia, later possibly Bulgaria and Romania.

Another complication lies in the fact that neither the new members nor the EU want to cut the ties that exist between the new members and their neighbours in the east such as Ukraine and Belarus.[8] Flexible border regimes seem to be the answer, but they require specific management skills and resources.

It is therefore no surprise that the concept of 'burden-sharing' started to play an important role in the papers presented by EU Commission and Council in the follow-up to the Laeken Summit of December 2001 (Commission of the European Communities 2002; Council of the European Union 2001a). The ideas developed include redistribution of resources between the Member States, financing of common equipment from the EU budget, and the creation of a European Border Guard/European Corps of Border Guards. A major argument for the latter proposal relates to the 'invaluable expertise' of

---

[7] It should not be overlooked though that customs obtains a re-compensation for additional tasks: 25 percent of the EU duties collected may be kept by national customs as an 'expense allowance'.

[8] According to Prodi, there 'shall be no new Iron Curtain' (Reuters 9.3.2002)

the border staff from the 'old' Member States that could thus be exploited for the benefit of all.

The Current Tool-set of EU and Schengen for Enhancing Uniform Border Management

In light of the legal and structural difficulties described above, EU and Schengen have continuously tried to 'soften' the bumpy road to better co-operation in border matters.

Customs instruments

The abolition of internal customs borders and simultaneous creation of a Common Customs Tariff (CCT) towards countries external to the EU were among the basic objectives of the EEC Treaty of 1957 (see Treaty of Rome 1957; The Treaty of Amsterdam 1997). Difficulties immediately arose, and although there was soon a common European legislation (the abolition of internal customs borders was achieved in July 1968, i.e., 18 months ahead of schedule!), the legislator had not foreseen the need for any rules on how to ensure the smooth and equivalent application of this legislation by the customs administrations of the six EEC Member States. Nor was there any type of administrative information exchange, leave alone co-operation, between the national services.

Because of this lack of administrative co-ordination, fraudsters would succeed in perpetrating the same type of customs fraud at various Community entry points: even when their trick had been uncovered at one point they could be sure that the news would not have been passed on to the neighbouring country, so they could commit the fraud again elsewhere.

As is common in the history of Schengen, the first remedy was not provided by the Community, but by Member States who took action themselves via traditional intergovernmental mechanisms. The Naples Convention of 1967 was an example of such old-style arrangements with safeguards such as a reciprocity clause that was not found any more in later Community legislation.

The Mutual Assistance Group (MAG)—created under this convention as sort of a customs-TREVI—continued to exist until the arrival of the Council 3rd Pillar structures under the Maastricht Treaty in 1993. MAG's activities, although confined since 1981 to non-Community matters, were widespread in organising the first Community-wide co-operation mechanism to combat crossborder fraud, in particular drug smuggling and other forms of trafficking. Since 1979, practical arrangements were developed with the Commission which subsequently financed (!) and hosted the meetings of MAG and its numerous sub-groups. Due to logistical support from the Commission, MAG was in particular able to conduct successful EC-wide operations to intercept drug smugglers in airports (Airline Transit Exercises since 1985) as well as drug consignments hidden in maritime and airborne containers (since 1988). A revised convention (Naples II) was signed by all Member States in 1997 (Council of the European Union 1997), but not yet ratified by all.

Notwithstanding the successes of MAG, the real dynamic in customs co-operation developed since 1981 on the Community 1st Pillar side. Alarmed by considerable financial losses to the EC budget through the evasion of customs duties, the first Community instrument on administrative assistance was passed with Regulation 1468/81 (Council of the European Union 1981),[9] containing much more stringent provisions than those of the parallel Naples Convention; there were no more diplomatic clauses such as reciprocity, and Member States were obliged to immediately inform each other and the Commission of any new type of fraud discovered and of any fraud case with 'ramifications to other Member States'.

Further innovations were achieved thanks to the important logistical and financial support that the customs service of the Commission (DG XXI, now DG TAXUD) was able to offer to the national services. Although Member States could still resist the temptation in the beginning, growing budgetary constraints at the national level helped to change their minds. From 1987 on,[10] the Commission was able, together with the Member States concerned, to conduct (and finance) joint investigative missions to third countries in order to resolve smuggling cases to the detriment of the Community budget (mainly fraudulent declarations of origin, infringements of quota rules, etc.).

Information technology was introduced already from the mid-1980s on, when this still represented an absolutely revolutionary approach: already by 1988, the SCENT (System Customs Enforcement NeT) information network linked up 150 computer terminals at customs headquarters and major border crossings all over the Community and allowed for speedy exchange on current fraud cases and risk assessments. By 1993, the number had risen to 350 terminals, for which, again, all costs were borne by Brussels. In addition, the Customs Information System (CIS) (Council of the European Union 1997, Title V), created in 1988, provided a database system on fraud-relevant data concerning commodities, means of transport, companies, individuals etc, accessible by all authorities designated by Member States or the Commission. CIS represented a cross-pillar instrument, as Member States were entitled to store even third Pillar information, with the Commission having no access to this part of the database (Council of the European Union 1997, Article 23 (3).

A policy of providing training and regular get-togethers at all levels played an important role in creating the EC-wide customs identity ('esprit de corps'), we can see today especially within the enforcement field: whenever

---

[9] This regulation was later amended by Regulation (EEC) No 945/87, and later replaced by Regulation (EC) No 515/97.
[10] Art. 14a Regulation 1468/81 as amended by Regulation (EEC) No 945/87, see Council of the European Communities 1987.

investigators saw a need to discuss case-related elements of an ongoing enquiry, DG XXI provided the meeting and translation facilities and reimbursed travel costs. The Matthaeus Program, operational since the early 1990s, offered numerous forms of joint training seminars and short term exchanges between operational border staff.

If one can speak today of coordinated EU border management in the customs rather than in the immigration/police field, this can also be attributed to an important resource factor: the EU allows national administrations to keep 10 percent, and since March 2002 even 25 percent, of the revenues they collect in customs duties, agricultural levies etc in order to finance their border infrastructure (Council of the European Union 2000). Financing is also available for joint operational activities along the external border through various programs such as INTERREG, TACIS, PHARE, CARDS, MEDA, in each case depending on the geographical context.

In conclusion, one can say that EU customs—although traditionally less in the ramp light than immigration and police services—have always been about 10 years ahead of their counterparts. In some aspects, it is quite evidently already done, in others it should be suggested to be done to a greater extent: that Schengen learns from the experience already made in the customs field.

The Schengen tools

The birth of 'Schengenland' occurred under much less favourable conditions than that of its customs counterpart. There was no straightforward Community policy backing it up politically and financially during the early days in the mid-1980s. Its initial motivations do not even seem clear, i.e., whether it was intended to be a security convention or a border control system (Boettcher 2000). Some suggest that it represented an ad hoc approach by police departments to resolve the problem of hot pursuit and certain isolated forms of crime (see 'Schengen and Europe' n.d.), which was subsequently enlarged to cover the wider issue of immigration. This view finds some support, for example in the aleatory fashion in which the 1990 Schengen Convention confined cross-border action to the sole crime areas of firearms and drugs.

In any case, Schengen represented a reaction of public security to the ever closer economic community: although the old internal borders were still in place, their efficiency was decreasing. Steadily growing transborder movements of goods and persons did not allow any longer for thorough routine checks, especially since the border authorities were not exempted from the downsizing of staff that occurred throughout the entire public sector during this period. With the predominance of economic objectives, there was also no question of slowing down traffic flows in order to achieve higher security standards.[11]

---

[11] This is clearly demonstrated by the evolving (Richtwerte) imposed on border staff: if there was a 1:1 relation between crossborder movements and controls in the pre-World War II times, this relation decreased in the post-war period to 1:10, 1:100.

New control philosophies emerged during these times: an issue frequently discussed in enforcement fora (Interpol) was the superiority of so-called 'hot finds' (detection of infringements on the basis of tip-offs or intelligence) over 'cold finds' (detection via routine checks). The techniques of risk assessment and targeting of suspects were also born. A further means of increasing efficiency was seen in the pooling of control and intelligence resources with the forces of neighbouring countries.

Schengen was a reply by 'sharp-end-practitioners' to a situation that had no direct coverage from any of the Community policies: the still existing reticence of Member States towards all forms of EC/EU involvement in the co-ordination process left no other solution but going the extra-Community path from the grass-roots. Nevertheless the central idea was clear: if European integration did not leave but one single border to filter out unwanted intrusions, the chances for success would be higher if the efforts of all control and enforcement services were pooled. The idea of 'integrated border management', used in the 2002 Border Communication, was born.

The concept: integration of what?

Basically, Schengen incorporates two different approaches: (1) to ensure that checks and surveillance at the external border are governed by common uniform principles (Schengen Convention 1990) (immigration aspect); and (2) to prevent criminals from taking undue advantage of the borderless area for *internal* escape (police aspect). It is evident that the police aspect mainly deals with action across internal borders (removed for the traveller but, in principle, not yet for police): hot pursuit, controlled delivery, apprehension, mutual legal assistance. Item (2) will therefore be left aside in this analysis—except for the bridge between both 'worlds' provided by Article 101 (1)(a) Schengen Convention, according to which the control authorities have the 'right to consult all data entered in SIS' and thus make the external border operate as barrage or filter from the point of internal security (Commission of the European Communities 2002, paragraph 9).

The Schengen external border rules

These rules, laid down in the 1990 Convention and spelt out in more detail by the Common Manual for External Borders, include the following:

- Crossing of borders is to occur only at (determined) border crossing points and during the fixed opening hours (Art. 3);

In the late-1980s, German customs still maintained the rule that one out of 100 containers should be thoroughly checked. This principle was abandoned soon after.

- Maximum stay of foreigners in common area is not to exceed 3 months; aliens representing a 'threat to public policy, national security or international relations of any' Schengen member is to be refused entry (Art. 5);
- Checks and surveillance are to have a Schengen-wide dimension: checking must be (a) systematic, (b) equivalent all along the external border and (c), although 'within the scope of national powers and national law, take account of the interests of all parties' (Art. 6). Especially the latter condition requires a genuine balancing act from the implementing authorities, i.e., to perform a non-harmonised international task with strictly national means. It is probably here where Schengen encounters its major practical difficulties.

A recent tool provides some limited help in this field, i.e., the 'EU Schengen Catalogue' which contains a collection of recommendations and best practises,[12] but of course cannot advise border officials of the more refined aspects of public order etc in various member countries. There are also some important ancillary provisions:

- Liability of carriers (Art. 26) and liability of those providing assistance to unlawful immigration for lucrative purposes (Art. 27);
- Horizontal provisions such as Articles 92–101 provide competent authorities with online and real-time access to the Schengen Information System (SIS). Its database, as the technical centrepiece of the entire Schengen construction, contains so-called 'alerts', i.e., a listing of certain aliens to whom entry is to be refused. Article 96 obliges, in particular, consular authorities to check SIS before issuing a visa;
- The involvement of consular authorities in the 'filtering process' as well as that of carriers represents a system of 'remote control' (Guiraudon 2002) in avoiding unwanted migration flows. It is based on earlier US experience (1902 Passenger Act, 1924 Immigration Act);
- From a theoretical point of view, these provisions ensure smooth operation of the system, all the more as there is a permanent control for the evaluation of border performance: SCEIS—the Standing Committee on the Evaluation and Implementation of Schengen (Schengen Executive Committee 1998).[13] SCEIS serves to (1) evaluate

---

[12] Adopted by the Council on 28.2.2002.
[13] The crucial role of SCEIS was reconfirmed by the Protocol integrating the Schengen *acquis* into the EU (cf. Council of the European Union 1999, p.30). From a critical point of view, it is noted that (1) SCEIS is not entitled to conduct unannounced visits, and (2) its evaluation reports do not give rise to any direct consequences such as penalties or financial/operational assistance.

new Member States in preparation of a Council decision to integrate them fully into the Schengen acquis; and (2) check whether existing Member States are implementing the *acquis* properly (e.g., France during the first quarter of 2002).

Weaknesses and Stumbling Blocks

Nevertheless, a number of weaknesses still represent major stumbling blocks and motivated the Laeken Summit, Commission and Council to urge for improvements.

Legal diversity

Despite all the co-ordination mechanisms, the basic problem remains the 'balancing act' between strictly national means and the multi-national task that Schengen imposes on all participating administrations while scrupulously respecting the diverse internal systems. It is the assessment of all involved that the border officials in many cases interpret security threats as well as SIS alerts on the basis of their national criteria rather than those of other Member States possibly concerned. This is no surprise and it would require over-exaggerated staff requirements if one would expect average officials to perform this extremely complex task. This situation is not going to change; on the contrary:

- The Council decisions integrating the legislative and operational Schengen *acquis* in the EU framework expressly maintain the separation between first and third Pillar aspects of that *acquis*, thus excluding that more coherent rules will be found in the short term.
- The internal legal orders of Member States remain outside the scope of fast track first Pillar legislation: legislative approximation under the 3rd Pillar advances rather slowly.
- With two non-EU members (Norway, Iceland) already participating and two more waiting for entry (Switzerland and Liechtenstein), diversity is likely to increase

Lack of resources, lack of burden-sharing

Different from the customs sector, Schengen members still obtain no compensation from the EU for ensuring border security; most costs must be covered by national budgets. This necessarily leads to safety deficits along the border depending on the resource potential of the Member States concerned. In the current EU, wealth and resource levels are still relatively balanced (GDP per capita lies mostly between 20,000 and 25,000 USD), with the new members envisaged, this will be drastically different, their average GDP per capita ranging between 8,000 and 10,000 USD.

Not only does the overall quality of equipment and training suffer where resources are low, but it will also be difficult to reach a certain degree of convergence in the equipment and training sector, such as has been put forward as a target by successive presidencies in the Council (Commission of the European Communities 2002, paragraph 18; Council of the European Union 2001a, paragraph 40). In addition, low income levels make public service more susceptible to risks of unreliability and corruption. So far no budgetary remedy is in sight that is similar to that available to EU customs administrations which receive a 25 percent share of the duties and other Community resources they collect.

Lack of a Schengen-wide training dimension

As a direct consequence of the suffering budgetary situation, Schengen border officials also lack a direct source of coherent training appropriate to their Schengen role.

Again to contrast: the Matthaeus (and successor) training campaigns have enabled thousands of customs officers since the early 1990s to become acquainted with the working methods and best practices of their counterparts. This includes joint training courses and short term exchanges (similar to that of the Erasmus program for students). Evaluation has always been extremely positive and the additional skills acquired represent but one benefit: most of the participating customs officers praise the personal contacts gained which facilitate future interagency co-operation along the border.

True enough, Article 7 of the Schengen Convention already foresees a bilateral exchange of liaison officers which serves *inter alia* to 'further training of officers manning checkpoints'. But the bilateral dimension prevents this exchange from happening on a large scale and thus from having the hoped for Schengen-wide effect.

Intermediate conclusion

There is no doubt that Schengen represents a venture in some way underprivileged in time, resources and legislative backing in comparison to its customs 'border colleague'. Police and immigration have come a long way during the past ten years, at a time when EU customs were already firmly established. There are certain advantages like the firm roots of customs in the first Pillar, majority vote legislation which Schengen border management will not be able to make up at short term. Nevertheless, a number of options remain which promise to make the border a reliable place.

The Road to Progress: Towards Common Border Management and the European Border Guard

The Commission and Council thoroughly explored the terrain in preparation for their 2002 initiatives and found that not all possible roads to better border management are equally viable. Some require profound ground works and must be eliminated for the short- and mid-term at least. In wise recognition of the prevailing political and legal situation, most proposals focus on the practical operational field

Legal order: item of minor action (Commission of the European Communities 2002, paragraphs 22–26; Council of the European Union 2001a, paragraphs 109–114).

One of the marathon tasks that are effectively out of reach would certainly consist in the profound remodelling of the legal landscape as would be required if one wished to eliminate the principle cause of the border guard dilemma. Given the previous JHA history that started from scratch half a generation ago, it would be premature and presumptuous to expect a radical change within the next 10–20 years, to harmonise or considerably approximate the 15 or more legal systems that Schengenland embraces.

Accordingly, both plans attributed a low profile to the general harmonisation aspect. They did not envisage, for the short- and mid-term, any profound changes of legislation, but rather advice and recommendation.

Rather than tackling formal legislation, they proposed to develop or recast certain practical manuals, such that they should obtain a certain legal status. The title 'Common Corpus of Legislation' does not appear fully appropriate for this section.

Short-term

- Recast the 'Common Manual on Checks at the External Border' (CMCEB);
- Add to CMCEB a section 'Best Practices' regarding all aspects of practical border management (organisation, infrastructure, staff, training etc);
- Develop a 'Practical Handbook' for border guards, to be available in electronic form. This publication would cover the same subjects as the 'Best Practices' compendium but be held in a more colloquial tone;
- Identify principles and adopt common measures on 'local border traffic'.

Mid-term

- Add new standards to the 'measures on the crossing of the external borders' (Art. 62(2)(a) TEC);
- Develop a formalised process of data/information exchange/processing between border and inland authorities;
- Determine powers possibly to be conferred to the European Corps of Border Guards/ECBG [COM];
- Determine possible geographical area of action for ECBG [COM];
- Envisage legal framework for a genuine inspection function [COM];
- Provide for financing of this policy on the basis of Art. 66 TEC (administrative co-operation).

The most important progress made in this area by mid-2005 concerned the Commission proposal for a European Border Code (Commission of the European Communities 2004), which would 'clarify, restructure, consolidate and develop rules on border controls on persons' developed within the Schengen intergovernmental framework, in particular the Common Manual (CMCEB).

Mechanism for co-ordination and co-operation

The centrepiece of this mechanism was intended to be the 'External borders practitioners common unit' (EBPCU) (Commission of the European Communities 2002, paragraphs 28–32; Council of the European Union 2001a, paragraphs 44–50), a forum composed of managers from the operational level (as opposed to a political forum, which is avoided). Due to its mixed attendance from visa (Art. 62, 63 TEC) and enforcement authorities such as police, customs, justice (Art. 61 (e), 62(1) TEC), this new body would provide a multidisciplinary approach; it would formally not require a new structure as it could grow out of the current SCIFA[14] group.

In view of the difficulties foreseen in the legislative field, the hope is that the EBPCU—on the basis of the reputation of the 'wise men' there assembled—will be able to establish a certain set of rules to be respected by all parties although there may be no legal obligation arising.

EBPCU's remit would be to (1) organise concrete joint action in border surveillance/control (Art. 66), and (2) exercise an inspection function over the various border authorities.

By mid-2005, the EBPCU-concept was replaced by the more pragmatic solution of a European Border Agency (EBA), established on 1 May 2005 with seat in Warsaw and the Finnish border guard Colonel Ilkka Laitinen as executive director. The agency is based on Community law (Council of the

---

[14] SCIFA stands for Strategic Committee for Immigration, Frontiers and Asylum.

European Union 2004), financed from the Community budget and will eventually have a staff of 100 officials. The agency does not exercise any direct operational tasks but it has far-reaching competences in coordinating training, joint operations, equipment policies, and will carry out risk analyses etc. It is expected that EBA, with a growing need for operational assistance, will develop into a body not too different from the European Border Guard originally intended.

In addition, there would be an exchange mechanism called 'Permanent process of data/information exchange and processing' (Commission of the European Communities 2002, paragraphs 33–35) not confined to any specific means of information but representing a 'process or code of conduct' under a special security procedure (Prosecure). Its purpose would be to deal appropriately with all sensitive information.

Common integrated risk analysis

This important mechanism designed to measure current risks and keep them under permanent observation would be set up under the supervision of the EBPCU. It would need to identify risks upstream (in third countries) and downstream (inside Schengen) from the external border as well as on the border itself (Commission of the European Communities 2002, paragraphs 38–39).

Staff and equipment (Commission of the European Communities 2002, paragraphs 40–44).

This item should promote a greater complementarity in national staff, staff training and equipment policies. It is to gradually reduce quantitative and qualitative disparities which are likely to create security distortions. Training would encompass the concept of a 'Common syllabus for the training of border guards', whereas the idea of a 'European Border Guards College' appears only as a far away vision. As regards equipment, the objective would be to identify a common policy on fixed and mobile border infrastructures, especially for the time when the new Member States are admitted to fully participate in the Schengen *acquis*. This may equally involve the use of advanced technology (e.g., satellite radio navigation) to supervise borders in a particularly difficult terrain. A specific feature should be that of interoperability, so that the equipment may easily be transferred to another section of the border without any compatibility problems.

Burden-sharing and the European Corps of Border Guards

As has been shown in the previous parts of this article, border conditions and the resource requirements for control and surveillance are extremely variable. Moreover, with the growing size of EU and Schengen, the share of the external border remaining for each member is subject to increasing imbalances, whereas neither in the short- nor even mid-term will there be a definite convergence between old and new members as regards living conditions and economic performance. Finally, the newcomers with few resources and no experience in EU or Schengen border management will shoulder the greater share of a more difficult borderline to protect. Burden-sharing thus emerges as an item of crucial importance for the benefit of the entire operation.

Nevertheless, the Commission Communication on border management tackled this issue with utmost delicacy, well aware that this was still old 3rd Pillar terrain and therefore particularly sensitive regarding any Community initiatives perceived as too far-reaching.

Basic burden-sharing options

The Commission plan recalls that, 'of course', Member States' budgets would remain the 'principle resources affected in border management' (as if their main concern should be to remain in charge of the financial burden) (Commission of the European Communities 2002, paragraph 46; Council of the European Union 2001a, paragraph 116). However, given the striking disparities in bearing the border burden, it is recalled that it would be in the interest of the Member States less burdened 'to take part in the joint protection effort'.

Practically speaking, a first redistribution of resources should take place via Article 66 TEC allowing the Council to take 'measures to ensure co-operation between the relevant departments' relating to the free movement of persons, as well as the EU ARGO programme already adopted in June 2002 (Council of the European Union 2002b).

Both options are subject to limitations: ARGO has an annual allocation of not more than 25 million Euro to be shared with areas such as the issuance of visas and the operation of the European asylum system. The Council decision itself calls it a 'modest forerunner' of more extensive activities to come (para 3). Measures under Article 66 TEC in turn still require a unanimous Council decision for adoption and thus encompass a certain unpredictability.

By all means financial contributions via bilateral agreements between the Member States should be avoided because they risk to become 'too complex and inequitable' (Commission of the European Communities 2002, paragraph 46).

An important factor of burden-sharing was seen, according to the Commission, in the PHARE programme for the future EU members which allocated important sums to various aspects of border management, notably under the JHA and cross-border headers (see PHARE Programme Types). However, these allocations ended with the accession in 2004.

European Corps of Border Guards—The Vision

The future ECBG, whose intended 'support function' towards national services is underlined, should work along the following lines (Paragraphs 48, 50):

- initially, handle only surveillance functions (possibly at the maritime border, where co-operation seems to be least developed at this stage), and switch to checking at crossing points only later;
- consist of staff having the prerogatives of public authority to perform these functions, irrespective of their nationality and their place of deployment.

This is a central question relating to 'constitutional grounds', as the Commission paper admits and which may not find a solution at short term.

However, certain conclusions can be drawn from bilateral/multilateral tests already performed by the Member States on the basis of the Seville Plan: according to the German Ministry of the Interior (Centre Land Borders, Berlin), a first joint operation (3–13 December 2002) on the German–Polish border, together with officials from Greece, Italy and the UK, involved 'Greek and Italian colleagues who were bestowed with executive powers, carrying out checks and controls (they stopped vehicles, asked for the requested documents and made S.I.S. checks).' There was no mention of any complicated procedures involved (Centre Land Borders 2002).

On the whole, the following functions would need to be fulfilled:

1. check identity documents, visa etc of persons crossing the border legally or illegally;
2. question aliens on the reasons of their stay or border crossing;
3. board ships and question the captain;
4. notify admission/refusal of entry to EU territory;
5. apprehend a person and hand him/her over to the competent national authorities;
6. be placed under the operational command of EBPCU. For the time being, recruitment of staff would be in form of temporary secondment from the Member States. In case of crisis, this 'nucleus' could be rapidly supplemented by a pool of national staff ('reservists'), mobilised by the EBPCU;
7. respect the powers of local authorities in matters not covered by Title IV (free movement of persons) or X TEC (customs). Even the exercise of the functions mentioned under point 2 above would need to be territorially confined, possibly a strip of 'several hundred metres of the land border and a portion of the territorial water';
8. be open at all hierarchical levels to any national of an EU Member State, provided he satisfies the requirements. This element will be of

paramount importance for the value-added of the ECBG—only when this body becomes detached from individual nationalities regardless of the part of the external border concerned, and takes advantage of the skills and motivation offered by a truly European staff, will this operation succeed. One should recall that this mobility is a quality that has always been required by the US Federal border services: 'It's law enforcement on a nationwide scale...from coast to coast, border to border' (US Customs recruitment message, February 2003);

9. have at its disposal equipment chosen by EBCPU and financed from the Community budget. This could avoid difficult balancing acts between national and EU interests.

From the few elements now known, one could draw the pessimistic conclusion that, given all the constitutional, sovereignty and national pride-related elements involved, Schengen and the EU will need another 50 years to make this new force operational. However, things may turn out differently: experience from other EU-related ventures have shown that pragmatic undertakings have often proved more successful than expected. Practice seems to overcome legal and other problems rather than the other way round.

It would therefore seem to have been a wise decision by the EU institutions to launch the border guard project before attempting to complete the Sisyphean task of establishing the 'Common Corpus of Legislation'. EU enforcement practitioners, as evidenced by almost 50 years of customs history, have always tended to tackle problems in a direct and pragmatic way; seemingly complicated problems of competence and legal form have at times dissipated like the morning fog in the sun, and appropriate legislative amendments were subsequently adopted.

Moreover, the ECBG project seems promising even in a landscape of still scattered legal orders: the combined skills of officials from the various countries would be capable of mastering not only the linguistic but also law-related problems that often exist in the practical application of the Schengen *acquis*. The greater impartiality of an EU 'federal' force may also be an advantage in managing a flexible border regime as is envisaged for parts of the eastern border.

By mid-2005, one can retrospectively state that the ECBG concept—although it did not materialise in its purest form envisaged—has lived on, finding a more modest implementation in the European Border Agency, which has been in place since May 2005. Although EBA has no direct operational function and for the time being there will be no guards with an EU uniform patrolling Europe's borders, the concept of burden-sharing between the Member States will become a matter of daily routine. It is even expected that EBA will relatively soon be requested by national services to play a greater operational role in border security, notably at hotspots of migratory movements. This could take the form of so-called rapid reaction forces composed of border officials from various EU Member States.

In order to further support this positive outlook, it seems reasonable to look at two forms of multi-national, border-related co-operation which have already accumulated a certain amount of practical experience:

Model 1: Joint French–German Centre of Police and Customs Co-operation, Kehl (Germany)

This centre, operating since 1998 as a Joint Investigative Team in the framework of Art. 34 (2)(b) TEU, Art. 47 Schengen Convention 1990 and on the basis of a bilateral agreement between France and Germany,[15] has a remit that is quite different from the future border guard. The Kehl Centre is (1) a specific enforcement structure (third Pillar) dealing with prevention and investigation of crime; and (2) situated on an internal border. Nevertheless, the experience gained in intra-EU and multi-agency co-operation is considered to be extremely useful. The Centre houses no less than 8 different agencies, some of which had no previous experience in inter-agency co-operation, not even on the national level.

The services are on the French side: *Gendarmerie nationale*, *Police nationale* (whereby the latter regroups three further sub-services, i.e., *Police de l'air et des frontières*, judicial police of the Strasbourg region with competence in 3 departments—Haut-Rhin, Bas-Rhin and Moselle—as well as the general police (*Sûreté publique*) of Strasbourg and *Douane française* (customs). On the German side it is: *Bundesgrenzschutz* (Federal Border Police), *Landespolizei* (State Police Forces) of Baden-Württemberg, *Landespolizei* of Rheinland-Pfalz and Saarland, and *Bundeszollverwaltung* (Customs). There is a joint 'coordinatorship' by Kriminaloberrat Belle (State Police BW) and Commissaire divisionnaire Willem (*Police nationale*).

All parties involved are full of praise for the smooth working procedures developed: the number of cross-border requests, including observations, has been rising steadily (8350 in 2001, and 9044 in 2002). On 10 February 2003, the ministers of both countries inaugurated the new and enlarged headquarters, calling this 'a milestone in security co-operation' (Bundesgrenzschutz 2003).

A number of similar centres have sprung up all over the EU since then:

- JC Luxembourg (Luxembourg/Belgium/Germany)
- CCPD Tournai (France/Belgium)
- CCPD Modane (France/Italy)
- CCPD Ventimiglia (France/Italy)
- CCPD Le Perthus (France/Spain)
- There is even one on Swiss territory: JC Geneva (Switzerland/France)

---

[15] Mondorf Agreement of 6.10.1997.

Others are planned, also on the borders with future members:

- JC Maas-Rhine (Germany/Belgium/Netherlands)
- JO Nickelsdorf (Austria/Hungary)
- JO Lingen (Germany/Netherlands)
- JC Frankfurt/Oder (Germany/Poland)
- JC Padburg (Germany/Denmark)
- JC Timisoara (Romania/Hungary)
- JC Galati (Romania/Ukraine/Moldavia)

Model 2: Multilateral Patrols on the External Border, Frankfurt/Oder (Germany)

In December 2002, a first joint border patrol[16] was carried out during 10 days on the German border with Poland. The tasks of the ad hoc force—host officers from German BGS together 2 police officers from Greece, 8 from Italy (Greeks and Italians were bestowed with public authority) and 7 UK immigration officers (without public authority)—included surveillance of the 'green border' as well as the stopping of vehicles, passport checks and interviews at border crossings. Acts of public authority were carried out, on equal footing, by the German, Greek and Italian colleagues, whereas the UK colleagues stood by 'in second line'.

Here again, results were positive and the local officers seemed convinced that the work with pooled resources (in particular linguistic skills and privileged contacts to the home authorities of the guest officers) were an important asset.

Conclusion

Although a coherent and homogeneous European area of freedom, security and justice combined with a common customs territory is not immediately in sight, signs are quite promising that the external borders of the EU and Schengenland will increasingly be under the joint protection of forces from all Member States.

This burden-sharing will not only be more equitable from the financial perspective and more reliable from the security point of view; in accordance with previous experience in the history of the EU, such a pragmatic approach may also prove to be a forerunner to a thorough legal framework for European 'federal' border management.

---

[16] Based on Art. 7 of the Schengen Convention and the spirit of Art. 66 of the TEC

References

BOETTCHER, DANIEL. 2000. 'The Impossibility of Schengen: A Multi-Level Game Analysis of the State of Refugees and Asylum in the European Union'. The Online Journal of Peace and Conflict Resolution, 2.5 (3.1). Available at URL: <www.trinstitute.org/ojpcr/3_1boettcher.htm>

BUNDESGRENZSCHUTZ. 2003. Press release of 10 February 2003.

CENTRE LAND BORDERS. 2002. Unpublished report.

CIA. 2002. *World Factbook 2002*.

COMMISSION OF THE EUROPEAN COMMUNITIES. 2002. Commission Communication of 7 may 2005, Paragraphs 9-114.

_____ 2004. COM (2004)391 final of 26 May 2004

'CONVENTION IMPLEMENTING THE SCHENGEN AGREEMENT'. 2000. *Official Journal of the European Union*, L 239, 22 September 2000.

COUNCIL OF THE EUROPEAN COMMUNITIES. 1987. 'Council Regulation (EEC) No 945/87 of 30 March 1987 amending Regulation (EEC) No 1468/81 on mutual assistance between the administrative authorities of the Member States and co-operation between the latter and the Commission to ensure the correct application of the law on customs or agricultural matters'. *Official Journal of the European Union*, L 90/3, 2 April 1987.

COUNCIL OF THE EUROPEAN UNION. 1981. 'Council Regulation (EEC) No 1468/81 of 19 May 1981'. *Official Journal of the European Union*, L 144.

_____ 1997. 'Council Act 98/C 24/01 of 18 December 1997'. *Official Journal of the European Union*, C 24 (23 January 1998).

_____ 1997. 'Council Regulation 515/97', Title V.

_____ 1997. 'Council Regulation 515/97', Article 23 (3).

_____ 1999. 'Council Decision 1999/435/EC'. *Official Journal of the European Union*, L 176.

_____ 2000. 'Council Decision 2000/597/EC'.

_____ 2002a. 'Council Plan for the management of the external borders (Doc. 10019/2).

_____ 2002b. 'Council Decision of 13 June 2002', *Official Journal of the European Union*, L 161 (19 June 2002).

_____ 2004. 'Council Regulation (EC) No 2007/2004 of 26 October 2004'. *Official Journal of the European Union*, L 349 (25 November 2004).

EUROPEAN COUNCIL. 2001. Conclusion no.42 of the Laeken European Council of 14 and 15 December 2001.

FEHÉRVÁRY, J. 2001. 'Europäisierung der Polizeiarbeit'. In Fehérváry and Stangl (eds) *Polizei zwischen Europa und den Regionen*. WUV Vienna.

'Glossary Justice and Home Affairs'. Website of the European Commission: Justice and Home Affairs Section . Available at URL: (Accessed 2 May 2006)
<http://europa.eu.int/comm/justice_home/glossary/wai/glossary_c_en.htm

GUIRAUDON, V. 2002. 'Controlling the EU border By Proxy ? The Delegation of Migration Control in Practice' 13th International Conference of Europeanists: New Approaches to the Study of Immigration, Chicago, 14–17 March 2002.

PEEK, J. 1994. 'International Police Cooperation Within Justified Political and Judicial Frameworks: Five Thesis on TREVI'. In *The Third Pillar of the European Union*, eds., J. Monar. and R. Morgan, 201–207. Brussels: European Interuniversity Press.

'Phare Programme Types: The National Programmes'. Website of the European Commission: Enlargement Section. Available at URL: <http://europa.eu.int/comm/enlargement/pas/phare/programmes/index.htm>

'Schengen and Europe: History of Schengen and Why it Developed'. Available at URL:
<http://www.ex.ac.uk/politics/pol_data/undergrad/rich/hist.htm>

SCHENGEN CONVENTION. 1985.

SCHENGEN CONVENTION. 1990.

SCHENGEN EXECUTIVE COMMITTEE. 1998. 'SCH/Com-ex (98) 26', *Official Journal of the European Union*, L 239 (22 September 2000).

SCHUMAN ROBERT. 1950. Speech delivered on 9 May 1950.

'Treaty of Rome'. 1957. URL: <http://www.bmdf.co.uk/rometreaty.pdf>

'The Treaty of Amsterdam'. 1997. *Official Journal of the European Union*, C 340/01, 10 November 1997.

Chapter 10

The Project of a European Border Guard: Origins, Models and Prospects in the Context of the EU's Integrated External Border Management

Jörg Monar

The creation of a common European Border Guard can surely be regarded as one of the most advanced and ambitious projects which has so far emanated from the discussion on the future development of the European Union (EU) as an 'area of freedom, security and justice'. It would be the most radical answer to the question of burden-sharing at external borders in the enlarged EU and presents formidable challenges in terms of its political feasibility, potential implications for national sovereignty and practical organisation. It is not surprising, therefore, that this idea has met a rather mixed reception both inside and outside of the EU Council.

After clarifying the historical and political background of the project of a European Border Guard this contribution will evaluate its potential and different models, addressing also the issue of democratic accountability. This will be followed by an analysis of recent progress made with the development of an integrated EU external border management from the Council Action Plan of June 2002 to the setting up of the EU External Borders Agency in May 2005, asking to what extent these are potential steps towards the creation of a European Border Guard.[1]

Political Background

Co-operation between EU Member States regarding issues of external border security started in a systematic way in the second half of the 1980s within the Schengen context. The objective of a full abolition of controls at internal borders between the Schengen countries was laid down by the Schengen Agreement of 14 June 1985. It was, to a large extent, based on the idea that

---

[1] Part of the information used for this contribution is based on the author's work as a specialist adviser to Sub-Committee F of the European Union Select Committee of the British House of Lords and cannot be attributed.

common standards, procedures and even certain common instruments—such as the Schengen Information System (SIS)—at external borders, should compensate for the 'loss' of controlling possibilities at internal borders. The Schengen system, when finally implemented in 1995, created de facto a single internal security zone encompassing all Schengen members in which the absence of any internal border controls meant that the external border parts of each individual Schengen member became a matter of common concern. Over the years the Schengen members have, therefore, not only further extended the corpus of common standards and procedures aimed at a high level of external border security, most of them laid down in the Schengen 'Border Manual', but also increased the sharing of information on border security relevant issues (not exclusively through the SIS) and other forms of co-operation such as the posting of liaison agents, common training projects and occasional co-ordinated or joint operations.

In the context of the completion of the Internal Market there was also a move in the EC as a whole towards increased co-operation on external border security issues, involving Ireland and the United Kingdom, in spite of their non-participation in Schengen. However, this move suffered a major setback in 1991 (and again in 1993) when the proposed EC external frontiers convention failed to be adopted, mainly because of the British–Spanish differences over Gibraltar. Yet this neither prevented the Member States from developing further bilateral and multilateral co-operation on border security issues (such as, the Franco–British co-operation on controls in the Channel area), nor from agreeing on a number of common EU texts on external border issues. These included the recommendations on effective control practices at external border for applicant countries (1997) and on the provision of forgery detection equipment at borders (1998). The launching of the 'Odysseus' programme in 1998, which allowed for common training measures, exchanges and studies in the area of external border crossings and controls, marked a further step towards a common EU approach beyond the limits of the Schengen group.

At the end of the 1990s a number of factors created an even more favourable context for an EU-wide common approach to external border security. Of primary importance was the entry into force of the Treaty of Amsterdam in 1999, which finally led to the incorporation of the Schengen system into the EU—with a continuing opt-out for Ireland and the United Kingdom, but an obligation for all newly acceding Member States to adopt the Schengen *acquis* in full. The Treaty also offered extended possibilities for the Union to act on external border issues. Yet there were also other favourable factors such as the increasing inclusion of external borders into EU strategies for the fight against cross-border crime and illegal immigration from the Tampere European Council of October 1999 onwards, mounting common concerns over security at the new post-enlargement external borders and, last but not least, the British and Irish opt-in into parts of the Schengen *acquis* since 1999.

The Emergence of the European Border Guard Project and its Different Models

With the big eastward enlargement fast approaching, it became clearer to EU Member States during 2000–2001 that the external border control capabilities of the future new Member States were not going to fulfil EU/Schengen standards by the time of accession in 2004, and that substantial EU help would be needed well beyond the time of accession. There were also more general concerns about external border security as an important instrument in the fight against illegal immigration and the various forms of cross-border crime. This was later reinforced by the events of 11 September 2001 and the effort to reduce terrorist risks, also through enhanced border controls. In spite of their common standards and procedures the Schengen countries were also acutely aware that differences in national legislation and administrative practice was causing security discrepancies between sections of external borders controlled by the different Member States. Persisting differences in interpretation of the rules on SIS alerts, for instance, affect both the efficiency and homogeneity of Schengen external border management.

All this led several Member States to give support to the idea of setting up a common European service for the safeguarding of EU external borders. The main arguments in favour of such a move were that it would provide an instrument of solidarity for sharing the burden of controlling external borders in the enlarged Union and allow for a better use of personnel and technical resources, as well as of available expertise, while at the same time marking a step forward for political integration. After the idea of creating a 'European Border Police' had been brought up in the Council by a joint initiative of Germany and Italy at the beginning of 2001, in October 2001 a group of countries including Belgium, France, Germany, Spain, and led by Italy embarked on a feasibility study on such a European Border Police, backed by the European Commission and financed on an 80 percent basis under the Odysseus-Programme (Bundesministerium des Innern 2002). Other Member States, including the UK, shared the view that more co-operation on external border issues was needed, but expressed reservations about the idea of creating a European Border Police corps.

The Laeken European Council of 14–15 December 2001 arrived at a carefully worded compromise on co-operation regarding external border issues. It gave the Council and the European Commission a mandate to work out 'arrangements for co-operation between services responsible for external border control and to examine the conditions in which a mechanism or common services to control external borders could be created' (Council of the European Union 2001)[2] The terms 'European Border Police' or 'European Border Guard', although already used by some Member States' governments,

---

[2] Conclusion No. 42 of the Laeken Council.

did not appear in the mandate.

In response to the Laeken mandate the European Commission presented on 7 May 2002 a Communication on the way 'towards an integrated management of external borders' to the Council and the European Parliament. Based on an analysis of the main challenges at external borders, and the current state of co-operation between Member States, this Communication proposed a gradual move towards an 'integrated management' of external borders, which would start with a consolidation and codification of common rules and standards for external border controls. It would continue, inter alia, with the creation of an 'External borders practitioners' common unit' and various other co-operation mechanisms, leading then to financial burden-sharing mechanisms, and, finally, to a 'European Corps of Border Guards'. The use of the term 'integrated management' by the Commission appeared doubly justified as the proposals were aimed at a progressive integration, both between the border security services of the different Member States, and between the different services in charge of external border security (border guard forces, customs, immigration services etc.).

The Commission placed a particular emphasis on enhancing operational synergies between services and on arriving at a more homogenous level of security at external borders. With its more long-term approach to the creation of a European Border Guard the Commission clearly made an effort to satisfy both the advocates and the sceptics of such a project, placing a lot of emphasis on the practical progress which could be achieved in various fields in the meantime. As all of the Member States could find substantial elements in the Communication which they were able to support, its reception was broadly positive, although several Member States did not agree with the Commission's view that integrated border management should ultimately lead to the creation of a European Border Guard Corps.

On 30 May 2002 the Italian-led feasibility study on the creation of a European Border Police was presented at a Ministerial Conference in Rome under the auspices of the Spanish Presidency (Feasibility study…2002). The feasibility study was based on the input of a number of national experts, most of whom tended to defend their national methods and organisational structures. This partially explains why the feasibility study—rather than coming out clearly for or against the creation of a European Border Police—advocated instead a complex network of national border police forces which would be linked by a number of important common elements. These would include 'centres' in different Member States specialising in different areas of border security expertise serving as 'knots' of the network, common units for special tasks (including a 'rapid response unit'), common risk assessment, a certain degree of financial burden-sharing and a common training curriculum.

While filled with detailed operational and organisational assessments and recommendations, the 'polycentric' network model proposed by the study was lacking in clarity, providing a mosaic of proposed structures and individual measures rather than a grand design. Even some of the participating Member

States were not fully satisfied, and a Brussels source seems even to have dismissed the entire study, rather harshly, as '80 pages of waffle' (Black and Carroll 2002). Yet in spite of its shortcomings the Italian feasibility study made it clear that there are indeed different possible models for a European Border Guard, which are ultimately based on different political concepts on how far 'integration' should go in the domain of external border controls. These models can be summarised as follows:

- The first model—which may be called the 'integrated force model'—would involve the creation, surely only in a longer-term perspective, of an integrated border guard force under the authority of the Council. It would have a common command structure and common training and equipment standards, financed through the EU budget. It would also be vested with full law enforcement powers at external borders, partially or (eventually) totally replacing national border police forces.
- The second model—which may be called the 'network model'—would mean the creation of a European Border Guard as a network of national border guard units. According to this model units would continue to exist as separate national forces, but they would be subject to common instructions issued by a Council body and based on common training and equipment standards. Certain parts of the national border guards could be trained and equipped to constitute a contingency reserve (or 'rapid response force') consisting of national units able to merge into joint units, and capable of being deployed at particular 'hot spots' at external borders upon request and approval by the Council body.

The first model would clearly be the most straightforward and efficient one from an organisational point of view, and would go furthest towards the creation of a comprehensive system of burden-sharing and mutual trust-building at external borders. Yet it would also be the most difficult to implement. The example of the establishment of the European police organisation, Europol— which after nearly a decade of development still does not have any operational powers—has shown how reluctant most Member States are to create any supranational body in the law enforcement field, and to confer law enforcement powers within their territory on officials from other Member States. This also applies to those Member States that would, in terms of burden-sharing, benefit most from the creation of such a force, (i.e., the new Central and Eastern European Member States). Having regained their full national sovereignty only at the end of the Cold War, most of these new Member States are wary of the creation of further supranational structures at the EU level restricting their sovereignty. A statement made by Colonel Marian Kasinski, Deputy Commander-in-Chief of the Polish Border Guard, in the context of an inquiry of the British House of Lords in 2003, that 'each one [i.e., country] should try to protect its own borders' is quite characteristic in this respect (House of Lords 2003).

Besides these fundamental political obstacles the integrated force model would necessitate substantial changes to national legislation, and in several countries even amendments to the constitution. The organisational difficulties would also be very considerable. An integrated force would need to be created through the merger of national forces, which up to now are marked by major differences in terms of tasks, structures, training and equipment. The language problems in an integrated border guard force consisting of officials from 25 different Member States could only be effectively resolved by agreement on one official language, which would, again, be politically quite sensitive and would require an unprecedented effort in language training.

The second 'network' model would clearly be more easy to implement as it would largely leave national forces legally and structurally untouched, bringing them, only gradually and to a limited extent, under a common regime of standards and procedures. Under the network model the creation of common structures is to be limited to: a steering body at the European level; a number of joint 'centres' for common analysis and co-ordination purposes; and the possibility of deploying specially earmarked units in joint operations as part of a 'rapid response force'. Although some organisational problems would also need to be resolved under a network model, especially as regards the creation and operation of the 'rapid response force', these would be on a much smaller scale than in the case of a permanent border guard force. The 'costs of change' imposed through gradual standardisation of training and equipment would overall be lower as separate national forces would remain the core elements of the system, and political resistance would, as a result, most likely be much more limited.

There are, however, also a number of specific problems with the network model of a European Border Guard. As separate national forces would continue to exist, the effectiveness of the network would heavily depend on all of these forces implementing external border control standards and procedures as uniformly as possible in line with the common guidelines issued by the Council body. The adoption of sufficiently precise, demanding, and timely common standards could turn out to be a major challenge in itself in an EU of 25 or more Member States.

An even bigger challenge would be to secure a sufficiently effective and uniform implementation of common standards, with national forces still being organised on different principles with different powers, different political and legal contexts and different cultures. With the principle being to base the network on existing national structures, Member States are most likely to resist any major changes to their national services in charge of border controls, especially if these are perceived to be costly and contrary to well established national traditions. It seems most unlikely, for instance, that a British government would wish to transform or replace its Immigration and Nationality Directorate (IND) to bring the British system closer to 'continental' models of border police forces. Major organisational cleavages would therefore continue to exist, affecting the effectiveness of the whole network.

Effective operational co-operation between the national forces would obviously be crucial for the success of a network European Border Guard. This would require a major effort in training, language learning and standardisation of equipment. The example of operation 'Ulysses' in the Western Mediterranean, which was partially impaired by language problems and incompatibilities between the participating ships' communication systems (*Independent* 2003), has shown how important and difficult to overcome these problems are. The standardisation and training efforts would require considerable pressure from the centre—raising again the question of sufficient political will—and substantial financial resources which would necessitate an effective system of burden-sharing through the EU budget if protracted negotiations over national contributions should be avoided.

Democratic Control and Accountability

The issue of democratic control and accountability seems a most appropriate one to address in a contribution prepared under the auspices of the Geneva Centre for the Democratic Control of Armed Forces. Yet this is clearly also an issue in its own right in the context of such a major political project because, whatever form of European Border Guard could eventually emerge, this structure is going to exercise public power at external borders—including the potential use of firearms—and will have to deal with persons, such as asylum seekers and illegal immigrants, who are particularly vulnerable from a fundamental rights perspective. The British NGO 'Justice' has already pointed out that, in contrast with Europol, a European Border Guard would most likely enjoy powers of a coercive nature, which is the basis of the NGO's 'extreme' concern regarding the protection of fundamental rights and adequate accountability in relation to operational activities of such a force (Justice 2003).

In terms of democratic control and accountability the first, 'integrated force' model would certainly pose quite fundamental challenges, as such a force with its own EU legal basis and competencies would most likely not be subject to any effective direct control by national parliaments. It is far from certain, however, that national governments would easily agree to make such a force fully subject to democratic control by the European Parliament, which has more often than not been regarded as a rival in control or even opponent (the traditional link between government and parliamentary majority not existing at the EU level). The example of Europol has shown that national governments tend to keep law enforcement authorities at the European level as far as possible outside the reach of the European Parliament. This could lead to a combination of weak national parliamentary control with non-existent European parliamentary control, which is clearly most undesirable in an area of law enforcement where the rights of individuals can be particularly vulnerable.

Yet the second, 'network force' model would also raise certain questions in terms of adequate democratic control and accountability. These apply, in particular, to the role of the Council body vested with the power to decide on common instructions for the 'network border guard'. While such a body would not be vested with any law enforcement powers, its instructions regarding common standards and joint operations could have a significant impact on control and law enforcement practices and operations at external borders requiring effective parliamentary control. As national parliaments would have no direct control over the adoption of these instructions, provision would need to be made for an adequate control by the European Parliament.

The June 2002 Action Plan and its Implementation

Differences over both the question of the actual need for a European Border Guard and the model to aim for resulted in the project losing some momentum after the presentation of the Italian feasibility study at the end of May 2002. Yet at the same time the Council had come under serious pressure to act on the external border security issues as, in their letter of 16 May 2002, Prime Ministers Tony Blair and José Maria Aznar, jointly called for more measures at external borders in the fight against illegal immigration in view of the June 2002 Seville European Council meeting intended to focus on illegal immigration. On 13 June 2002 the Council of Ministers agreed on a 'Plan for the management of the external borders of the Member States'. This took up most of the analysis and proposals of the Commission Communication, merging it only with some of the elements of the Italian-led feasibility study (such as the idea of creating a network structure) (Council of the European Union 2002). This Action Plan, which was then formally endorsed by the Seville European Council on 21–22 June 2002, was different from the Commission Communication mainly in that it placed distinctly less emphasis on common legislation and common financing in the field of border controls, and referred only in rather vague terms to a later 'possible decision' on the setting up of a European Corps of Border Guards, which would support but not replace national border police forces (Council of the European Union 2002). Instead the Plan, which is currently still in force, provides for a wide range of more immediate practical measures on 'integrated management' aimed at reinforcing operational co-ordination, common integrated risk analysis, measures on the side of training and equipment, the adoption of common minimum standards and enhanced burden-sharing between the Member States.

Overall the June 2002 Council Plan is clearly based on a very comprehensive concept of common EU external border management, aimed at an increasing synergy between the Member States' border guard services on a broad range of issues. Quite distinctive is its focus on measures of an operational rather than legal nature, which gives to the whole Plan a very 'pragmatic' orientation. On the basis of the 2002 Action Plan significant progress has been made towards the 'integrated management' of external borders through enhanced operational co-operation and co-ordination between national border guard forces, institutionalisation of the co-operation process regarding external borders, and burden-sharing in the domain of external border controls.

Regarding *operational co-operation*, there have been a considerable number of joint operations and projects (such as 'Ulysses', 'Triton', 'Rio III and IV', 'Nettuno I', 'Nettuno II', 'Semper Vigilia I' and 'Semper Vigilia II' in 2003 and 2004) in which land and/or sea border guard services from several Member States have participated. 'Nettuno II' and 'Semper Vigilia II' (both carried out in 2004) can be taken as examples of the active involvement of the new Member States in such operations: 'Nettuno II', which was targeted at illegal immigration by sea and involved units from Cyprus, Greece, France and the United Kingdom, was hosted by Cyprus, and Poland played a key role in the coordinated mixed team controls carried out in the context of 'Semper Vigilia II', alongside Germany, Italy, Austria and the United Kingdom. Although not always an unqualified success in terms of results, significant experiences have been gained as regards interoperability and co-ordination problems, co-operation mechanisms have been improved and the operations have helped to create new networks and better mutual understanding between participating forces. On the downside one has to mention that in all of these operations only some of the Member States have participated, that non-participating Member States have not always been kept effectively informed, and that the reporting and evaluation procedures have often not been effective (Council of the European Union, Presidency Report 2003).

In relation to *institutionalisation*, major steps forward have been taken, in particular with the creation of the Risk Analysis Centre (RAC) in Helsinki and the Ad-hoc Training Centre (ACT) in Vienna. On the basis of the Common Integrated Risk Analysis Model (CIRAM) the Helsinki centre has proven its value for both periodical reports on the border security risks situation—one under each Presidency—and the analysis of specific border security problems or border areas. The Member States submit each month written information to the RAC on investigations regarding networks of traffickers in human beings and the methods they are using, new routes used by traffickers and illegal immigrants, the use of fraudulent methods to obtain visa and the use of false documents (Council of the European Union, UK Delegation 2004).

The training modules of the Vienna Ad-hoc Centre for Border Guard Training have been instrumental in encouraging the practical approximation of control standards (especially customs and administrative standards) and in providing specific organisational, legal and linguistic knowledge to border guards engaged in multinational operations. The other centres—the Centre for Land Borders (CLB) in Berlin, the Air Borders Centre (ACB) in Rome, the Eastern Centre for Sea Borders (ECSB) in Piraeus (Greece) and the Western Centre for Sea Borders (WCSB) in Madrid—have mainly played a planning, co-ordination and supporting role for joint operations. Co-ordination and information exchange between these different structures has improved over time (Council of the European Union 2004). The centres have also started to work on common rules and procedures for the carrying out of joint operations.[3] Yet there are still many shortcomings, such as: the non-systematic application of the integrated risk analysis model; underdeveloped analytical capacities of the centres; the absence of more comprehensive common standards based training programme; and the fact that only a varying part of the Member States participates in the various centres.

As regards *burden-sharing* there has been a clear move towards financial solidarity, first with the introduction of the ARGO programme in 2002, whose financial framework for measures regarding the management of external borders was upgraded in 2004, and secondly with the introduction of the Euro 960 million Schengen facility for the new Member States (2004–2006). The ARGO project has been used primarily as a funding instrument for measures regarding external borders right from the start[4] and provides much of the funding for the above mentioned Centres. Yet the ARGO programme only provides for co-funding of 60 percent (in exceptional cases 80 percent), and with an overall ceiling for 2005 of just under Euro 6.7 million,[5] its overall financial envelope remains a rather modest one.[6]

In relation to the Schengen facility, it has to be noted that it is obviously only a temporary instrument which was part of a special accession deal for new Member States—especially Poland—with particularly heavy responsibilities at the new EU external borders. Burden-sharing can, of course, also take an operational form, and joint operations and the establishment of the new EU External Border Agency (see below) can also be regarded as a step towards institutionalised solidarity. The Hague programme on the strengthening of the area of freedom, security and justice, which was approved by the European Council on 4 November 2004, rightly stresses the importance of financial solidarity and—with the provision for the creation of a Community border management fund by the end of 2006—takes a further step in this direction.[7] In May 2005 the Commission proposed a total of Euro 2.152 billion

---

[3] See the last non-classified report on the activities of the ESBC, EU Council document 9469/04, 13 May 2004.

[4] In its First Annual Report on the implementation of the ARGO project (2002-2003) the Commission reported on page 4 that eight out of ten projects were dealing with external border security issues: <http://europa.eu.int/comm/justice_home/funding/argo/doc/annual_staff_working_argo_en.pdf)>.

[5] <See the Commission Work programme for ARGO 2005: http://europa.eu.int/comm/justice_home/funding/argo/doc/annual_work_programme_2005_en.pdf>

[6] See list of the projects funded in 2004: <http://europa.eu.int/comm/justice_home/funding/argo/doc/list_grants_awarded_2004_01_en.pdf>

[7] See paragraph 1.7.1. (pp. 14–15) of the Programme, EU Council document 16054/04, 13 December 2004.

for this fund over the period 2007–2013,[8] an impressive total, which will, however, be heavily dependent on the overall framework of the 2007–2013 Financial Perspective on which the European Council failed to reach agreement in June 2005.

Overall, the progress made with the implementation of the objectives set in the June 2002 Council Plan is quite impressive. However, five years ago few experts would have thought it likely that Member States would by now be carrying out joint patrolling operations in the Mediterranean, or work on the basis of a Common Risk Analysis Model. Driven at least partially by the challenges of border security in the enlarged EU, the Member States have clearly already gone quite some way in the direction of regarding EU external border controls as a common challenge requiring common action. While formally no step further has been taken towards the creation of a European Border Guard, the implementation of the 2002 Action Plan has led to the putting into place of at least some elements of the 'network model', especially regarding operational co-ordination and common training and risk assessment.

Yet in spite of the progress made, four major problems have also become apparent, which seriously limit the effectiveness of the EU's current 'integrated management' of external borders. The first problem is that there is quite clearly not a uniform level of commitment of Member States to the joint projects. In most cases only some of the Member States have participated in a given project and often enough some of them left it at a declaration of interest or even did not fully deliver what they promised. While this voluntary participation and flexibility in the implementation has the advantage of allowing different groups of Member States to explore different ways forward at the same time, it is clearly not optimal in terms of developing an EU common approach and drawing maximum benefits from the different know-how, capabilities and geographical situations of the Member States.

The second problem is that projects have often been introduced and carried out very much on an 'ad hoc' basis without a strategic plan or effective co-ordination. More often than not individual Member States have taken the lead on an individual project and carried it out together with interested partners without paying much attention to overlaps or potential synergy effects with other projects.

The third problem is the absence of a proper legal framework for seconding border guard officers to other Member States. In most cases it has limited their role in common operations to a mere observer status without any executive powers. As a result, even in cases where multinational teams have formally been created at external borders, these have in most cases remained 'national teams' from an operational perspective.

---

[8] See European Commission: The Hague Programme: 10 priorities […] 10. Financial Resources adequate to policy objectives, May 2005 <http://europa.eu.int/rapid/pressReleasesAction.do?reference=MEMO/05/230&format=HTML&aged=0&language=EN&guiLanguage=en>.

The fourth problem is funding difficulties. In many cases the availability of EU funding for co-operation projects has a major impact on the degree of their success. Projects may even not take off at all if no such funding is available. Yet currently these funding possibilities are limited to a small number of EU programmes and their mobilisation is subject to rather restrictive conditions and cumbersome procedures.

Varying standards and practices in the implementation of border controls also continue to be a major challenge. The Schengen countries have introduced a system of mutual evaluations of Member States on a rotating basis, based on questionnaires and multinational inspection missions. Yet these so-called Schengen evaluations normally allow the evaluated administrations plenty of time 'to get things right' before inspection missions arrive, and are only carried out at intervals of several years for the individual Member States, normally resulting in reports which are drafted in a rather careful and diplomatic language (European Parliament 2005).The reports also have no judicial follow-up and are kept confidential, so that the pressure generated by this peer review process has tended to be rather limited. The Hague Programme tries to address this deficit by providing for the supplementing of the existing Schengen evaluation system with a new supervisory mechanism which will also include unannounced visits.[9]

The New EU External Borders Agency

Some of the above problems, especially those on the co-ordination side, are going to be addressed by a new institution, which had just been established at the time of writing. Well aware of the need for better co-ordination and evaluation mechanisms and driven forward by a strong initiative from the Greek Presidency at the European Council in Thessaloniki in June 2003, the Member States agreed, on 16 October 2004, on the establishment of an Agency for the Management of Operational Co-operation at the External Borders (Treaty Establishing a Constitution for Europe 2004). The main tasks of the Agency—for which the acronym FRONTEX has been introduced—comprise: the co-ordination of operational co-operation of Member States in the field of external border controls; providing assistance to Member States in the training of national border guards (including the establishment of common training standards); the carrying out of risk analyses; developing research relevant for the control and surveillance of external borders; and providing assistance to Member States in circumstances requiring increased technical and operational assistance at external borders as well as necessary support in organising joint return operations of rejected asylum seekers and illegal immigrants.

The seat of the Agency, whose first structures were put into place in

---

[9] See Hague Programme, p. 15, and the Council and Commission Action Plan implementing the Hague Programme, adopted on 10 June 2005, EU Council document 9778/2/05 REV2, p.10.

May 2005, is in Warsaw, which can be taken as an indication of the importance attached to the responsibilities of the new Member States as regards the control of EU external borders. On 25 May 2005 the Finnish Colonel Ilka Laitinen was appointed as its first Executive Director. He had previously been the director of the Risk Analysis Centre (see above) whose functions will be taken over by the Agency, which was allocated a budget of Euro 6 million for 2005 and Euro 10 million for 2006.[10] The Agency, which is planned to have 57 members of staff (European Commission 2005), will be mainly funded from the EC budget and has been vested with quite substantial operational powers which go distinctly beyond those of other agencies in the justice and home affairs domain, such as Europol and Eurojust. According to Article 2 of the Regulation it shall not only evaluate but also approve and coordinate proposals for joint operations and pilot projects made by Member States. It can also itself, and in agreement with the Member State(s) concerned, launch initiatives for joint operations and pilot projects in co-operation with Member States. In cases in which individual Member States are faced with particular difficulties at external borders requiring increased technical and operational assistance, the Agency can organise this assistance by coordinating the support provided by other Member States and deploying its own experts (Article 8). It can also decide to put its technical equipment at the disposal of Member States participating in the joint operations or pilot projects.

A particular feature of the Agency is that it can, on the basis of a decision of its Management Board and subject to the consent of the Member States concerned, decide upon the setting up of 'specialised branches' in the Member States which will at least initially be the operational and training centres already established (see above) and specialised in the different aspects of control and surveillance of the land, air and maritime borders respectively (Article 16). The Agency's 'specialised branches' will have the task to develop best practices with regard to the particular types of external borders for which they are responsible, and the Agency will ensure the coherence and uniformity of such best practices. The national 'branches' can also be used by the Agency for the practical organisation of joint operations and external borders and pilot projects.

Finally, the Agency has also been vested with an important monitoring and evaluation function: It has the formal responsibility for evaluating the results of the joint operations and pilot projects and make a comprehensive comparative analysis of those results with a view to enhancing the quality, coherence and efficiency of future operations and projects.

The establishment of the new Border Management Agency must be regarded as an important step towards a more integrated and 'institutionalised'

---

[10] Colonel Ilka Laitinen appointed as Executive Director of EU Borders Agency, May 2005. Available at URL:
<http://www.intermin.fi/intermin/home.nsf/pages/2CC06F4498C6D307C225700D0080CE78>.

management of external borders. An important element of progress is the solidarity dimension introduced by the emergency support possibility provided for by Article 8 of the Regulation (see above), and the 'promotion of solidarity' between the Member States is actually mentioned amongst the reasons for its establishment in Article 1. While the Agency does not constitute any 'European Border Guard' as such, it certainly creates some sort of a coordinating command structure and, through the 'specialised branches', gives to the Agency a direct reach into national border guard forces which could at a later stage considerably facilitate the build-up of specialised integrated contingency reserves ('rapid response forces') or, a more remote possibility, fully fledged European Border Guard units. It should also be noted that with the establishment of the Agency a key element of the 'network model'—the creation of a central coordinating body with the possibility to issue instructions to national border guard forces—has been put into place, although the scope of these instructions is likely to remain, at least initially, quite limited.

The issue of democratic control has been addressed in the Regulation establishing the Agency, but only to a limited extent. According to Article 20(b) and (c) of the Regulation, the Management Board of the Agency has to forward both its annual Report and its work programme for the following year to the European Parliament, and by virtue of Article 25(2) the Agency's Executive Director can be asked by the European Parliament to report to it on the carrying out of his tasks. Because of the EC budgetary funding provided for the Agency, the European Parliament has also some leverage regarding the Agency through its budgetary powers. Whether these controlling powers can be considered sufficient will depend on the development of the Agency's role and its openness towards parliamentary scrutiny.

Conclusions

The creation of a European Border Guard—whether in the form of a fully fledged integrated force or of a more or less developed network of national forces—is clearly one of the most ambitious and controversial projects which has come up in the context of the EU's 'area of freedom, security and justice' so far. In terms of its innovative approach and the potential challenges it poses to the principles of national sovereignty and territoriality, it can be compared to the development of Europol into a European police force with cross-border operational powers and the establishment of a European Public Prosecutor's Office. In spite of an initial firework of ideas during 2001–2002, the time has clearly not yet come for the most advanced model of such a European structure, the integrated force model. Apart from the lack of any concrete progress in this direction, one of the most telling indicators for that is the EU Constitutional Treaty: Although the concept of a European Border Guard was discussed in the European Convention's Working Party X, the Convention left it in the end at a mere reference in the Constitutional Treaty (Treaty Establishing a Constitution for Europe 2004) to the less controversial term 'integrated management system for external borders' (Article III-265), a term which was vague enough to pass the subsequent Intergovernmental Conference without any objections from the governments.

Yet the EU governments have clearly come to understand that in a Union in which internal borders have lost much of their former security functions, the external borders of every individual Member State are very much a matter of concern to all of them, this even more so if some of the new Member States clearly continue to have some capability problems in this respect. And at a time when illegal immigration and international terrorism figure amongst the primary perceived threats, this common concern is likely to increase rather than decrease. As a result the political rationale of the idea of a European Border Guard—arriving at effective burden-sharing and mutual trust through the build-up of common structures for external border security—is a very powerful one. The Council Action Plan of June 2002 and the establishment of the new EU External Border Agency in May 2005 have provided substantial starting points for the gradual development of at least an EU network structure of border guard forces. The various operational projects which have already been initiated in implementation of the Action Plan and the at least potentially quite significant functions given to the Agency indicate that the Member States are at least willing to engage in and experiment with the creation of common structures and to enhance cross-border operational co-operation. This emerging, and currently still rather imperfect, patchwork of 'integrated external border management' can be regarded as an excellent laboratory for the development of more effective common approaches and structures and may over time well prepare the ground for an organisational form worth the name of a European Border Guard.

References

BLACK, IAN AND RORY CARROLL. 2002. Article in *The Guardian*, 31 May 2002.

BUNDESMINISTERIUM DES INNERN. 2002. 'Schily: Guter Start auf dem Weg zur Europäischen Grenzpolizei'.(Press Communication). Berlin, 30 May 2002.

COUNCIL OF THE EUROPEAN UNION. 2001. Laeken Council, Conclusion No. 42 of the Laeken Council.

_____ 2002. Council document 10019/02 of 14 June 2002.

_____ 2003. 'Presidency Report on the implementation of programmes, ad hoc centres, pilot projects and joint operations'. EU Council document 10058/1/03 REV 1 of 11 June 2003.

_____ 2004. Council Regulation (EC) 2007/2004. *Official Journal of the European Union*, No. L 349/1, 25 November 2004.

_____ 2004. EU Council document 16054/04, 13 December 2004.

_____ 2004. 'Non-classified Report on the Activities of the ESBC'.

EU Council document 9469/04, 13 May 2004.

_____ 2004. 'Report on the 7th Meeting of the Participants of the Centre for Land Borders'. EU Council document 6736/04, 27 February 2004.

_____ 2004. United Kingdom Delegation, Risk Analysis Centre (RAC): Information analysis. EU Council document 12208/04, 9 September 2004.

_____ 2005. 'The Council and Commission Action Plan Implementing the Hague Programme'. Adopted on 10 June 2005, EU Council document 9778/2/05 REV2.

EUROPEAN COMMISSION. 2002-03. 'First Annual Report on the implementation of the ARGO project'.

_____ 2005. 'Basic facts about the External Borders Agency'.Memo/05/230,30 June 2005. Available at URL: <http://europa.eu.int/rapid/pressReleasesAction.do?reference=MEMO/05/230&format=HTML&aged=0&language=EN&guiLanguage=en>

_____ 2005. 'The Hague Programme: 10 Priorities [...] 10. Financial Resources Adequate to Policy Objectives'. May 2005. URL: <http://europa.eu.int/rapid/pressReleasesAction.do?reference=MEMO/05/230&format=HTML&aged=0&language=EN&guiLanguage=en>.

_____ 2005. 'Work programme for ARGO 2005'. Available at URL: <http://europa.eu.int/comm/justice_home/funding/argo/doc/annual_work_programme_2005_en.pdf>

EUROPEAN PARLIAMENT, COMMITTEE ON CIVIL LIBERTIES, JUSTICE AND HOME AFFAIRS. 2005. 'Report on the Proposal for a Regulation of the European Parliament and of the Council Establishing a Community Code on the Rules Governing the Movement of Persons Across Borders'. (Rapporteur: Michael Cashman). EP document no. A6- 0188/2005 of 15 June 2005; p. 64-65.

'Feasibility Study for the Setting-up of a European Border Police – Final Report'. 2002. Rome

HOUSE OF LORDS. 2003. 'Minutes of Evidence Taken Before the Select Committee on the European Union'. (Sub-Committee F, provisional transcript) Warsaw, 4 March 2003.

The Independent. 2003. 'Mediterranean Joint Patrols Fail to Stop Migrants'. 11 March 2003.

'Justice Submission to the House of Lords Inquiry into the European Border Guard, Paragraph 7. February 2003

'Treaty Establishing a Constitution for Europe'. 2004.*Official Journal of the European Union*, C 310/1, 16 December 2004.

Chapter 11

Integrated Borderlands?

Eberhard Bort

Hopes and Fears

The substantial enlargement of the European Union in 2004 was, in many quarters, seen as a great opportunity: one hundred million new citizens, new markets, greater stability and prosperity for all. Yet, the eastward move of the boundaries of the EU has also given rise to new fears. What about security at the new external frontier? Can these, borderlands that include countries like Russia, Ukraine or Belarus be policed properly and efficiently? Can the new member states be trusted? Can they carry the burden of controlling effectively their external EU borders? Or do we need a joint border guard, sharing both the costs and the responsibility for the EU external frontiers?

Borders have always existed as this set of opposites. They cut off, delimit, serve as barriers; yet they can also be bridges, channels of trade and communication. The control of borders and their security function can sit uneasily with the need to transcend boundaries for the sake of stability on both sides of the border. With new surveillance and control technologies and an increasingly globalised market, border regions have come to the fore again. The be-all and end-all of border management seems to reach far beyond the actual borderline, particularly in tracing and combating the origins and sources of cross-border crime. It is understandable that, in the security community, the concerns of control prevail over the concerns of openness; openness—for trade and communication—is often perceived as a threat. If, on the other hand, economic and social stability in the borderlands is seen as a consequence of open boundaries, then this stability could be a major factor in the provision of security as well. Negotiating the proper compromise between short-term fears and long-term hopes seems to be of crucial importance.

Traditionally, border regions have been marked by their peripherality and remoteness from the core of the state they belong to, not only in the geographical sense, but also administratively, socially and culturally. Yet, in disputed borderlands, the borderland culture could be instrumentalised as an identity marker for the 'homeland'. Underdevelopment was often a consequence of this peripheral location, as, to give but one historical example, in the *Zonenrandgebiet* in the former Federal Republic of Germany, the strip of land along the Iron Curtain which suffered from being cut off from its natural hinterland, lacking investment and infrastructural development.

The difference that had developed between the internal borderlands of the EU and the situation at its external boundaries was, by the time of the demise of the Berlin Wall, instructive. Forty years of increasingly intensive cross-border co-operation along the internal frontiers had produced a dense web of cross-border networks and institutionalised transfrontier regions as one of the building stones of a regional Europe. This chapter will look at the experience of cross-border integration at the EU's internal frontiers and how the attempt to translate and emulate that process on the future internal frontiers with the new democracies in the former Eastern bloc has fared. Finally, the author will attempt to assess whether this process can be furthered with a view of getting the balance right between security/control on the one hand, and co-operation/openness on the other, at the post-enlargement external frontier of the EU.

A useful framework for looking at border relations is the categorisation developed by Oscar Martinez (1994). He distinguishes four different modes—or stages—of borderlands:

1. *Alienated borderlands*: rigidly controlled, often militarised; political and military tensions allow for very little, if any, exchange across the border. The border is closed and 'borderlanders' on each side perceive of each other as aliens.
2. *Co-existent borderlands*: contacts are made possible by international arrangements, but are difficult, as control is clearly prioritised over permeability. Limited exchange takes place, but long-term co-operation is deemed undesirable for political or military reasons.
3. *Interdependent borderlands*: where 'interdependence creates many opportunities for borderlands to establish social relationships across the boundary as well as allowing for significant transculturation to take place' (Martinez 1994, p.5). Borders are semi-open; economies are linked across the boundary, but concerns lead to careful monitoring, particularly on issues such as immigration and crime. Contacts are frequent, mutual trade and exchange across the frontier assume a complementary character, and a common borderland mentality is developed on both sides of the border, but the border is only open insofar as the states' interests are not damaged.
4. *Integrated borderlands*: pooled sovereignty; all barriers and obstacles to cross-border communication, exchange and movement of people, goods, services and capital have been removed and a common cultural and political cross-border identity develops.

Although these are 'ideal-typical' definitions, it is not difficult to allocate practical examples to these four stages (which can, as envisaged by Martinez, be seen as stages in an evolution): (1) is exemplified by the historical example of the bipolar Cold War frontier, the 'Iron Curtain', as symbolised by the Berlin Wall. Other examples include the Korean border or the 'Green Line' separating Turkish and Greek Cypriots; (2) could be represented by the borders between former Soviet Republics, such as Belarus and Poland; (3) is clearly Martinez's model for the US–Mexico border where, under the umbrella of NAFTA, goods and capital may flow relatively unhindered across the internal border of the free trade area, but movement of people is restricted, and border control is a high priority; (4) could be the internal frontiers of the post-Schengen European Union, classically expressed in the close cross-border relations along the German–Dutch (Euregio) or German–French borders, including the German provision of transferring sovereignty rights to institutions straddling the frontier (Beyerlin 1998, p.127).

Cross-Border Co-operation at Europe's Internal Borderlands

Peripheral borderlands are one of the legacies of the nation-state. It is because of the memory of that fact that the new rhetoric of the lasting importance of the nation-state is viewed with a degree of scepticism in the borderlands of Europe. Regionalism, and in particular cross-border regionalism, has been a tool to place formerly peripheral regions at the heart of developments. Full integration, including the transfer and pooling of sovereignty rights, cannot coexist with the classical notion of the nation-state.

Notwithstanding the changing phases of this discourse, transfrontier co-operation between local and regional authorities has become the practice at all EU internal frontiers, including sea frontiers such as the English Channel and the Baltic Sea. Co-operation began in the 1950s as a series of informal contacts which were gradually transformed into systematic institutionalised meetings of regional and local authorities.[1] The free movement of goods and people was already envisaged in the Treaty of Rome (1957), the founding document of the European (Economic) Community. With the introduction of the Single Market in 1993, based on the 1986 Single European Act, the economic functions (customs, tariffs, etc.) of borders inside the EU were further eroded. Since 1995, a blurring of the distinction between international and sub-state boundaries within the EU has occurred through the progressive implementation of the 1985 Schengen Agreement and the 1990 Schengen Convention.

A framework for cross-border co-operation between Regional and Local Authorities was provided by the 1980 (Madrid) Outline Convention on Transfrontier Co-operation; an annex to the Convention provided a model agreement for these authorities. An additional protocol came into force in 1994, allowing the transfer of transfrontier agreements from public international law to the administrative law of the states concerned.

The main categories of transfrontier agreements are intergovernmental treaties, conventions or recommendations; treaties such as the Bonn Treaty of 5 March 1975, setting up the tripartite commission for the Upper Rhine and the

---

[1] For a historical overview of cross-border co-operation see Gross and Schmitt-Egner 1994; Brunn and Schmitt-Egner 1998; Raich 1995; Scott et al. 1997.

bipartite commission for the Middle Rhine; private law agreements between local authorities (and sometimes other organisations); informal agreements between local authorities, sometimes including other organisations which result in de facto regular co-operation; and intermittent consultations about common problems.

Co-operation arrangements range from fairly elaborate institutional structures, such as the Euregio on the Dutch–German border[2] to a simple agreed pattern of regular meetings of executives of local or regional authorities such as the Working Committee for the Pyrenées. Overlapping areas of transfrontier co-operation are common. For example, there are now two Euroregions for the Pyrenées and a series of local associations, as well as the Working Committee for the Pyrenées. The regions involved in ARGE ALP (Working Community of the Eastern Alps) and the ALPE ADRIA (Working Community of the Eastern Alps) overlap, with four regions (Lombardy, South Tyrol–Trentino, Salzburg and Bavaria) being members of both.

Reasons behind the promotion of cross-border co-operation include: resolving the practical difficulties created by the frontier; developing good neighbourly relations; obtaining remedies for harm; and gaining information about decisions and developments which may affect the material interests of neighbouring regions. A less explicit intention involves dependent regions seeking to influence decision-making processes of the economically stronger neighbouring regions. A good example is provided by the dormitory towns in France which are in a dependent relationship vis-à-vis the Swiss cities of Basel and Geneva; similarly, Barcelona exerts an economic attraction across the Catalan–French frontier; most regions in the Alpine arc in Switzerland and Austria, which have small populations, are exposed to overwhelming economic and social influences from densely populated and highly industrialised regions in the surrounding plains of Lombardy, Bavaria and Rhone–Alpes.

Other motives for co-operation have changed over time. The first forms of transfrontier co-operation between local governments across the Rhine originated in the early 1950s as part of a movement for Franco–German reconciliation. In the early 1960s, the focus changed from reconciliation to overcoming difficulties created by the frontier for economic development, particularly in the field of industrial location and land-use planning. Many other examples in widely separated European frontier regions illustrate the interest in infrastructure planning, the development of transport facilities, the sharing of services such as sewage and waste disposal, and similar matters. In the aftermath of the protest movements of the 1960s, a new concern about the environment emerged, leading to direct action campaigns and the establishment of pressure groups and green parties. This affected the agenda of transfrontier co-operation and, in some places, created a popular basis for it.

Mobilising the opposition against the concentration of nuclear power stations on the Upper Rhine in the 1970s may not have resulted in a reversal of

---

[2] For an organisation chart of the Euro-region see Scott et al. 1995, p.123

state policies in the short term (with the possible exception of abandoning one projected nuclear power station at Wyhl), but it did create new transfrontier networks of environmental campaigners (and a radio station, Radio Dreyeckland). The International Lake Constance Conference was set up, which saved the lake from environmental catastrophe. There were other successes in Saar–Lor–Lux, the Danube and the Alpine region. Transfrontier groupings of ecologists are to be found in other regions, for example on the Basque littoral. This was 'bottom up' pressure to engage in transfrontier co-operation, contrasting with previous elite co-operation.

In the second half of the 1970s and a part of the 1980s (a period often described as one of 'euro-stagnation'), the promoters of European integration took an interest in transfrontier co-operation. Some participants in transfrontier associations came to regard themselves as at the forefront of the European movement. Another phase was apparent after the 1986 Single European Act and the passage to the Single Market. Economic interests have come again to the fore—adaptation of local economies previously dependent on the frontier and frontier controls, new opportunities for joint ventures with the dismantling of frontier controls and, above all, the prospect of EU financial aid for frontier regions.

A good practical example of the evolution of cross-border co-operation, even straddling the EU frontier, is the Upper Rhine Region, embracing the borderlands of France, Germany and Switzerland. Attempts at establishing a model of co-operation was first mooted in the early 1960s, and led to the foundation of Regio Basiliensis, encompassing about 500,000 people in and around Basel. After the Treaty of Bonn (1975), the 'Comité Tripartite' was formed, with a remit to coordinate economic, transport, environmental, cultural and media policies. In 1991, the Upper Rhine Conference replaced the tripartite (and bipartite) committees. 1995 saw the foundation of the Council of the Regio TriRhena, including Basel, Mulhouse, Colmar and Freiburg, with about 2.1 million people. It is the southern partner within the Upper Rhine Euroregion, which reaches from Basel and Colmar to Strasbourg, Offenburg, Karlsruhe and Landau (the latter also part of PAMINA[3]), an area with a population of 5.7 million.[4] In 1998, following the Karlsruhe Agreement of 1996, it introduced a cross-border 'parliament', the Upper Rhine Council, with 73 elected representatives.[5] The region has developed an integrated expertise in life sciences, with 40 university institutes and six technical colleges and three hundred firms working in the area, and not just in tailor-made facilities like the

---

3   PAMINA - Palatinate, Middle Rhine and North Alsace.
4   Cross-border co-operation in the Upper Rhine area is reminiscent of Russian matrioshka dolls: the Regio Basiliensis within the Regio TriRhena within the Euregio.
5   It cannot really be called a parliament, as only half the Baden-Württemberg members are MPs, the other half are mayors and elected *Landräte*, with no specific mandate to represent the region; the Swiss representatives come closest to the paliamentary tag, as they are delegates from the cantonal parliaments.

Bio-Tech Park Freiburg, the Bio Park Colmar or the Innovation Centre in Altschwil/Basle. Integrated curricula for the 78,000 students at Basel, Mulhouse, Freiburg and Strasbourg have also been designed.

But it has not all been smooth sailing. There have been difficulties along the way, and some of them have yet to be resolved. The different constitutional and administrative structures of states, which also produce striking inequalities in budgetary powers and resources,[6] cause difficulties for transfrontier co-operation. The most obvious manifestation of differences is the varying extent of central government involvement in transfrontier co-operation. A striking example is France, all of whose neighbours have more decentralised systems in which central governments play a much smaller role. The French central government, represented by the Prefects, is always very much present.

From the start, the EEC/EC provided indirect support for transfrontier co-operation. The European Commission promoted inter-regional networking, the development of regional institutions and direct contact between the regions and the European Commission. The direct application of European law to the environmental and social spheres, direct contacts between the regions and the Commission since 1975 through the European Fund for Regional Development (FEDER), helped to give a European dimension to the activities of regional and local government and, therefore, to inter-regional co-operation. As the EC became increasingly important as a source of funds, permanent offices were established in Brussels by regional authorities, by their associations, by various specialised associations of frontier regions, mountain regions, peripheral and maritime regions, and by the Association of European Border Regions (AEBR, founded in 1971). In 1996, AEBR jointly initiated with the European Commission LACE-TAP (Linkage Assistance and Co-operation for the European Border Regions – Technical Assistance Programme). The representation of local authorities in the Economic and Social Council and in the multitude of consultative committees of the European Union, and regional representation in the Committee of the Regions, all help to erode the previously clear distinction between the national and sub-national levels of government.

Aimed at reducing the negative impact of frontiers through the provision of support for joint transfrontier projects, programmes such as INTERREG I (1990–1994), INTERREG II (1995–1999) and INTERREG III (2000–2006) were introduced. The less well-known RECITE I Programme (Regions and Cities for Europe) has financed 36 inter-regional co-operation projects in which 249 regional and local authorities are involved. The record of INTERREG I in promoting transfrontier co-operation between local and regional authorities was flawed because, among other factors, of the lack of co-

---

[6] There is an enormous disparity in budgets even of rich regions. In the 'four motors' association of the most dynamic French, Spanish, Italian and German regions, Rhône–Alpes had a budget in 1997 of Euro 1 billion, compared with 9 billion for Lombardy and 30 billion for Baden–Württemberg.

ordination with other EC programmes and unclear guidelines. Also, the distribution of funds was unbalanced—63 percent of the EU contribution went to the European periphery—for improving communications infrastructure on the borders of Greece and between Spain and Portugal. INTERREG I was, in these cases, handled by representatives of the central governments, contrary to the intention of the programme.

INTERREG II took some of the criticisms into account. The regions were much better prepared, and the programme succeeded in federating interests separated by the international frontier. Environmental protection, tourism, transfrontier footpaths and foot bridges, promotion of bilingualism, educational and cultural co-operation and many other small projects were financed. The provision of full and reliable information about developments on the other side of the frontier was a frequent basis for successful projects. Information services have been set up, sometimes offices covering enquiries about employment issues, tax, how to build business partnerships, about consumer rights, the organisation of meetings and working groups, and so on. Fine examples are the four INFOBEST offices (Kehl, Lauterbourg, Vogelgrun–Breisach, Weil–Huningue) on the frontier between France and Germany. Other initiatives include joint or co-operative tourist information services, transfrontier guides and hotel booking services, transfrontier travel timetables and maps, and consumer rights bureaus.

INTERREG III shows a commitment to continuing and developing co-operation between local and regional authorities across the internal frontiers. A new map of regional groupings and a new list of priority areas are intended to give the programme greater focus. The practice of working together, often on detailed matters, and the treatment of the whole of the EU as a single territory divided into large transnational regions, is intended to encourage the development of transfrontier communities of interest.

Although the EU has often played a central role in much of this co-operation, some has taken place independently of the EU framework. The most compelling examples of the relative unimportance of the EC/EU as the essential impetus of transfrontier co-operation are associations in the Alps–Adriatic triangle ARGE ALP for the Alpine region stretching from Baden–Württemberg and Bavaria in the north to Lombardy in the south and Salzburg in the east and including the Swiss cantons of Graubünden, St Gallen and Ticino, and ALPE ADRIA, stretching from Bavaria to Slovenia and Croatia (Strassoldo 1998). These associations, unusually, have at certain times had a highly political profile. Initially this was because they were interpreted, in certain Italian and Yugoslav circles, as evidence of a Bavarian–German attempt to regain influence towards the south-east. More recently, ALPE ADRIA was supportive, from the beginning, of the separatist aims of Slovenia and Croatia in the early 1990s, with the result that both remain members, even though they stand out as two sovereign states in an association of regional governments.

Practical problems in frontier regions create pressure for further reform of the current arrangements. Sometimes problems are trivial, but they illustrate that applying the label of 'integrated borderlands' to the internal EU frontiers might be premature. For example, the dismantling of frontier controls and the reciprocal granting of social security rights within the European Union have not solved some of the difficulties faced by transfrontier workers—long-term sickness is an example of incompatibilities between regulations on both sides of the border resulting in individuals having neither rights to sick pay nor unemployment benefit on either side of the frontier.

The flow of information across frontiers is of paramount importance, particularly where a large and dynamic city is a transfrontier neighbour or an especially dynamic activity, such as the technological park at Aachen, is located just across the border. Information about changes in economic activity, investment patterns, demand for labour, new local and central government policies, planning decisions, pollution and environmental measures, is of fundamental importance. Sometimes this information is publicly available, but local and regional policy makers on the other side of a frontier may not be aware of it in the absence of regular channels of communication and face-to-face contacts.

Without belittling the achievements so far, transfrontier institutions or associations still lack real political weight and influence. This can be explained by a plethora of reasons: lack of impact among the populations in the frontier regions, political divisions, lack of resources, lack of a sense of transfrontier solidarity, constitutional obstacles and reticence or indifference of central governments. There is often very little public awareness of this form of co-operation. The practical achievements of transfrontier institutions are often mundane, and not especially newsworthy.

There is also little evidence that the frontier as a marker of the limits of political identity has been effaced from the mentality of the populations of the frontier regions (e.g., PAMINA 1995). Sometimes transfrontier ethno-national identities sustain institutional co-operation—for example in Tyrol and in the Basque region—but this is rare and, where it occurs, tends to raise anxieties and opposition at the centres of the states concerned. For example, in January 1996 the Italian government opposed the opening of a joint office in Brussels representing the Euroregion Tyrol.

Some transfrontier co-operative projects are not indeed welcomed wholeheartedly by the affected populations. Opposition may delay, if not prevent, eventual implementation of cross-border projects. An example is the controversial Somport tunnel under the Pyrenees which provoked a militant, and partially successful, environmentalist campaign against it. Another example is the rebellion of mayors of the French communes in the 1980s against a proposed solution for Rhine pollution—the dumping of saline waste in disused mine shafts—on the grounds that this would damage the water table. A similar case, which surfaced in the 1980s and early 1990s, was the pollution of the river Meuse with heavy metals from the old industrial area around Liège in Belgium, which conflicted with the Dutch use of the Meuse for the extraction of drinking water. Such disputes tend to reinforce national stereotypes and traditional animosities.

It is a paradox of transfrontier co-operation (whether of an intergovernmental or inter-regional form) that, although the intention is to remove the source of conflicts, as transfrontier contacts become closer, it has the potential to trigger new conflicts. Sometimes popular sentiment is expressed against lowering the (culturally and economically) protective frontier as, for example, when in the early summer of 1997 thousands of Danes formed a human chain on the German–Danish frontier chanting 'the frontier must stay', in protest against the institution of a Euroregion along that border.

Moving on from this protective perception of frontiers, what about the security aspect at internal frontiers? Has the 'borderless Europe' become a free-roaming paradise for criminals? Schengen, now signed by all but two EU member states (UK and Ireland), and implemented in 15 member states, abolished border controls (passport controls, border police check points) at the internal frontiers, and transferred those border controls, standardised and supervised by the Schengen Control Committee, to the external frontiers of 'Schengenland'.

The general purpose of frontiers in the sovereign state was to establish absolute physical control over a finite area and to exercise exclusive legal, administrative and social controls over its inhabitants. But the traditional attributes of 'sovereignty' are clearly being eroded in Europe and frontiers are losing their hard-edged clarity (Anderson 1996, p.189).

Schengen also entails a transformation of the borderline into a spatial concept of borders, which has been seen in the light of advancing surveillance technology and the need to combat cross-border crime at the *locus* of its origin (or destination) rather than at the border, as a return of the marches, or the *limes* (Foucher 1998, pp.235–6). 'Controlled delivery' has become a key concept in combating illegal drug trafficking. If the police receive information of a drugs transport, a collaborative effort involving police forces of different countries is undertaken to track the drugs from their origin to their distribution. National EU police forces have built up their presence in non-EU states in order to combat organised cross-border crime far from the actual national and/or EU border line (Kummer 2002). 'The spatial approach,' claims Dr Horst Eichel of the German Ministry of the Interior, 'clearly ought to take precedence over the purely linear approach to geographic boundaries. The latter is no longer a match for today's challenges, because individual and collective security begins beyond our borders and continues well on this side of them' (cited in Molle 1996, p.6).

But this opening of frontiers has also caused fears. What is apparent is that people in Europe seem to harbour an unfocused, general anxiety about frontiers no longer providing the protection they once (allegedly) did. Organised cross-border crime, trafficking of drugs and other smuggled goods and organised human trafficking seem to indicate that frontier controls are no longer as effective as they once were. This may be changing as populations become more accustomed to the absence of frontier controls at the internal frontiers. The absence of controls is widely welcomed in frontier regions. In general, the French—normally very sensitive to these matters—seem to have adopted a reasonably relaxed attitude about open frontiers, and those living in the frontier regions seem very pleased with the new situation. Law enforcement agencies seem to have adapted to the new situation without undue difficulty. The nature of frontiers is perceived as changing. New information technology for surveillance and identity control is widely seen as a key factor in securing efficient frontier controls, rather than checking at a physical border line.

Despite these difficulties and problems, which show that integrating the internal borderlands of the EU is an ongoing process and not yet an accomplished goal, transfrontier co-operation has already proven its worth in the sharing of services and, sometimes, joint investments—in emergency, hospital and waste disposal services and sewage disposal. They seem to illustrate that, in Martinez's classification, the internal borderlands of the EU have not yet achieved the status of fully integrated borderlands.

Adaptations

In response to the opening of the Iron Curtain, Euroregions were set up from the Finnish–Russian border down to Austria, Slovakia, Hungary and Slovenia (Bort 1998, pp.91–108; Bort 1997, pp.20–31). Euroregions have thus become a general feature of the eastern frontier, often aided by staff trained in the Euroregions at the internal EU borders. They range from Kuhmo–Kostamuksha (1992) on the Finnish–Russian border (Tikkanen and Käkönen 1997), the Euroregion Baltyk, involving Poland, Lithuania, Latvia, Kaliningrad, Bornholm (Denmark) and Sweden (1998);[7] the German–Polish border region with the Euregios of Neisse-Nysa-Nisa, founded in Zittau in 1991; Spree-Neisse-Bober (1993); Pro Europa Viadrina (1993) and Pomerania (1995);[8] the three Euregios on the German–Czech border—Elbe–Labe (1992), Erzgebirge (1992), Egrensis—to Sumova/Bayerischer Wald/Mühlviertel in the borderlands of Germany, the Czech Republic and Austria, and the Businesspark Heiligenberg–Szentgotthárd at the Austro–Hungarian border. Further south, at the Slovene frontiers, it was already well-established through the *Arbeitsgemeinschaft Alpenländer*. (For a comprehensive review of cross-border co-operation in the eastern borderlands of the pre-enlarged EU see Neuss, et al. 1998.)

Yet, while the 'pooling' of sovereignty has become widely accepted in the West, newly regained independence has made sovereignty as an idea more precious for the Eastern neighbours. Close co-operation in the borderlands has been viewed in Prague and Warsaw as an erosion of territorial sovereignty and a threat to national and cultural identity. In particular, it has been considered as a

---

[7] Main objectives are the 'Via Baltica' motorway link and an upgraded railway from the Polish-Lithuanian border to Kaunas.

[8] Including the Szczecin industrial centre, the island of Bornholm/Denmark, and Sweden. It was formally established in December 1995 as a pilot project for Baltic Sea partnership.

means of expanding German influence. Although there has been a subsequent modification of opinion, in June 1993, Václav Klaus called the Euroregions 'a German attempt at "creeping" reconquest of the Sudetenland' (Gerner 1997, p.157). This runs counter to an underlying motive in Central and Eastern Europe of wanting EU membership as a tool to dilute or contain German influence in Central Europe, in the same way as Ireland used its EU membership after 1973 as a means to re-define its relationship with neighbouring ex-colonial Britain (Bort 1997, pp.26–27).

Despite these reservations, transfrontier co-operation is spreading even further east, as the foundation of the first exclusively Eastern European Euroregion, the Carpathian Euroregion, in February 1993 indicates (Kurcz 1999). Under the guidance (and financial aid) of the Institute of East–West Studies in New York, the foreign ministers of Hungary, Poland, Slovakia and Ukraine, representing around a dozen regions and a population of over 100 million people, signed the agreement on transfrontier co-operation. Since the break-up of the area in different nation-states in the aftermath of the First World War, the number of road and rail links has shrunk. Transport and telecommunication are priority areas for co-operation (Gerner 1997, pp.156–7). The difficulties here are more accentuated than in the West, or even at the pre-enlargement eastern frontier. The Carpathian Euroregion may illustrate this. It covers five different national territories, its population speaks eight different languages and follows five different religions (Suchanek 1996). The Carpathian Euroregion is an example of macro-regional co-operation, such as the Baltic Sea co-operation or the ARGE Donauländer, which cover areas larger than some of the member states of the EU (Weissmann 1997, pp.85–90). Euroregions have also been created between the Czech Republic and Poland (Euroregion Glacensis, 1996) at the Bug, in the Tatra, and around Niemen/Neman/Nemunas,[9] as well as in the borders between Romania and Moldova (Euroregion Low 1998).

The ostensible purposes of transfrontier regionalism in the eastern borderlands are threefold:
- Economic co-operation: investment in infrastructure, technology transfer, coordinated planning, optimising the use of resources and European funds, and making the border more permeable for transfrontier workers;
- the environment,[10] focusing on sustainable development and tourism;[11]

---

[9] The quadrilateral agreement establishing the Euroregion 'Niemen' was signed on 9 February 1996 by Poland, Lithuania, Belarus and Russia (Kaliningrad). Yet Russian (Kaliningrad) co-operation lagged behind; and reluctance on the part of Belarus meant that little progress was made beyond statements of intent (Koscharow 1997, p.3; see also Neubauer 1997).

[10] An example of environmental co-operation is the Sewage Project Bärenstein/Vejprty in the borderlands of Saxony and the Czech Republic opened in 1996. PHARE/CBC and INTERREG II provided capital grants for the project. This pilot project is embedded in a wider strategy of the Saxon State Ministry for the En-

- and cultural exchange, based on common traditions, education and communication, forging, or reviving, a common regional identity.[12]

Wherever possible, at internal or external frontiers, Euroregions are linked to common cultural and historical experience but they are primarily pragmatic associations for economic development. They are funded by the EU's INTERREG and PHARE/CBC programs. A key role in giving impetus to the Euroregions is often played by split or twin towns along the eastern frontier, from Frankfurt/Oder and Slubice through Guben/Gubin and Görlitz/Zgoralec on the German–Polish frontier (Horn 1997) to Goriza and Nova Gorica (Strassoldo 1999) and Trieste and Koper on the Italian–Slovene border (Richter-Malabotta 1998; Skok 1998).

The publicly stated objectives of transfrontier regions are impressive and ambitious. An example is the Euroregion on the German–Polish frontier, Pro Europa Viadrina, initiated in 1993 by Frankfurt an der Oder, Eisenhüttenstadt, four German counties and two Polish community associations. Beneath general objectives of improvement in living standards and economic performance and the promotion of European unity by creating an integrated trans-boundary region, six primary objectives and 27 individual objectives are listed. Neither the elaborate nature of the mechanisms for consultation nor the policy areas covered by formal agreements give an accurate picture of the success of co-operation. Undoubtedly, Euroregions like Pro Europa Viadrina helped in the preparations for EU accession. In September 2005, Franfurt/Oder saw the opening of a new 'Infopoint Europe Direct', and some projects have been significant successes—for example, the German–Polish 'Youth Factory' in Frankfurt/Oder, where German and Polish apprentices share their training, or the German–Polish Viadrina University at Frankfurt/Oder (and its partnership with the University of Poznan), which received a funding boost of 55 million Euros in July 2005 to internationalise its research and teaching (Klesmann 2005). In general, though, the evidence

---

vironment and State Development, 'Cross-border sewage and Drinking Water Solutions on the Oder', supported by the EU LIFE programme. In the Euroregion Spree–Neisse–Bober, a similar sewage plant at Guben/Gubin was built with support from INTERREG II.

[11] Peripheral zones often have unspoiled resources, which provide a basis for sustainable, environmentally friendly tourism. An example is the Danube national park between Austria and Hungary, agreed in October 1996.

[12] Examples include Czech, Bavarian and Austrian borderlands, as illustrated by *Glas ohne Grenzen*, a guide to the glass museums and collections in the Bayerischer Wald, Böhmerwald and Mühlviertel. There are cultural festivals like 'Mittel Europa', or Bavarian–Bohemian 'Kulturtage' in Weiden, as well as programmes for the stocking of Czech libraries with the literature from across the border, or the provision of German–Czech one-year school exchanges and financial support for Czech language courses in German adult education centres.

available about the Euroregions on the eastern frontier of Germany suggests a certain lack of progress in fulfilling their objectives.[13]

Stanislaw Tillich, on the other hand, Saxony's Minister for European Affairs, is on record with a much more positive verdict. According to him, the co-operation with the eastern neighbours has 'developed as well as the co-operation between German border regions with France, Belgium or the Netherlands.' A report of his Ministry supports this:

> Since 1990, a dense network of contacts, joint projects, subsidised measures, agreements and working groups has been formed, which guarantees that the continuous dialogue is not disrupted (cited in Sattler 2001).

But this dialogue covers, first and foremost, environmental clean-ups and initiatives in a particularly affected area. Otherwise, the translation and translocation of cross-border co-operation from the former internal to the former external frontier has been slower. And the problems at the present external frontier are even bigger. But progress is being made. A good example of how this translation process works is the proposal by the coordinators of German–Polish relations, the Polish diplomat and academic Irena Lipowicz, and the rector of the European University Viadrina at Frankfurt/Oder, Gesine Schwan, to establish a Viadrina Mark II at the Polish–Ukrainian border, a project they hope will get EU backing (Herold 2005).

Challenges and Opportunities

Economic inequality is the single most important obstacle to the flourishing of transfrontier co-operation. Within the EU, especially along the German frontiers, there was a rough approximation of levels of economic development when authorities started collaborating across their borders. Although the eastern borderlands of the Federal Republic of Germany suffered—and continue to suffer as a result of their peripheral location[14]—the eastern frontier of the European Union became, before 1989, a profound economic divide which left a legacy of extreme economic inequality. This legacy has four effects hindering transfrontier co-operation. First, the amount of money the eastern partners can contribute to joint projects is minimal unless there are grants from EU programs or other western sources. Second, and partly as a consequence of

---

[13] Among the few concrete German–Polish joint ventures in the Polish borderlands are the Volkswagen investments in Gorzów Wielkopolski (Landsberg) where cables and leads are manufactured, and Poznan where VW built a car factory.

[14] Unemployment rates vary widely on the German–Polish and German–Czech borders. In the Euroregion Pomerania there is 25 percent unemployment on the German (rural) side, only 6.3 percent around Szczecin; in the Euroregion Elbe–Labe the figures are 14.5 percent (German) and 5.5 percent (Czech).

the first, countries bordering the EU to the east have anxieties about economic and political subordination to the western partners. Third, complex financial procedures involving the EU and central governments lead to long delays, from application to actual payment of grants, and to disillusionment in the frontier regions (Kennard 1997). Fourth, central governments and other regions in the Central and Eastern European countries sometimes object to the regions bordering on the EU being privileged by cross-border initiatives and subsidies, over the regions in the interior in even greater need of economic development. By challenging state centralism, these apparently privileged western frontier regions can cause perceptions of threats to the geographical integrity of the state itself (Dauderstadt 1996).

A second obstacle to co-operation is the fact that the present eastern frontier of the EU is a distinctive language barrier, which makes cross-border communication difficult. A survey in the Czech borderlands found 41 percent of the respondents quoting the language barrier as the biggest obstacle to improving cross-border co-operation (Jerabek 1998, pp.55–56).[15] Forced population movements during and after the Second World War meant that, on the Finno–Russian border, the Finnish-speaking Karelians were mostly resettled in Finland. Along parts of the Polish–German border incomers predominate on both sides of the frontier: on the Polish side, eastern Poles were resettled from areas annexed by the USSR; and on the eastern front of the former GDR, Germans from Pomerania and East Prussia (which Germany lost to Poland and the Soviet Union after the war) found refuge. The Sudeten Germans were expelled by Czechoslovakia following the Benes decrees; large numbers of ethnic Germans were driven out of Hungary, Romania and Yugoslavia after the war. The political frontiers are therefore more clearly functioning as language frontiers than they were in 1939. Moreover, incentives to learn the neighbouring languages are asymmetrical; Poles and Czechs learn German (because there is an economic advantage), but very few Germans or Austrians learn Polish, Czech, Slovakian, or Hungarian, let alone the Slavic languages of the Balkans.[16]

Nationalist sentiment is another factor which hinders transfrontier co-operation. Anti-Polish attitudes are evident in the borderlands of the former GDR. There are fears, especially among the older generation of Poles and Czechs, partly fuelled by memories of the war, partly by long years of anti-capitalist propaganda, of western expansion and domination. Surveys in the

---

[15] Differences in 'national character' and different wage and wealth levels came second and third; among secondary obstacles, historical legacy replaced language as the main issue of concern.

[16] Euroregions are promoting the mutual learning of languages, as in the 'Sptkania' project of the Euroregion Spree–Neisse–Bober, involving seven elementary schools in Poland and Germany, respectively.

borderlands show that these xenophobic feelings may diminish through closer contact and interaction, but this is not inevitable (Heffner 1998).[17]

More positively, transfrontier co-operation is now seen as a resilient development and survives periods of stress in high politics and diplomatic relations. For example, in the German–Czech borderlands co-operation continued despite disagreements between the countries on other matters. Difficult negotiations between Germany and the Czech Republic took place about the property of, and compensation for, the Sudeten Germans prior to the accord of January 1997. Nonetheless, co-operation developed contemporaneously between the Technical University of Chemnitz and the West Bohemian University of Pilsen, which both recruit a large percentage of their students from the border regions. The universities are considered as 'two poles of cross-border co-operation' (Doukoupil 1998, p.87) in the German–Czech borderlands.[18] It prospered despite the unfavourable general political climate.

In the borderlands, any functional change of frontiers is felt immediately, and there is an awareness of the difficulties of transfrontier co-operation (Krafke et al. 1997). Overall, cross-border co-operation along the eastern frontier is evaluated positively, as enhancing communications and collaboration, and contributing to stability (Roch 1999). 56 percent of respondents in a poll in the German–Czech borderlands, for example, saw the role of the Elbe–Labe Euroregion as positive for the development of German–Czech relations. 54 percent expected the intensity of co-operation to increase, because it was beneficial for mutual economic development (Jerabek 1998). Despite some German impatience, respondents thought that remarkable progress had been achieved in a relatively short period of time (Jaedicke and Schwab 1999).

Cross-border co-operation is also seen as a major contribution towards solving, or at least easing, minority problems:

> The integration of transportation and communication systems, common efforts for environment protection and co-operation in trade and education, etc., etc. facilitate the contacts among the members of the national minorities separated by the borders. It relieves the burden of being separated and belonging to different national states and, by promoting civic activities and associations on both sides of the border, it solves the conflicts of dual loyalty. These regional integrations ... accelerate local socio-economic development and make the national borders transparent for different kinds of minorities

---

[17] Yet, close encounters with wealth and wage differences or with phenomena like street prostitution can also have a negative effect on the perception of 'the other'.

[18] This is also the case for universities along the Baltic coast, in Szczecin, Greifswald and Rostock.

without changing the national borders and creating new frustrated minorities (Agh 1998, p.209).

Against all this stand the fears that open borders bring with them the real and perceived threats posed by cross-border crime. The dangers of cross-border crime—drug trafficking, illegal weapons trade, car and cigarette smuggling, money laundering, fraud and corruption, human smuggling, etc.—must not be underestimated (Bort 2002). At 'their most extreme, substantial rises in the proportion of illegality in international economic activity can destabilise national economies' (Holmes 2001, p.193). The rise in internal and cross-border crime in Eastern Europe, and particularly in the countries of the former Soviet Union, can be pinned down to the difficult transitional situation in these countries: post-communist states attempting, in Claus Offe's term, a 'triple transition': the rapid and simultaneous transformation of their political systems, their economic systems, and their boundaries and identities (Offe 1996).

As at the US–Mexican border, the southern and eastern frontiers of the European Union demonstrate that the 'promotion of borderless economies based on free market principles in many ways contradicts and undermines ... efforts to keep borders closed to the clandestine movements of drugs and migrant labour' (Andreas 1996, p.51). Yet, despite these efforts to tighten border controls, even erecting what has euphemistically been dubbed the 'tortilla curtain', a metal wall along the border south of San Diego, and combining military and law enforcement agencies, 'many clandestine border crossers are adapting rather than being deterred.' The economic factors, 'underlying push–pull factors' (Andreas 1996, p.68), have frustrated repeated attempts at closing the US–Mexican border for illegal migrants. Operation 'Wetback' (under Richard Nixon) and, more recently, operation 'Gatekeeper' caused 'immediate economic damage, tensions between social groups and [had] almost zero effect on illegal immigration' (Bigo 1998, p.159; see also Nevins 2001).

Exporting Stability

In view of the looming EU enlargement, the Spanish presidency of the EU in the first half of 2002 made the fight against illegal migration a top priority. For Spanish Prime Minister José Maria Aznar, international terrorism and 'intensifying the struggle against illegal immigration' were the two dominant challenges for the EU (Woodworth 2002). The topic has not gone away. The terrorist bomb attacks in Madrid and London have intensified this resolve, as could be seen at the emergency counter-terrorism summit in July 2005 (Travis 2005).

A joint border police, shared visa standards, the development of a common visa database and increased powers for Europol were part of a Spanish 'action plan' discussed by a meeting of the EU Ministers of the Interior at Santiago in February 2002, biometric data and compulsory electronic fingerprinting on ID cards were on the agenda in July 2005. Brandenburg's Justice and European Affairs Minister Kurt Schelter, one of the German architects of Schengen, explicitly supported the idea of a common European border police. He also pointed out that police co-operation between Germany, the EU and the neighbouring applicant countries still needed 'completion'—synchronised, spy-proof communication frequencies, and the networking of search computers, were only two measures he mentioned (Heinen 2002). For the EU Commission, Justice Commissioner Antonio Vitorino introduced a strategy for a joint 'European Corps of Border Guards', beginning with a concept that he called 'integrated border protection'—the border authorities of the EU working together in a common body for risk assessment, co-ordination of measures in times of crisis and working towards harmonised methods and techniques. This External Borders Agency (FRONTEX), situated in Warsaw, began operating on 30 June 2005. The common European border force would start operating at airports, the route most used by illegal immigrants.[19] Vitorino expected the commonly financed body to be in place by 2007 (Bolesch 2002). This ambitious deadline looks increasingly unlikely to be met. But there are also serious problems of democratic oversight of such a joint border guard. References in the Commission's proposals to data protection, human rights considerations, protection of asylum seekers' rights are scarce, and there is 'no discussion of rules that would have to govern such a Corps as regards…judicial and political accountability' (Peers 2003, p.100).

One of the overarching strategies by EU agencies in the preparation of the candidate countries for accession was assisting them in becoming capable of managing the future eastern frontier of the EU as a Schengen border. Without having much of an input into the evolving Schengen regime, the long shadow of Schengen reached to the Bug and Carpathian regions and changed the candidate countries' border regimes. The efficient policing of their external non-EU frontiers became a condition for entry into the European Union. The equation looks simple: the candidate countries' EU borders would be opened to the degree that they closed their frontiers to their eastern neighbours.

Thus, some of the poorest countries of the EU have to carry the burden of guarding the security of the wealthy western EU states. Moreover, it is important to take into account the future of the countries beyond the new external EU frontier. Joanna Apap, a senior research fellow at the Centre for European Policy Studies, has warned:

> If we start creating a new Berlin Wall and, with it, the marginalisation of countries on the other side, we risk that

---

[19] In preparation for their plans for a common border police force, 20 European countries carried out a joint crackdown on 25 airports between 25 April and 21 May 2002. More than 4500 illegal immigrants were identified and almost one thousand false identity documents seized. Five hundred sanctions against airlines were imposed.

these nations will be unmotivated from trying to progress. They may also not co-operate on security with police (cited in Castle 2002).

When the President of Belarus, in the autumn of 2002, was refused a visa for the NATO summit in Prague he threatened to 'open the frontier and let thousands of refugees and drug dealers escape to Western Europe.' The Europeans would 'come crawling and begging us to cooperate in the fight against drug trafficking and illegal migration.'[20]

Kaliningrad, a Russian enclave, is to be cut off from Russia by the EU's external Schengen frontier once Poland and Lithuania will have joined the EU. The EU has rejected demands for a sealed corridor through which Russians in transit could travel, arguing instead in favour of multi-entry visas. But any visa demands met with fierce Russian resistance. The wealth gradient between Kaliningrad and its neighbours is already very steep, and has increased since Lithuania and Poland joined the EU (Bäurle 2004; Paulikas 2005). Some feared that Kaliningrad could become an 'open door' for illegal immigration and cross-border crime (Fairlie 2001; Middel 2002). On the other hand, people in Kaliningrad feared that, due to strengthened border controls, 'petty illegal over the border trade, Kaliningrad's lifeblood, will almost come to a complete halt' (Lavelle 2004). In October 2002, after months of acrimonious debate, the EU and Russia agreed to a compromise. Lithuania was to regulate using a simple 'transit document'. By November this had become a multiple re-entry transit pass which, until the end of 2004, could be used in conjunction with internal Russian identification documents rather than international passports. The EU also agreed to a feasibility study for a 'rail corridor'—an upgraded non-stop high-speed railway connection between Kaliningrad and Russia, which would offer the long-term possibility of transit without identity checks (Wernicke 2002; Holtom 2005). In the short-term, there still are worries in Lithuania that this agreement could compromise the country's unhindered entry into Schengen (Urban 2002), envisaged for October 2007. For Kaliningrad, there are long-term concerns. Only a comprehensive development plan, with substantial contributions from both the EU and Russia, will prevent the enclave from becoming a permanent problem zone (Timmermann 2002). It did not bode well that for the 750-year celebrations in Kaliningrad, the enclave's immediate neighbours were not invited. This 'decision not to invite the Polish and Lithuanian leaders has been construed as a deliberate diplomatic snub, adding a sour note to the celebrations' (Grammaticas 2005).

Poland's appeals regarding an active EU policy of economic co-operation must not go unheard. Otherwise we enter into a vicious circle at the future eastern frontier of the EU: sealing the frontier will enhance the misery

---

[20] In Belarus, every year about three thousand people are caught attempting to illegally cross the frontier into Poland, Lithuania or Latvia (*Süddeutsche Zeitung*, 15 November 2002).

beyond the border and thus reinforce the pressure on the border, which in turn will spurn attempts at closing the border even more hermetically.[21] Marek Borowski, a member of the Polish parliament, emphasised Poland's position:

> In joining the European Union, Poland would not like to be a bulwark for an affluent, isolationist Europe. We believe that the gradual involvement of Ukraine in the common economic space is in the unquestionable interest of the EU. It is at the least as important as good co-operation with the Kaliningrad district of the Russian Federation (2002).

Poland is interested in a new EU eastern policy, 'which would eventually bring Poland's eastern neighbours in from the cold' (Harding 2004).

Lurking behind discussions about the frontier regime at the future EU borders is the debate about the *finalité d'Europe*. Will there be a perspective for Ukraine, or is it too big to be incorporated, too close to Russia to be part of the EU? And what about Belarus, the ailing partner of Russia? And what about Russia itself? 'Where does Europe stop?' Romano Prodi, the former Commission President, asked in an interview in a Dutch newspaper. And his answer was: 'The Balkan nations will probably join, they are part of this. Turkey is an official candidate, that is clear.[22] But Morocco, Ukraine or Moldova. I see no reason for that' (*De Volkskrant* 2002). Bavaria's Prime Minister, Edmund Stoiber, has frequently declared his firm opposition to Turkish EU membership, while Chancellor Gerhard Schröder cautiously encouraged Turkey in its aspirations (Graw 2003; *Süddeutsche Zeitung* 2003). The French 'Non' to the draft EU constitution, although not officially linked to Turkey's EU aspirations, was widely interpreted as having been a vote against Turkish membership.

Two names recur through Turkish commentary and analysis—those of Nicholas Sarkozy, a favourite for the 2007 French presidential election, and Angela Merkel, leader of the German Christian Democrats (CDU), tipped to win the next German elections. Both have made very clear their opposition to Turkish membership. A Merkel–Sarkozy axis could, it is thought, cause real problems for Turkey (Dymond 2005).

Despite these ominous signs, accession talks with Turkey started in October 2005, after Turkey signed a customs protocol with the enlarged EU

---

21 The example of the US–Mexican border has shown that this concept does not work. While the US government poured more money than ever into the fortification of the 'tortilla curtain', a record number of illegal immigrants entered the country.

22 Only a few weeks before Prodi's interview, the European Convention's convener, Valerie Giscard d'Estaing had publicly denied Turkey's membership aspirations.

(insisting that this would not constitute formal recognition of the Greek–Cypriot government).[23]

The debate about a joint border police is ambiguous, too. Is it, as Prodi emphasised, a matter of shared burden (it being unfair to leave the accession states shouldering the entire weight of securing the EU's external frontiers) or a matter of not trusting the new member states with the task of keeping criminals out of EU territory?

What is doubtless is that the dichotomy of open/closed borders does not work. If the aim is the building of trust through international and cross-border co-operation at borders of the EU, it is necessary to achieve a balance between economic, administrative and security co-operation. Danuta Hübner, when Secretary of State for European Integration and Poland's representative in the Convention on the Future of Europe (and by 2005 a Commissioner for Euroregions), put it in a nutshell: 'The best recipe to counteract importing instability is to export stability' (2002).

As the pre-enlargement eastern frontier has been transformed from the Iron Curtain type 'alienated borderlands' into 'interdependent', if not 'integrated borderlands', the EU would be ill-advised to define its current external frontier as a rigid barrier; presently perhaps best described as 'co-existent', these borderlands must become at least 'interdependent' or, in Raimund Krämer's typology, a 'co-operative border' (1997), balancing security, protection, communication and exchange, enhancing trust and growing stability across the frontier. A security strategy alone will not suffice. To the chagrin of security strategists, a degree of 'illegality at the margins' (Bigo 1998, p.161) might be inevitable and have to be accepted during this transition. The flexible and adaptable structures provided by Euroregions seem to offer the best space for negotiating and achieving that balance.

References

ÁGH, A. 1998. *The Politics of Central Europe*. London: Sage.

ANDERSON, M., 1996. *Frontiers: Territory and State Formation in the Modern World*. Cambridge: Polity Press.

ANDREAS, P. 1996. U.S.–Mexico: Open Markets, Closed Border. *Foreign Affairs*, 103: 51–69.

BÄURLE, P. 2004. 'Viel Treibholz schwimmt durch diese Stadt', *Freitag*, 23 (April).

---

[23] In a Eurobarometer survey for the European Commission in June 2005, more than one-half of Europe's citizens expressed opposition to Turkey's accession to the EU. Austria and France pledged to hold referendums on Turkey's eventual entry. Britain and Belgium belong to the countries strongly supporting Turkish membership (Watt 2005).

BEYERLIN, U., 1998. 'Neue rechtliche Entwicklungen der regionalen und grenzüberschreitenden Zusammenarbeit'. In *Grenzüberschreitende Zusammenarbeit in Europa: Theorie — Empirie — Praxis*, eds., G. Brunn and P. Schmitt-Egner. Baden-Baden: Nomos.

BIGO, D. 1998. 'Frontiers and Security in the European Union: The Illusion of Migration Control'. In *The Frontiers of Europe*, eds. M. Anderson and E. Bort. London: Cassell.

BOLESCH, C. 2002. 'Neuer Vorstoss für EU-weiten Grenzschutz'. *Süddeutsche Zeitung*, 8 May 2002

BOROWSKI, M. 2002. 'Poles must play a part in Europe'. *The Independent*, 8 July 2002.

BORT, E. 1997. 'Crossing the EU Frontier: Eastern Enlargement of the EU, Cross-Border Regionalism and State Sovereignty'. *Interregiones*, 6.

_____ 1998. 'Mitteleuropa: The Difficult Frontier'. In *The Frontiers of Europe*, eds. M. Anderson and E. Bort. London: Cassell.

_____ 2002. 'Illegal Migration and Cross-Border Crime: Challenges at the Eastern Frontier of the European union'. In *Europe Unbound: Enlarging and Reshaping the Boundaries of the European Union*, ed., J. Zielonka. London: Routledge.

BRUNN, G., and Schmitt-Egner, P. (eds) 1998. *Grenzüberschreitende Zusammenarbeit in Europa: Theorie–Empirie–Praxis*. Baden-Baden: Nomos.

CASTLE, S. 2002. 'Russia finally Bows to EU Pressure for Kaliningrad 'Visas'. *The Independent*, 12 November 2002.

DAUDERSTÄDT, M. 1996. 'Ostmitteleuropas Demokratien im Spannungsfeld von Transformation und Integration'. *Integration*, 4: 208–223.

De Volkskrant, 27 November 2002.

DOUKOUPIL, J. 1998. 'Entwicklung und Zusammenarbeit im tschechisch-deutschen Grenzgebiet'. In *Grenzübergreifende Kooperation im östlichen Mitteleuropa*, eds., B. Neuss, P. Jurczek and W. Hilz. Tübingen: Europäisches Zentrum für Föderalismusforschung.

DYMOND, J. 2005. 'French cloud Turkey's EU dreams', BBC News online, 31 May 2005.

FAIRLIE, L.D. (ed.) 2001. *Are Borders Barriers?: EU Enlargement and the Russian Region of Kaliningrad*. Berlin: Institut für Europäische Politik.

FOUCHER, M. 1998. 'The Geopolitics of European Frontiers'. In *The Frontiers of Europe*, eds., M. Anderson and E. Bort. London: Cassell.

GERNER, K. 1997. 'The Evolving Political Role of Borders and Border Regions in Central Europe'. In *Borders and Border Regions in Europe and North America*, eds., J. Scott et al. San Diego: San Diego State University Press.

GRAMMATICAS, D. 2005. 'Kaliningrad Marks Key Anniversary', BBC News online, 3 July 2005.

GRAW, A. 2003. 'Die Union und die Türkei'. *Die Welt*, 10 January 2003

GROSS, B., AND SCHMITT-EGNER, P. 1994. *Europas kooperierende Regionen: Rahmenbedingungen und Praxis grenzüberschreitender Zusammenarbeit deutscher Grenzregionen in Europa*. Baden-Baden: Nomos.

HARDING, L. 2004. 'On Patrol Along the EU's New Eastern Frontier'. *The Guardian*, 28 April 2004.

HEFFNER, K. 1998. 'Entwicklung und Zusammenarbeit im deutsch-polnischen Grenzraum'. In *Grenzübergreifende Kooperation im östlichen Mitteleuropa*, eds., B. Neuss, P. Jurczek and W. Hilz. Tübingen: Europäisches Zentrum für Föderalismusforschung.

HEINEN, G. 2002. 'Eine europäische Grenzpolizei wäre nötig'. *Die Welt*, 4 April 2002.

HEROLD, F. 2005. 'Pläne für Gründung einer Viadrina II'. *Berliner Zeitung*, 22 February 2005.

HOLMES, L. 2001. 'Crime, Corruption and Politics: International and Transnational Factors'. In *Democratic Consolidation in Eastern Europe: International and Transnational Factors*, eds., J. Zielonka and A. Pravda. Oxford: Oxford University Press.

HOLTOM. P. 2005. *The Kaliningrad Test in Russian–EU Relations*. Leiden: Brill Academic.

HORN, J. 1997. *Auf dem Weg zur 'Euro-Stadt'? Die deutsch-polnische Zusammenarbeit in den an der Oder und Neiße geteilten Städten*. Berlin: Bundesinstitut für ostwissenschaftliche und internationale Studien.

HÜBNER, D. 2002. 'The European Union - open to citizens, open to the world'. Contribution to the Convention on the Future of Europe, 3 April 2002.

JAEDICKE, W., and SCHWAB, O. 1999. 'Brücke oder Bedrohung? Haltungen zur Kooperation in deutsch-polnischen Grenzregionen'. *Welttrends*, 22: 27–43.

JERÁBEK, M. 1998. 'Regionalentwicklung und grenzüberschreitende Zusammenarbeitr im tschechisch-deutschen Grenzraum'. In *Grenzübergreifende Kooperation im östlichen Mitteleuropa*, eds., B. Neuss, P. Jurczek and W. Hilz. Tübingen: Europäisches Zentrum für Föderalismusforschung.

KENNARD, A. 1997. 'A Perspective on German-Polish Cross-Border Co-operation and European Integration'. In *Schengen and the Southern Frontier of the European Union*, eds., M. Anderson and E. Bort. Edinburgh: International Social Sciences Institute.

KLESMANN, M. 2005. 'Viadrina wird internationaler'. *Berliner Zeitung*, 12 April 2005.

KOSCHAROW, A. 1997. Euroregion Neman: Das Projekt steht. Nun muss es realisiert werden. W & U.

KRÄFKE, S., S. HEEG and R. STEIN. 1997. *Regionen im Umbruch*. Franfurt a.M.: Campus.

KRÄMER, R. 1997. *Grenzen der Europäischen Union*, Potsdam: Brandenburgische Landeszentrale für politische Bildung.

KUMMER, J. 2002. 'Front gegen Verbrechen beginnt im Ausland', *Welt am Sonntag*, 25 November 2002.

KURCZ, Z. 1999. 'Polnische Grenzregionen im Vergleich'. *Welttrends*, 19: 63–74.

LAVELLE, P. 2004. 'The Kaliningrad Experiment'. *The Washington Times*, 3 May 2004.

MARTINEZ, O. J., 1994. 'The Dynamics of Border Integration: New Approaches to Border Analysis'. In *Global Boundaries*, ed., C. Schofield, 1–15. London: Routledge.

MIDDEL, A. 2002. 'Kaliningrad: Putin nimmt das Angebot der EU an'. *Die Welt*, 12 November 2002.

MOLLE, P. 1996. *External Borders Pilot Projec: Placement Report*. Strasbourg: Centre des Études Européennes.

NEUBAUER, M., 1997. 'Verflechtungen bis zur Tatra und zum Bug'. *Franken Post*, 26 January 1997.

NEUSS, B., P. JURCZEK and W. HILZ, (eds.). *Grenzübergreifende Kooperation im östlichen Mitteleuropa*. Tübingen: Europäisches Zentrum für Föderalismusforschung.

NEVINS, J. 2001. *Operation Gatekeeper: The Rise of the Illegal alien and the Remaking of the US–Mexico Boundary*. New York and London: Routledge.

OFFE, C. 1996. 'Capitalism by Design? Democratic Theory Facing the Triple Transition in Eastern Europe'. *Social Research*, 58(2): 3–13.

PAMINA. 1995. 'Comportements socio-économiques de la population dans l'espace PAMINA 1994'. Karlsruhe: PAMINA.

PAULIKAS, S. 2005. 'Kaliningrad: The Forgotten Land'. *BBC News online*, 26 March 2005.

PEERS, S. 2003. 'Memorandum by Statewatch'. In *Proposals for a European Border Guard*. House of Lords Select Committee on the European Union (Session 2002-3), 29th Report, 99–102. London: The Stationery Office.

RAICH, S., 1995. *Grenzüberschreitende Zusammenarbeit in einem 'Europa der Regionen'*. Baden-Baden: Nomos.

RICHTER-MALABOTTA, M. 1998. 'Some Aspects of Regional and Transfrontier Co-operation in a Changing Europe'. In *Schengen and the Southern Frontier of the European Union*, eds., M. Anderson and E. Bort. Edinburgh: International Social Sciences Institute.

ROCH, I. 1999. 'Grenzüberschreitende Regionalentwicklung—Basis europäischer Integration?' *Welttrends*, 22: 44-62.

SATTLER, K. O. 2001. 'Erfreuliche Aufhellung im Schwarzen Dreieck: Transnationaler Umweltschutz im sächsisch-böhmisch-schlesischen Ländereck'. *Das Parlament*, 17 August 2001.

SCOTT, J., A. SWEEDLER, P. GANSTER, and W. D. EBERWEIN, (eds.) 1997. *Borders and Border Regions in Europe and North America*. San Diego: San Diego State University Press.

SKOK, M. 1998. 'Selective Integration? Schengen Restrictions and the Dynamic of Transborder Connections between Slovenia and Italy'. In *Schengen and the Southern Frontier of the European Union*, eds. M. Anderson and E. Bort. Edinburgh: International Social Sciences Institute.

STRASSOLDO, R., 1999. 'Studying Borders in the Gorizia Area'. In *The Boundaries of Understanding*, eds., E. Bort and R. Keat, R. Edinburgh: International Social Sciences Institute.

SUCHANEK, I. 1996. 'Problems and Possibilities for Political Co-operation in the Carpathian Euroregion: The Role of Local Government'. University of Cambridge (Global Fellows Initiative) Occasional Paper No.5. Cambridge.

Süddeutsche Zeitung. 'Stoiber lehnt EU-Beitritt der Türkei strikt ab'. 3 September 2003

TIKKANEN, V., and J. KÄKÖNEN. 1997. 'The evolution of Co-operation in the Kuhmo-Kostamuksha Region of the Finnish–Russian Border'. In *Borders and Border Regions in Europe and North America*, eds., J. Scott et al. San Diego: San Diego State University Press.

TIMMERMANN, H. 2002. 'Strategische Partnerschaft: Wie kann die EU Russland stärker einbinden?' *Integration*, 4: 297–310.

TRAVIS, A. 2005. 'Clarke presses for EU fingerprint plan'. *The Guardian*, 13 July 2005.

URBAN, T. 2002. 'Zweifel am Nachbarn'. *Süddeutsche Zeitung*, 12 November 2002.

WATT, N. 2005. 'Europeans reject Turkey, poll shows'. *The Guardian*, 19 July 2005.

WEISSMANN, O. 1997. 'Arbeitsgemeinschaft Donauländer: Multi-Regional Co-operation for a Common Europe'. In *Schengen and EU Enlargement: Security and Co-operation at the Eastern Frontier of the European Union*, eds. M. Anderson and E. Bort. Edinburgh: International Social Sciences Institute.

WERNICKE, C. 2002. 'EU verzichtet auf Visa zwischen Kaliningrad und Russland'. *Süddeutsche Zeitung*, 23 October 2002.

WOODWORTH, P. 2002. 'Aznar says EU Must Combat Terrorism and Illegal Immigration'. *The Irish Times*, 7 June 2002.

Chapter 12

Switzerland: Between Intergovernmental Co-operation and Schengen Association

Sandra Lavenex

'Schengen' has become a ubiquitous term in Switzerland's political landscape.[1] The question of an eventual association with the Schengen Agreement dominates not only the debates on the reform of the system of internal security in Switzerland, the modernisation of the police, or the asylum law—it has also become a key issue in Switzerland's general relations with the EU. The outcome of the current negotiations on an association with the Schengen and Dublin Agreements between Switzerland and the European Union will be decisive not only for Switzerland's formal place in the evolving European co-operation in justice and home affairs. It will also be decisive for the fate of the other nine dossiers involved in the current round of bilateral negotiations and, herewith, will have important implications for the future and sustainability of the strategy of approximation to the EU via bilateral sectoral agreements pursued by Switzerland.

Why has the question of an association with the Schengen Agreement gained such a great prominence in Switzerland, and which are the implications of such an association? What would happen in absence of such an agreement?

This chapter seeks to provide an overview of the stakes involved in processes of justice and home affairs integration associated with the Schengen Agreement as well as the Dublin Convention for Switzerland as a non-member state and to reflect about the meaning of a formal association to this still primarily intergovernmental area of co-operation. In contrast to the conventional 'monolithic' view of the EU *acquis* as a strongly formalised form of supranational governance which would preclude participation to non-member states, it shall be argued that the area of justice and home affairs is more open towards less hierarchical modes of co-operation below the threshold of membership. Thus, notwithstanding the exact outcome of the

---

[1] Editors' note: This article was written shortly before the referendum of 5 June 2005, in which 54.6 percent of voters supported Switzerland joining the Schengen and Dublin agreements. The accords will not formally enter into force until 2008 at the earliest.

current bilateral negotiations, it will be argued that even without formal association, Switzerland already is—90 percent—a Schengen member. This is largely due to a parallel development of internal security concerns and strategies with those of neighbouring countries, as well as a variety of unilateral, bilateral and multilateral channels of adaptation and co-operation which continue to be in place today.

In reflecting about the implications of these formal and informal channels of integration, two levels of adaptation will be discussed: alignment at the level of public policy and changes at the level of political institutions. Whereas the adaptation pressure at the level of policies and laws is relatively small (given the already large degree of convergence), it will be argued that the relevance of the Schengen Agreement for Switzerland lies at a deeper institutional level. 'Schengenisation'—understood as the deliberate and unintentional, negotiated and unilateral adaptation to the EU's emerging 'area of freedom, security and justice'—is presented as a symbol for a more profound transformation of some central political institutions, in particular federalism and direct democracy, under the influence of European integration and internationalisation.

The chapter discusses the relationship between Schengen and Switzerland in four steps. It starts with a brief presentation of Switzerland's overarching institutional links with the EU and of the strategy of bilateral sectoral association. The second section maps the geographical and political position of Switzerland in the evolving European 'area of freedom, security and justice'. After scrutinising the status quo of unilateral, bilateral and multilateral exchange in the various areas covered by the Schengen and Dublin Conventions, the third section looks more specifically at the contents of the Schengen and Dublin *acquis* and at the reasons for Switzerland's interest in a formal association with these agreements. The fourth section addresses the potential consequences of such an association and the conditions for the transposition of the relevant provisions at the level of public policies and political institutions. After having discussed both the current level of interaction and the potential chances and challenges of a formal association, the last section of the chapter returns to the question of the current bilateral negotiations and concludes with some reflections on the broader significance of Schengen and justice and home affairs co-operation for Switzerland as a non-member state as well as for the enlarging European Union.

Subsidiary Integration via Bilateral Sectoral Agreements

The strategy of integration in the European Union via bilateral sectoral treaties was endorsed by the Swiss government as a 'second-best' alternative after membership in the European Economic Area (EEA) had been turned down by a popular referendum in 1992. Apart from general isolationist tendencies in Swiss public opinion, two issues had an important impact on this negative vote. The first is the fact that the Swiss government, realising the wide scope of obligations emanating from the EEA and the lack of institutional mechanisms for participation in decision-making, had tabled an application for full membership in the EU.[2] The result was that, in the perception of the public, the question of EEA membership became one of joining the Union. The second main motive behind this negative vote which is also of some relevance for Switzerland's stance vis-à-vis the Schengen Agreement consisted of opposition against the introduction of free movement of persons within the EU (Kriesi et al. 1993).

Faced with the impossibility of joining either the EEA or the EU, the Swiss government endorsed the subsidiary strategy of association through separate sectoral agreements. Between 1994 and 1999, seven bilateral treaties were negotiated in form of a package which entered into force on 1 June 2002. The treaties cover civil aviation, public procurement, agricultural trade, overland transport, technical barriers to trade, research, and—upon the insistence of the EU—also free movement of persons.[3]

After the successful conclusion of these first agreements, a second round of negotiations was launched. This deals with the so-called leftovers from the first bilateral negotiations (retirement pensions, processed agricultural products, the environment, statistics, media and education, vocational training and young people) as well as two additional dossiers tabled by the EU and Switzerland respectively: the fight against fraud and the taxation of savings on request of the EU, and co-operation in justice and police matters as well as asylum and immigration (or 'Schengen/Dublin') on Swiss request. Whereas initially the fate of this second round of negotiations seemed to depend upon the capacity to find a consensus regarding co-operation against fiscal offences which would allow Switzerland to maintain its banking secrecy, it now centres on the institutional aspects of an association to the Schengen Agreement. After a compromise was found in the negotiations concerning fraud and taxation of savings, the conclusion of these negotiations now depends on whether the EU is willing to respond to Switzerland's request for a mechanism that would allow for special consultations in the case of future developments in the Schengen *acquis* which would impair 'vital interests' of Switzerland, such as direct democracy.[4]

---

[2] Herewith, the Swiss government converged with the governments of the other members of the European Free Trade Association (EFTA) which, with the exception of Norway (where membership was rejected by a popular referendum in 1994), Liechtenstein and Iceland, joined the EU in 1995.

[3] In addition, it should be mentioned that since 1972, Switzerland has a free trade agreement with the EU.

[4] On these developments see *Neue Zürcher Zeitung* of 8 April 2002: 'Pokerpartie um Schengen'.

Switzerland in the European 'Area of Freedom, Security and Justice'

Geographically, Switzerland is positioned at the heart of 'Schengenland'. Surrounded by EU member states, Switzerland is also economically deeply integrated into the common market. In the year 2000, 77.7 percent of Swiss imports originated from the EU, and 60.4 percent of its exports went into the EU.[5] In terms of people, 70 percent of the foreign population living in Switzerland are from EU countries. With a total share of foreigners at nearly 20 percent, EU citizens make up roughly 14 percent of the total Swiss population. Apart from persons legally resident, Switzerland also has the highest number of border commuters in the EU. Roughly 150,000 persons come every day to work in Switzerland while residing in one of the neighbouring member states. As a consequence of this deep interdependence as well as the importance of the tourism industry, the Swiss borders are necessarily permeable ones. According to estimates from the Federal Office of Justice and the Police, cross-border movements amount to some 700,000 persons crossing the Swiss borders every day, compared to approximately 320,000 vehicles entering or leaving the country.

Apart from the bilateral sectoral agreements presented above, Switzerland's integration in the European area of freedom, security and justice has been facilitated by different avenues of co-operation and adaptation which have developed at three different levels: multilaterally in relations with the EU and its member states; bilaterally with individual neighbouring countries; and unilaterally through internal processes of adaptation.

Relations with the EU

The current set up of Swiss–EU relations has been strongly influenced by the intensification of economic and political integration spurred by the Single European Act (1987) and the Treaty on the European Union as concluded in Maastricht and revised at Amsterdam and Nice. Although it was only with the Amsterdam Treaty of 1997 that the Schengen Agreement was incorporated into the EU framework, it is important to note that, at an intergovernmental level, co-operation between law and order officials has a longer tradition in which Switzerland has—at some stages—played an active role. Thus, if today Switzerland is seeking to conclude a formal association agreement with the Schengen and Dublin Conventions, this does not mean that no co-operation has developed outside of this formal association; nor are the current negotiations the first attempt to secure a formal role in these agreements.

---

5   Source: Swiss customs authorities (*Oberzolldirektion*).

The intergovernmental period

Apart from the global Interpol system, intra-European co-operation in police and judicial as well as immigration matters started in the Council of Europe before becoming gradually concentrated in European Community structures. Here, Switzerland was a full member and played an active role in specialised intergovernmental groups such as the Pompidou[6] group dealing with the fight against drug-related crime, the CAHAR[7] group dealing with asylum, or the Committee on Migration, Refugees and Demography (CMDG). Influenced by growing concerns with terrorism in the 1970s, two other intergovernmental groups were set up outside existing international institutions in which Swiss police and intelligence services co-operated with their counterparts in the EC member states and Austria: the 'Club of Vienna' and the 'Club of Bern' (both created in 1978, see Bigo 1996; Busch 1988). The fact that shortly before, the so-called Trevi Group[8] had been created as the first intergovernmental forum against terrorism composed exclusively of EC member states suggests that this proliferation of co-operation forums was a means of including non-member states in the evolving networks of police co-operation (Lange 1999, p.150).

The foundation for many of the instruments which constitute today the Schengen and Dublin *acquis* was laid in a period of purely intergovernmental co-operation outside the legal framework of the EC/EU, in which Switzerland could play an active role. Even in the 1980s, when the Schengen Implementation Agreement was negotiated, Switzerland—as well as some other non-member states such as Austria and Sweden, but also Australia, Canada, and the USA—maintained close links with its EC partners and were allowed to participate in the meetings of the Trevi Group as well as its sub-groups dealing with terrorism, police training and equipment, immigration, organised crime, and later the establishment of the European Drugs Unit and the European Police Office (Europol) (Busch 1988, 49ff.; Lange 1999, p.151). Similarly, in the domain of (illegal) immigration and asylum, Switzerland was a founding member of the Intergovernmental Consultations on Asylum (IGC) set up in 1986 among a number of 'like-minded' refugee-receiving countries in Western Europe, North-America and Australia.[9]

---

[6] Named after the then acting French President Georges Pompidou and created in 1971.
[7] Ad Hoc Committee of Experts on the Legal Aspects of Refugees set up in 1977. On its work see Lavenex 2001, pp.76–82.
[8] The meaning of the acronym Trevi is contested: one interpretation refers to the fountain with the same name in Rome where the first meeting of the group took place, a second sees it as the acronym for 'Terrorism, Radicalism, Extremism, Violence International', and a third opinion alludes to the name of the then acting police director in the Dutch Ministry of Justice Fonteijn.
[9] The IGC has its seat in Geneva.

The quest for association

Thus, Switzerland was not unprepared when the Schengen Implementation Agreement and the Dublin Convention were signed in 1990. In fact, due to its geographical location surrounded by EU member states and its high numbers of asylum seekers, Switzerland had an immediate interest in joining the Dublin Convention establishing the exclusive responsibility of one (member) state for the examination of an asylum claim. Ironically, it was the first country to introduce, already in 1990, the domestic legal basis for implementing this system of responsibility by way of an urgent governmental decree.[10] In the same year, the federal government set up an expert committee to examine the question of an eventual association with the Schengen Agreement, which concluded in 1993 that such an association would be desirable in order to prevent Switzerland from becoming an 'island of insecurity' in Europe.[11]

However, the introduction of justice and home affairs into the EU framework with the Maastricht Treaty and the failure to join the European Economic Area (EEA) in 1992 delayed these prospects. Although the possibility of concluding a parallel agreement to the Dublin Convention had been seriously discussed in 1990, this was subsequently opposed by the EU and its member states. First, Switzerland was put off with the argument that the member states wanted to await the entry into force of the Convention before negotiating an association. Then, when it finally became operational in 1997, the member states rejected a renewed demand with the argument that the Convention would first have to be translated into EC law in accordance with the upcoming Amsterdam Treaty. Whereas these developments show that, not surprisingly, the EU member states have little interest in integrating Switzerland which would be a 'net beneficiary' of the system of responsibility allocation given its geographical location and its high numbers of asylum seekers, they are also a reaction to Switzerland's selective approach concerning Schengen. This is mainly because initially, the latter tried to be associated with the police co-operation and, in particular, the Schengen Information System (SIS) without, however, adhering to the core of the Agreement, which is the abolition of internal border controls.

Faced with these limitations, the Swiss government has sought to include the themes 'Schengen' and 'Dublin' in its strategy of association on a sectoral basis through the conclusion of bilateral agreements with the EU and its member states. Although the EU rejected this aim in the first round of negotiations, the Swiss government added a unilateral declaration to the 1999

---

[10] Federal Decree of 22 June 1990 on the asylum procedure (BBl 1990 II 573). By contrast, Germany and France, the two countries who initiated the Schengen process in 1984, introduced the necessary changes only three years later in the context of incisive reforms of their constitutions and aliens/asylum laws (Lavenex 2001).

[11] See the final report of the Expert Commission set up under Nationalrat Leuba of 1993.

treaties in which it emphasised its aim to come to an agreement in JHA (Hailbronner 2000). This was eventually accepted in 2001 when the EU requested Switzerland's co-operation in fighting fraud and in taxation matters (see above).

Meanwhile, Switzerland has acknowledged the need to accept the Schengen *acquis* in full, and will also seek an association with other elements of EU justice and home affairs co-operation such as Europol,[12] Eurojust, or the European Police Academy.

Trans-frontier co-operation and regional integration

Whereas at the national level Switzerland's integration into EU structures and processes has faced both internal and external obstacles, its border regions have some of the most dynamic examples of trans-frontier co-operation in Europe. The region of Basel is seen as a pioneer in this respect. Already in the 1960s, the rapidly expanding Basel economy prompted the setting up of a planning office, the Regio Basiliensis, which turned the upper Rhine (with Alsace and Baden-Württemberg) into one of the most intense areas of co-operation involving universities, transport, the banking sector, and the development of a common labour market (Anderson 1996, 120ff.). In addition, and supported by its federal structure, Switzerland has been participating in the EU's Interreg programme from its onset in 1991. With the third Interreg initiative (2000–2006), the scope of co-operation has been widened from the border regions to all European regions, allowing in the Swiss case for the participation of all 26 Cantons. Although focused on economic and social affairs,[13] the strengthening of links and interaction at the level of the regions or the Cantons provides the context for an intensifying exchange among the regional police as well as border guards (see also Bort in this volume).[14] Considering the historically sensitive nature of national borders and their control, this growing integration of border regions may be seen as a deeper condition for the level of permeability and cross-national co-operation implied by the Schengen Agreement as well as the bilateral co-operation agreements concluded between Switzerland and its neighbouring countries (see below). In other words, trans-

---

[12] A co-operation agreement has already been drafted in April 2002 which will enter into force as soon as the overarching bilateral agreement is concluded.
[13] Priorities for action under Interreg III are, *inter alia*, the promotion of urban and rural development, the support for small and medium-sized enterprises, the development of local employment initiatives and the integration of cross-border labour markets, co-operation in research and education, improving environmental protection and transport systems as well as increasing co-operation in legal and administrative areas.
[14] In Switzerland, five regions have entered into cross-border co-operation: Oberrhein Mitte-Süd (around Basel), Alpenrhein/Bodensee/Hochrhein (around lake of Konstanz), Franche-Compté/Suisse (across the Jura mountains with France), Rhone-Alps (around Geneva) as well as around Lugano with Italy.

frontier co-operation has contributed to the 'de-dramatisation' (Walters 2000, p.564) of the border. In the words of Eberhard Bort, 'frontiers, historical dividing lines, separating rather than linking, have been transformed into junctions of regions or states; frontiers, historically often disputed, and the focus of territorial conflicts, have turned into border-lands with intensified exchanges and a high degree of interdependence...' (Bort 1998, p.99).

Multilateral forums of co-operation

Although the institutionalisation of Maastricht's 'third pillar' and its consolidation as well as partial communitarisation have concentrated justice and home affairs co-operation in the EU structures, some older intergovernmental forums continue to exist and new ones have developed in which Switzerland has maintained participation. This is the case for Interpol, the IGC or the respective initiatives within the Council of Europe. Furthermore, Switzerland has concluded a multilateral Alpine Security Partnership (*Alpensicherheitspartnerschaft*) with its neighbouring countries (Austria, France, Germany, Italy and Liechtenstein) which aims at deepening co-operation in justice and home affairs. An interesting development is Switzerland's engagement in forums which deal primarily with the current and future eastern borders of the EU and the fight against illegal immigration and organised crime. Although geographically Switzerland is 'shielded' by the surrounding member states, it is an active member of the so-called Budapest Group[15] and was co-initiator of the International Centre for Migration Policy Development (ICMPD) created in 1993 and located in Vienna, which seeks to develop innovative governmental approaches to migration in co-operation with the countries of Central and Eastern Europe and, more recently, also the Maghreb countries.[16] Yet, notwithstanding its full integration in multilateral intergovernmental as well as regional co-operation processes, the intensification of internal security co-operation within the EU and its growing formalisation and legalisation within supranational structures have prompted the Swiss government to seek an official association with these developments.

---

[15] The Budapest Group is an intergovernmental forum for the fight against illegal immigration and organised group especially in Central and Eastern Europe.

[16] In addition, the activities of the government-sponsored Geneva Centre of the Democratic Control of the Armed Forces (DCAF) which organised the workshop at which these contributions were presented also document the engagement of Switzerland in the strengthening of the EU's Eastern external borders and its involvement in capacity-building in these countries.

Subsidiary strategy: bilateral co-operation agreements with neighbouring countries

Pending the outcome of an eventual treaty with the EU and the Schengen states, Switzerland has concluded a number of bilateral readmission[17] and police co-operation agreements with its neighbours. These agreements are a clear indicator of Switzerland's strong degree of integration in the evolving practices of police co-operation in Europe: although not an EU member, Switzerland has concluded agreements which exceed in substantial respects the Schengen *acquis*. This is the case for the agreements concluded in 1999 with Austria and, especially, Germany.[18] The fact that this agreement allows for more co-operation than among EU member states illustrates the strong degree of flexibility involved in European justice and home affairs co-operation and the various opportunities for formal and informal 'closer co-operation', including with non-member states. The main differences with the Schengen Agreement concern mutual assistance in the case of major events such as catastrophes or severe accidents; the possibility of secret investigations; the absence of geographic or temporal limitations on hot pursuit and transborder observation; the possibility to extend transborder observation to non-suspected contact persons (friends, family) of suspected criminals and to carry it out for preventive purposes; and the exchange of electronic data including data on undesired entries. Given its extensive scope, this agreement has been repeatedly presented as a model for EU member state co-operation in the Schengen framework (Busch 2001). In order to assure the smooth functioning of the agreements, Police and Customs Co-operation Centres were set up with France in Geneva and Italy in Chiasso. In addition, all bilateral agreements allow for co-operation in training purposes as well as the exchange of personnel and the deployment of mixed patrols in the border region.

The third track: unilateral adaptation

Apart from direct negotiations with the EU, participation in multilateral and regional frameworks, and bilateral co-operation with its neighbours, Switzerland has also sought a gradual approximation to the emerging 'area of

---

17 Between 1993 and 2003, Switzerland signed readmission agreements with 20 countries: Albania, Austria, Bosnia and Herzegovina, Bulgaria, Croatia, Estonia, France, Germany, Hong-Kong, Hungary, Italy, Liechtenstein, Latvia, Lithuania, Macedonia, Nigeria, Romania, Senegal, Sri Lanka and Yugoslavia.

18 Police co-operation agreements were concluded with France and Italy in 1998 (BBl 1999, 1485ff.) and Germany as well as Austria and Liechtenstein in 1999 (BBl 2000, 862ff.). The agreement with Italy hitherto precludes the possibility of transfrontier pursuits and observation and, like the one concluded with France, does not allow for the electronic exchange of information. The Accord with Austria/Liechtenstein is similar to the Schengen Agreement but also includes mutual assistance in the case of major events such as catastrophes or severe accidents.

freedom, security and justice' by adapting unilaterally to the evolving justice and home affairs *acquis*. Whereas much of today's convergence is due to parallel developments and unintentional processes of policy diffusion and learning,[19] Switzerland has also pursued a more deliberate form of adaptation. Already in the early 1990s, the federal government endorsed the doctrine of autonomous adaptation or autonomous follow-up (*autonomer Nachvollzug*) according to which the Swiss legislation, upon adoption, is checked for its compatibility with EC and EU legislation and—if necessary and viable—adapted.[20] Thus, many aspects of the Swiss legislation concerning asylum, immigration, visas, border checks, or data protection have long been aligned with European developments (see below).

Why Schengen/Dublin? Swiss Motives for an Association

As demonstrated in the previous section, Switzerland is not only at the heart of 'Schengenland' but is already well integrated in the emerging structures of European co-operation in matters of internal security co-operation. Against the background of its participation in multilateral forums, as well as the far-reaching co-operation agreements with the neighbouring countries at both the national and regional level, the question may be raised whether a formal association agreement with 'Schengen' and 'Dublin' is really necessary. This question seems particularly justified if one considers the degree of political contention existing between the EU and some member states and Switzerland in these matters (see above) and the unpopularity of these negotiations in Switzerland. Whereas the Dublin Convention is generally accepted as a potentially useful mechanism to reduce the number of asylum seekers, the Schengen Agreement is particularly unpopular because of its connections with administrative and judicial co-operation against fraud and fiscal offences and the potential challenges to Swiss banking secrecy; its implications for the organisation of the police forces and in particular the federal division of competences between the central government, the cantons and local governments; the question of compatibility with direct democracy; and, more broadly, its implications for popular images of national sovereignty and independence.

Whereas current political debates in Switzerland suggest that an eventual association agreement might be voted down in a popular referendum, two arguments of the federal government stand out in the justification of such

---

[19] On the various modes of externalities exerted by European integration on third countries see Lavenex and Uçarer 2002.

[20] This strategy goes back to the doctrine of former Secretary of State Franz Blankart who, when drafting the 1988 Report on the Swiss situation in the European integration process (*Bericht über die Stellung der Schweiz im Europäischen Integrationpsprozess* of 24 August 1988) argued that Switzerland should be made fit for joining in order not to join (see Zbinden 1988, p.251).

an agreement: First, the expected benefits from the Dublin Convention and the Eurodac system in alleviating the problems related to asylum seekers, and second, access to the Schengen Information System (SIS).

As mentioned above, Switzerland has sought selective access to these two instruments since the early 1990s and has had to accept that the EU would allow its participation only if it accepted the Schengen Agreement as a whole. Faced with continuously high numbers of asylum seekers, rising costs and an unabated politicisation of the asylum question, the Federal Office for Refugees has strong expectations for an association to the Dublin Convention. Whereas national provisions (including the safe third country rule) and the readmission agreements concluded with the neighbouring countries would allow the rejection of asylum seekers coming from one of these countries in a simplified procedure, both the difficulty to determine and control the provenance of the asylum seekers and the difficulty to ensure the readmission of these persons motivate the desire for full participation in the Dublin system, including access to the Eurodac database. In the absence of such an association, so goes the argument, Switzerland would risk being turned into the 'accumulation basin' (*'Reserveasylland'*) in which all otherwise rejected asylum seekers end up (e.g., example Bundesamt für Flüchtlinge 1998/1999, 24f.; Gerber 1999, p.5).

While the EU has always argued that 'Dublin' was not to be had without 'Schengen', access to the SIS is the second outstanding argument for a formal association. Although most of the bilateral police co-operation agreements allow for the electronic exchange of relevant data, they only cover that of the contracting parties and not the fifteen Schengen countries.[21] Especially in light of the Eastern enlargement of the Union, this limitation is seen as a major handicap in the safeguarding of internal security by the Swiss authorities.

Schengen's Impact on Switzerland

As a consequence of the different layers of co-operation existing below and beyond a formal association with the Schengen agreement, it is difficult to say which additional implications a formal association would have. Indeed, the field of justice and home affairs in the EU, but also in relations with third countries in Western and Eastern Europe, is characterised by a plethora of relations between national public officials acting at various levels of government and often rather independent from EU institutions and sometimes also national politicians and parliaments (Curtin and Meijers 1995).[22] In this last section of the chapter, I will discuss potential challenges posed by the Schengen and

---

[21] These are thirteen EU member states (without the UK and Ireland) and the associated countries Norway and Iceland.

[22] This is also true for Switzerland. Concerning the low involvement of the Swiss parliament in the conclusion of bilateral police co-operation agreements see Busch (1998).

Dublin Conventions for Switzerland in two respects: challenges to public policies and political institutions. It will be argued that whereas at the level of public policies both unilateral adaptation and pre-existing frameworks of co-operation have promoted a high level of conformity with European provisions, the Schengen Agreement and the broader processes of justice and home affairs co-operation associated with it do have an important impact on domestic institutional structures, in particular federalism and direct democracy.

Compatibility of public policies

At the level of public policies, an association to the Schengen Agreement would require only marginal adaptation of Swiss laws. As mentioned above, the Swiss asylum and immigration provisions have been largely brought in line with European measures. The current revision of the asylum law will also harmonise the notion of safe third country with that stipulated in the 1992 London Resolutions of the EU Justice and Home Affairs Ministers. Whereas some doubts could have been raised as to whether the current system of juridical safeguards against negative asylum decisions is compatible with the levels of protection proposed in the (not yet adopted) Commission proposals concerning a minimum standards in the asylum procedure, the inclusion of the current federal appeal commission in the new Federal Administrative Court will conform with these standards. In the area of immigration too, the current law as well as the planned revisions are compatible with the European provisions adopted so far. One example of increased compatibility is the introduction of sanctions against carriers responsible for the illegal entry of undocumented immigrants provided for in the draft Aliens Law.

A second area in which Switzerland has unilaterally adapted to EC legislation is visa policy. Since 2000, Switzerland has exempted nationals from certain Middle Eastern countries[23] as well as Thailand from the necessity to acquire a Swiss visa if they are in possession of a Schengen visa (which is valid for travel purposes not exceeding three months). This measure was introduced in order to counter the perceived negative effects of the necessity to purchase a distinct Swiss visa for the number of persons coming, thus harming both the tourism industry and commerce. In addition to these economic effects, participation in the common visa system is expected to reduce administrative costs. Therefore an association would require only minimal adaptations; in particular, Switzerland would have to abolish the visa requirement for three countries[24] and introduce it for another thirteen (USIS 2002).[25]

---

[23] These are Bahrain, Kuwait, Oman, Qatar, Saudi Arabia and the United Arab Emirates.
[24] Macao, Bulgaria and Romania (in these cases, the abolition is imminent).
[25] These are South Africa, Bahamas, Barbados, the Dominican Republic, Grenada, Jamaica, Kiribati, Saint-Kitts-and-Nevis, St. Lucia, St Vincent and Grenadine, the Salomon Islands, Trinidad and Tobago, as well as Tobago.

Although formally an external border of the EU, control standards at Switzerland's borders with Italy, France, Austria, or Germany resemble already today more an internal border of the EU than an external one. Switzerland has also increasingly adapted to the methods stipulated by the Schengen Agreement and its border manual. Already today, most controls are carried out by mobile forces inside the territory; of the 105 border posts, only 30 are staffed on a permanent basis. Likewise, only 1–3 percent of the estimated 700,000 border crossings per day are effectively controlled. Thus, although physically the Swiss frontiers are maintained, their management resembles much more that at internal EU borders than that stipulated by the Schengen Agreement for external borders. In the case of an association, adaptation will be limited mainly to the system of immigration control at international airports where the Schengen manual will have to be implemented. Much to the relief of popular fears, however, the physical aspect of the Swiss borders will be preserved: since Switzerland is not party to the European Customs Union, controls on goods will be maintained.

Apprehensions that the Schengen Agreement would conflict with the Swiss militia army system (in which members of the military keep their weapon at home) were alleviated in the course of the negotiations. Likewise, a second issue regulated in the Annex to the Schengen Agreement, the measures against the trafficking in drugs, will not require any adaptation of existing laws in Switzerland.

Regarding police co-operation and the SIS, only minor adaptations are needed. The existing bilateral agreements with neighbouring countries (see above) will remain in place insofar as they exceed the scope of the Schengen Agreement. With regard to the SIS, provisions regarding data protection should be in line with European legislation. Both the SIS and the Eurodac database for asylum seekers will require some adaptations in cantonal legislation for their implementation. In particular, each canton will have to nominate a responsible independent control authority. Another unproblematic measure will be the creation of a SIRENE[26] office which will act as the human interface responsible for the exchange of data and the national counterpart for the SIRENE office of the other countries participating in the SIS.

Having discussed most aspects of the Schengen Agreement, one area remains where some apprehensions exist as to whether the *acquis* and/or its future development is compatible with Swiss legislation: co-operation in juridical matters and, in particular, administrative and judicial co-operation in the case of indirect taxes. Similar to the controversial negotiations relating to an agreement on fraud and taxation on savings, the problem here is that Swiss law allows for administrative and judicial co-operation in cases of fiscal fraud, but not fiscal offences such as tax evasion. Whereas the Schengen Agreement so far only covers indirect taxes, this problem will increase when it will be extended as intended to direct taxes such as income taxes. In this case, the requirement of

---

[26] Supplementary Information Request at the National Entry.

administrative and judicial co-operation is likely to jeopardise the banking secrecy guaranteed in Swiss law—which is not only seen as a long-standing tradition, but also a major economic asset. These apprehensions concerning the future development of the Schengen *acquis* that Switzerland would be bound to implement in the case of an association are the reason behind the current stalemate in the bilateral negotiations. These apprehensions are particularly weighty in the light of Swiss direct democracy which, in the case of unpopular developments in the Schengen *acquis*, might jeopardise Switzerland's association.

Consequences for Swiss federalism

Europeanisation and internationalisation impact the internal division of competences in federalist states in several ways. The direction of this impact is not entirely clear-cut: whereas many aspects point to a strengthening of the central state vis-à-vis subnational units, Europeanisation has also opened up new venues for the participation of regions in foreign relations, thus fostering their institutional capacities (Conzelmann and Knodt 2002). In this case, Switzerland is not very different from its European neighbours (Aubert et al. 2001; Hänni 2000). However, both its status as a non-member state and the scope of cantonal competencies lend the question of federalism a particular weight in Switzerland.[27] The importance of this question becomes clear from the genesis of the Swiss state, which was built upon sovereign cantons and enshrined the notion of subsidiarity as a central principle in its constitution, giving the cantons a significant degree of autonomy (Abderhalden 1999; Linder and Vatter 2001). This is particularly crucial in the area of internal security which, in contrast to many other areas of co-operation with the EU, touches core aspects of sovereign statehood (see for example Walker 1993) and, in particular, the cantons' traditional police monopoly.

Studies on the reconfiguration of internal security systems in other federalist European countries highlight numerous changes in the organisation of the (sub)national police systems under the influence of European integration (Lange 1999, 231 ff). In the case of Germany, for instance, Europeanisation has contributed to a levelling out of traditional differences in the police organisation of the *Länder* and a widening of competences at the federal level (Lange 1999, p.409). Several developments point to a similar trend in Switzerland. Whereas originally the federal level had only very limited powers relating mainly to the security of the state (i.e., the political police), it has gradually developed more and more competences especially with regard to transnational organised crime, money laundering, and trafficking in drugs and people. Likewise, these competences have been enlarged from information, co-ordination and analytical functions to include also a genuine investigation capacity and, with this, the nucleus of a federal police.

---

[27] For a recent analysis of Swiss federalism see Vatter and Wälti (2003).

Although these developments may be seen as a necessary adaptation to the changing nature of security threats, they are also a function of increased intergovernmental networking and co-operation as well as of the need to find national partners to deal with their European counterparts. Indeed, this pressure for stronger centralisation is also confirmed in the reports drafted by an interdepartmental committee which was set up in 1999 with the task of reviewing the system of internal security in Switzerland (USIS). In particular, the committee concluded that the capacities of communal and cantonal police corps were not suited to facing the new challenges of international crime, migration and other internal security issues and that this federal division of competences also posed a problem for international co-operation in the context of the Schengen Agreement (USIS 2001). The same problem was stated with regard to the competence for border controls which, until now, has mainly resided with the cantonal authorities.[28] As a consequence, the cantons have hitherto taken an ambiguous stance to the new round of bilateral negotiations and have questioned the urgency of having a formal association with the Schengen Agreement (Konferenz der Kantonsregierungen 2002).[29]

Consequences for direct democracy

A specific problematique of an association with the Schengen and Dublin Conventions is related to the institutional set-up of such an association and the problems of legitimacy and democratic accountability that go with it. This problematique derives from the fact that an association would bind Switzerland not only to the provisions included in the agreement but also to all future measures adopted by the Schengen and EU countries which fall into the scope of the Schengen and Dublin *acquis*.[30] Switzerland would be allowed to participate through joint committees in decision-shaping, but not decision-making. Whereas this obligation to dynamic adaptation is also included in the association agreement concluded with Norway and Iceland (see Brochman and Lavenex 2002), it is particularly sensitive for Switzerland as it may conflict with popular rights enshrined in the constitution.

According to the Swiss constitution, future measures taken within the Schengen/Dublin *acquis* could conflict with the optional referendum which as

---

[28] In practice, the border cantons share the border control functions with the federal border police (*Grenzwachtkorps*): the border police has been delegated the task of controls at border points on roads, on boats as well as the green borders. The cantonal police realises the controls at international airports at in international trains (USIS 2001, 73ff). Due to problems of staffing, a special section of the Swiss army (*Festungswachtkorps*) has also become involved in border control.

[29] See also *Neue Zürcher Zeitung* of 18.5.2001 'Nach Schengen—und zu welchem Preis?' and *Neue Zürcher Zeitung* of 17.3.2002: 'Niemand will nach Schengen'.

[30] From the seven bilateral agreements concluded in the first round of negotiations, only one, the agreement on air transport, has such a dynamic component.

guaranteed in Article 141 of the Federal Constitution.[31] Although it is difficult to say how often the optional referendum would be taken in practice, an estimation on the basis of the evolution of the Schengen/Dublin *acquis* between March 1995 and 2002 comes to the conclusion that around 12 percent of all measures adopted would have qualified for the rights enshrined in Article 141 of the Constitution (Interdepartmentale Arbeitsgruppe PESEUS 2002, p.7).

Whereas also here one can say that increasing internationalisation and Europeanisation impose manifold limitations on the ideal and the procedures of direct democracy which, most of the time, play outside the scope of the general public's awareness, the obligation to comply with the future evolution of the Schengen/Dublin *acquis* is particularly sensitive. This results on the one hand from the fact that although participating in general deliberations, Switzerland—as a non-EU member state—would not be allowed to vote for or against upcoming measures. On the other hand, it derives from Schengen's and Dublin's pertinence for individual rights and fundamental freedoms and, herewith, the rights of every man and woman. Whereas already in the EU, co-operation in justice and home affairs has faced enduring criticism as to its lack of democratic accountability and transparency, the democratic deficit is exacerbated in the associated countries which remain outside of the formal decision-making mechanisms.

It seems that the Swiss negotiations have recognised that the commitment to an automatic adaptation to future elements of the Schengen/Dublin *acquis* might collide with constitutional rights and that these rights might seriously inhibit the Swiss government to live up to its obligations under an association. A first step to alleviate this dilemma was the negotiation of a two-year transition phase before a new measure is implemented which would allow for the conducting of an eventual optional referendum.[32] The

---

[31] Article 141 of the Federal Constitution on the Optional Referendum reads:
'The following are submitted to the vote of the People at the request of any 50,000 citizens entitled to vote, or of eight Cantons, declared within a period of no more than 18 months from the official publication of the act in question: a. Federal Laws; b. Federal laws declared urgent with a validity exceeding one year; c. Federal decrees to the extent the Constitution or statute law prescribes this; d. International treaties which: 1. are of unlimited duration and may not be terminated; 2. provide for the entry into an international organisation; 3. contain important provisions which create binding legal rules or require the adaption of federal law in order to become effective.' On 9 February 2003 the People agreed to the removal of both the old Art. 1d/3 (involve a multilateral unification of law) and (2) The Federal Assembly may submit other international treaties to optional referendum. In particular, the referendum falling under Art. 141 (1) a. (Federal Laws) and Art. 141 (1) c3 (International treaties which contain important provisions..) could be taken against future developments of the Schengen/Dublin *acquis*.'

[32] This two year period exceeds significantly the limits awarded to the Nordic associated countries for the adoption of future measures in cases which impact on their national constitutions—Iceland 4 weeks and Norway 6 months.

second step is the request for a special consultation mechanism with the EU partners which, however, has not been specified so far.

Conclusion

Soon, Switzerland might become the third non-EU member state participating in those sections of the area of freedom, security and justice which are regulated by the Schengen and Dublin Conventions. Although the question of a formal association is pending, this chapter has argued that already today, Switzerland may be considered as a 90 percent Schengen country. Its strong degree of integration in the evolving framework of internal security co-operation is underpinned by a variety of multilateral, bilateral and unilateral channels and is illustrative of the strong inter- and trans-governmental dynamics which are at play in the co-ordination of justice and home affairs. Thus, like many other aspects of the Schengen *acquis* which become codified under European law, an association would mainly formalise already existing practices. At the same time, however, this chapter has argued that the question of an association with the Schengen Agreement is symbolic of more fundamental changes at work inside Switzerland's political system. Although linked to more general processes of internationalisation and Europeanisation, the Schengen Agreement has important implications for two fundamental features of the Swiss state—federalism and direct democracy.

Although this chapter has focused on the implications of Schengen for Switzerland, the institutional questions addressed above will also have repercussions for the functioning of justice and home affairs co-operation in the enlarging EU. Whether formally associated or not, Switzerland's participation in the emerging area of freedom, security, and justice will bring yet another degree of flexibility in an already fragmented policy field, thus probably strengthening the already predominant intergovernmental elements in this core area of political unification.

References

ABDERHALDEN, URSULA. 2000. 'Die Geschichte des schweizerischen Bundesstaates'. In *Schweizerischer Föderalismus und europäische Integration. Die Rolle der Kantone in einem sich wandelnden internationalen Kontext*, ed., Peter Hänni, 5–48. Zürich: Schulthess.

ALBERT, MATHIAS, DAVID JACOBSON and YOSEF LAPID (eds.). 2001. *Identities, Borders, Orders. Rethinking International Relations Theory*. Minneapolis: University of Minnesota Press.

ANDERSON, MALCOLM. 1996. *Frontiers. Territory and State Formation in the Modern World*. London: Polity Press.

ANDERSON, MALCOLM and EBERHARD BORT (eds.). 1998. *The Frontiers of Europe*. London: Pinter.

BORT, EBERHARD. 1998. 'Mitteleuropa: The Difficult Frontier'. In *The Frontiers of Europe*, eds., Malcolm Anderson and Eberhard Bort, 91–108. London: Pinter.

BUNDESAMT FÜR FLÜCHTLINGE. 1998–99. *Asyl Schweiz. Ein Überblick über den Asylbereich*. Bern: Bundesamt für Flüchtlinge.

BUSCH, HEINER. 1988. 'Von Interpol zu TREVI. Polizeiliche Zusammenarbeit in Europa'. *Bürgerrechte und Polizei/CILIP*, 30: 38–55.

―――――――― 1998. 'Die Schweiz als Zwei-Dritte-Schengen-Land. Verträge mit den Nachbarn verändern auch die Hausordnung der Schweiz'. *WoZ*, 15.

―――――――― 2001. 'Offene Grenzen – aber nur für die Polizei. Verrechtlichung grenzüberschreitender Polizei-Aktionen'. *Bürgerrechte & Polizei/CILIP*, 60 (2).

CONZELMANN, THOMAS and MICHÈLE KNODT (eds.). 2002. *Regionales Europa – Europäisierte Regionen*. Frankfurt/New York: Campus.

CURTIN, DEIRDRE and HERMAN MEIJERS. 1995. 'The Principle of Open Government in Schengen and the European Union: Democratic Retrogression?'. *Common Market Law Review*, 32 (2): 391–442.

FISCHER, ALEX, SARAH NICOLET and PASCAL SCIARINI. 2002. 'Europeanisation of a non-EU Country: The Case of Swiss Immigration Policy'. *West European Politics* 25 (4): 143–170.

GERBER, JEAN-DANIEL. 1999. 'Passé et Futur d'une Politique d'Asile. Réfléxion sur les Nouvelles Perspectives'. Exposé Devant le Congrés du Parti Libéral Suisse. Morges, 22 September 1999. Bundesamt für Flüchtlinge.

HÄNNI, PETER (ed.). 2000. *Schweizerischer Föderalismus und europäische Integration. Die Rolle der Kantone in einem sich wandelnden internationalen Kontext*. Zürich: Schulthess.

HAILBRONNER, KAY. 2000. *Kompatibilität des Schweizer Asylverfahrens mit Harmonisierungsbestrebungen im Asylrecht der Europäischen Union*. Zürich: Schulthess.

INTERDEPARTMENTALE ARBEITSGRUPPE PESEUS. 2002. *PESEUS VI. Referendum und Weiterentwicklung des Schengen-Acquis*. Bern.

KNELANGEN, WILHELM. 2001. *Das Politikfeld innere Sicherheit im Integrationsprozess. Die Entstehung einer europäischen Politik der inneren Sicherheit*. Opladen: Leske und Budrich.

KONFERENZ DER KANTONSREGIERUNGEN (ed.). 2001. 'Die Kantone vor der Herausforderung eines EU-Beitritts'. Bericht der Arbeitsgruppe Europa-Reformen der Kantone. Zürich: Schulthess.

―――――――― 2002. 'Bemerkungen zur vorläufigen Würdigung des Bundesrates von Schengen/Dublin vor Aufnahme von

Verhandlungen'. Verabschiedet von der Plenarversammlung der KdK am 25. Januar 2002.

LANGE, HANS-JÜRGEN. 1999. *Innere Sicherheit im Politischen System der Bundesrepublik Deutschland*. Opladen: Leske und Budrich.

LAVENEX, SANDRA. 2001. *The Europeanisation of Refugee Policies. Between Human Rights and Internal Security*. Aldershot: Ashgate.

LINDER, WOLF and ADRIAN VATTER. 2001. 'Institutions and Outcomes of Swiss Federalism: The Role of the Cantons in Swiss Politics. *West European Politics*, 24 (2): 95–122.

SCHWOK, RENE, and NICOLAS LEVRAT. 2001. 'Switzerland's relations with the EU after the adoption of the Seven Bilateral Agreements'. *European Foreign Affairs Review*, 6(3): 335–354.

USIS. 2001. 'Teil II Grobe Soll-Varianten, Sofortmassnahmen'. Bern, 12 September 2001.

USIS. 2002.'3ᵉ partie. Etude détaillée'. Bern, 24 September 2002.

VATTER, ADRIAN and SONJA WÄLTI. 2003. 'Swiss Federalism in Comparative Perspective'. Special Issue of the *Swiss Political Science Review*, 9(1).

WALKER, NEIL. 1994. 'European Integration and European Policing: A Complex Relationship'. In *Policing across national boundaries*, eds., Malcolm Anderson and Monica den Boer, 22–45. London: Pinter.

WALTERS, WILLIAM. 2000. 'Mapping Schengenland: Denaturalizing the Border'. *Environment and Planning D: Society and Space*, 20: 561–580.

ZBINDEN, MARTIN. 1998. 'Von der Neutralität zur direkten Demokratie: die Entwicklung der schweizerischen Integrationspolitik' In *Der Beitritt der Schweiz zur Europäischen Union: Brennpunkte und Auswirkungen*, eds., Thomas Cottier and Alwin R Kpse, 213–269. Zürich: Schulthess.

Part IV

Comparative Perspectives

Chapter 13

Border Issues: Transnational Crime and Terrorism

Louise I. Shelley

The fall of the Iron Curtain and deliberate policies to open borders to promote trade changed the dynamics of border control at the end of the 20th century. Cross-border mobility has increased dramatically in Europe since the Schengen agreement and NAFTA (North American Free Trade Agreement). At the same time, the rise in legitimate border crossings has coincided with an enormous growth in illegitimate border crossings as millions of people seek entrance into the affluent countries of Western Europe and North America (Andreas and Snyder 2000).

Individuals cross the border not just at the physical perimeter of a country but also at airports. Therefore, the regulation of borders requires monitoring of all forms of crossings by all forms of transport. Facilitating this massive movement of people is computer technology, which allows individuals to meet and connect in ways that were not previously imaginable. The increased movement of people and goods, one aspect of globalisation, has coincided with increasing economic and demographic disparity between developed and developing countries. There are powerful economic forces driving individuals from their homes in the developing and transitional world to the more affluent countries. Unable to enter the developed countries legally, there has been an enormous increase in transnational crime groups facilitating illegal immigration. The growth of international terrorism whose targets often lie outside the terrorists' home country has placed enhanced emphasis on border control ever since the events of 11 September 2001.

The rise of regional conflicts, network-based transnational crime, and terrorism, seriously undermine the ability of both weak and strong states to control their borders. However, the need to secure defensible borders is even more important as transnational criminals and terrorists have enormous motivation to cross the borders to realise their financial and/or political objectives. Therefore, there is a great disproportionality between those seeking to violate border regulation and the capacity of even the most affluent states to safeguard their borders. The present commitment in North America and Europe to promote international trade often far outweighs their willingness and capacity to establish meaningful border controls to realise their objectives in an era with great concerns about transnational crime and terrorism.

Regional Perspectives

Apart from the most affluent countries, most of the world's states have little capacity to guard their borders. The problems of insufficient financial resources, inadequate training, low pay and corruption, mean that effective border security is a reality only in very few regions of the world. Even the affluent states of Australia and Japan, whose island status isolates them from some problems of cross-border crime and terrorism, are not immune from them.

The emergence of regional conflicts in the post-Cold War era has increased the desire of those affected to escape conflicts and has limited the capacity of states to control their borders (Berdal and Malone 2000). The prospect for continued turmoil in many regions because of enduring conflicts and local, regional or international tensions ensures future challenges to effective border control in many parts of the globe.

In the fifteen years since the collapse of the Berlin Wall, Europeans have become increasingly concerned with cross-border crime that appears to be circulating ever more easily within the European Union. The penetration of crime groups from Eastern Europe, Asia and Latin America has made organised crime a primary security concern for the European Union (EU 2002). The linkage between transnational crime and terrorism has become evident in the European investigations that followed the 11 September attacks. Those investigations revealed that many terrorists supported themselves through such organised crime activity as credit card fraud and counterfeiting (Shelley and Picarelli 2002).

Driving the United States' heightened concerns with border issues are, of course, the terrorist acts of 11 September. Prior to this date, American border concerns were focused primarily on the illegal entry of drugs and people into the United States (Andreas 2000). Homeland security is increasingly concerned with guarding borders and entry into the United States. Although potential terrorists had been detained prior to 11 September at US borders, it was not until the second attack on the World Trade Center and the attack on the Pentagon that the United States reoriented its policies in focusing more attention on border controls.

American policy on border patrol now seeks to control transnational crime both at home and abroad. The US border patrol is being retrained to pay more attention to these issues and American foreign assistance programs focus on border guard training in regions of instability and at high risk of terrorism.[1] There is also more focus on combating trafficking in nuclear materials and safeguarding border regions.

---

[1] The Transnational Crime and Corruption Center at American University is developing new curriculum for the US border patrol; see also the report of INL on the State Department website, <http://www.state.gov/g/inl/corr/c2167.htm>, for foreign assistance.

In many of the less affluent states and transitional countries, border controls are often meaningless in practical terms. Border patrols are insufficiently trained and equipped. Moreover, low salaries and poor living conditions make members of the border patrol prone to corruption. This can mean looking the other way when human beings and commercial freight cross the border illegally, or it can involve significant payments to the border guards to allow illicit movement across borders. In some parts of the world, border crossings that appear legitimate are facilitated by false or forged documents. Sometimes this movement is facilitated by corrupt personnel in consular missions who provide fake passports and visas for significant sums of money.

Vulnerability of Border Areas

Certain categories of border areas are particularly vulnerable to the problems of transnational crime and terrorism. These include regions with: (1) lengthy exposed borders and/or a high volume of border crossings; (2) transitional states where the control mechanisms of the central state do not function effectively; 3) areas of great political or regional conflict or where the state has lost control over part of its territory; (4) countries with very high levels of corruption on at least one side of the border; (5) countries in which there is government complicity in transnational crime or terrorism.

Lengthy borders

Managing borders is most difficult where there are thousands of kilometres of borders and limited controls over those extended borders. Border control officers may seek to channel border crossings through selected points along the US–Canada border, the US–Mexico and Russia–China borders, but many individuals cross at unregulated crossings (Thompson 2003).

For example, Chinese nationals are smuggled into the United States through unregulated territory of Indian reserves on the US–Canada border, and Latin Americans enter the United States through a national park on the southern US border that has a limited border guard presence. The same crossing points can be used by both transnational criminals and terrorists.

In the Asian context, where there are less resources expended on controlling lengthy borders the consequences can be particularly pernicious. For example, Russian–Chinese crime groups were recently apprehended near the Russian–Mongolian border trafficking radioactive materials. Although this case was detected, the enormous Russian–Mongolian and Russian–Chinese borders provide ample opportunities for illicit crossings. Remote and mountainous areas in Central Asia similarly provide ample opportunities for the movement of criminals, terrorists and illicit commodities.

The Tajik–Afghan border stretches for more than a thousand kilometres. Loosely guarded, with extensive corruption on both sides of the border; there are ample opportunities for the massive drug production of

Afghanistan to move into Tajikistan (Kupchinsky 2003). Apart from the Russian military, Russian border guards in Tajikistan have been heavily implicated in the drug trade. Trafficking has also been engaged in by the specialised units designated to fight organised crime and the drug trade. In 2003, a warrant officer from the border guard service of the Russian Federal Security Service was caught with 12 kg of heroin, and later that year another warrant officer from the same service was caught with eight kg of heroin ('V Tajikistane zaderzhan rossiyskiy pogranichniks 12 kg geroina', *Interfax*, 5 May 2004).

Not only do the drugs move but also the criminal networks which distribute these drugs. This problem existed before the most recent war in Afghanistan but has been compounded by the need to earn money in the post-war period. Terrorist networks also move across this loosely guarded border to obtain revenues from the drug trade to further finance their operations.

Heavily frequented borders

Borders that serve as transit points for large numbers of people are particularly vulnerable to illegal crossings by criminals and terrorists. The Dutch airport of Schiphol is one of the busiest airport hubs in Europe. The Dutch explain the enormous presence of transnational crime in their country as a consequence of the ability of individuals to easily enter through their airport and extensive ports. For this reason, the Netherlands is the gateway for many drugs into Europe and has a great diversity of transnational crime groups.

Millions of border crossings between the US–Mexico and US–Canada borders allow illicit trade to enter with the licit (Andreas 2001). The implementation of NAFTA to enhance cross-border trade and the movement of goods in North American has augmented the number of border crossings. The vast proportion of illicit drugs and migrants enter through the southern border. Potential terrorists have been apprehended at the US–Canadian border, including the Algerian Ahmed Ressam, who plotted to blow up the Los Angeles airport (Powell and Haughney 2001). It is not precluded that some potential terrorists have traversed the southern US border but with over one hundred million border crossings on the southern border of the US, finding potential terrorists is like finding a 'needle in a haystack'. US officials are increasingly concerned because a larger proportion of the apprehended aliens at the US–Mexican border are not Mexican and may be members of terrorist groups.(World Net Daily, 9 June 2005).[2]

---

[2] In 2002, the numbers were 252 million passengers, 86 million cars, 4.4 million trucks, and about 600,000 trains at the US Mexico borders. According to the new Customs and Border Protection unit in the Department of Homeland Security <www.CBP.gov>

Transitional states where control mechanisms do not function effectively

The term 'transitional state' most generally applies to the countries of the former Soviet Union, which are in transition from a communist system to a more democratic polity and more open market economy. Yet there are other states which can also be defined as transitional, such as South Africa, which is in transition from an authoritarian state to a more open democratic one, or Mexico, which is in transition from a one-party political system to a more multi-party system.

One of the key elements of this transition process is the dismantling of the police controls of the authoritarian state. Among the first to be dismantled are the tight border controls that existed in former socialist states and South Africa (Gastrow 1998). In addition, the expulsion of some former law enforcement personnel, and the voluntary departure of others, has made the states less policed. Compounding the problem is the fact that former members of the police and security apparatus in former socialist countries have often gone over into the private security sector, forming their own security forces that differ in name only from organised crime (Volkov 2002).

In these societies, transnational criminals and terrorists can operate with almost total impunity. They can find safe havens or even fertile territory in which to operate. In the states of the former Soviet Union and Eastern Europe, one finds not only indigenous crime groups but groups from many other parts of the world that are investing in these countries or hiring personnel from the region. In the Eastern part of Russia in particular, one finds crime groups from China, Japan, and Korea (Nomokonov 2001). In the western parts of Russia and Ukraine, there are Nigerian, Colombian and Italian crime groups operating. Since the war in Afghanistan, individuals associated with the terrorist networks have been detained in Ukraine and are reported to have taken refuge in Georgia (Peuch 2002).

A similar phenomenon is observed in South Africa. In the decade since the end of apartheid, South Africa has received transnational crime groups from many regions of the world. Law enforcement bodies have identified groups from other parts of Africa, the Indian sub-continent and Russia. Some of these groups operate there, entering through the less tightly controlled borders, whereas others use the superb transportation and banking infrastructure as a base for their operations throughout the African sub-continent (Gastrow 1998). Some of the trade in 'blood diamonds', where diamonds are traded for arms used in regional conflicts, occurs throughout South Africa (Gordema 2002). Transnational crime and terrorism are inseparable in these cases and capitalise on the limited border controls in much of Africa to achieve their goals.

Areas of regional and political conflict

Areas of regional and political conflict do not have defensible borders. The rise of regional conflicts in many parts of the world since the end of the Cold War makes many states unable to maintain effective border management (Reno 2000). Whereas there were twelve such conflicts in 1989, there were thirty-seven registered in 1997. Some of those conflicts were particularly associated with the rise of transnational crime and terrorism. Moreover, the failure to solve those conflicts meant that many of them have had a spill-over effect on adjoining countries. Among the most prominent of such conflicts has been the ongoing guerrilla war in Colombia, the Balkan conflicts within Europe and the Chechen conflict within Russia, with spill-over impact in the Caucasus. Also significant have been the numerous regional wars, among which the most notable in Africa include the conflicts in Sierra Leone, Niger, and Burundi, and in Asia, the conflict in Sri Lanka.

The conflicts persist when there are significant natural resources which can be traded for illicit commodities (Reno 2000; Duffield 2000). Therefore, the nexus of transnational crime and terrorism fuelled the Balkan conflicts; the drug trade prolongs the conflict in Colombia; the vast arms and drug trade saturate the porous borders around Chechnya; and Tamil tigers facilitate the proliferation of the drug trade. Drugs moved internationally by transnational crime groups and terrorists help exacerbate regional conflicts (Duffield 2000). The inability to control cross-border movement in these conflict regions ensures the perpetuation both of the conflicts and the illicit activities which fund them.

States that lack control over their territory

The centralised state which maintains control over its borders is far from a reality in many parts of the world. Only the most affluent states have the resources to effectively control their territory. Many states in Western Europe have chosen to cede control to a larger unit under the Schengen agreement, which places responsibility on the peripheral states of the union (Anderson 1996). In Europe, there is a large amount of illicit movement into regions at the edges of Western Europe. Spain now estimates that it has 300,000 women illegally engaging in prostitution (Gomez-Cespedes and Stangeland, 2004). The majority of these women originate in Latin America and to a lesser extent come from Eastern Europe and Africa. This figure does not include the illegal male migrants often smuggled in from North Africa via the Mediterranean.

A very large illicit movement of people previously occurred between Italy and Albania (Hysi, 2004). Greece has many trafficked people from the Balkans and Eastern Europe because of its inadequate border controls. Millions are detained each year on the US–Mexico border for trying to enter illegally (Winer 1997). Within this very large illicit movement of people there are often a certain number of potential terrorists who have managed to obtain legitimate work and study visas that allow them to live legally in Europe and the United States. The investigations of the bombings in London in July 2005 and in the 11 September investigations revealed that individuals were able to enter the states with visas.

In other regions of the world, the absence of border controls is a result of different factors. Unlike in the Schengen case where countries have chosen to open their borders, in other parts of the world, the absence of state controls has made its states lose control over their borders. For example, the central government of Colombia has failed to control many areas on its borders with Brazil and Venezuela. This contributed to the recent bombing in Venezuela where the perpetrators crossed the border from Colombia. In Georgia, unresolved conflicts in Abkhazia and Ossetia provide fertile ground for drug trade between the East and points west and a lively trade in all forms of contraband (Ciklauri and Lammich 2000). This conflict exemplifies the problem of the weak state.

Yet a weak state can result from other conditions as well. Corruption of security and law enforcement personnel and the absence of financial resources to pay for personnel are important contributors to weak border controls. Also important may be the absence of political will to control one's borders that are often an artificial creation of colonial rule. In many national situations there is a loss of control over territory even though there is an intense desire by the central state to reassert control over separatist territory. But without financial and human resources, the state cannot achieve its objective. The previously discussed Georgian and Colombian cases epitomise this phenomenon.

Countries with very high levels of corruption

Border and customs officials are frequently among the most corrupted of law enforcement officials (Rose-Ackerman 1999). Often this corruption is the result of very low salaries paid by the government, which provide an existence below the subsistence level. But in other cases, individuals expend large sums to obtain positions in border and customs services because of the significant opportunities for personal enrichment.

Integrity on one side of the border is not sufficient to ensure adequate controls. Cases of corruption of the US border and customs patrol are rare. The chances of detection and prosecution are high. In contrast, on the Mexican side of the border there is a very high level of corruption of law enforcement personnel. Effective border management is difficult to maintain when there is such a variance in levels of integrity. The problem has become more acute as there has been increasing violence on the US–Mexican border. As controls have increased, the costs of being smuggled across the border have increased, and so have the incentives to corrupt officials on the border.

In some cases, corruption occurs not at the actual border but in the consular offices which award visas to enter the country. Organised crime groups have penetrated the visa sections of US consulates in Prague, Kyiv and India permitting criminals to enter.[3] In the Balkans, corrupt officials of some Western European countries sell visas to sex traffickers permitting women to enter into Europe after which they can be moved within Europe without problems by the traffickers. Widespread corruption is a major impediment to effective border management.

Government complicity in transnational crime or corruption

The problem of government complicity is much broader than the concept of the 'rogue state', which is seen as supporting terrorism. There are many regions of the world where officials gain personally by tolerating significant cross-border trade in contraband. One of the most notable examples of this is the tri-border area of Argentina, Brazil and Paraguay. The illicit cross-border trade in Paraguay is a significant part of the economy and provides significant personal revenues for the national leadership. This tri-border region also is a focal point of terrorists. Without effective border controls, terrorists planned and executed a bombing of the Jewish community centre in Argentina using this region as their base.

A significant illicit trade that fuelled transnational crime and terrorists, occurred between Albania and Italy. This was facilitated not only by the links between the crime groups, but the law enforcement on both sides of the border (Hysi, 2004). Italian officials were able to stop Cosa Nostra co-operation with terrorists not by tightening border controls, but instead by revealing to the Cosa Nostra the nature of their trading partners (Author's interviews with Deputy Chief Prosecutor in Palermo in October 2002). Informing the members of the highly nationalistic Cosa Nostra that their trading partners were not just engaged in illicit commerce, but were actually terrorists supporting their operations through illegal cross-border trade, halted these trade relationships. Italian prosecutors were more successful in curtailing this illegal cross-border trade by understanding the mentality of the crime group than by using repressive measures. Repressive measures, however, have been used to stop the extensive cross-border flows of people, as has been seen recently between Albania and Italy. Smuggling of migrants was almost eliminated by 2002 because repressive measures were used between 2000 and 2002. In 2000–2001, 663 rubber dinghies carrying 18,000 illegal immigrants were sent back from Italy to Albania (Hysi, 2004).

This discussion suggests that there are many structural impediments to effective border control. Despite this fact, terrorists and transnational criminals seek to diminish their risk of detection by segmenting their activities.

---

[3] This is based on information obtained from the FBI under the Freedom of Information Act on Kyiv, interviews with the investigator in the Indian case, and press reports of the Prague case which led to prosecutions.

Segmentation of Terrorism and Transnational Organised Crime to Minimise Risks

The terrorists and criminals try to span different jurisdictions to minimise the risk of effective enforcement. Furthermore, the operations are segmented with the planning going on in one country, the financing going on in another country, with the operation carried out in a third locale. Criminals capitalise on the existence of borders where legislation is not harmonised by operating as networks across continents shifting their operations on the basis of feasibility and calculated risks.

Illustrative of this is that the terrorists behind the 11 September 2001 attacks planned their crime in Hamburg, received training in Afghanistan, funding from the Middle East and perpetrated their crime in the United States. The failure to coordinate law enforcement and intelligence internationally and domestically permitted the terrorists to plan the multi-faceted operation without detection.

The same segmentation can be seen in the illicit drug trade. The drugs can be produced in South America, marketed in the United States and the profits laundered in the Caribbean. With Asian trafficking networks, the drugs move from Asian to European markets through many routes with the profits repatriated, placed in offshore locales or moved internationally through the system of underground banking (Geopolitical Observatory of Drugs 1996).

The planning of crime and terrorist operations using cell phones and computer communications moving through cyberspace means that the protection of borders has even less meaning as there are no tangible borders in cyberspace (Shelley 2002).

Intersection of Border Control and Terrorism

Managing borders to prevent transnational crime and terrorism requires multi-faceted strategies. These include not only addressing the terrorists who seek to enter, but the materials used to carry out their operations and the commodities and assets used to finance their operations. Enhancing physical controls is only part of the strategy. While Ahmed Ressam tried to cross the US–Canada border with the materials needed to bomb the Los Angeles airport, others enter the country in other ways often separate from the materials needed to carry out their operations.

The perpetrators of the attacks on 11 September entered the US on student and tourist visas. Therefore, greater controls need to be placed on visa issuance as a form of border protection. In countries where potential terrorists can easily enter without visa scrutiny or by bribing border guards, terrorists can find a safe haven—a place to hide out or a base of operations to plan their activities in another country. Examples of this include the planning in Thailand of the bombing in Bali, Indonesia, and the movement of terrorists into the Pankisi gorge in Georgia. The movement into these safe havens is sometimes facilitated by transnational crime groups. Individuals are able to reside during their sometimes long planning stages thanks to large pay-offs to local officials. The money for these pay-offs is often generated from illicit activities.

The movement of the terrorists is only one component of the terrorist act. Frequently significant materials must be transported including arms, nuclear materials, or the raw components for a bomb, as in the Ahmed Ressam case. Organised crime groups are important actors in the transport sector in many countries. Therefore, necessary links form between the terrorists and crime groups as they seek to move their commodities. Crime groups, as in the previously cited Chinese–Mongolian case, were called in to transport the nuclear materials.

Terrorist activities do not require as much financing as a large-scale military engagement, but there are significant expenses to maintain terrorist cells, obtain intelligence and run operations. The activity which most often funds terrorist activities is the drug trade. This occurs on a massive scale out of Afghanistan, where it constituted a vital part of funding of the Taliban. But the drug trade has also funded terrorist groups in Sri Lanka and Colombia and other regions of the world. In some parts of the world, cross-border trade in diamonds funds terrorist activities (Gordema 2002). Therefore, the control of the commodities which fund terrorist activities is as necessary a part of border control as is the control of the people who carry out these acts.

The control of potential terrorists, materials and the sources of terrorist financing are all needed if one is to successfully address terrorism. Yet they require different strategies to combat these problems at borders. Border patrol cannot simply be reactive; it must be informed by intelligence and a fuller understanding of terrorism and its diverse forms.

Recommended Structural Reforms

The implementation of effective border defences to protect against terrorism requires major structural changes in border management including new forms of training, institutional change and greater reliance on intelligence. To begin with, border guards must be trained to think and not just act reflexively. Often those serving on the border are the lowest level of military or law enforcement personnel, and do not have the education or the background to understand and react to the problems that they face on the border.

The problems of corruption in the border services of many countries remain fundamental obstacles to effective border control. In many developing and transitional countries, border patrol personnel are paid less than the survival wage in their countries and it is presumed that they will enhance their incomes through bribes. Terrorists, having such strong political motivations, are willing to expend large amounts of money to obtain entry into a particular country or to move their arms and supplies across borders. To secure their results, they bribe border guards, customs and consular officials to obtain needed documents and secure passage.

Border guards need to receive adequate professional training and compensation. There needs to be appropriate oversight of their activities. Border control and customs also need to be more closely integrated. In some countries, there is significant corruption in one sector but not as much in the other, yet cleaning up one sector without the other results in porous borders. Control of borders cannot occur with a segmental approach—it requires greater integrity in all aspects of law enforcement at the border.

The current interest in intelligence-led policing applies to the border sector. In fact, the co-ordination of intelligence and border security may be more important than in day-to-day police work. The increasing number of people and goods crossing the borders means that the detection of the illegal within the large legitimate movement of people and goods is extremely difficult. Therefore, without the information which comes from intelligence on suspicious shipments of commodities and people, there is great difficulty in finding the potential terrorist threat. Whereas Ressam's suspicious behaviour alerted customs officials on the US–Canadian border, there are many more potential terrorists in different parts of the world who do not arouse any suspicion. Without information that can help target law enforcement, there is little chance that border officials can serve an effective preventive function.

International Assistance in Border and Customs Issues to Control Organised Crime and Terrorism

The opening of borders in Europe and the collapse of the Soviet Union made border assistance a paramount concern of international assistance programs. This was only heightened after the events of 11 September. Yet international assistance can go only so far in countries where the central government has lost control over much of its territory. The problems of separatism, regional conflicts and inefficient central governments undermine border assistance programs from their inception. In many cases, the central government lacks the political will to address these problems. Problems of internal order and domestic stability are more important than what occurs at the periphery of the country.

Existing border assistance programs provided by many different foreign aid donors are not coordinated. The assistance programs become like 'competing missionaries' trying to influence the shape of border policies to their terms of reference. Therefore, European and American border assistance programs are often trying to achieve the same results in one country or region without adequate co-ordination, whereby the recipient country becomes confused as to the nature of the laws they should adopt, how they should reshape their border patrol institutions and how they should shape their national priorities.

The countries offering assistance more often provide technical advisors rather than the funds needed to shape and develop a border service. The border patrol of the Soviet Union could not service the fifteen new countries. In the territory of the former USSR, few Soviet successor states, except the Baltic countries, have had the financial resources to develop and establish a national border patrol. Therefore, the poorly paid and equipped border patrol has survived by extraction of bribes from those seeking to move across borders. The enforcement of borders is often not such a new task as in the Soviet successor states, but it is one that is constantly under-funded. In poorer countries, the competition for national resources often places border control at the end of the priority list. International assistance from countries seeking to limit terrorism through enhanced border controls is not sufficient to compensate for their failure to allocate limited domestic resources to this task.

Conclusion

Globalisation has increased cross-border flows of goods and people. It has also placed increased pressure on border managers to facilitate this movement. The commercial imperatives of a globalised world are often at cross-purposes with the increased security needed to combat terrorists and the weapons needed to promote their objectives.

The convergence of transnational crime and terrorism in many cases facilitates illicit cross-border flows. Terrorists use the services of human traffickers and smugglers to facilitate their border crossings. Within the large illicit flows of people seeking greater opportunities in the developed world are some individuals with ideological rather than economic motivations, namely terrorists. These cross-border flows, facilitated by crime networks, are not limited to the nexus of the developed and developing world. They also occur within the transitional countries and developing countries in Asia, Africa, Eastern Europe and Latin America. The importance of the terrorist–crime nexus is not fully appreciated as security specialists have tended to focus exclusively on combating terrorism.

The rise of regional conflicts in the 1990s and the start of the 21st century have facilitated the movement of terrorists across borders. When countries lose control over their territories, they cannot provide controls over their borders. In these societies where there is no central authority of the state, terrorists can be provided safe haven and can move when they need to execute their activities. The recent military actions in Afghanistan and Iraq have left a large swathe of the Middle East and Central Asia without border controls. Terrorists can regroup in adjoining territories, rebuilding their financial coffers through the drug trade and securing unrestricted access to a large range of countries lacking adequate border defence.

The focus on border control to limit terrorism cannot be limited simply to curtailing the movement of people. It must also be concerned with controlling the weapons that are needed to commit their acts and restricting the financial resources of the terrorists by cutting off their profits from the drug trade and other illicit businesses, which fund their activities. These are formidable challenges considering that even a well equipped and financed border and customs service, such as exists in the United States, can interdict at most only one-third of the drugs targeted to enter the country. In other regions of the world, the possibilities are much more limited.

In the Cold War era and prior to globalisation, border control was as central issue as it is today. Today border issues are central to key concerns of the 21st century—the need to control and combat transnational crime and terrorism. These challenges are particularly formidable because they conflict with some of the fundamental objectives of the contemporary world—the promotion of free movement of goods and people. It is at borders that the interests of countries and regions conflict. Border issues will thus remain a primary challenge of the 21st century.

References

ANDERSON, M. et al. 1996. *Policing the European Union: Theory, Law and Practice*. Oxford: Clarendon Press.

ANDREAS, P. 2000. *Political Economy of Global Smuggling: Policing the US-Mexico Divide*. Ithaca and London: Cornell University Press.

_____ 2001. 'The Transformation of Migrant Smuggling Across the US-Mexican Border'. In *Global Human Smuggling: Comparative Perspectives*, eds., D. Kyle and R. Koslowski. Baltimore: Johns Hopkins University Press.

ANDREAS, P. and T. SNYDER. (eds). 2000. *Wall Around the West: State Borders and Immigration Controls in North America and Europe*. Lanham: Rowman & Littlefield Publishers.

BERDAL, M. and D.M. MALONE. (eds). 2000. *Greed and Grievance: Economic Agendas in Civil Wars*. Boulder: Lynne Rienner.

CIKLAURI, E. and S. LAMMICH. 2000. 'Menschenraub und Menschenhandel im Kaukasus'. *Osteuropa*, 30.

COLLIER, P. 2000. 'Doing Well out of War: An Economic Perspective'. In *Greed and Grievance: Economic Agendas in Civil Wars*, eds. M. Berdal and D.M. Malone. Boulder: Lynne Rienner.

European Union Organized Crime Situation Report 2002. Available at URL: <http://www.europol.eu.int/index.asp?page=EUOrganisedCrimeSitRep2002>

DUFFIELD, M. 2000. 'Globalization, Transborder Trade and War Economics'. In *Greed and Grievance: Economic Agendas in Civil Wars*, eds. M. Berdal and D.M. Malone. Boulder: Lynne Rienner.

FIJNAUT, C. et al. 1998. *Organized Crime in the Netherlands*. Hague, Boston.

GASTROW, P. 1998. 'Organized Crime and the State's Response in South Africa'. *Transnational Organized Crime*, 4 (1).

GEOPOLITICAL OBSERVATORY OF DRUGS. 1996. *The Geopolitics of Drugs*. Boston.

GOMEZ-CESPEDES, A. and P. STANGELAND. 2004. 'Organized Crime in Spain'. In *Organized Crime in Europe: Manifestations and Policies in the European Union and Beyond*, eds., C. Fijnaut and L. Paoli. Dordrecht: Springer.

GORDEMA CHARLES. 2002. 'Diamonds and Other Precious Stones in Armed Conflicts and Law Enforcement Cooperation in Southern Africa'. ISS paper no. 57. Available at URL: <www.iss.co.za>

HYSI, V. 2004. 'Organized Crime in Albania'. In *Organized Crime in Europe: Manifestations and Policies in the European Union and Beyond*, eds., C. Fijnaut and L. Paoli. Dordrecht: Springer.

KUPCHINSKY, R. 2003. 'The Russian Narco-Business'. *RFE/RL Organized Crime and Terror Watch*, 3 (19), 5 June 2003. Available at URL: <www.rferl.org.corruptionwatch>

Interviews with Deputy Chief prosecutor in Palermo in October 2002

LOS, M. and A. ZYBERTOWICZ. 2000. *Privatizing the Police State: The Case of Poland*. New York: St. Martin's Press.

NOMOKONOV, V.A. 2001. *Transnatsional'naia organizovannaia prestupnost': definitisii i realnost*. Vladivostok.

PEUCH, J.C. 2002. 'Georgia: What are the Motives for U.S. Sending Elite Troops'. *RFE/RL* 27 February 2002. Available at URL: <http://www.rferl.org/nca/features/2002/02/27022002095326.asp.>

POWELL, M. and C. HAUGHNEY. 2001. 'Los Angeles Airport Intended Target, Terrorism Plot Defendant Tells Jury'. *Washington Post*, 4 July 2001.

RENO, W. 2000. 'Shadow States and the Political Economy of Civil Wars'. In *Greed and Grievance: Economic Agendas in Civil Wars*, eds. M. Berdal and D.M. Malone. Boulder: Lynne Rienner.

ROSE-ACKERMAN, S. 1999. *Corruption and Government: Causes, Consequences and Reform*. Cambridge: Cambridge University Press.

SHELLEY, L.I. 2002. 'Organized Crime, Terrorism and Cybercrime'. A paper prepared for the 5th International Security Forum. Available at URL: <http://www.isn.ethz.ch/5isf/5/Papers/Shelley_paper_IV-4.pdf>

SHELLEY, L.I. and J. PICARELLI. 2002. 'Methods not Motives: Implications of the Convergence of International Organized Crime and Terrorism'. *Police Practice and Research: An International Journal*, 3 (4).

THOMPSON, G. 2003. 'In Border Town, Migrant Crackdown Rankles.' *New York Times*, 5 June 2003.

VOLKOV, V. 2002. *Violent Entrepreneurs: The Use of Force in the Making of Russian Capitalism*. Ithaca: Cornell University Press.

WINER, J.M. 1997. 'Alien Smuggling: Elements of the Problem and the US Response'. *Transnational Organized Crime*, 3 (1).

WORLD NET DAILY, 2005. 'Non-Mex illegal crossings surge'. 9 June 2005. Available at URL: <http://www.worldnetdaily.com/news/article.asp?ARTICLE_ID=44673> (Accessed on 20 September 2005).

Chapter 14

Border Management Issues in NAFTA

Martha Cottam

The vision of free trade underlying the North American Free Trade Agreement (NAFTA) is one of open and free movement of goods, services and capital (but not people) across borders, co-operation and collaboration in economic enterprise, and increased economic interdependence bringing prosperity to member states. The vision includes the option of the expansion of NAFTA throughout the western hemisphere. While the proponents of NAFTA emphasise positive economic outcomes, the dependence of those outcomes on open borders inevitably brings with it the prospect of greater opportunities for transnational criminal activities, supplemented after 11 September 2001 with the prospect of terrorists using the open borders to enter the United States. Therefore, NAFTA is an arena in which co-operation and collaboration by authorities and civilians in Mexico, the United States, and Canada is necessary and expected despite significant differences in economic practices and legal restrictions on border management authorities. In practice, NAFTA border management offers examples of the best of successful border management collaboration, as well as the worst failures in cooperative border management.

Managing the borders between the US, Canada, and Mexico is not an easy task. The US–Mexico border is 2,000 miles long and the US–Canada border is about 5,500 miles long, (including Alaska). The number of agencies involved in border management on the US side alone is astounding, and includes agencies in the Department of Homeland Security—particularly the Immigration and Customs Enforcement (ICE, formerly known as the Immigration and Naturalization Service), Customs and Border Patrol (CBP), the Coast Guard, the Federal Bureau of Investigation (FBI), the Drug Enforcement Agency (DEA), state and local police agencies, and the military or National Guard from time to time. These agencies often have overlapping jurisdictions and tasks, meaning that bureaucratic competition and in-fighting are inevitably present in border management. Canada and Mexico also have complex federal systems with multiple agencies involved in border matters. Moreover, the political and legal systems of the three countries are also very different, meaning that agencies involved in border management often do not have exact counterparts with which they can coordinate across the border.

Finally, the central issues involved in managing these particular borders are perceived differently in each country. One issue concerns the inherent conflict between moving towards open borders that facilitate trade while ensuring that this does not simultaneously facilitate trade in drugs, weapons, and other illicit items. Immigration is also a central issue. Unlike the European Union, NAFTA does not have as a goal the free flow of workers. Rather, the United States has long sought to halt the flow of illegal immigrants from Mexico, while being relatively unconcerned about the flow of Canadians into the US. Mexicans must obtain visas to enter the United States but Canadians need only present identification (although there has recently been discussion of requiring passports for entry into the US from Canada and other countries). American concerns about the flow of people across the borders have expanded to include concerns about terrorists entering the US.

Perceptions of these issues vary in each of the three countries. Canadians and Mexicans tend to view drug trafficking as a law enforcement issue and drug abuse as a public health issue. Americans see the use of illicit drugs more as a problem of crime and morality. Canada and Mexico regard demand reduction as the key to ending international narcotics trafficking, while American policy has emphasised the law enforcement–supply side. Mexicans perceive immigration of undocumented workers from Mexico into the US as a natural by-product of a high-wage market in the north and a matter that should be addressed through diplomatic agreement as to how that immigration can be regulated. Many Americans prefer a steel wall at the border to prevent the perceived hordes of undocumented aliens from swarming across the frontier. And when it comes to the issue of terrorists entering the US through Canada, nothing will rile a Canadian faster than an assertion that the 9/11 terrorists came through Canada (none did) and that Canada's more liberal immigration laws enable terrorists to infiltrate the US. Americans, on the other hand, regularly cite those laws as being responsible for terrorists' access to the US.

These and other differences in perceptions of border management issues may lead one to expect an equal degree of difficulty in engaging in cooperative border management arrangements on the two borders. Nothing could be further from the truth. There is a vast difference between US–Canada interactions and US–Mexico interactions. This is best illustrated by examining each border and its pattern of co-operation (or lack thereof). The paper will conclude with some explanations of the causes of the differences between the northern and southern NAFTA borders.

Mexico-United States Border Management

The US–Mexico border has received top priority from the United States, particularly since Mexico became the primary transit country for cocaine entering the US. The central issues in US–Mexico border management, both before and after NAFTA's creation, have been illegal immigration by Mexican nationals into the US and the trafficking of narcotics, particularly cocaine, across the border into the US. Relations between Mexico and the US are complicated by a history of US conquest of Mexican territory through war, nationalism and mutual stereotyping, and implementation problems (more so on the US than the Mexican side) caused by competing bureaucracies. Nevertheless, the border was essentially a free zone until drugs became a concern in the late 1960s. The disparity in the number of Border Patrol agents on the southern and northern borders of the US, approximately 7,000 and 300 respectively before 11 September 2001, and about 10,000 and 1,200 respectively after that date, shows the extent to which the US is more concerned with its southern than its northern border.

Drugs and related issues

Issues affecting border management in the context of the war on drugs include disputes over American unilateralism, the importance of addressing the supply of drugs through Mexico versus the demand for drugs in the United States, the attitudes and behaviour of DEA agents, the problem of corruption, and the American policy of certification/decertification. American unilateralism, the behaviour of the DEA, and the certification policy are all deeply threatening to Mexican concerns about their territorial sovereignty. American violation of Mexico's sovereignty can be traced back to the war of 1848, which resulted in the US annexation of one-third of Mexico's land.

The US expressed concern about narcotics coming into the US from Mexico periodically during the 20th century, establishing early on a pattern of pressuring Mexico to adopt a policy towards narcotics that was similar to that of the US (Craig 1989, p.72). Consumption may be a US problem, but as US demand grew and the drug industry evolved, the drug trade had an increasing impact on Mexico's political and justice systems. In 1987 President de la Madrid elevated narco-trafficking to the realm of a national security issue for Mexico. One-third of Mexico's defence budget became directed towards drug control (Toro 1995, p.33).

Mexico's role in the international narcotics industry began as a major source of heroin and marijuana. After the mid-1970s Mexican eradication and interdiction efforts, under the auspices of Operation Co-operation and aided by American equipment, drastically reduced the supply of Mexican marijuana to the US. Mexico's share of the market fell from 75 percent in 1976 to 9 percent by 1983. Its share increased again to 32 percent in 1986 (Chabat 1994, p.379; Ruiz-Cabanas 1989, p.48). Mexico's role as a source of heroin declined as it went from supplying 85 percent of the US market in the early 1970s down to 37 percent by 1980 (Chabat 1994, p.379). Drug trafficking patterns changed as growers and traffickers adapted to the pressures imposed by law enforcement interdiction and eradication efforts, and Mexico became a major transit route for cocaine from the Andes, particularly after the Caribbean–south Florida routes were largely shut down in the 1980s. Mexican policy was also affected by the economic downturn of the 1980s and again in 1994, as well as the pervasive efforts of the drug industry to employ its vast resources in corrupting Mexico's criminal justice system. Throughout this period US demand for illegal narcotics remained powerful. By the mid-1990s Mexico was 'a principal transit route for

South American cocaine, a major source of marijuana and heroin, as well as a major supplier of methamphetamine to the illicit market in the US', according to the 1997 International Narcotics Strategy Report (p.140).

Bilateral drug-related issues with Mexico made headlines in the early 1970s when the US embarked on Operation Intercept. As people crossing the border were subjected to great scrutiny and searched, this operation constituted a unilateral decision by the US to essentially close border traffic. Mexico quickly complied with US demands that it improve its drug interdiction efforts. The years that followed saw increased US anti-drug aid to Mexico, the establishment of Mexico's Northern Border Response Force (NBRF) at US urging, and increased collaboration (operational planning, intelligence sharing) between Mexican military and police officials and US military counter-narcotics officials as well as civilian law enforcement agencies. Numerous institutional arrangements have been designed to promote co-operation. These include the US–Mexico High Level Contact Group (HLCG), established in 1996, wherein top level officials from both countries discuss anti-trafficking measures and policies; Bilateral Border Task Forces (BTFs); and the Border Liaison Mechanism (BLM), designed to improve communication at the border. BLMs hold quarterly meetings of law enforcement personnel, representatives of border inspection agencies and civilians, and run many joint training programs (White House, ONDCP 1997). The involvement of the Mexican military in anti-drug efforts increased during the late 1980s with US approval and assistance. After several disastrous raids on suspected drug bases the military's involvement diminished, but increased again after 1994 when the Zedillo administration came into office. Currently, the United States provides training and intelligence support for the Mexican military's anti-drug forces. Despite these efforts to promote co-operation, there are a number of problems that hinder full and effective co-operation at the border.

Beginning with Operation Intercept I and II (1969 and 1985 respectively), the US has attempted to direct Mexico's internal and international approach towards drug production and trafficking. Anti-narcotics trafficking programs along the US–Mexican border would seemingly require co-operation, but little consultation took place until the late 1990s. Operation Alliance, for example, which began in 1986, 'was the primary coordinating body for collaborative drug enforcement efforts in the border region...Its joint-command structure included senior officers from the Customs Service, Coast Guard, DEA, FBI, and INS–Border Patrol as well as representatives from various law enforcement agencies in each of the four border states' (Dunn 1996, p.113). Nevertheless, it had no representative from Mexico. The parallel operation at the US–Canada border, Project Northern Star, did involve the participation of Canadian law enforcement (Mendel 1995). Even Operations Co-operation and Condor, long hailed as a highlight in the history of US–Mexico co-operation in the drug war in the 1970s, consisted of the United States furnishing 'aircraft, technology and instruction. Mexicans would furnish money, men and a desire to master the arts of crop destruction and trafficker interdiction' as taught by the Americans (Craig 1989, p.77).

As the drug industry in Mexico, and its impact on Mexico, changed during the 1980s, so did US–Mexico interaction. Mexican policy-makers were consistently sensitive about implications for Mexican sovereignty and rejected US suggestions for collaboration that they perceived to threaten Mexican territorial integrity (such as joint border patrols allowing incursions across the border by US law enforcement personnel in pursuit of drug smugglers). The bilateral relationship reached a crisis point in 1985 when DEA agent Enrique Camarena was tortured and murdered in Mexico by drug traffickers (narcos) and/or corrupt Mexican police with ties to the traffickers. The US responded with Operation Intercept II and increased attention to corruption in the Mexican criminal justice system. Recriminations issued from both sides of the border and both US–Mexican relations and US drug policy in general changed.

US drug policy became more nationalistic and unilateral than ever after the Camarena murder. The US policy instruments used in the bilateral drug war became increasingly militarised and the US flouted international law when Humberto Alvarez Macháin, one of those involved in Camarena's murder, was kidnapped and brought to the US to stand trial. Although most suspects were brought to trial in Mexico, two were brought to trial in the US. The DEA paid Mexican nationals to capture the two in Mexico and, through collaboration between Mexican police and DEA agents, smuggle them into the US. The Mexican government protested. Ultimately, the Alvarez Macháin case went all the way to the US Supreme Court which upheld the abduction in 1992, thereby asserting a US right to take extraterritorial legal action, which is, and was, generally considered a violation of international law.

As mentioned, Mexican nationalism is intensely sensitive to any perceived effort by non-nationals to exercise power or decision-making authority on Mexican soil. Any such action is perceived as a challenge to the authority of the Mexican state, is associated with the Mexican historical experiences of invasion, and is simply not considered acceptable. International narcotics matters inflame these sensitivities since co-operation among the various countries involved implies at a minimum an overlap of law enforcement activities. Mexico tends to be very cautious about such interaction given a perceived tendency for the US to take advantage of cooperative endeavours and maximise its own interests and priorities. Mexican elites tend to believe that if concessions are made on this issue which diminish Mexican sovereignty, the US would soon be making similar demands in other issue areas, such as immigration. Reuter and Ronfeldt (1992) argue that the declaration of narcotics production and trafficking as a national security issue was based not only on concerns about the narcos' violation of Mexican law and sovereignty, but also concerns about US pressures to deviate from strict observance of Mexican sovereignty. The Mexican preference for eradication rather than interdiction in the 1970s is a reflection of the desire not to endorse the presence of US law enforcement personnel on Mexican territory. Although Mexico has accepted DEA training, along with US equipment and aid, it considers it extremely important that this technical assistance not translate into decision-making authority. Mexicans will decide how the drug war operates in Mexico. This has frustrated American policy-makers who have long wanted Mexico to follow the American approach to international narcotics control.

All matters concerning the operation of US law enforcement personnel on Mexican soil are also evaluated through the prism of protecting Mexico's territorial sovereignty. These include permitting border crossings by US law enforcement personnel engaged in the hot pursuit of criminals, which Mexico has refused to allow, over-flights of Mexican territory by US intelligence aircraft tracking drug traffickers, which was agreed upon only after difficult and complex negotiations under the careful scrutiny of Mexican nationalists, and the issue of permitting DEA agents to carry weapons on Mexican soil. This last issue has been a particularly contentious one, in that it provides a flash point for Mexican nationalism and long-term DEA resentment about the Camarena case. Mexico has repeatedly been asked to permit DEA agents to carry weapons on its territory, and has repeatedly refused.

Another extremely important issue is certification, a process wherein the United States executive branch must certify before Congress every year that countries involved in narcotics production or trafficking are cooperating with the US or abiding by the United Nation's 1988 Convention Against Illicit Traffic in Narcotics and Psychotropic Substances. If a country is not certified, it is punished with the termination of US assistance unrelated to the drug war, and US rejection of that country's efforts to secure aid through international financial institutions. Thus, the US gives itself the privilege of determining not only whether other countries are doing what the US wants for the benefit of US citizens, but also whether other countries are complying with the United Nations agreement. Mexico was threatened with decertification a number of times during the 1990s. Mexico refuses to recognise the certification process, regarding it as a possible violation of international law, and a certain illustration of American arrogance and imperialism. It is threatening, but most importantly, the certification process is infuriating to Mexicans. Anger is expressed in the press and by Mexican political leaders through denunciations of American arrogance in 'grading' other countries. Some Mexicans would prefer complete decertification to conditional certification, which they liken to a parent scolding a child for behaving badly, but promising forgiveness for good behaviour. In 1997, the last time Mexico was threatened with decertification, the Mexican Congress voted unanimously to condemn certification in principle as an insult to national sovereignty (*Washington Post*, 28 February 1997). Mexican officials speculated that if decertification had occurred, Mexico would have expelled all DEA agents from its soil. They regarded the public condemnation of Mexican corruption in Congressional debates on 13 March 1997 as an insult to every honest Mexican, of which, they noted, there were many. They condemned American hypocrisy, noting that most of the marijuana consumed in the US is grown in the US (*Washington Post*, 28 February 1997). Finally, they considered it remarkable that their American counterparts would tell them that they need to understand US politics, the role of Congress, and not take all the Mexico bashing seriously, while simultaneously not themselves taking into consideration Mexican politics. It would not have been possible for Mexican officials to fail to condemn the United States, given the strength of Mexican nationalism. As one official expressed it, Mexican '...society as a whole will react very angrily to the decision and the government will have to reflect that. There is no way the government is going to say to its citizens, "we've been defamed, but don't worry about it." That's not going to happen' (quoted in the *Washington Post*, 28 February 1997, p.16). In addition, Mexicans repeatedly argue that the United States is doing too little to reduce demand for drugs and that this is central to a solution to the problem of drug trafficking across the US–Mexico border.

Mexican officials have also complained repeatedly that a central problem in controlling narcotics is controlling the supply of guns smuggled into Mexico from the US. It is estimated that up to 80 percent of guns used in violence involving drug traffickers are smuggled into Mexico from the US. Mexico has asked the US to make a better effort to suppress the trade, including enforcing current US laws and developing stronger laws to control weapons. The basic US response has been two-fold: first, this is really a Mexican demand problem which should be dealt with by Mexican authorities, rather than a supply problem (from the Mexican side this argument is completely hypocritical since it is the inverse of the US position on the drug problem). Second, guns are legal in the US and changing the law to require tighter control would be politically difficult (again, this strikes Mexicans as hypocritical—Mexico is asked to change its laws and approach to the problem of drugs, but that does not apply to the US position on guns). The issue has not been resolved, even though a number of meetings and agreements have been arranged to address the problem. While the Mexican government has expressed its concerns about the flow of weapons from the US and the High Level Contact Group has a Bi-National Firearms Trafficking Working Group, the fact remains that the US has not made a major effort to halt the cross-border flow of weapons. Weapons are freely traded and sold informally in the US. The Bureau of Alcohol, Tobacco and Firearms does not have enough inspectors to monitor the vast number of gun dealers, and is limited to one inspection per year per gun dealer. The difficulty the United States has in addressing the free flow of weapons is only partly a product of the power of the National Rifle Association interest group. The notion of citizens having a right to a personal weapon, and resistance to any effort to impose limits, go to the heart of American political culture and national identity.

Another issue hindering co-operation in border management is the problem of corruption. The United States regards corruption in Mexico as, to quote a recent ONDCP fact sheet, 'the principal impediment to counter-drug success' (White House ONDCP 2002, p.1). American officials' desire for co-operation with their Mexican counterparts is limited because of their fears that the US would be sharing information with corrupt policy-makers and law enforcement personnel. Americans believe that corruption indicates a lack of political will and endangers US operatives. This perspective led to American demands for Mexican institutional reform along the lines of American law enforcement, vetted units with polygraphs administered by US investigators, and justified unilateralism in operations, all of which are political irritants and inhibitors of good co-operation between the two countries. The vetted units issue was the subject of conflict for some time, as the US, particularly the DEA, insisted that it could not work with Mexican officers whom it could not trust. Only special units vetted by the US are considered trustworthy. Initial demands by the US that the US create such units and screen officers were rejected by Mexico, but subsequent bilateral agreements led to the creation of joint units to conduct vetting.

One of the principle constraints on co-operation that results from American suspicions regarding Mexican corruption is the unwillingness to share information. In 1997, for example, DEA Director Tom Constantine stated that 'there is not one single law enforcement institution in Mexico with whom DEA has a trusting relationship' (US Congress 1997, H961). This attitude inevitably perpetuates a vicious circle. Americans officials interpret Mexico's lack of progress in anti-narcotics as a sign of Mexican corruption, and they consequently refuse to share information. Without relevant information, Mexican officials fail to apprehend narcos, which is again interpreted as an indicator of corruption by the American side. Successes in Mexican efforts to break the cartels have been evaluated favourably by American officials. In 2001 the DEA announced that for the first time they were able to share sensitive drug information with Mexican officers, whose very honesty the DEA takes credit for. In July 2002, US drug czar John Walters praised Mexico's successes, saying 'Mexico has done an outstanding job' (quoted in the *Christian Science Monitor*, 9 July 2002). The successes, including high profile arrests of Benjamin Arellano Félix, Adán Medrano Rodriguez, and Albino Quintero Meraz, all important narcos, were attributed to shared information by officials from both countries.

In part, improvements in co-operation such as these are a result of a campaign by Mexican President Vicente Fox's administration to change US policies and perceptions about the border, and Mexican policies related to the drug war. Major traffickers and a governor have been arrested; the Mexican Supreme Court has determined that under some circumstances the extradition of Mexican citizens to the US for trial does not violate the constitution; and corrupt officials continue to be purged from the military, police and justice agencies. The Fox administration has insisted on greater partnership and equality. It has asked the US, and the Bush administration, to help develop a 'master plan for the fight against organized crime, drug trafficking and violence', to share information, to 'arrest and prosecut[e] American weapons dealers who are arming Mexican crime syndicates', and to create genuine co-operation among Mexican and US law enforcement agencies. As noted by a Mexican academic, US agencies have 'typically treated the Mexican agencies as servants. Servants are not allowed to ask questions. They are only supposed to follow orders. That attitude has to change.' The national security advisor to the Fox Administration, Adolfo Aguilar Zinser, made the same point. It is time for US agencies to 'trust' Mexico and not 'expect us to be the recipient of unilateral demands' (quoted in the *New York Times*, 11 April 2001, p.A8). As the journalists note, that 'will require a small revolution in the way American law enforcement and intelligence services regard Mexico' (ibid).

Nevertheless, there is general reluctance to share information with Mexican law enforcement, and any trust that has been established tends to ebb and flow. In June 2005 Mexican federal troops took over law enforcement in Nuevo Laredo, Mexico when most the city's police were taken into custody under suspicion of being involved in drug trafficking, and cartel-related violence had crossed the border into the US. Not only is corruption in Mexico an on-going problem, but American officials are increasingly concerned that that corruption, along with narco-trafficking activities, can be used by terrorists to gain entry into the US (*Los Angeles Times*, 13 May 2005).

Immigration and border security

A second general area of importance in border management along the US–Mexico border concerns the flow of undocumented workers. This policy area also has a long and complex history with large variations in US responses to Mexican immigrants. The most recent campaign to reduce illegal immigrants and to expel those who managed to cross the border began in the 1990s, but was initiated by the Immigration Reform and Control Act of 1986. This Act introduced employer sanctions for hiring illegal immigrants as well as giving illegal immigrants who had been in the US for some time a limited time offer to acquire citizenship. Concerns about illegal immigration and control of the borders emerged in the United States in the 1970s and continued fairly consistently. The budget for the Immigration and Naturalization Service and its law enforcement arm, the Border Patrol, increased as did the number of officers, and this was particularly notable in the 1990s. In 1994 the INS initiated Operation Gatekeeper (followed by Operations Hold the Line and Hard Line), which not only failed to stem the flow of illegal immigrants, but by making border crossings more difficult, increased the hardships faced by those immigrants. This, in turn, necessitated a Border Safety Initiative wherein both governments agreed that efforts had to be made to protect immigrants from smugglers, bandits, and threats to safety and well-being stemming from the harsh terrain they traversed. Interestingly, while NAFTA promoted economic integration, the US government became increasingly concerned that it did not bring more Mexicans into the United States.

With the inauguration of Presidents Bush and Fox, there were initial indications that movement on the immigration issue would be forthcoming. The Fox administration insisted that the US: rethink its policies on an open border and illegal immigration; do more to protect immigrants from dying while crossing (the result of increased border patrol which has forced illegal immigrants away from populous areas into desert as they seek a way across, resulting in about 400 dying each year by drowning or heat exhaustion); increase the number of resident visas; expand guest worker programs; and grant legal status to 3 million Mexicans in the US illegally. The Bush administration appeared to be interested in pursuing these ideas until the terrorist attacks on 9/11. At that point, Mexico and the Fox administration's campaign for immigration reforms evaporated from the US radar screen. This, in turn, resulted in the resignation of Mexico's foreign minister, Jorge Cantaneda in January 2003, for having failed to achieve his major goal for Mexican foreign policy. Mexico's strategy shifted to emphasise forging agreements at the state and local levels on the border. President Fox never gave up his efforts to persuade the Bush administration to get Congressional approval of immigration reforms that would grant legal status to the eight to twelve million illegal Mexicans residing in the US. However Congress remains resistant and Bush is not enthusiastic about expending political capital on reforms. Indeed, public resistance to such reforms has been evident in the formation of vigilante squads attempting to apprehend illegal immigrants in the spring of 2005 along the Arizona border with Mexico (Pilant 2005).

Post-9/11 border management

After the terrorist attacks of 11 September 2001, the United States created a new Department of Homeland Security (DHS) which now controls most aspects of everyday border protection. Customs and Immigration were reorganised and are now housed in DHS. As mentioned, after 9/11 the number of Border Patrol agents along the southern border dramatically increased to around ten thousand. Interest in the war on drugs has diminished on the US side but catching illegal drugs and people crossing the southern border remains the primary activity of law enforcement along the southern border of the US. Interestingly the Bush administration expressed little public concern that terrorists would cross into the US from the south until 2004. Since then more and more public expressions of concern about terrorists using people and drug smuggling operations to their advantage began to appear in the press. Control of the border has tightened and it is no longer possible for people in small border towns to cross over 'informally'. There have been numerous US–Mexico meetings since 9/11 to discuss border security issues and Presidents Bush and Fox signed a 'smart border' agreement focusing on three areas— infrastructure development, the flow of people and the flow of goods across the border. Nevertheless, the statement is quite general and vague. It includes provisions such as agreements to identify individuals who pose a threat, to establish a joint US–Mexico Advanced Passenger Information exchange mechanism, and to develop systems to exchange customs data rapidly. Mexicans are still required to have visas (now called 'laser visas') and Mexicans who wish to have clearance to enter the US through fast lanes are vetted by American authorities. Another recent development in border management is the installation of a DEA, FBI, and CIA operation to watch for illegal immigrants crossing into Mexico from Guatemala and Belize, a border that Mexico has had difficulty policing and through which people from Central and South American along with India and China cross on their way to the US (*Excelsior*, 6 February 2003).

Canada–US Border Management

Border management in the northern part of NAFTA involves the same US agencies that operate along the southern border. In Canada, the principal border organisations are the Royal Canadian Mounted Police (RCMP), Citizenship and Immigration Canada (CIC), and the Canada Customs and Revenue Agency (CCRA). The RCMP has specific national responsibilities and acts as the provincial police in eight of Canada's provinces. Ontario and Quebec provinces have their own provincial police forces. In addition, Canada created the Public Safety and Emergency Preparedness Canada (PSEPC), the Canadian equivalent of DHS, in December 2001. Nevertheless, co-operation and co-ordination with the US is necessarily complicated in terms of the number of agencies involved because of the complexity and decentralisation on the United States side.

The track record of co-operation at the state-to-state level at the northern border is the polar opposite of that along the southern border. Most Canadian visitors to the US are not required to have visas to enter the United States, however Mexican nationals are. There are programs to facilitate travel by frequent border crossers by pre-clearing them. It is a crime in Canada to conspire to violate US laws. The central criminal activities are the same as those along the Mexico–US border: drug trafficking, gun running and illegal immigration. In addition there are issues such as telemarketing and cyber crime across this border, criminal activities not involving actual physical border crossings. The latter includes, as an issue of great concern to the US, the entrance of anti-US terrorists to the US via Canada, attributed by Americans in part to Canada's liberal immigration policy and the fact that it does not require visas for 29 countries from which the US does require visas. These different approaches also make it easy for Mexicans to come into the US illegally. It is sometimes cheaper to buy a ticket to Canada, which requires no visa from Mexicans, and enter the US through Canada than it is to hire a coyote (human smuggler) to take one across the southern border.

The collaboration and co-operation between the United States and Canada is so intense and has such a long history that only a few of the many agreements can be discussed here. Among the more important state-to-state efforts at co-operation in the 1990s are, for example, the Canada–United States Accord on Our Shared Border of 1995. The Accord suggested initiatives regarding promotion of international trade; facilitation of border crossing by individuals; preventing drug trafficking, smuggling and illegal immigration; and reducing costs to governments and the public. It established a coordinating committee with members from the United States Immigration and Naturalization Service (INS), Citizenship and Immigration Canada (CIC), US Customs

Service, Canada Customs and Revenue Agency (CCRA), the US Department of State, and Foreign Affairs and International Trade Canada (CIC 2000). Also in 1990 the US and Canada signed a mutual legal assistance treaty which allows the exchange of information to be used in legal proceedings against suspected criminals. In 1994 the two countries signed an asset sharing agreement so that assets seized from criminals during joint investigations can be divided between the jurisdictions.

The Shared Border accord was enhanced by the Canada–US Cross Border Crime Forum that has met annually since 1997. The forum, which is chaired by the Solicitor General of Canada and the US Attorney General, brings together more than 60 officials from both countries to discuss transnational crime problems. In 1999 Prime Minister Chrétien and President Clinton introduced the Canada–US Partnership Forum (CUSP) to 'promote high-level dialogue among governments, border communities, and stakeholders on border management'. This was an effort to 'streamline, harmonize, and collaborate on border policies and management; expand co-operation to increase efficiencies in customs, immigration, law enforcement, and environmental protection at and beyond the border; and collaborate on threats outside Canada and the United States' (US Department of State 2000, p.1). Additional agreements designed to accomplish goals set forth in these agreements are USINS–CIC Border Vision and Cross-Border Crime Forum. Clearly, the border and its management are the subject of top-level executive attention and multi-level and multi-agency co-operation. Integrated Border Enforcement Teams (IBETs), which are interagency law enforcement teams, were established in 1997. There are also Integrated Marine Enforcement Teams (IMETS) and Integrated Border Intelligence Teams (IBITs) in operation.

Drugs and related issues

In terms of the drug problem, in the case of Canada and the United States, despite different philosophies regarding drug abuse and the drug war, co-operation and collaboration takes place on an equitable basis. The US spends about $18 billion a year on the war on drugs, about 70 percent of that on law enforcement. Canada's basic approach (Fisher 1998), in rhetoric if not always policy, is that drugs, especially marijuana, are a social problem. Policy needs to seek to reduce the harm done to individuals and society, and that means focusing on treatment, with prevention through law enforcement being the last preference, and then focused mainly on hard drugs and trafficking, not on consumption. About 70 percent of Canada's drug effort is targeted on treatment and prevention. Moreover, Canada is apparently on the verge of decriminalising marijuana, which American officials are not happy about, but which has elicited few public comments. US drug czar John Walters, however, did denounce the Canadian parliamentary recommendation that marijuana be decriminalised, saying that it would be a 'dangerous threat' to the United States and that it would cause delays at border crossings (*Globe and Mail*, 16 December 2002).

Drug trafficking between the US and Canada has increased substantially, as indicated by a 400 percent increase in arrests between October 1998 and April 1999 (US Congress 1999). The flow of drugs across the northern NAFTA border is quite extensive. Powerful marijuana grown in Canada called BC Bud, which has a much higher street value than regular marijuana, heroin from Southeast Asia, and precursor chemicals for producing methamphetamine are imported from Canada into the US. The US is a transit country for South American cocaine, via Mexico, going to Canada. Liquid hashish and marijuana also travel from the US to Canada. In 1998 the US seized 4,413 pounds of drugs along the border with Canada, comprised of: 614.77 pounds of cocaine; 3.84 pounds of heroin; and 3,794.63 pounds of marijuana. In contrast, 'Customs seized 31,769 pounds of cocaine, 830,891 pounds of marijuana, and 407 pounds of heroin' at the US–Mexico border in 1998 (US GAO 1999, p.23). A more recent development is the influx of pseudoephedrine into the US from Canada for use in making methamphetamines. Pseudoephedrine is a controlled substance in the US but not in Canada.

Law enforcement agencies working in the drug control area operate very cooperatively at this border. Information is shared, databases are shared, operations are jointly planned and carried out, and there is trust among border officials. The language of government statements regarding the relationship in the realm of drug trafficking is glowing. Differences between the US and Canada in laws and perspectives on the drug war are not interpreted by Americans as indications that the Canadians are corrupt, unreliable, or not doing their share to 'protect' American consumers from illegal substances. For example, in a press interview announcing the successful arrest of more than 100 people in Operation Mountain Express III in January 2002, US officials praised their Canadian counterparts for their contribution to the operation, calling it a 'great example of law enforcement agencies working together' (DEA 2002, p.3). When questioned about Canadian law, the following exchange took place:

> Q. You thank the Canadian law enforcement agencies for their role in assisting you in this. But do you not think that the Canadian government has been negligent in not clamping down on the use of pseudoephedrine in Canada sooner?
>
> Mr. Hutchinson (DEA Director): Let me just say from a very positive standpoint we want them to move expeditiously. This is very important to what we are trying to accomplish in the United States, and we urge the Canadian government to move as quickly as possible to enact regulatory legislation....
>
> Mr. Bonner: Could I just add one thing to that? And that is I want to echo Administrator Hutchinson's comment, and that is that we had incredibly good co-operation from Canadian law enforcement... In fact, they were extremely helpful...(DEA 2002, p.5).

Canadians voice some of the same complaints Mexicans have about US behaviour: the drug problem is created and sustained in the US, yet the US wants concessions, legal changes and different policy priorities, but offers little in return except threats, and does not recognise the need for Canada to protect its own systems of law and norms of justice. As one Canadian official stated, Canadians do not 'point fingers at others', casting blame on them for international drug trafficking, and Canadians do not like it when the US points its finger at Canada (Author's interview, 27 October 2002). Like the Mexicans, the Canadians complain that the US does too little to address the demand for drugs in the US and that it does too little to address weapons smuggling from the US. (The same official mentioned above stated that his American counterparts actually advise Canada to adopt America's weaker gun control approach.) A policy of harm reduction 'would mean a significant erosion of the traditional prohibition ideology on the North American continent [and] would have to be launched against enormous American pressure and sanctions that might far exceed the area of drug control, a rather grim prospect for Canada, a country so unilaterally dependent on the United States in socio-economic terms' (Fisher 1998, p.174). Canada has not yet changed completely to a harm reduction policy because of real or predicted pressures. Another example is the US 1999 International Narcotics Control Strategy Report which explicitly presents as one of its goals to 'work to strengthen [Canadian] legislation and regulatory practice in an effort to bring them more in line with U.S. practice' (US Department of State 1999, p.5). Demands for banking regulation reform to assist the US in controlling money laundering or changes in border control mechanisms (e.g., visa requirements) to help in US immigration at the northern border have a long history.

Nevertheless, despite American bossiness, the American perspective on drug trafficking across the northern border is quite unlike the attitude towards Mexico's role in drug trafficking. Americans see drug trafficking across the northern border as a two-way street—they acknowledge that drugs cross from the US into Canada—and, most significantly, that the culprits are criminals rather than the citizens of Canada (or, parenthetically, the United States). For example, the Deputy Chief of the US Border Patrol in Blaine, Washington, explained the problem as follows:

> The US/Canada Border is significantly different than our border with Mexico in that most of the smuggling on our Southern Border is northbound, whereas smuggling along the Border in Blaine Sector is both north and south. In fact, it is common to have the same smugglers moving illegal contraband in both directions. Their bottom line is profit (US Congress 1999, p.17).

The implication is that Mexicans themselves are to blame rather than criminal organisations. This difference in perception exists despite the fact that corruption occurs in the US (a former FBI official stated that law enforcement in the US is thoroughly corrupted thirty miles deep from the Mexican border) and in Canada (in August 2000, for example, US Customs and DEA officers seized 240 pounds of BC Bud from a Canadian military vehicle crossing into the US). Moreover, the Deputy Chief's statement discounts the extent to which the drug industry thrives on two-way business at the southern border, particularly in weapons smuggling from the US to Mexico.

Project North Star (1990) perhaps best illustrates the differences in co-operation at the state-to-state level when the two borders are examined. In contrast to Operation Alliance, Operation North Star was developed with the participation of Canadian law enforcement and military personnel. It was designed to improve and systematise co-operation in drug trafficking, as well as the smuggling of tobacco, liquor and weapons into Canada from the US (Mendel 1995). This reflects both an understanding that Canadian officials had to be involved in the development of the plan and that smuggling is two-way. The organisation and decision-making practices also reflect an assumption of equality between the two state parties. Law enforcement efforts are integrated through three Joint Co-ordination Groups composed of four law enforcement members from each US border state (reflecting the policing levels in the US—state, county, municipal and national guard) and a RCMP officer from each province, plus provincial police representatives from Quebec and Ontario. The North Star strategy developed by these groups was based on consensus.

Immigration

As mentioned, neither Canada nor the United States have been concerned about 'illegal' immigration of Canadians or Americans. There has always been a considerable amount of economic and social interaction, with many border families having members of either Canadian or US citizenship. From the US standpoint, the central immigration issue has been the perceived ease with which third country immigrants can enter the US through Canada. US officials do repeatedly express frustration with Canada's immigration and visa policies, which, as mentioned above, are far more liberal than those in the United States. This, US officials believe, facilitates illegal immigration from countries like Mexico or China through Canada to the US, and, more importantly, makes it easier for terrorists intent on attacking the US to get into the country. Indeed, a number of individuals with alleged ties to terrorist organisations or with alleged intentions of committing a violent act against the United States were intercepted crossing into the US from Canada before 11 September 2001.

However, this frustration is expressed in, for Americans, very polite and respectful terms. For example, the Sheriff of Whatcom County, Washington State said, 'our friends to the north, the Canadians, are good neighbours but I must tell you that I too am troubled by their liberal immigration policies' (US Congress 1999, p.37). Another example is the explanation given by an INS official to Congress in 1999:

In the fall of last year, the director of the Canadian Security Intelligence Service (CSIS) testified before his Senate that CSIS was investigating 50 terrorist organizations that had established infrastructures in his country. Put simply, this is because Canada, like the United States, has a long and cherished tradition of embracing immigrants and openness of expression. And, as with the United States, one of the challenges for their democracy is in striking the right balance between openness and guarding against becoming a refuge for terrorists from abroad.

In combating terrorism, in particular, the challenge for United States and Canadian officials is the rapid and timely exchange of information on such individuals, who pose a shared threat. While most exchanges of information follow established formal protocols, there is also considerable personal liaison between officers and direct communication between INS and Canadian agencies (US Congress 1999, p.13).

The State Department's report on CUSP makes a similarly equitable comment, noting that Canada and the United States have visa-waivers for countries for which the other does not and that 'legal changes in one or both countries can be useful in some cases, such as the amendment before the US Congress in 2000 that would allow US consular officers overseas to share visa application information with Canadian consular offices' (2000, p.14). Note that both countries are deemed to share in responsibility, both could and conceivably should change their laws, and the example refers to change by the US.

Close co-operation between local authorities regarding terrorists also existed before 9/11. Already in place was a Bilateral Consultative Group on Counterterrorism that works on preventive measures. Another working group is the Integrated Border Enforcement Team which involves agencies from Washington State and British Colombia and which has been very effective in increasing the interdiction of contraband (US Department of State 2000).

Post-9/11 border management

Despite strains in the US–Canada relationship caused by American accusations that Canada is 'the Achilles heel' of American security against terrorists entering the US, co-operation between the two NAFTA partners with regard to border management is, if anything, stronger than ever. This is not to minimise the extent to which Canadians are angered by such accusations. As recently as January 2003 the Canadian Ambassador to the US, Michael Kergin, wrote an editorial in the *Washington Times* titled 'Stop Blaming Canada', in which he denounced false US accusations that five terrorists had entered the US from Canada. In addition, on 17 September 2002 the Canadian government issued travel advisory warnings to Canadians born in Syria, Sudan, Libya, Iran and Iraq who were planning to travel to the US because of racial profiling and mistreatment by American customs agents (*New York Times*, 8 November 2002).

On the other hand, US and Canadian officials moved quickly to overcome delays at border crossings caused by the terrorist attacks, and to develop a 'smart border' plan. Among the agreements was the extension of IBET teams across the entire border (they had previously been located at the Washington State/British Columbia border). The rapid crossing program was temporarily halted but efforts were immediately underway to restore them. FAST lanes are now operative for pre-approved commercial traffic. The NEXUS program, whereby individuals apply for pre-approval to cross the border regularly, is operative at a number of border crossings. Indicative of the level of trust between law enforcement in the two countries, as well as at the executive levels, Canada does the criminal record check for NEXUS applicants from Canada, and Americans only check backgrounds of American applicants. The two countries use the same databases on criminal behaviour (Author's interview at Douglas/Peace Arch, 12 July 2002).

More broadly, Canada and the US issued a 'summary of Smart Border Action Plan Status' on 6 December 2002, detailing the agreements developed in the months since 11 September 2001, and they are quite extensive, ranging from plans for continuing easy commerce across the border, to maritime co-operation, programs for cooperative work in biosecurity, science, technology, visa policy co-ordination, a 'safe third country' agreement that is designed to share in the management of asylum seekers from third countries by vetting them before the leave their home country, visa policy co-ordination, joint facilities, and so on. There are thirty points in the document.

Conclusions

Clearly the levels of co-operation, trust, and collaboration are vastly different at the two NAFTA borders. Of course the borders are different: the crime problems fit the same categories—drug trafficking, normal crime, and illegal border crossing—but are very different in degree, and the borders reflect unequal levels of economic development and political power among Canada, Mexico and the US. NAFTA seems to have encouraged the promotion of a 'seamless' border with Canada and the development of a virtual war to prevent the same thing from occurring on the southern US border. More to the point, the US has promoted the seamless northern border, and an iron fence along the southern border. Co-operation along the northern border illustrates excellent practices in border management. Information is shared, law enforcement agencies work well together, agreements are forged at the federal level, and issues are approached through well-oiled working groups that meet regularly. On the southern border those same patterns of co-operation occur irregularly, and are often accompanied by acrimonious accusations of malfeasance. In addition, the fact that this paper on NAFTA border management has no section on Canada–Mexico interaction shows the extent to which NAFTA border management is determined by US decisions. Co-operation is much greater in the north than it is in the south. While this can be explained in part by the unequal economic development among the partners, and the consequent American desire to protect itself from Mexico's poverty, there are more subtle factors that explain the differences in co-operation.

It is useful to separate the two borders and the two issues discussed above, drugs and immigration at the north and the south of NAFTA. Much of the border control problem is driven by the insatiable demand for drugs in the US. The political psychology of nationalism leads to the expectation that proud, nationalistic people, and that is what Americans are, cannot blame themselves for their problems. (Controlling the flow of drugs was too sensitive a topic for inclusion in the NAFTA talks.) And in the case of drug trafficking across these two borders, Americans manage to blame someone else for America's drug problem—Mexicans on the southern border and criminals along the northern border. Why the difference? It has much to do with the stereotypes and images held by Americans of the other two societies. Mexicans are seen as inferior, susceptible to corruption, and in need of American instruction. Canadians are perceived as equals and therefore much like Americans, so corruption cannot explain the flow of drugs, and if not a blind eye, an eye with a big cataract, is turned towards that possibility. Moreover, the perception of relative equality enables Americans to admit that drugs (and other illegal goods) flow both ways, and it also enables them to accept without complaining the fact the American law enforcement personnel are prohibited from carrying weapons in Canada. In Mexico, however, the DEA complains loudly and often about the same prohibition.

Of course, co-operation between Canada and the United States is not without its problems. The Canadians do complain about the Americans' high handedness. But the interaction and the complaints are nowhere near the extreme that they are in the US–Mexico relationship. This raises the question of why, if the US perceives Canadians as equals, it still is accused of imperial-like behaviour. There are three possible explanations. First, American arrogance may be a result of American nationalism and the assumption that if American identity is threatened, someone has to do something and quickly. This is illustrated in the terrorist border crossing issue (but still American official policy statements reflect the normal diplomatic courtesies expected among equals). Second, it may reflect the fact that Canada is perceived as an ally, but being weaker in capability, its fit is less than perfect. Or third, it may be a consequence of Canadian nationalistic sensitivities which are alert to being bossed around by a more powerful neighbour combined with some sense of insecurity or doubt about Canadian national identity.

The immigration issue follows a similar pattern, with one interesting difference. Along the southern border it is the Mexicans that the US wants to keep out. Mexican money and produce, other than drugs, are welcome, but not the people. Along the northern border it is terrorists that the US wants to keep out. Canadians can be trusted, with some prodding from the US, to do their part. Mexico's government can be put on hold until it is convenient for the US to discuss the immigration issue. The interesting question here is why is the US not more concerned about terrorists entering the US from Mexico? True, the number of border patrol agents along the southern border did increase significantly after the terrorist attack, as they did along the northern border, but there is nothing as elaborate as the US–Canada smart border plan of action for the southern border. Perhaps it is attributable to the simple fact that American authorities have not caught suspected terrorists entering the US from the south (although there have been some false alarms). Or perhaps it is attributable to the American assumption that if a terrorist had the choice of going to Canada versus going to Mexico, he would naturally go to Canada. In any case, Canada and Canadians are regarded as an equal ally in border management, whereas Mexico and Mexicans are not. Instead, they are seen as weak, corrupt, and in need of American guidance.

References

CHABAT, JORGE. 1994. 'Drug Trafficking in U.S.–Mexican Relations'. In *Drug trafficking in the Americas*, eds., Bruce Bagley and William Walker III. Miami: University of Miami Press.

CRAIG, RICHARD. 1989. 'U.S. Narcotics Policy Toward Mexico'. In *The Drug Connection in U.S.-Mexican Relations*, eds., Guadalupe Gonzalez and Marta Tienda. San Diego: Center for US–Mexican Studies, University of California, San Diego.

DUNN, TIMOTHY J. 1996. *The Militarization of the U.S.–Mexico Border*. Austin: University of Texas, Center for Mexican American Studies.

FISHER, BENEDIKT. 1998. 'Prohibition as the Art of Political Diplomacy: The Benign Guises of the "War on Drugs" in Canada'. In *The New War on Drugs: Symbolic Politics and Criminal Justice Policy*, eds., E.L. Jensen. and J. Gerber, 157–175. Cincinnati: Anderson.

MENDEL, WILLIAM H., COLONEL (ret.). 1995. 'Countering the Drug Threat with Interagency Teamwork'. In *Global Dimensions of High Intensity Crime and Low Intensity Conflict*, ed., Graham H. Turbiville, 206–230. Chicago: Office of International Criminal Justice, University of Illinois at Chicago.

PILANT, LOIS. 2005. 'Taking on Borders. On the Frontline with the Minuteman Project'. *Law Enforcement News*, 31 (634).

REUTER, PETER AND RONFELDT, DAVID. 1992. 'Quest for Integrity: The Mexican–US Drug Issue in the 1980s'. *Journal of Interamerican Studies and World Affairs*, 34 (3): 89–153.

RUIZ-CABAÑAS, MIGUEL. 1992. 'Mexico's Permanent Campaign: Costs, Benefits, Implications'. In *Drug Policy in the Americas*, ed. Peter Smith. Boulder: Westview Press.

TORO, MARÍA CELIA. 1995. *Mexico's "War" on Drugs: Causes and Consequences*. Boulder: Lynne Rienner.

UNITED STATES CONGRESS. 1997. *Congressional Record*, 143 (32), 13 March 1997.

—————— 1999. Law Enforcement Problems at the Border Between the United States and Canada: Drug Smuggling, Illegal Immigration, and Terrorism. Hearing before the Subcommittee on Immigration and Claims of the Committee of the Judiciary, House of Representatives, 106th Cong. 1st session, 14 April 1999. Washington, DC: US Government Printing Office

UNITED STATES, DEPARTMENT OF STATE. 1997. 'International Narcotics Control Strategy Report, March 1997'. Bureau for International Narcotics and Law Enforcement Affairs. Washington, DC: GPO.

—————— 1999. 'International Narcotics Strategy Report'. Available at URL: <http://www.usis.usemb.se/drugs/1998/canmex.html>

—————— 2000. 'Canada–U.S. Partnership Forum Report: Building a Border for the 21st Century'. December 2000. Available at URL: <http://www.state.gov/www/regions/wha/0012_cusp_report.html>

UNITED STATES DEA (Drug Enforcement Administration) 2002. 'More than 100 Arrested in Nationwide Methamphetamine Investigation'. Available at URL: <http://www.dea.gov/major/me3/html>

US, GAO. 1997. 'Drug Control. Reauthorization of the Office of National Drug Control Policy. Statement of Norman J. Rabkin, Director, Administration of Justice Issues, General Government Division'. Washington, DC: GAO, GAO/T-GGD-97-97.

—————— 1999. 'US–Mexico Border. Issues and Challenges Confronting the United States and Mexico'. Washington, DC: GAO/NSIAD-99-190

WHITE HOUSE (ONDCP). 1997. 'The National Drug Control Strategy, 1997'. Washington, DC: The White House, Office of National Drug Control Policy.

—————— 1997. 'Institutional Counterdrug Co-operation'. Available at URL: <http://www.whitehousedrugpolicy.gov/publications/enforce/rpttocong/usmexinstit.html>

—————— 2002. 'Fact Sheet: Bilateral Cooperation with Mexico'. <http://www.whitehousedrugpolicy.gov/publications/international/factsht/mexico.html>.

Chapter 15

The Factor of Trust and the Importance of Inter-agency Co-operation in the Fight Against Transnational Organised Crime: the US–Mexican Example

Edgardo Buscaglia and Samuel González-Ruíz

This article examines the factor of trust and the importance of inter-agency co-operation as determinant elements for an effective fight against transnational organised crime. First, the links between organised crime and corruption will be explored to establish the necessity of confronting these two phenomena simultaneously if any success in the matter is to be achieved in the future. Second, the importance of collaboration at national, regional and international levels in the fight against organised crime will be explained. Finally, we will address the struggle by Mexico and the United States against organised crime at the border, as an excellent example of the multiple difficulties encountered in a relationship of co-operation between law enforcement officials of two countries.

The Link between Organised Crime and Corruption

During the last decades of the 20th century, after the end of the Cold War, a process of globalisation has been developing in the world leading to, among other effects, the intensification of economic, ideological, political, cultural and multiple social consequences (Kacowiks 2001). This process has caused everyday activities to be more and more influenced by factors and events taking place in other parts of the world; in the same way, practices and decisions of local groups and communities can have important regional or international effects (Silva Machado 2001). Unfortunately, the process of globalisation has also created negative consequences, as it has been accompanied during the last decades by the parallel growth of two phenomena, closely related to each other, which constitute a serious threat to the world's security and political stability. These two phenomena are transnational organised crime and corruption.

Criminological discussion about organised crime has for some decades now used legal definitions drawn from the American RICO[1] and the Italian

---

[1] RICO stands for Racketeer Influenced and Corrupt Organizations Act.

Rognoni-La Torre Statutes. The focus has centred on the hierarchy, structure and harm done by organised crime. At the same time, increases in the scale and scope of organised criminal activities within and across countries clearly depend upon the implicit or explicit support from corrupt public officials. The United Nations Convention against Transnational Organised Crime gathered 124 government signatories in Palermo in December 2000, and contains a practical definition of organised crime codified in Article 2. An Organised Crime Group is a 'structure of three or more persons, existing for a period of time and acting in concert with the aim of committing one or more serious crimes or offences in order to obtain, directly or indirectly a financial or other material benefit.' The links between organised crime and public sector corruption, which can broadly be understood as the abuse of public power for private profit, are not new (Friedrich 2002). Through the use of corruption organised criminal groups have been able to distort police investigations, derail criminal processes against them, bribe members of the judiciary, and hire the best private attorneys, thanks to the extremely lucrative nature of their business. In other words, they have utilised public sector corruption as a means for confronting states with impunity and subverting or degrading the rule of law (González Ruíz et al. 2002). In some other cases public sector corruption has been a central prerequisite for the development of organised crime, as in several of the countries that once constituted the former Soviet Union (Shelley 2002).

This close link has also been confirmed in a recent study of the United Nations in which 43 organised crime groups in 18 countries from different regions of the globe were analysed. The main objectives of the study were: the building of a substantial data-base, the development of a comparative study of the phenomenon, the creation of an organised crime typology, and, in the future, the possibility of monitoring global organised crime trends.

The profile of the organised crime groups surveyed showed that almost two-thirds of the groups are hierarchical in some way and only one-third of the groups were loosely organised. The vast majority participate in only one primary criminal activity, yet at the same time take part in some secondary activities with the intention of achieving the main activity, which in a large number of cases is drug trafficking. The level of trans-border activities was also an important finding from this work, showing that a large number of the groups extend their criminal activities across three, four or more states. Moreover, the degree to which the criminal groups penetrated the legitimate economy of the country or countries where they were based and the cross-over between legitimate and illegitimate activities in those countries was a common aspect in a large number of cases. Concerning the use of political influence, which is closely linked to the issues of corruption and the penetration into the legitimate economy; one-third of the groups were said to have political influence at the local or regional level; in seven cases the groups were regarded to have some influence at national level in the country of intervention; and in five cases to have some influence in a country or countries outside of their base state. Finally, regarding corruption as a necessary tool for organised crime, in the overall majority of cases, corruption was shown to be a key element for the undertaking of organised crime activities. What is more, 30 of the groups used corruption occasionally or regularly for the fulfilment of their primary activities (Van Dijk et al. 2002). In this context, the need for fighting and controlling public sector corruption at the same time as organised crime constitutes a necessary strategy for criminal justice practitioners in any country of the world.

In the case of corruption and its connection to organised crime, five different levels of relationship can be distinguished between these two phenomena:

1. The first level involves the promise, offer or giving of any benefit that improperly affects the actions or decisions of a public official; the offer or giving at this level is a one time operation, such as, for example, to obtain a passport, license, or advance information about police activities with the purpose of achieving a criminal gain.
2. The second level consists of 'Continuous Acts of Bribery', when the public official is on the payroll of the organisation ensuring thereby a continuous flow of information and protection from police intrusion into criminal activities. At this level organised crime obtains constant access to confidential information allowing it to maintain patterns of illegal activity and remain one step ahead of the police or law enforcement authorities.
3. At the third level governmental agencies are sporadically infiltrated at lower ranking official positions. Employment in law enforcement agencies, judicial and prosecutors' office is gained for members and friends of organised crime. The infiltration is mostly accomplished through two main channels. One is through the application for job vacancies within government or law enforcement agencies by one or more members or friends of an organised criminal group, and the second by literally 'buying the job' through bribes or blackmailing officials to place the member or friend in the government post.
4. At the fourth stage we can find that penetration of the state has taken place (Shelly 2002). The infiltration of the government can encompass entire branches or top officials in law enforcement, prosecutors' office and other sensitive government offices. Again two main channels can be distinguished by which organised criminal groups infiltrate higher levels of government. One is the use of bribery and blackmail to promote officers previously corrupted by their organisation to higher ranks with broader access to information. This is soon thereafter repaid to organised crime with increased protection and access to more useful secret police information. The second way is the use of bribery, blackmail and coercion to control the chief decision-maker of an entire branch of government. At this level of infiltration organised crime can continue operating with very little risk of discovery or successful prosecution. Organised crime can maintain market control with the support of government officials and gain control over entire sectors of the economy.

5. At this last level organised crime infiltrates the political arena. Political infiltration is accomplished by giving money or media support or by participating in political campaigns, corrupting the democratic election process; lobbying other politicians for support using bribery and blackmail; exploiting organised crime members' family links, and creating 'debts' for politicians to 'repay' later by using blackmail and extortion. There are many examples of benefits obtained by organised crime when it penetrates the political arena; such as friendly prosecutors and judges, the legitimisation of organised crime though alliances with elected political figures, the monopolisation of entire economic sectors by criminal activities, and the legalisation of the organised criminal group's activities by influencing law makers.

Collaboration at National, Regional and International Levels

In the fight against transnational organised crime and its close links to corruption, information about criminal activities in the home country or other countries in which a criminal group operates represents the keystone of any criminal investigation in these matters. In addition, the amount of information that a criminal investigation at national level can collect, most of the time only corresponds to a small fraction of the complex phenomenon that organised crime represents.

Take, for instance, the example of drug trafficking. A policeman who seizes a container with drugs in Europe will never be in a position to secure enough information or evidence for a possible prosecution of the suspects who are transporting drugs from the producing or transit country without the help of law enforcement officials of all the states involved. In most of the large and complex cases related to organised crime, possible evidence and witnesses are located in at least two different countries, and often dispersed across several different countries across the world. International collaboration, therefore, is a crucial element for a winning outcome in this fight.

The problem of collaboration between law enforcement officials at national, regional and international levels is not a simple one. Even at national and sub-national levels, strong competition between agencies can exist. Individuals and law enforcement agencies compete among each other to obtain credit for successful investigations. This is one of the main reasons why law enforcement officials and agencies keep information within their own jurisdiction; there is, as well, the necessity to show evidence of successful investigations, justifying by this means bigger budgets for future assignments.

Differences or disputes between police, prosecutors and investigating magistrates also occur frequently. Learning to work together in their respective spheres of jurisdiction is a key factor for achieving success in investigating complex criminal cases. Consequently, the management of every law enforcement organisation should stress the necessity of a process of co-ordination with other agencies, whether in the same country or abroad. This process has to be developed starting from high level officials and extending to lower levels of the organisation, as well as across sectors.

Law enforcement officials, prosecutors and investigating magistrates should always keep in mind that every time they fail to cooperate as in the sharing information among individuals and agencies, the victims of organised crime suffer the consequences. Law enforcement officials often argue that if they were able to link and process information from criminal investigations presently in the hands of police and prosecutors around the globe, it would be possible to indict most of the largest organised criminal groups in the world.

The importance of fighting corruption in law enforcement agencies in order to enhance co-operation for combating organised crime around the world has been stressed before. It is a well known fact that in many countries corruption of police and prosecutors represents a reality which compromises anti-organised crime operations. However, on many occasions reports about corrupted public officials form part of disinformation campaigns, launched by criminal organisations to generate distrust among law enforcement agencies at national and international level. Examples of disinformation campaigns can be found in several cases related to the fight against the Mafia in Italy, the Colombian drug cartels and the Mexican fight against organised crime and corruption. In all the examples mentioned above, disinformation was developed and disseminated by organised criminal groups to impede co-operation among officials at national and international levels.

Some organised criminal groups employ former policemen and military personnel, since they know former colleagues and the methods used by the law enforcement agencies they once worked for. Furthermore, through the use of intelligence and disinformation campaigns, criminal organisations seek to discredit honest officers they were unable to bribe. These practices include, among others, the use of corrupt journalists to disseminate false and incriminating information. Unfortunately in some countries, public sector corruption is at present time a real and serious problem that hampers the fight against organised crime.

Fear for the safety of law enforcement officials is a very important matter. It is vital not to risk the lives of law enforcement personnel, witnesses, confidential sources or their families. At the same time, the development of a system that allows law enforcement counterparts at national or international level to experiment and test to see if they can trust each other constitutes an essential issue to enhance collaboration in the future. A good strategy can induce law enforcement officials to share information with counterparts. After making sure that witnesses or persons involved are not placed at any risk, all the information which is not relevant for their specific criminal investigation, but could be useful for other national or international agencies, should be shared. Relevant information can be shared effectively and more rapidly through the application of article 20 of the Palermo Convention (Convention against Transnational Organized Crime of 2000). This would entail the start of a pattern of collaboration among law enforcement agencies and officials. Every time success in a criminal investigation is achieved through the use of information provided by other agencies, the relationship of collaboration and trust would be strengthened at the same time.

An investigator will face two main problems in terms of international collaboration. First, there are differences in the legal systems involved, such as Continental Law or Common Law or Islamic Law approaches. A good solution to this problem could be the possibility of using the allegation of 'conspiracy' as a criminal offence, or the concept of 'membership' as participation in criminal activities (Article 6, Palermo Convention 2000). Second, the role of a criminal investigator can be carried out by policemen, prosecutors and investigating magistrates, depending on the country in which the criminal investigation takes place and the legal tradition being followed. This conflict of legal traditions can affect an international investigation, whether in its initiating stage or in the process of attempting to search and seize profits of crime in a foreign country.

Other problems and obstacles in the fight against organised crime are related to political factors or the sovereignty of the countries involved. As in any other business, criminal organisations operate wherever there is less risk to do so. The *Global Trends Report* of the United Nations showed that countries that have lower standards in laws and the implementation of them are also countries with high levels of organised crime and corruption (UNODC 2002). This same relationship can also be found to exist in countries that show high levels of abuse in judicial discretion in criminal cases (Buscaglia and Van Dijk et al. 2003).

In this context, the Palermo Convention confirms the political commitment of the international community to enhance collaboration among agencies and individuals, promoting mechanisms to exchange information through any possible means in accordance with article 18 of the international instrument.[2] Through the use of 'joint investigations', it is now possible to conduct more complex investigations with positive effects in the fight against transnational organised crime around the world.[3]

There are many ways to obtain international collaboration. One such way is direct collaboration through liaison officers. Many countries have devel-

---

[2] Palermo Convention, Article 18, Paragraph 4: 'Without prejudice to domestic law, the competent authorities of a State Party may, without prior request, transmit information relating to criminal matters to a competent authority in another State Party where they believe that such information could assist the authority in undertaking or successfully concluding inquiries and criminal proceedings or could result in a request formulated by the latter State Party pursuant to this Convention.'

[3] Palermo Convention, Article 19, Joint investigations: 'States Parties shall consider concluding bilateral or multilateral agreements or arrangements whereby, in relation to matters that are the subject of investigations, prosecutions or judicial proceedings in one or more States, the competent authorities concerned may establish joint investigative bodies. In the absence of such agreements or arrangements, joint investigations may be undertaken by agreement on a case-by-case basis. The States Parties involved shall ensure that the sovereignty of the State Party in whose territory such investigation is to take place is fully respected.'

oped the position of 'liaison officer' to facilitate the exchange of information among agencies at national and international levels. Another means of fostering international collaboration is through Interpol or a mutual legal assistance agreement developed in accordance with article 18 of the Palermo Convention or Article 7 of the Vienna Convention of 1988 (United Nations Convention against Illicit Traffic in Narcotic Drugs and Psychotropic Substances, 1988). Finally, states can develop co-operation among main elements of their justice systems.

Additionally, differences between Mutual Legal Assistance (MLA) and Rogatory systems must be kept in mind. Mutual Legal Assistance is a system ruled by treaties and other international legal instruments. The request of co-operation goes from a central authority of the requesting state to the central authority of the state whose assistance is requested; therefore, it is a faster and more effective system. Law enforcement authorities often commit the mistake of considering their national legal system as the only possible one. However, most successful experiences in MLA and Rogatory systems are achieved when both are considered as a bridge between the legal systems of the requested and the requesting state.

The US–Mexican Case

The United States–Mexican fight against organised crime in the border region constitutes an excellent example of the multiple factors and difficulties encountered in developing co-operation between law enforcement officials of two countries with great differences in their legal culture and economic resources. The study of those factors is of great importance for determining the type of criminal organisation states are dealing with and the share of the markets controlled by them, such as in the case of cocaine.

After an initial period of consolidation of the Mexican criminal organisations, negotiations between the Colombian and the Mexican drug cartels over transport and routes fell under the control of Mexican organised crime, which raised their fees to 35 percent of the value of the shipments transported through Mexican territory and, finally, pressured the Colombian cartels into sharing 50 percent of the value of the shipment. By this time, between 50–70 percent of the cocaine consumed in the United States was transported trough Mexico, marking the beginning of large-scale distribution by Mexican criminal organisations in the United States (González and Cesar 2001).

The beginning of the 1990s also saw the decline in the retail value of heroin and marijuana produced in Mexico, a consequence of the increase in the consumption of cocaine in the United States. In this period, public sector corruption related to drug trafficking appeared to be at its highest level and was a key element for the undertaking of the cartels' activities.

An unprecedented case study by the United Nations with the Mexican Unit against Organised Crime to monitor and follow-up investigations of organised crime, in order to determine the structure of its organisation and operations, its criminal activities, modus operandi and links with the licit/illicit environments, is presently in progress. The case study, based on the Falcone Checklist Questionnaire, also has the purpose of assisting the unit's work in developing preventive tools and determining possible investigative and prosecutorial strategies.[4] This study has shown that, at present time, 43 percent of organised Mexican criminal groups are cells, 51 percent are criminal networks and only six percent are hierarchical groups. The relevance of this finding cannot be underestimated. As the case of Mexico shows, by identifying the structure of organised crime, authorities can develop proper anti-crime strategies that fit the scale and nature of the operations of each criminal group. The Falcone checklist is a tool that serves the purpose of providing the necessary inputs to address this need.

It is important to mention that the study has confirmed a direct relationship between drugs related organised crime and kidnappings. While 23 percent of the organised criminal groups in Mexico conduct kidnappings as one of their primary activities, an additional 12 percent conduct kidnappings as a secondary activity.

Concerning the actual level of trans-border activities and geographical jurisdiction of these criminal groups, 57 percent of them are transnational, of which 40 percent extend their activities in two or three countries, while 17 percent involve criminal activities in more than three countries.

Approximately 40 percent of organised crime in Mexico uses corruption of judicial officers in order to avoid or block investigations or prosecutions. These cells or criminal networks that use judicial corruption as part of their normal operational procedures also engage in drug trafficking as their primary related activity. Prosecutors are the most frequently corrupted group, occurring in almost 90 percent of the sampled cases.

Organised criminal groups in Mexico focus their activities within well defined areas. According to the sampled cases, between 60 and 75 percent of the resources used by criminal networks to commit crimes are recycled. Kidnapping and corruption go hand in hand, and the latter is mainly focused on state authorities.

---

[4] The Falcone Checklist Questionnaire is the product of a process of evolution of an investigative tool originally developed by the Centre for International Crime Prevention of the United Nations ODC. The questionnaire received further valuable imputes from UNICRI, TRANSCRIME, and the Ministry of Justice of the Netherlands to work as an academic tool. Samuel González and Edgardo Buscaglia realised that it could also be used as an investigative tool and adapted it for real case investigation purposes in seminars for law enforcement officials in Colombia, Peru, Central-America and Mexico. The results presented in this article are based in an adaptation by Jose Luis Santiago Vasconcelos, actual head of the Mexican Unit against Organized Crime of the Federal Prosecutor's Office in Mexico. Contribution for this was also given by Cesar Prieto Palma and José C. García-González. The statistical analysis support was given by Fabrizio Sarrica.

In this context, establishing trust in the region between public authorities and between the law enforcement agencies of the two countries is not an easy matter. There is competition over the credit to be given for work done and a lack of confidence in the work of other agencies, which is greatly increased by the disinformation campaigns conducted by drug trafficking groups in the region. It must not be forgotten that many of the members of those organised crime groups were trained in police or military schools and hence are well aware of organisational culture and sensitivities.

As is well known, the Arellano Felix family and the Carrillo Fuentes cartel, among others in the region, engaged, while they could, in extensive counter-intelligence activities, mainly through the use of informers working with Mexican and United States police agencies, and at the same time supplied information to harm rival gangs in the region (for example, by stopping drug deliveries of such gangs). They gave information leading to seizures of small amounts of drugs while larger quantities were moved through at the same time at other points. They had relations with the press, based in part on the natural interest of journalists in being informed about the drug trafficking situation, but sometimes involved journalists who were friends of the criminals or whom they simply paid and controlled. This is one of the factors that makes it so difficult to combat drug trafficking and organised crime in Mexico. Sometimes these links between corruption and organised crime rose to the highest levels of law enforcement, as when General Jesus Gutierrez Rebollo, the Mexican drug czar, was revealed in 1997 to be on the payroll of the Amado Carrillo Fuentes organisation.

Following this scandal all previous efforts of co-operation and trust between the two countries were crushed, leading the US House of Representatives to declare Mexico 'a delinquent ally in the war against drugs' (Dettmer 1997). Since then, great effort has been undertaken to rebuild a relationship of trust and co-operation in the fight against transnational organised crime between the governments and law enforcement officials of the two states. This episode is only one of many examples of the difficult conditions surrounding the fight against organised crime in Mexico and the United States.

In May 2001, thanks to continued efforts in Mexico and the United States, Everardo Arturo 'Kitty' Paez Martínez—an important member of the Arellano Felix Family—was extradited to the United States. He had been held since October 1997 in the federal maximum security prison of Almoloya de Juárez. This was accomplished thanks to the efforts of the Tijuana/San Diego Group, a task force formed by federal agencies of Mexico and the United States.

The Binational Group was formed in that same period and helped to put seven of the ten criminal leaders of the Tijuana cartel of 1996 behind bars, while another two died. As a result Emilio 'El CP' Valdez Mainero was arrested at Coronado, California, on the basis of a request for detention for extradition purposes submitted by Mexico in September 1996. He was sentenced by the San Diego federal court to 30 years imprisonment for offences committed in his United States prison, pending the extradition proceedings. When he finishes his time in prison, he will be extradited to Mexico for another trial. Everardo Arturo 'Kitty' Paez Martínez, arrested in 1997 in Tijuana at the request of the United States government, was sent to the maximum security prison in Almoloya de Juárez. The Ministry for Foreign Affairs granted an extradition request. That decision was challenged in the courts but, after lengthy proceedings, Paez was extradited to the United States. He was the first important Mexican criminal to be extradited to that country for drug trafficking. Amado Cruz Anguiano has been held since February 1998 in the maximum security prison of Almoloya de Juárez, having been convicted of laundering money for the Arellano Félix Organisation. Ismael 'El Mayel' Higuera Guerrero was arrested in May 2000. He is also in the Almoloya de Juárez maximum security prison and is now undergoing trial. Jesús Labra Áviles, arrested in February 2000, is also being held in the same prison. David 'El CH' Baron Corona died on 17 November 1997 in an attempt to kill Jesús Blancornelas, editor of the Mexican newspaper *Zeta*. Unfortunately Blancornelas' bodyguard was killed in that incident.

Of the 1996 leadership of the Tijuana cartel, Benjamín Arellano Felix was arrested in March 2002, just a few weeks after his brother Ramon was killed in a gunfight with rival gangs in Sinaloa, Mexico. Benjamin is now undergoing trial in the same maximum security prison as the rest of his colleagues and only Manuel 'El Caballo' Aguirre Galindo has so far evaded arrest.

The activities of the Binational Group also permitted, for the first time, the issue in the United States of arrest warrants against Benjamín and Ramón Arellano Félix, the latter becoming one of the ten criminals on the FBI's list of most-wanted fugitives until his death.

Each society has its own view of the drug problem, which reflects the way it is affected by drugs, whether it is predominantly a consumer country or region (Europe and the United States), an area of transit and production (Mexico and Latin America), or a country that generates illicit resources or constitutes a tax haven where, *inter alia*, the money accumulated by drug traffickers is laundered. The consequences are vastly different and so are, inevitably, the perspectives and approaches of policy-makers and researchers. The multiplicity of approaches to the drug problem sometimes makes it difficult to appreciate the need to take into account all elements of the problem in trying to develop real solutions.

In the year 2000 the United Nations launched a programme in which key components of the fight against drugs were identified as preventing trafficking, consolidating national institutions, preventing displacement of illicit cultivation, supporting country efforts, and implementing alternative development (UNODCCP 2000). Initiatives should concentrate on: reducing the demand for drugs at the same time as curtailing supply; strengthening programmes for sanctioning those responsible for drug trafficking; generating support in the community for the officials entrusted with combating organised crime; developing anti-corruption mechanisms in different countries; working with civil society to develop techniques for the elimination of violence; developing effective programmes for confiscating the assets of drug traffickers; and promoting measures to punish money-launderers. Only by addressing these many facets will it be possible to reduce the social burden for society created by the drug problem in the 21st century.

References

BUSCAGLIA, EDGARDO and JAN VAN DIJK 2003. 'Global Trends in Controlling Public Sector Corruption and Organized Crime'. In *Forum on Crime and Society*, December 2003, 23–45. United Nations Office on Drugs and Crime. United Nations Press.

DETTMER, JAIME. 1997. 'U.S. Drug Warriors Knock on Heaven's Door'. *Insight*, April. Washington, D.C.

FRIEDRICH, CARL J. 2002. 'Corruption. Concepts in Historical Perspective'. In *Political Corruption: Concepts and Contexts*, ed. Arnold J. Heidenheimer. London: Transaction Publishers.

GONZÁLEZ RUÍZ, SAMUEL, BUSCAGLIA, EDGARDO, GARCÍA GONZÁLEZ, JOSÉ CRUZ, and PRIETO, CESAR. 2002. 'Corrupción y Delincuencia Organizada: Un Estrecho Vínculo'. *Revista de la Universidad Católica de Chile*, no. 76 (August/ September 2002): 55–62.

GONZÁLEZ, SAMUEL AND PRIETO, CESAR. 2001. 'La Experiencia Mexicana contra la Mafia Organizada'. In *La Lucha contra la Delincuencia Organizada y la Corrupción*. PNUFID: Lima.

KACOWIKS, ARIEL M. 2001. *Globalization and Poverty: Possible Links, Possible Solutions*. Department of International Relations, Hebrew University of Jerusalem, Israel, July 2001: 7–11.

SHELLEY, LOUISE. 2002. 'The penetration of state and private sector structures by criminal networks: Its impact on governance in Russia and other states of the former Soviet Union'. Seminar on the impact of organised crime and corruption on governance in the SADC region. Pretoria, 18–19 April 2002.

SILVA MACHADO, JORGE A. 2001. 'Concepto de Globalización'. Forum Global 2001.

'United Nations Convention against Illicit Traffic in Narcotic Drugs and Psychotropic Substances'. 1998. Adopted by the Conference at its 6th plenary meeting, on 19 December 1988. Available at URL: <http://untreaty.un.org/English/TreatyEvent2003/Texts/treaty7E.pdf>

'United Nations Convention Against Transnational Organized Crime'. 2001. G.A. Res. 25, annex I, U.N. GAOR, 55th Sess., Supp. No. 49, at 44, U.N. Doc. A/45/49 (Vol. I).

UNITED NATIONS OFFICE ON DRUGS AND CRIME (UNODC). 2002. *Global Trends Report*. Center for International Crime Prevention.

UNITED NATIONS OFFICE FOR DRUG CONTROL AND CRIME PREVENTION (UNODCCP). 2000. *World Drug Report 2000*. Oxford: Oxford University Press. Available at URL: http://www.unodc.org/unodc/world_drug_report_2000.html

UNITED STATES. DEPARTMENT OF STATE. 2002. 'International Narcotics Control Strategy Report (INCSR)'.

VAN DIJK, JAN, MARK SHAW and EDGARDO BUSCAGLIA. 2002. 'The TOC Convention and the Need for Comparative Research: Some Illustrations from the Work of the UN Centre for International Crime Prevention'. In *The Containment of Transnational Organized Crime: Comments on the UN Convention of December 2000*, eds., Hans-Jörg Albrecht and Cyrille Fijnaut, 31–54. Freiburg: Editions iuscrim.

Part V

Conclusion

Conclusion:
Border management as an element of security sector governance

Marina Caparini and Otwin Marenin

This volume was generated by interest in the evolving security sector reform (SSR) agenda that has been increasingly shaping the way policy-makers, scholars and security practitioners think about and approach the provision of security. In particular, we were struck by the observation that while there have been rapid and far-reaching developments in the border control policies of North American and European states over the past decade and especially in the past five years, the aspect of democratic control and oversight of border security agencies has been neglected both in the literature and—as has been confirmed by various authors in this collection—in practice.

Security sector reform is based on the idea that those state organs and institutions that play an important role in providing security should, on the one hand, be efficient and effective, and on the other hand, should be managed and overseen in a way that reflects the values of liberal democracy—that is, with greater transparency, accountability and democratic control. Judging the efficiency and effectiveness of border guarding is problematic, however, given the problematique of border control in a globalised world: witness the ability of smugglers and traffickers to re-route flows around barriers and other increased security measures, and the practical and political impossibility of any system of border management checking every cargo container that enters national territory, given the widespread emphasis on economic liberalisation and freer trade. A more fundamental critique has been advanced by various observers that often the real, but undeclared, priority underlying efforts to ramp up border security is maintaining *the image* of the state as able to exercise sovereignty in conditions of globalisation and effectively control who and what has access to its territory. So, for example, Andreas (2000) comments that US law enforcement efforts aimed at controlling drug flows over the US–Mexican border have provided 'highly visible but misleading indicators of government resolve—increased arrests, seizures, and so on—helped sustain this image and obscured the failings and flaws of the enforcement effort'.

Managing border security institutions in a way that is consistent with the principles of democratic control, accountability and oversight that are held to view other security institutions in a democracy also encounters challenges. Border guarding tends to take place away from the public eye, often at the periphery of the state in remote areas far from view. The subjects of border guarding—especially non-citizens and asylum seekers who attempt to gain entry into Western states—have little or no voice in the usual forums. Little attention has focused in the public discourse of border management on human rights of migrants, privacy issues, or the need to balance perceived security considerations with other values, such as freedom or justice.

Democratic control and oversight have been neglected elements in the border security discourse in Europe, particularly with respect to the imperative of strengthening external border controls by new member states and candidates for future membership. Contributors have discussed the prevailing absence of democratic control and oversight institutions and mechanisms. Guiraudon, for example, describes how the secretive intergovernmental process of justice and home affairs (JHA) cooperation, and the ignoring by European Commission and Council policy-makers of advisory boards established to act as watchdogs for EU rules, has compromised democratic control in border and immigration controls. Recent developments such as growing exchange of data between states and other forms of international cooperation also raise serious concerns about democratic oversight. Legislative oversight has been lacking, both at the EU and national level, in the development of EU approaches to internal security and border management. Monika Sie Dhian Ho notes that in the EU, there is insufficient legislation governing the powers and accountability of multinational teams conducting joint controls. There has been very rapid development of activities such as joint operations, ad hoc centres etc, but little or no effort to implement corresponding accountability structures and mechanisms. She notes the need for an EU institutional structure to prepare, coordinate, monitor and evaluate these joint activities, foster more transparency, and ensure they are subject to legal rules and parliamentary oversight.

The inadequate attention paid to democratic oversight and accountability with regard to border management in the EU context is also seen more generally across the 'area of freedom, security and justice' (AFSJ), where, as has been noted elsewhere, 'the reactive, security-centred approach may have an in-built tendency to marginalize familiar constitutional constraints, such as the proper balancing of fundamental values, the primacy of democratic decision, due process in individual cases, and a robust system of separation and diversification of powers and of institutional checks and balances' (Walker 2004, p.13). The fast pace of the security-focused policy agenda and institutional development has not been matched by the establishment of safeguards for protection of rights and freedoms such as oversight arrangements.

More than a decade ago, Didier Bigo criticised the emergence of a 'security continuum' in Europe, which linked illegal immigrants and asylum-seekers with organised crime, drug trafficking and terrorism (Bigo 1994, p.165). The spread of the ideology and practice of economic liberalisation and freer trade coincide with the effects of globalisation—technology, telecommunications, economic and cultural influences that transcend the nation-state and create relations of interdependence. At the same time, the securitisation of social and economic issues and resulting moral panics about the influx of 'illegal immigrants' and their putative linkages to serious forms of crime and terrorism have taken hold in public debates about immigration and border control. Political discourse in Europe and North America about removing barriers to trade and the flow of goods has been linked to reassuring domestic populations about the state's capacity to enforce migration controls and prevent uncontrolled migration and the entry of contraband. The contributions to this volume suggest that, contrary to the popular view that globalisation greatly diminishes the relevance of national borders, in some ways borders have acquired ever more symbolic importance through state efforts to improve its perceived control over how the state's population is constituted. Those state efforts now include the use of sophisticated surveillance technologies, stricter visa requirements and law enforcement measures, including interagency and international cooperation, to exclude those elements deemed to be undesirable.

One of the principal concerns of the European Union today is the protection of its external borders. The internal security policy field, now known within the EU context as the 'area of freedom, security and justice' (AFSJ), is a concept which emerged from the 1997 Treaty of Amsterdam but which brought together various bodies of law and practice in the inter-related areas of external border management, asylum, cooperation among police, customs and judicial authorities, and coordinated policies against organised crime, drug trafficking and terrorism. The AFSJ originated in the effort to develop compensatory measures to control movement across the EU's external borders and monitor internal populations as a result of the free movement created within the EU's internal market, and the perceived security deficit resulting from the removal of internal frontiers. The field is undergoing rapid development through legal harmonisation and enhanced practical cooperation, driven in part by EU enlargement, but also supposedly by emerging security threats and challenges of the post-9-11 era.

New member states from Central and Eastern Europe are expected to implement the Schengen and JHA *acquis* and bear a disproportionate share of the burden in managing the EU's new external borders. The EU has further been able to 'thicken' its external border by convincing states that are not yet members but are candidates or hope for eventual entry into the EU to invest in strengthening their border controls and adopting safe third country policies with respect to asylum-seekers. In effect, the EU has been able to create a buffer zone consisting of its neighbouring countries, most of whom specifically seek entry to the EU.

While the EU has provided technical assistance and advice to build institutional capacity of the new member states for effective border management, what has been lacking according to several contributors to this volume is any emphasis on creating democratic oversight and accountability mechanisms to accompany the efforts to boost effectiveness of state border guard and policing institutions. While this is not only a problem concerning the new member states, it is of most concern with regard to them because of their recent transition from authoritarian state socialism in which border control was militarised and internal security structures were pillars of the repressive regime. While democratic control over other parts of the security sector has been formally implemented, the substantive existence of accountability and democratic oversight is still developing and needs to be improved in various areas. Moreover, the states of Central and Eastern Europe tend to have far weaker civil societies and other mechanisms by which state power is constrained and held accountable.

The security continuum has been seen not only in the European context, but also in North America, where the events of 11 September 2001 and the resulting dominance of counter-terrorism over the domestic political agenda have focused ever more resources on law enforcement issues involved in border control. American efforts have sought to improve the perceived effectiveness of the functioning of its borders as security barriers while facilitating legitimate trade and people flows. These trends have directly affected Canada and Mexico. Due to Canada's high level of exports to the US market and its need to avoid harmful effects of unilateral US security measures on cross-border trade, the Canadian government has had to respond to American criticisms of lax border control and implement a broad array of measures tightening its border security. Signing onto the 31-point 'smart borders' agreement with the US in December 2001, border control has similarly risen to the top of Canada's national political agenda.

The events of 11 September 2001 and the subsequent counter-terrorism agenda that has dominated the political agenda in the US has had important effects at the Canada–US border, and for human rights of Canadian citizens. Maher Arar, a Canadian citizen who was born in Syria, while travelling back to Canada from Tunisia was detained during a stop-over in New York's JFK airport and interrogated by American officials in October 2002. Accused of being a member of al-Qaida, he was subsequently deported to Jordan and ultimately Syria, where he was imprisoned, interrogated and tortured for more than a year until his release in late 2003. Due to the public furor and media attention generated by this incident and the lawsuits Mr. Arar has launched against the US and Canadian governments, the Canadian government launched a Commission of Inquiry to investigate the incident. While the investigation continues, the incident demonstrated the growing transnational impacts of security policies and practices. It specifically revealed the potential for harmful consequences of profiling and renditions in U.S. border management practices, particularly for the human and civil rights. The rendition, which apparently occurred with information provided by Canada's RCMP, constituted a transnational action whose subject was a Canadian citizen. Although Arar's efforts succeeded in the establishment of the Commission of Inquiry, the incident also underscored the gap between Canadian oversight mechanisms and such transnational action: the Arar Commission does not have jurisdiction to require US officials to appear before it, and these same have declined invitations by the Commission to appear before it and explain their role in the affair. So, although there is increasing bilateral and transnational cooperation between US and Canadian border management, law enforcement and national security institutions, oversight structures have not kept pace.

The securitisation of border control has also contributed to lack of transparency, including vis-à-vis formal oversight mechanisms. One example is provided by the Canadian Senate Committee on National Security and Defence, which in a recent report on Canadian border security, commented on the secrecy of government officials:

> Secrecy – particularly in the field of security – is too often the government default position. Openness should be the default position and secrecy the exception. Secrecy about security hides bureaucratic inefficiency and protects governments that aren't doing what they should be doing to protect their citizens.
> This Committee keeps asking questions about risk and measures supposedly being taken to avoid risk. Too often, we are not getting answers (Senate Committee on National Security and Defence 2005, p. 16).

Obviously, types of border control challenges vary according to who one's neighbours are. Neighbouring countries that have a high 'economic step', or a large difference between their respective levels of economic development, serve as flashpoints for border control. An example in Europe is the border between Spain and Morocco, in particular the Spanish enclave cities of Ceuta and Melilla, which have become springboards for large numbers of Africans seeking to scale the fences and enter Spain and the EU. The present US focus is on influencing perceptions that it is cracking down on illegal immigration by the increasing militarisation of the border, the establishment of a fence, and the deployment of up to 6000 National Guard troops on the border with Mexico. This 'border security' dilemma is rooted in a similar high economic step that has seen the number of illegal immigrants residing in the US increase from less than 4 million in 1986 to nearly 12 million by 2006 (Alden 2006, p.4). An issue frequently overlooked, remittances, illustrates the strong disincentives to more rigorous efforts by source states at combating uncontrolled migration from their territories. For many developing countries, remittances are one of the main sources of hard currency, outstripping foreign direct investment and tourism.

Attention of US policy-makers is often focused on the supply side; the US–Mexican border has become increasingly militarised and will be the site of a fence. Yet the pull factor or demand side of American agricultural, industrial and service sectors that rely on low cost labour is frequently omitted from the discourse. In a similar fashion, the demand side of the drug trafficking problem (high US levels of consumption of illegal drugs) is generally not addressed in talk and action surrounding the war on drugs.

Comparing developments in North America and Europe reveals that there has been a fundamental difference between the two regions. Both have been characterised by the emergence of regional economic integration. While the North American Free Trade Agreement (NAFTA) has focused on facilitating the movement of goods, capital and services, the EU has sought to facilitate the free movement of goods, capital, services and people. Even with the enlargement of the EU to include numerous Central and Eastern European states, the long-term objective has been to achieve the relatively free movement of people throughout any of the Member States, whether for work, leisure or family reasons. This has not been the case with NAFTA, specifically with regard to Mexican labour flows to the US. In effect, NAFTA enables differentiated access to the US labour market, with Canadians enjoying much greater access compared to Mexican nationals.

Another trend of concern in border management is the growing involvement of private actors (corporate firms such as airline carriers) in surveillance and migration control functions and thereby in security governance. Guiraudon explores the shift of responsibility for migration control towards private firms ('third parties') through the application of carrier sanctions, which occurred without adequate consultation of the industry. The delegation of migration control authority to private firms also constitutes a move towards risk management in migration control, more specifically, the privatisation of risk management. With the shift of responsibility to private companies and the move towards risk management, migration control becomes less a policy issue and more a technical one in which private firms avoid dealing with the essentially political question through fulfilling technical requirements. Thus, while enlarging the number of actors involved in security governance, the evolution of border management suggests a concomitant qualitative shift towards technical solutions and approaches.

Developments since 11 September 2001 in Europe and North America suggest that, far from losing their relevance in a context of globalisation and economic liberalisation, borders have acquired a new importance and state efforts to implement better control measures have underlined the role of the regulatory state in determining who and what have legitimate access to the territory of the state (Andreas 2003, p.110). While the actual effectiveness of border policing in stopping (as opposed to re-routing) inflows of undesired people and articles has been questioned, the day-to-day activities of border guards clearly have symbolic importance in underscoring the authority and legitimacy of state power. Democratic security governance requires that the means and mechanisms of accountability respond to the realities of evolving forms of border management if they are to be effective and legitimate. Unfortunately, the contributions to this volume indicate that whilst international cooperation in border management is increasing, the experience in both the EU and North America suggest resistance of state administrations and governments to implementing effective governance structures, and specifically accountability and oversight mechanisms for these enhanced cooperative arrangements.

References

ALDEN, EDWARD. 2006. 'Doubt over Bush focus on border security force', *Financial Times*, 17 May 20064.

ANDREAS, PETER. 2000. 'U.S.–Mexico Drug Control in the Age of Free Trade', *Borderlines* 66, vol. 8, no. 4 (April).

_____ 2003. 'Redrawing the Line: Borders and Security in the Twenty-first Century', *International Security*, vol. 8, no. 2 (Fall): 78–111.

BIGO, DIDIER. 1994. 'The European Internal Security Field: Stakes and Rivalries in a Newly Developing Area of Police Intervention'. In Malcolm Anderson and Monica den Boer, eds., *Policing Across National Boundaries* (London: Pinter).

SENATE COMMITTEE ON NATIONAL SECURITY AND DEFENCE. 2005. *Borderline Insecure*. Ottawa: Government of Canada.

WALKER, NEIL. 'In Search of the Area of Freedom, Security and Justice: A Constitutional Odyssey' In *Europe's Area of Freedom, Security and Justice*, Neil Walker, ed., (Oxford: Oxford University Press and the Academy of European Law, European University Institute, 2004)

Note on Authors

Eberhard BORT, a graduate in English and German of Tübingen University, is the Academic Coordinator of the Institute of Governance and a Lecturer in Politics at the University of Edinburgh. Previously, he worked at Tübingen University in British and Irish Studies with Christopher Harvie, taught in German Studies at Trinity College, Dublin, and at the University of Puget Sound, Tacoma, Wa., USA. Between 1995 and 1998 he worked with Malcolm Anderson on an ESRC-funded research project on 'The Internal and External Frontiers of the European Union'. From 1997 to 1999 he was Associate Director of the International Social Sciences Institute at Edinburgh University

Edgardo BUSCAGLIA is an Adviser to UNITAR (United Nations). He is a Senior Fellow at Columbia Law School (New York, USA) and a Fellow at the Hoover Institution at Stanford University (California, USA). He has advised and worked in technical assistances to counter organised crime and public sector corruption in 67 countries worldwide. He holds a post-doctorate and doctorate in law and in economics from the Universities of California in Berkeley and the University of Illinois in Urbana Champaign.

Marina CAPARINI is Senior Fellow, Research Division, DCAF. She writes on security sector governance, with a focus on the privatisation of security, internal security institutions and civil society. Her recent publications include *Civil Society and the Security Sector* (co-edited with Philipp Fluri and Ferenc Molnar, 2006) *Democratic Governance of Civil–Military Relations in Europe: Learning from Crisis and Institutional Change* (co-edited with Hans Born, Karl Haltiner and Jürgen Kuhlmann, 2006); *Privatizing Security: Law, Practice and Governance of Private Military and Security Companies* (co-authored with Fred Schreier, 2005); and 'The Relevance of Civil Society: A Response to Herbert Wulf' in the Dialogue Series on Security Sector Reform, *Berghof Handbook for Conflict Transformation* (2004).

Martha COTTAM is a Professor at the Department of Political Science of the Washington State University. Her major theoretical research interests concern the impact of political-psychological factors in decision making and negotiations in international politics in general, bargaining between governmental and non-governmental international actors, perceptions in the war on drugs, and border politics. Other areas of research interest include US-Latin American relations and North-South conflict and cooperation.

Daphné GOGOU is Principal Administrator, European Commission, Brussels, Belgium Home Affairs in Brussels, Belgium. She has worked in the visa and management of external border section dealing in particular with relations between the EU and a number of 3rd countries. Prior to joining the Directorate in 2001, Mrs Gogou served from 1992, as an attorney in the Legal Affairs Units of the Directorate General for Telecommunications (until 1996) and the Directorate General for Environment. She earned her LLM in European Law in the Institute of European Studies in Brussels and also an LLM on International Economic Law in the University of Dijon in France. She was admitted to the bar of Athens, Greece in 1983.

Samuel GONZÁLEZ–RUÍZ is a Professor of Law at the University of Sevilla (Spain) and worked as an interregional adviser to the United Nations Office for Drug Control and Crime Prevention. He has been the head of the Specialized Unit on Organized Crime in México, Chief of Staff to the General Attorney (Procurador General) of México and Deputy Director of the National Institute of Criminal Sciences in Mexico. He has a doctorate in law from Milan-Bologna University.

Virginie GUIRAUDON is a permanent research fellow at the National Center for Scientific Research (CNRS) in Lille, France. She holds a Ph. D. in Government from Harvard University where she focused on explaining the evolution of the rights granted to foreigners in France, Germany and the Netherlands since 1974. She has been a Jean Monnet Fellow at the European University Institute in Florence, a visiting fellow at the Center for International Studies at Princeton University and a recipient of the Descartes-Huygens prize whose tenure she spent at the university of Nijmegen. She was also awarded the CNRS bronze medal for best young researcher and the European Union Studies Association best paper prize. She is the author of Les politiques d'immigration en Europe (l'Harmattan, 2000) and co-editor of Controlling a New Migration World (Routledge, 2001).

Alice HILLS received a PhD in war studies from King's College, London. She is Senior Lecturer in conflict, development & security at the School of Politics and International Studies, University of Leeds. Previously she taught defence studies for King's College, London at the Joint Services Command and Staff College, lectured in policing and public safety at the University of Leicester, acted as a course director in crisis management for the Home Office, and was a research assistant in the Cabinet Office. She was a senior research associate at the Centre for Defence Studies, University of London (2004), a member of the international border security advisory board, Geneva Centre for the Democratic Control of Armed Forces (2001-03), and a visiting research fellow at the Institute of Defence and Strategic Studies, Singapore (2001).

Peter HOBBING is an Associate Research Fellow at CEPS. His professional background at the European Commission has included relevant positions in the DGs responsible for trade control (TAXUD) and security (JAI/JLS); he also gathered operational experience in border matters as an officer of the German border security services.

Rey KOSLOWSKI is Associate Professor of Political Science and Public Policy, Rockefeller College of Public Affairs and Policy, University at Albany (SUNY). He also holds a joint appointment on the Informatics Faculty of Albany's College of Computing and Information. Further, he is Director of the Center for Policy Research Program on Border Control and Homeland Security. His primary teaching and research interests are in the field of international relations dealing with international organization, European integration, international migration, information technology, and homeland security.

Sandra LAVENEX is Professor of International Relations and Global Governance at the University of Lucerne in Switzerland. Her research focuses on international migration and refugee policies, the internationalisation of justice and home affairs, and EU-association relations with non-member states.

Otwin MARENIN is Professor of Political Science and Criminal Justice at Washington State University. His research and publications have focused on comparative politics and criminal justice issues and, more recently, on issues in international and comparative policing, international police assistance and training efforts, criminal justice in Third World countries, and policing in Native American communities. Recent publications in this area include the edited book with Marina Caparini, *Transforming Police in Central and Eastern Europe* (2004).

Jörg MONAR is Professor of Contemporary European Studies and Co-Director of the Sussex European Institute (University of Sussex) as well as associate Director of the One Europe or Several? Programme. His research focuses on institutional development of the EU, EU justice and home affairs, Common Foreign and Security Policy, and external economic relations and EU citizenship issues.

Kurt SCHELTER, as a lawyer in European affairs, is heading office of a German law firm in Brussels and is an expert in the field of internal security, border management, Schengen and organized crime. As Professor of Law at the University of Munich he also lectures on constitutional, administrative, and European law.

Louise SHELLEY is a Professor in the School of International Service and in the Department of Justice, Law and Society at American University. As the founder and Director of the Transnational Crime & Corruption Center she is a leading expert on transnational crime and terrorism with a particular focus on the former Soviet Union.

Monika SIE DHIAN HO is senior researcher at the Netherlands Scientific Council for Government Policy in The Hague. Her research fields concern institutional reform and democratization of the EU, justice and home affairs cooperation in the EU, and differentiated forms of European integration.

Geneva Centre for the Democratic Control of Armed Forces (DCAF)

Heiner Hänggi;
Theodor H. Winkler (Eds.)
Challenges of Security Sector Governance
The war in Iraq in spring 2003 was a further indication of the 'resecuritisation' of international relations triggered by the terrorist attacks of September 11, 2001. However, the new (or renewed) primacy of security will be of a rather different nature as compared to the Cold War period. The underlying assumption of the essays in this volume is that security issues will increasingly be approached from a governance perspective and that, in this context, the internal dimension of security governance – security sector governance – is an issue whose rapidly growing importance has not yet been duly recognised.
2003, 312 S., 23,90 €, br., ISBN 3-8258-7158-4

Marina Caparini; Otwin Marenin (Eds.)
Transforming Police in Central and Eastern Europe
Process and Progress
The issue of police reform in countries in transition from state socialism toward more democratic forms of governance has risen to practical prominence in recent years. The collapse of the Soviet Union initiated fundamental changes in aspirations, ideologies and governing practices among former members of the socialist camp. Reforming policing systems which had served primarily to protect the party-states from their opponents into systems which serve and protect civic society has come to be seen as an essential prerequisite and concomitant of the democratisation process in transitional countries. The chapters in this book describe what has happened to the policing systems in 14 countries in Central and eastern Europe; what reforms in ideology, organisation, policies and practices have been undertaken; what has changed in the way policing is done; and assessment of whether the policing system has moved closer toward democratic policing. In combining descriptions of reforms and assessments of whether reforms have moved policing systems toward more democratic forms, the book provides a comparative overview of what has been achieved since 1989 and what has been learned so far about how to reform policing systems along democratic lines. Such lessons offer insights for further reform in transitional countries and for Western democracies as well, and we hope will stimulate more theoretical discussions of the nature and dynamics of policing systems, state-society relations, and the role of processes of democratisation of policing systems.
2004, 376 S., 29,90 €, br., ISBN 3-8258-7485-0

Alan Bryden; Heiner Hänggi (Eds.)
Reform and Reconstruction of the Security Sector
Security sector reform (SSR) is widely recognised as key to conflict prevention, peace-building, sustainable development and democratisation. SSR has gained most practical relevance in the context of post-conflict reconstruction of so-called 'failed states' and states emerging from violent internal or inter-state conflict. As this volume shows, almost all states need to reform their security sectors to a greater or lesser extent, according to the specific security, political and socio-economic contexts, as well as in response to the new security challenges resulting from globalisation and post-9/11 developments. Contributions from academics and practitioners elaborate on both the conceptual underpinnings and the practical realities of security sector reform and – a crucial aspect of post-conflict peace-building – security sector reconstruction.
2004, 296 S., 29,90 €, gb., ISBN 3-8258-7770-1

Bernardo Arévalo de León;
José Beltrán Doña;
Philipp H. Fluri (Eds.)
Hacia una Política de Seguridad para la Democracia en Guatemala
Investigación Acción Participativa (IAP) y Reforma del Sector Seguridad
Esta obra, compilada por Bernardo Arévalo, José Beltrán y Philipp Fluri, es un esfuerzo que acredita varios logros; uno de ellos es

L**IT** Verlag Münster – Berlin – Hamburg – London – Wien
Fresnostr. 2 48159 Münster
Tel.: 0251 – 62 032 22 – Fax: 0251 – 23 19 72
e-Mail: vertrieb@lit-verlag.de – http://www.lit-verlag.de

el enriquecedor enfoque actualizado sobre diversos temas de las relaciones cívico militares, con la participación del Estado – Fuerzas Armadas – Sociedad, en forma de un rico debate en el que han intervenido fructíferamente especialistas civiles y militares de Guatemala y del extranjero. Otro logro es, evidentemente, mostrarnos la madurez que un diálogo de esta naturaleza ha alcanzado a lo largo de los años; algo extraordinario comparado con los enconados abordajes de la temática que se hacían a principios de los años 90 para llegar a consensos que trasciendan; lo cual retroalimenta nuestro optimismo en el futuro del país.Helen Mack Chang, Fundación Myrna Mack, Directora
2005, 352 S., 34,80 €, br., ISBN 3-8258-8692-1

Alan Bryden; Heiner Hänggi (Eds.)
Security Governance in Post-Conflict Peacebuilding
Post-conflict peacebuilding has become a primary concern of international politics. Indeed, the UN reform agenda – including the creation of a Peacebuilding Commission – makes clear that more must be done to prevent societies from falling back into violent struggle. Building up domestic capacity to provide security in an accountable manner plays a crucial role in this context. Applying a security governance perspective, this volume examines a number of key issues that must be addressed by both post-conflict societies and the international community as they confront the task of rebuilding after armed conflict – including security sector reform (SSR), disarmament, demobilisation and reintegration (DDR), rule of law and transitional justice.
2005, 304 S., 29,90 €, br., ISBN 3-8258-9019-8

Marina Caparini; Philipp Fluri; Ferenc Molnar (Eds.)
Civil Society and the Security Sector
Concepts and Practices in New Democracies
This volume analyses the role of civil society in the reform and oversight of the security sector in post- communist countries as a key aspect of the transition towards democracy. It is widely accepted that civil society actors have an important contribution to make in the governance of the security sector. However, that specific role has not been subject to much close or comparative examination. This book constitutes an attempt to examine and compare experiences of civil society participation in security oversight across Central and Eastern Europe. The first part of the volume presents the reader with the theoretical and conceptual background against which the potential role of civil society in security sector governance can be understood and assessed. The remainder of the book is comprised of nine country studies of civil society engagement with the security sector. Reviewing developments over the past 15 years of regime transformation in the region, the book draws upon a rich variety of cases that cast light on the different experiences, challenges, and successes of civil society actors and the media in democratisation, security sector reform, and the exercise of democratic oversight of the security sector.
2006, 264 S., 29,90 €, br., ISBN 3-8258-9364-2

George C. Marshall European Center for Security Studies

Jürgen Kuhlmann; Jean Callaghan (Editors)
Military and Society in 21st Century Europe
A Comparative Analysis
After the Cold War came to an end, European countries in both East and West faced the common question of how their military organizations and those of their neighbors would respond to shifts in international relations affecting their economies, their perception of globalized threats, and cross-national security management. It is undisputed, for example, that in well-developed democratic societies, the challenge to the legitimacy of the military in society, the decreasing subjective apprehension of threat, and growing opposition to systems of universal conscription have been linked to gains in wealth and living standards. This volume seeks, by empirically measuring social indicators, to assess the current state of civil-military relations in a number

LIT Verlag Münster – Berlin – Hamburg – London – Wien
Fresnostr. 2 48159 Münster
Tel.: 0251 – 62 032 22 – Fax: 0251 – 23 19 72
e-Mail: vertrieb@lit-verlag.de – http://www.lit-verlag.de

of countries in Eastern Europe (Bulgaria, Czech Republic, Hungary, Romania, Russia) as well as the state of relations in several of their Western European counterparts (France, Germany, Italy, the Netherlands). The country studies describe and analyze the differing positions of the military in their specific national settings.
Bd. 1, 2000, 384 S., 35,90 €, br.,
ISBN 3-8258-4449-8

Jürgen Rose;
Johannes Ch. Traut (Editors)
Federalism and Decentralization
Perspectives for the Transformation Process in Eastern and Central Europe
The Marshall Center research project on "Federalism and Decentralization in Eastern and Central Europe" was designed to cooperatively explore ways to promote the decentralization of formerly centralized political structures in Central and East European States, and to present models of federalism that could help introduce or strengthen federal structures in these countries. It was developed by the research department of the Marshall Center in cooperation with two reputable institutes, the European Center for Research on Federalism at the University of Tübingen and the German Institute for Research on Federalism at the University of Hannover.
Bd. 2, 2001, 384 S., 45,90 €, gb.,
ISBN 3-8258-5156-7

Jean Callaghan;
Mathias Schönborn (Editors)
Warriors in Peacekeeping
Points of tension in complex cultural encounters. A comparative study based on experiences in Bosnia
This book makes an extraordinary contribution to broadening and deepening understanding of the complex range of relations in modern peacekeeping operations, including interactions between national contingents and their respective chains of command and their relations with other contingents in the field, as well as with regional authorities, scores of NGOs, and the Its findings help to identify "points of tension" in peacekeeping operations in Bosnia-Herzegovina, where, for the first time, contingents from more than 35 countries had to cooperate, each of which had their own, quite different, This volume provides both descriptive and analytical insights based upon these experiences that are applicable to contemporary international peacekeeping operations all over the world.
2004, 456 S., 45,90 €, gb., ISBN 3-8258-5172-9

COMPAS Group on Security and Defence Studies
edited by Preben Bonnén
(Trinity College, Toronto),
Robert Momich
(Trinity College, Toronto),
Goran S. Pesic
(Trinity College, Toronto),
Teemu Palosaari (University of Helsinki)

Preben Bonnén
Towards A Common European Security and Defence Policy
The Ways and Means of Making It a Reality
As a significant global economic player, the EU has increasingly become self-conscious in areas of foreign and security policy. Recent experience has made clear that if the EU is to have a truly effective common policy on foreign and security policy, it must have the capacity to take more responsibility for regional security. For the EU to play such a role, its ability to manage and project military force will need to be significantly enhanced, particularly in terms of its institutions and military capability. For the same reason the EU made a strong commitment to developing an effective EU led crisis management capacity. By 2003 the EU must be in a position to deploy within 60 days up to 50,000–60,000 troops capable of a full range of so-called Petersberg tasks including: humanitarian and rescue missions, peacekeeping, combat force tasks in crisis management and peacemaking missions. According to the EU however the initiative should not be seen as a duplication

LIT Verlag Münster – Berlin – Hamburg – London – Wien
Fresnostr. 2 48159 Münster
Tel.: 0251 – 62 032 22 – Fax: 0251 – 23 19 72
e-Mail: vertrieb@lit-verlag.de – http://www.lit-verlag.de

of NATO. Neither should the establishment of a European Force be confused with the concept of a European army. Whether a European army, or a common defence for Europe is more capable of handling the future needs and challenges of the EU is not the subject of this book. Essentially it is about whether a military crisis management system is practical and realistic and how the planned initiatives within the agreed limits are to be transformed into operative policy.
Bd. 1, 2003, 208 S., 24,90 €, br., ISBN 3-8258-6711-0

Transatlantic Public Policy Series
edited by Prof. Dr. Eberhard Bohne (Deutsche Hochschule für Verwaltungswissenschaft, Speyer), Prof. Dr. Charles Bonser (Indiana University) and Prof. Dr. Ken Spencer (University of Birmingham)

Eberhard Bohne; Charles F. Bonser; Kenneth Spencer (eds.)
Transatlantic Perspectives on Liberalization and Democratic Governance
The first volume of the new *Transatlantic Public Policy Series* comprises contributions by members of the Transatlantic Policy Consortium (TPC). Earlier versions of the papers published in this volume have been presented and discussed at the TPC Colloquium in Speyer, Germany, in June 2003 on the theme of Liberalization and Democratic Governance. They centre around subthemes which are critical on both sides of the Atlantic: the role of the state with social and economic actors, policy development and regulatory challenges to the state and the changing nature of democratic institutions and participation. Some contributions represent updated versions of papers originally prepared for the TPC Colloquium in Pittsburgh, Pennsylvania/USA, in September 2001 on public service ethics at both national and international levels. The earlier publication of these papers fell victim to the terrorist attacks of that time. The volume provides a unique insight into European and US-American public policy issues and thinking.
Bd. 1, 2004, 544 S., 34,90 €, br., ISBN 3-8258-7284-x

David J. Eaton (Ed.)
The End of Sovereignty?
A Transatlantic Perspective
The second volume of the Transatlantic Public Policy Series comprises contributions by members of the Transatlantic Policy Consortium (TPC). The 17 provocative contributions focus on the concept of internal and external sovereignty which is critical on both sides of the Atlantic. It is not easy to articulate the domain and limits of the state's control of its resources, its capacity to coerce activities within its borders, its powers to treat other states as co-equals across a border, or even implement its own defense, trade or regulatory policies. The volume provides a unique insight into these problems from a European and US perspective.
Bd. 2, 2006, 480 S., 39,90 €, br., ISBN 3-8258-9285-9

Berghof Research Center for Constructive Conflict Management
Berghof Forschungszentrum für konstruktive Konfliktbearbeitung (Berlin)

Martina Fischer (Ed.)
Peacebuilding and Civil Society in Bosnia-Herzegovina
Ten Years after Dayton
The Dayton Accords ended the war in Bosnia-Herzegovina in 1995. The 10th anniversary gives reason to investigate the post-war period, today's realities and future perspectives. Bosnian authors and international experts express their views on recent developments. Insiders and outsiders, working in the conflict and on its transformation, have been invited to tackle the questions: Which conflict lines mark the present society? Did peacebuilding activities address the underlying causes? What are obstacles for conflict transformation? What are the potentials and limits of

international support? What does civil society mean in Bosnia and how is it related to statebuilding and democratisation? How can people constructively deal with the past in order to design the future in the region of former Yugoslavia? The book gives an overview on an important research focus of the Berghof Research Center, highlighting the work of its most important cooperation partners.
2006, 488 S., 29,90 €, br., ISBN 3-8258-8793-6

Gesellschaftliche Transformationen/Societal Transformations

hrsg. von /edited by Eckhard Dittrich, Nikolai Genov, Raj Kollmorgen, Ingrid Oswald, Heiko Schrader, Melanie Tatur

Heiko Schrader (Ed.)
Trust and Social Transformation
Theoretical approaches and empirical findings from Russia
Bd. 1, 2004, 208 S., 19,90 €, br.,
ISBN 3-8258-7866-x

Nikolai Genov (Ed.)
Ethnic Relations in South Eastern Europe
Problems of Social Inclusion and Exclusion
Bd. 4, 2004, 152 S., 19,90 €, br.,
ISBN 3-8258-7869-4

Rainer Neef; Philippe Adair (Eds.)
Informal Economies and Social Transformation in Romania
Bd. 5, 2005, 248 S., 19,90 €, br.,
ISBN 3-8258-8296-9

Nikolai Genov (Hg.)
Ethnicity and Educational Policies in South Eastern Europe
The crosscutting area of interethnic relations and educational policies is the locus of most intriguing scientific and practical issues in South Eastern Europe. They concern economic, political and cultural dimensions of social action and social order, touch upon sensitive relationships between individual and collective human rights and imply integration or disintegration of societal systems.
Bd. 7, 2005, 216 S., 24,90 €, br.,
ISBN 3-8258-8594-1

Reinhard Golz (Ed.)
Internationalization, Cultural Difference and Migration
Challenges and Perspectives of Intercultural Education
The articles of this book discuss social and educational challenges in migration and transformation processes in selected countries of Europe, North America and Africa. The authors discuss problems of human rights, the increasing cultural diversity, and the identity crises resulting from these processes. They concentrate on pedagogical and sociopsychological issues and refer to new research contexts on migration processes and their perspectives for intercultural education.
Bd. 8, 2005, 232 S., 29,90 €, br.,
ISBN 3-8258-8755-3

Nikolai Genov (Ed.)
Ethnicity and Mass Media in South Eastern Europe
Not the mass media, but other powerful domestic and international factors provoked the ethnic conflicts in South Eastern Europe and determined the paths and mechanisms of their settlement. Nevertheless, it is a proven fact that on various occasions the use of guns was well prepared by hate speech used by the mass media in their coverage of interethnic relations. And vice versa, the efforts to find solutions for interethnic tensions and conflicts have been often facilitated by the moderate or neutral coverage of events by the mass media.
Bd. 9, 2006, 200 S., 24,90 €, br.,
ISBN 3-8258-9348-0

LIT Verlag Münster – Berlin – Hamburg – London – Wien
Fresnostr. 2 48159 Münster
Tel.: 0251 – 62 032 22 – Fax: 0251 – 23 19 72
e-Mail: vertrieb@lit-verlag.de – http://www.lit-verlag.de